WAR
ON
PEACE

Ronan Farrow

WAR
ON
PEACE

**The End of Diplomacy and the
Decline of American Influence**

**WILLIAM
COLLINS**

William Collins
An imprint of HarperCollins*Publishers*
1 London Bridge Street
London SE1 9GF

www.WilliamCollinsBooks.com

First published in Great Britain in 2018 by William Collins
First published in the United States by W. W. Norton & Company, Inc. in 2018

7

A catalogue record for this book is
available from the British Library

ISBN 978-0-00-757562-6 (hardback)
ISBN 978-0-00-757563-3 (trade paperback)

Designed by Ellen Cipriano

Printed and bound in Great Britain by
CPI Group (UK) Ltd, Croydon, CR0 4YY

MIX
Paper from
responsible sources
FSC
www.fsc.org   FSC® C007454

This book is produced from independently certified FSC paper
to ensure responsible forest management.

For more information visit: www.harpercollins.co.uk/green

For Mom.

CONTENTS

PART II: SHOOT FIRST, ASK QUESTIONS NEVER

PART III: PRESENT AT THE DESTRUCTION

EPILOGUE: THE TOOL OF FIRST RESORT

PROLOGUE

MAHOGANY ROW MASSACRE

AMMAN, JORDAN, 2017

[A]ppoint an ambassador who is versed in all sciences, who understands hints, expressions of the face and gestures. . . . The army depends on the official placed in charge of it . . . peace and its opposite, war, on the ambassador. For the ambassador alone makes and separates allies; the ambassador transacts that business by which kings are disunited or not.

—THE *MANUSMRITI*, HINDU SCRIPTURE, CA. 1000 BCE

THE DIPLOMAT HAD NO CLUE that his career was over. Before stepping into the secure section of the American embassy, he'd slipped his phone into one of the cubbies on the wall outside, according to protocol. The diplomat had been following protocol for thirty-five years, as walls crumbled and empires fell, as the world grew smaller and cables became teleconferences and the expansive language of diplomacy reduced to the gnomic and officious patter of email. He had missed a few calls and the first email that came in was terse. The director general of the Foreign Service had been trying to reach him. They needed to speak immediately.

The diplomat's name was Thomas Countryman, which seems like it must be made up, but is not. He was sitting at a borrowed desk in the political section at the heart of the low, sprawling embassy complex in Jordan's posh Abdoun neighborhood. The embassy was an American contractor's studied homage to the Middle East: sand-colored stone, with a red diamond-shaped motif on the shatterproof windows that said, "local, but not too local." Like most American embassies in this part of the world, there was no avoiding the sense that it was a fortress. "We'd build a moat if we could," a Foreign Service officer stationed there once muttered to me as our armored SUV made its way through the facility's concrete and steel barriers, past armored personnel carriers full of uniformed soldiers.

It was January 25, 2017. Countryman was America's senior official on arms control, a mission that was, quite literally, a matter of life and death. He oversaw the State Department's work on the fragile nuclear deal with Iran, and its response to apocalyptic threats from the regime in North Korea. His trip that January was a moonshot: the latest in decades of negotiations over nuclear disarmament in the Middle East. Nuclear-free zones had been established around the world, from Latin America to parts of Africa and Europe. No one thought Israel was going to suddenly surrender its nukes. But incremental steps—like getting states in the region to ratify treaties they had already signed banning nuclear *tests*, if not the weapons themselves—might someday be achievable. Even that was "a fairly quixotic quest, because the Arabs and the Israelis have radically different views." Tom Countryman had a flair for understatement.

The work this mission entailed was classic, old-school diplomacy, which is to say it was frustrating and involved a lot of jet lag. Years of careful cajoling and mediating had brought the Middle Eastern states closer than ever to at least assenting to a conference. There was dialogue in the hopes of future dialogue, which is easier to mock than to achieve. That evening, Countryman and his British and Russian counterparts would meet officials from Egypt, Jordan, Saudi Arabia, and Kuwait to press the importance of nonproliferation diplomacy. The next day, he'd go on to Rome for a meeting with his counterparts from around the world. "It was an important meeting," he told me later, "if not a decisive one." He punctuated this with a hollow little laugh, which is not so much an indictment of the comedic qualities of Tom Countryman as it is an indictment of the comedic qualities of nuclear proliferation in the Middle East.

Countryman had landed in Amman the previous day and checked into the InterContinental. Then he went straight to a meeting with his Arab League counterpart over coffee and cigarettes. Countryman took the coffee *mazboot*, or black with sugar, in the local fashion. For the cigarettes, he favored Marlboro Lights, as often as possible. (A life of travel and negotiation hadn't been conducive to quitting. "I'm trying," he said later, before vaping unhappily.)

The next day, it was over to dinner with British and Russian officials. Not all of Countryman's counterparts had his years of experience and relationships. The British point person had changed several times in the preceding years. His Russian counterpart had sent a deputy. That would make it harder. In high-wire acts of persuasion, every ounce of diplomatic experience in the room counted.

Diplomats perform many essential functions—spiriting Americans out of crises, holding together developing economies, hammering out deals between governments. This last mandate can sometimes give the job the feel of Thanksgiving dinner with your most difficult relatives, only lasting a lifetime and taking place in the most dangerous locations on earth. A diplomat's weapon is persuasion, deployed on conversational fronts at the margins of international summits, in dimly lit hotel bars, or as bombs fall in war zones.

Tom Countryman had, since joining the Foreign Service in 1982, weathered all of these vagaries of diplomacy. He had served in the former Yugoslavia and in Cairo during Desert Storm. He had emerged unscathed from travels through Afghanistan and the bureaucracy of the United Nations. He'd picked up Serbian and Croatian, as well as Arabic, Italian, and Greek along the way. Even his English carried a puzzling accent from all of those places, or maybe none of them at all. Tom Countryman had a flat, uninflected voice and an odd way with vowels that made him sound like a text-to-speech application or a Bond villain. An internet troll excoriating him as "one of those faceless bureaucrats in the State Department" called it "a strange bureaucratic accent I guess you obtain by not being around real people your whole working career," which encapsulates another facet of being a diplomat: they work in the places the military works, but they're not exactly welcomed home with ticker-tape parades.

But this particular troll was wrong: Tom Countryman was not faceless. He had a face, and not one you'd lose in a crowd. A slight man with a flinty, searching gaze, he often wore his salt-and-pepper hair clipped short in the front and long behind, tumbling gloriously over his neat suits. It was a diplomat's mullet: peace in the front, war in the back. ("Sick mane," one conservative outlet crowed. "King of the party.") He had a reputation for frank, unbureaucratic answers in public statements and Senate hearings. But he never strayed from his devotion to the State Department and his belief that its work protected the United States. In a work of fiction, naming him Countryman would have been annoying as hell.

SITTING UNDER THE FLUORESCENT LIGHTS of the political section that day in Jordan, Countryman looked at the email for a moment and then sent back the number of his desk. The director general of the Foreign Service, Ambassador Arnold Chacon, called back quickly. "This is not happy news," Chacon began, as Countryman recalled the conversation. The White House, Chacon said, had just accepted Countryman's resignation, effective as of the end of the week. Chacon was sorry. "I wasn't expecting that it was about me," Countryman remembered between puffs at his e-cigarette. "I didn't have any idea." But there he was, a few hours before a critical confrontation with foreign governments, getting shit-canned.

When there's a changing of the guard in Washington, Senate-confirmed officials submit brief, one- or two-sentence notes tendering their resignations. It's a formality, a tradition. It is almost universally assumed that nonpartisan career officers like Tom Countryman will remain in place. This is a practical matter. Career Foreign Service officers are the foundation of the American government abroad, an imperfect structure that came to replace the incompetence and corruption of the spoils system. Only career officials have the decades of institutional knowledge required to keep the nation's agencies running, and while every administration takes issue with the intransigence and unaccountability of these "lifers," no one could remember any administration dismissing them in significant numbers.

The president doesn't technically have the power to fire career Foreign Service officers, just to remove them from their jobs. But there's an "up or out" rule: if you're not in a presidentially appointed job after a certain number of years at a senior level—Countryman's level—you have to retire. Being relieved of this job was the end of his career; it was just a question of how long he wanted to draw it out. He opted for a quick end. It was Wednesday. When the resignation took effect on Friday, he'd leave.

They decided he'd attend the meeting with the Arabs that night. "What about the Rome meeting?" Countryman asked. It was one of the rare opportunities for the United States to press its nonproliferation agenda with world powers. "It's important." Chacon agreed, but the forty-eight hours Countryman had been given wouldn't be enough for that. A less-senior officer would have to suffice in his place. "Okay, thanks for informing me," Countryman said simply. "I'll be coming back home." For a man with a mullet, Tom Countryman was resistant to spectacle.

Others were less sanguine. His wife Dubravka had met him during his first tour in the former Yugoslavia and they'd had a thirty-year Foreign Service romance. She had a degree in education and talent as a painter, but she'd set aside her ambitions to move around the world every few years with him, helping to make ends meet as an interpreter while raising their two sons. Her father had been a diplomat, so she knew the sacrifices of the job—but she also understood the general expectation of respect for senior diplomats, in her native Yugoslavia and in the United States. This was something else. "It's not fair," she said when Countryman called her, minutes after he got the news, "and it's not fair to me."

She was shocked. The less-senior officer replacing him in Rome—being sent to navigate one of the world's most treacherous multilateral issues from a position of scant authority—was shocked. The Italians were shocked. The Arabs, that night, were shocked. Countryman waited until the end of the session, after the Arabs had related the grievances (and the Arabs had a lot of grievances) they wanted addressed before they'd sit down with the Israelis. Then he told them he'd relate the results of their conversation to a successor, because this was his final meeting as an American diplomat. One by one, they took his hands in theirs and exchanged words of respect—for him, and for a shared tradition that seemed, suddenly, to face an uncertain future.

It WAS JUST FIVE DAYS into the new Trump administration, and rumor and paranoia gripped America's diplomats. On the campaign trail, Trump had offered little by way of specifics about diplomacy. "America First," went the campaign mantra. He wanted to "stop sending foreign aid to countries that hate us," though it was, at the time, unclear whether this meant development aid or military assistance or both. ("Nobody can do that better than me," he added helpfully.)

Tom Countryman was one of many senior officials who emerged from their first meetings with the Trump transition team alarmed. "The transition was a joke," he remembered. "Any other administration changeover, there were people who were knowledgeable about foreign affairs, there were people who had experience in government, and they had a systematic effort to collect information and feed it to a new team. In this case, none of those things were true." He presented the transition team with detailed briefing papers on nonproliferation issues, marked "sensitive but unclassified," since few members of the team had security clearances. But they showed little interest in nuclear weapons. What they did show was a "deep distrust for professional public servants," Countryman said. They hadn't come to learn, he realized with a sinking feeling. They'd come to cut.

Then the firings began. Typically, even politically appointed ambassadors in important places, especially ones without overly partisan reputations, stay on until a replacement is confirmed, sometimes for months. The Trump administration broke from that tradition: shortly after taking office, the new administration ordered all politically appointed ambassadors to depart immediately, faster than usual. *Pack your bags, hit the road.*

After that, the transition team asked State Department management to draw up a list of all noncareer officers across the Department. Countryman began to fear that the next target would be the contractors hired under an authority specifically designed to bring subject matter experts into American diplomacy. The Department was full of these. They played pivotal roles in offices overseeing the most sensitive areas of American foreign policy, including in Tom Countryman's. "These were the best possible experts on issues like Korea and Pakistan," he remembered. "And in the arms-control bureau there were a number of them that were not easily replaceable." They were "necessary." The United States couldn't afford to lose them. But "the concern that they were going to dump everyone they could dump was palpable." And so he'd spent the weeks leading up to that day in Jordan quietly lobbying State Department management, helping them devise arguments against what he feared might be a wave of firings of the Department's experts.

In fact, that's what he'd assumed the call was about. What was unthinkable, ahistorical, seemingly senseless, was that it would in fact be about career officials like him. Countryman insisted it was no great sob story for him personally. He had been around a long time. He had his pension. But it was a troubling affront to institutional culture. Tom Countryman had an unimpeachable record of service across Republican and Democratic administrations. He'd had a few contentious moments in Senate hearings, but they'd earned him more respect than ire. Senators "would come up to me after and say, 'I really like the way you shoot straight,'" he recalled. Perhaps, he speculated, the administration was trying to send a message that the United States was no longer interested in arms control. Or maybe they'd gotten into his private Facebook account where, during the campaign, he'd posted criticism of Trump to a small circle of friends. "To this day, I don't know why I was singled out."

IN FACT, TOM COUNTRYMAN had not been singled out. The White House, Chacon told him, was relieving six career diplomats of their jobs that day. Some were more explicable than Countryman. Under Secretary of State for Management Patrick Kennedy, who served around the world for more than forty years, had been involved with both the secretary of state's email accounts and diplomatic security, and had spent the preceding year swept up in the torrent of campaign coverage of Hillary Clinton's email server and the controversy surrounding Benghazi. David Malcolm Robinson had been assistant secretary of state for conflict and stabilization operations, a bureau with an amorphous portfolio that conservative critics said amounted to that deadliest of terms in Washington: "nation building." But three others—assistant secretaries who worked under Kennedy and had nothing, as far as anyone could tell, to do with Benghazi, had also gotten the axe. "That was just petty," said Countryman. "Vindictive."

It was just the beginning. A few weeks later, on Valentine's Day,

Erin Clancy's phone rang—the personal one she kept in a beat-up blue wooden case. She had just landed at John Wayne Airport in Orange County and was standing in the February California sunlight, in her jeans and T-shirt, waiting for a rental car. "Hold on the line," said the scheduler. "We're having an emergency team meeting." The team was the deputy secretary of state's, where Clancy, a career Foreign Service officer, was posted. She sat within spitting distance of the secretary of state on the seventh floor: through the secure crash door, past where the sagging drop ceilings and linoleum floors end and the opulent wood-paneled receiving rooms begin, in the legendary corridor of power known as Mahogany Row. Jobs on Mahogany Row were elite postings, held by the best of the Foreign Service; the Ferraris of State Department personnel, but more reliable.

Clancy held on the line. Her partner, a State Department alum, gave her a searching look. Erin shrugged: *beats me.* The fired officials so far had at least been in Senate-confirmed roles. Her team consisted entirely of working-level officers, and the most elite and protected of them at that. They'd assumed they were safe.

In the weeks since Tom Countryman and the other senior officials cleared out their desks, the Department had been dead quiet. By this time in most administrations, the deputy secretary's office would be humming with activity, helping a new secretary of state jump-start his or her agenda. In this case, the new administration had yet to even nominate a deputy secretary of state and wouldn't for months to come. When the last deputy, Tony Blinken, was in the job, Clancy and the rest of her team had arrived at 7 a.m. and worked twelve- to fourteen-hour days. Now they sat with little to do, taking long coffee breaks at 9 a.m. each day, waiting for orders that never came. "No one's asking us for anything, we're totally cut off, we're not invited to meetings, we had to fight for every White House meeting," she remembered. "Our morning meetings were, 'well, have you heard this rumor?' That was no way to formulate US foreign policy." Eventually, the acting deputy, Tom Shannon, told them they might as well take a break. So Clancy had caught a flight out of DC that morning, to see her mother.

When Yuri Kim, the deputy secretary's chief of staff and a fellow Foreign Service officer, came on the line, her voice was solemn. "Great," she began, in a tone that suggested this would not, in fact, be great. "Thanks everyone for your time. We just found out that we're all being asked to *move on*." The entire deputy secretary's staff was assembled: five in the room back on Mahogany Row, two on the phone. Everyone spoke at once. "How?" they asked. "Why?" They should go to their union, one suggested. They should go to the press, offered another. "Your assignments are broken," Clancy remembered being told. "Who knows if you have your next job, maybe you don't. It's utter chaos. And it's out of the blue. No reason."

Kim, usually a fierce advocate for her team, became mechanical. They had forty-eight hours. There would be a meeting with the office of human resources the next day to walk them through next steps. They should use the little time they had left to start making preparations.

When the call was over, Clancy hung up and turned to her partner, dumbfounded. "We're all being fired."

Like a lot of young diplomats, Erin Clancy had joined the Foreign Service after 9/11. She wanted to make the world safer. She moved to the Middle East for six years. She'd been in Damascus when the American embassy there was overrun by protesters. She'd narrowly avoided kidnapping. She'd worked long hours with low pay. As with Countryman, the Foreign Service officers on her team couldn't be fired altogether. But they could be removed from their jobs. This wasn't just a career setback. For many, it was the difference between making ends meet and not. Foreign Service officers don't earn overtime. Instead, assignments with backbreaking hours get a pay differential, a bonus of 18 percent for the deputy secretary's team. No one goes into this career expecting riches. Including the differential, Clancy was making $91,000 a year.

But they bid on these jobs knowing they were guaranteed for a year. Many had planned their family's lives around that income. The dismissals felt wanton and without regard for their service.

Offices across the seventh floor of the State Department were having identical emergency meetings that day. The deputy for management's staff learned their recently departed boss would not be replaced. They too, would be let go. The same went for the office of the State Department counselor, a role some secretaries of state have maintained, and others not. According to several people present that day, Margaret Peterlin, chief of staff to incoming secretary of state Rex Tillerson, sat down in counselor Kristie Kenney's office for their first one-on-one meeting that Valentine's Day. Peterlin's first question to Kenney, a veteran ambassador and one of the most senior women in the Foreign Service: How soon could she leave?

By some back-of-the-napkin calculations from insiders, the jobs of more than half of the career staff on Mahogany Row were threatened that day. At the eleventh hour, Erin Clancy and the deputy's team got a reprieve: Acting Deputy Secretary Tom Shannon had put his foot down. They'd live to see another day. But the other teams moved on.

When I met up with Clancy, she was in her T-shirt and jeans again, sitting in the sun outside a Los Angeles café. She still had her job, but she was back home, regrouping, thinking about next steps. Maybe she should run for office, she mused—it might be a better way to make a difference at this point. Eventually, she decided to stay, going on to a posting at the United States Mission to the United Nations. She, like many still working at the State Department, wasn't giving up. But her confidence in her profession had been shaken. "The culture of the State Department is so eroded," she remarked. It was an institution more than a dozen career diplomats told me they barely recognized, one in which their expertise had been profoundly devalued. Squinting into the afternoon sun, Erin Clancy paused. "We are truly seen as outsiders," she said.

Members of Rex Tillerson's team were adamant that they hadn't been aware of the firings, which, in some cases, took place after the Trump transition team had begun to interface with the Department, but before Tillerson was confirmed. (Other dismissals or attempted dismissals, like Clancy's, took place after Tillerson's confirmation.) In the first days of 2018, when I asked Tillerson about Countryman and the wave of forced retirements, the secretary of state stared at me, unblinking, then said: "I'm not familiar with that one." A little over a month later, Tillerson was gone too: another casualty of a fickle president and a State Department in disarray.

IN SOME WAYS, the world had changed and left professional diplomats like Countryman and Clancy behind. A strain of populism that, from America's earliest days, opposed and denigrated internationalism, was on the rise across the Western world. The foreign policy establishment that underpinned diplomatic acts of creation from NATO to the World Bank after World War II had long since disintegrated into vicious partisanship. Technology had made the work of the diplomat less meaningful and special. For the basic function of delivering messages in foreign lands, email was more efficient than any ambassador. The prestige and power of the Foreign Service were in decline.

Some of the skepticism of American diplomacy was earned. The State Department was often slow, ponderous, and turfy. Its structures and training were outdated in the face of modern tests of American influence from cyberterrorism to radical Islam. Eyes in many a White House have rolled when the subject of "State's objections" has been raised. But for a complex set of new challenges—penetrating cultural barriers in a fraught relationship with China; pulling North Korea back from threats of nuclear war; containing a modern Iran pursuing regional hegemony—specialized experts trained in the art of hardnosed negotiation remain indispensable. Evolving technology and a rising military offer no substitute. In these crises, sidelining diplomacy is not an inevitability of global change: it is a choice, made again and again by administrations Democratic and Republican.

"Unprecedented," blared *Foreign Policy* and a host of other publications on what was being described as the Trump administration's "assault" or "war" on the State Department. But for all the ways in which the developments were shocking, to describe them as unprecedented was simply not true. The Trump administration brought to a new extreme a trend that had, in fact, been gathering force since September 11, 2001. From Mogadishu to Damascus to Islamabad, the United States cast civilian dialogue to the side, replacing the tools of diplomacy with direct, tactical deals between our military and foreign forces. At home, White Houses filled with generals. The last of the diplomats, keepers of a fading discipline that has saved American lives and created structures that stabilized the world, often never made it into the room. Around the world, uniformed officers increasingly handled the negotiation, economic reconstruction, and infrastructure development for which we once had a devoted body of trained specialists. As a result, a different set of relationships has come to form the bedrock of American foreign policy. Where civilians are not empowered to negotiate, military-to-military dealings still flourish. America has changed whom it brings to the table, and, by extension, it has changed who sits at the other side. Foreign ministries are still there. But foreign militaries and militias often have the better seats.

These relationships are not new, nor are they inherently a negative. "America's military might, used judiciously and with strategic precision, is a critical tool of diplomacy," James Baker, George H. W. Bush's secretary of state, said, embodying a more hawkish strain of foreign policy. "I've always said 'diplomacy works best when it comes in a mailed fist.'" The question is of balance. In many of America's engagements around the world, those military alliances have now eclipsed the kind of civilian diplomacy that once counterbalanced them, with disastrous results.

These trends have been apparent since 2001, but their roots stretch even further back. By the time terrorists toppled the Twin Towers, the stage had been set for this crisis of modern diplomacy for at least a decade. Bill Clinton ran on the promise of domestic reinvestment—it was, as Clinton's strategist James Carville noted in a statement that became the indelible brand of their campaign, "the economy, stupid,"—and quickly set about slashing America's civilian presence around the world. When Republicans took control of Congress in 1994 and Jesse Helms—he of the jowls and the racism and the fevered isolationism—became chair of the Senate Foreign Relations Committee, the nosedive accelerated. Clinton's first secretary of state, the late Warren Christopher, championed what he called a "tough budget for tough times." Christopher's successor, Madeleine Albright, defended Clinton's personal commitment to international engagement, but conceded that, in the wake of the Cold War, "there really was a sense that we needed to pay attention to domestic issues."

Over the course of the 1990s, the United States' international affairs budget tumbled by 30 percent, on a par with the cuts requested years later by the Trump administration. Here's what happened then: the State Department pulled the plug on twenty-six consulates and fifty missions of the United States Agency for International Development (USAID). The timing could hardly have been worse. With the disintegration of the Soviet Union and Yugoslavia, the United States needed a slew of new outposts to stabilize the region and gain footholds of American influence in spaces vacated by the Soviets. While some were indeed created, by the mid-1990s, the United States had fewer embassies and consulates than it did at the height of the Cold War. Even remaining outposts felt the shift—Christopher sheepishly told a congressional committee that the embassy in Beijing reeked of sewer gas, while in Sarajevo, diplomats desperate to receive news had to jerry-rig a satellite dish to the roof using a barbecue grill.

In 1999, the Arms Control and Disarmament Agency and the United States Information Agency were both shuttered and their respective mandates folded into a shrinking and overstretched State Department. The Cold War was over, the logic went. When would the United States possibly need to worry about rising nuclear powers, or information warfare against an ideological enemy's insidious propaganda machine? Two decades later, Iran's and North Korea's nuclear aspirations and the Islamic State's global recruitment are among the United States' most pressing international challenges. But by then, the specialized, trained workforces devoted to those challenges had been wiped out. Thomas Friedman raced to the scene with a visual metaphor, lamenting that the United States was "turning its back on the past and the future of U.S. foreign policy for the sake of the present." (The point was certainly valid, though one wondered where the nation's back was now facing. Maybe we were spinning? Let's say we were spinning.)

So it was that on September 11, 2001, the State Department was 20 percent short of staff, and those who remained were undertrained and under-resourced. The United States needed diplomacy more than ever, and it was nowhere to be found.

THE BUSH ADMINISTRATION SCRAMBLED to reinvest. "We resourced the Department like never before," then–secretary of state Colin Powell recalled. But it was growth born of a new, militarized form of foreign policy. Funding that made it to State was increasingly drawn from "Overseas Contingency Operations"—earmarked specifically for advancing the Global War on Terrorism. Promoting democracy, supporting economic development, helping migrants—all of these missions were repackaged under a new counterterrorism mantle. "Soft" categories of the State Department's budget—that is, anything not directly related to the immediate goals of combatting terrorism—flatlined, in many cases permanently. Defense spending, on the other hand, skyrocketed to historic extremes, far outpacing the modest growth at State. "The State Department has ceded a lot of authority to the Defense Department since 2001," Albright reflected.

Diplomats slipped to the periphery of the policy process. Especially during the early days of the Iraq War, Bush concentrated power at the White House; specifically, under Vice President Dick Cheney. Cheney built a close rapport with Secretary of Defense Donald Rumsfeld, but had little time for Powell. "The VP had very, very strong views and he communicated them directly to the president," recalled Powell. The Bush White House had "two NSCs during that period. One led by Condi [Rice, then the national security advisor] and one led by the VP. Anything going to the president after it left the NSC went to the VP's NSC and the problem I'd have from time to time is that . . . access is everything in politics and he was over there all the time." It was a challenge former secretaries of state invariably recalled facing, to one extent or another. "There is the interesting psychological fact that the secretary of state's office is ten minutes' car ride from the White House and the security advisor is right down the hall," said Henry Kissinger, recalling his time in both roles under presidents Nixon and Ford. "The temptations of propinquity are very great."

During the Bush administration, those dynamics cut the State Department out of even explicitly diplomatic decisions. Powell learned of Bush's plan to withdraw from the Kyoto Protocol on climate change only after it had been decided, and pleaded with Rice for more time to warn America's allies of the radical move. He raced to the White House to press the case. Rice informed him that it was too late.

But State's exclusion was most profound in the Global War on Terrorism, which an ascendant Pentagon seized as its exclusive domain. That the invasion of Iraq and the period immediately after were dominated by the Pentagon was inevitable. But, later, Bush handed over reconstruction and democracy-building activities, which had historically been the domain of the State Department and USAID, to uniformed officers with the Coalition Provisional Authority, reporting to the secretary of defense. Powell and his officials at State counseled caution, but were unable to penetrate the policymaking process, which had become entirely preoccupied with tactics—in Powell's view, at the expense of strategy. "Mr. Rumsfeld felt that he had a strategy that did not reflect Powell thinking," he recalled. "And he could do it on the low end and on small. My concern was probably, yeah, he beat the crap out of this army ten years ago, I have no doubt about them getting to Baghdad, but we didn't take over the country to run a country." Powell never used the phrase "the Pottery Barn rule," as a journalist later dubbed his thinking, but he did tell the president, "If you break it, you own it." It was, he later told me with a heavy sigh, "a massive strategic failure both politically and militarily."

More specifically, it was a string of successive strategic failures. The Pentagon disbanded the Iraqi security forces, turning loose hundreds of thousands of armed and unemployed Iraqi young men and laying the foundations for a deadly insurgency. Taxpayer dollars from the massive $4-billion Commander's Emergency Response Program, which essentially gave military brass the authority to undertake USAID-style development projects, was later found to be flowing directly to those insurgents. The State Department's legal adviser is typically consulted on questions of law regarding the treatment of enemy combatants, but Powell's Department was not involved in conversations about the administration's expanding use of military commissions—aspects of which were later found to be unconstitutional by the Supreme Court.

As the disasters of Iraq deepened, a bruised Bush administration did attempt to shift additional resources into diplomacy and development. The White House pledged to double the size of USAID's Foreign Service, and began to speak of rebalancing civilian and military roles and empowering the US ambassador in Iraq. The supposed rebalancing was more pantomime than meaningful policy—there was no redressing the yawning chasm of resources and influence between military and civilian leadership in the war—but there was, at least, an understanding that military policymaking had proved toxic.

THE LESSON DIDN'T STICK. In a haze of nostalgia, liberal commentators sometimes frame Barack Obama as a champion of diplomacy, worlds apart from the pugnacious Trump era. They remember him in a packed auditorium at Cairo University offering dialogue and calm to the Muslim world. "Events in Iraq have reminded America of the need to use diplomacy and build international consensus to resolve our problems whenever possible," he said in that speech. And the Obama administration would, especially in its second term, yield several examples of the effectiveness of empowering diplomats, with the Iran deal, the Paris climate change accord, and a thaw in relations with Cuba. But it also, especially in its first term, accelerated several of the same trends that have conspired to ravage America's diplomatic capacity during the Trump administration.

Obama, to a lesser extent than Trump but a greater extent than many before him, surrounded himself with retired generals or other military officers in senior positions. That included National Security Advisor General Jim Jones, General Douglas Lute as Jones's deputy for Afghanistan, General David Petraeus as head of the CIA, and Admiral Dennis Blair and General James Clapper as successive directors of national intelligence. Growth in the State Department budget continued to flow from Overseas Contingency Operation funds, directed explicitly toward military goals. Defense spending continued its rise. The trend was not linear: sequestration—the automatic spending cuts of 2013—ravaged both the Pentagon and the State Department. But the imbalance between defense and diplomatic spending continued to grow. "The Defense Department budget is always very much larger, and for good reason, I mean I agree with that, but the ratio between the two keeps getting worse and worse," Madeleine Albright said.

Over the course of his presidency, Barack Obama approved more than double the dollar value of arms deals with foreign regimes than George W. Bush had before him. In fact, the Obama administration sold more arms than any other since World War II. When I pressed Hillary Clinton on those facts, she seemed taken aback. "I'm not saying it was perfect," she told me. "As you made out, there were decisions that had increased military commitments associated with them." In the end, however, she felt the Obama administration had gotten "more right than wrong," when it came to the militarization of foreign policy. She cited, as an example, the emphasis on diplomacy that accompanied the Afghanistan review in which she participated. But that review was held up, by both State Department and White House officials, as a deep source of regret and an acute example of the exclusion of civilians from meaningful foreign policymaking. In secret memoranda sent directly to Clinton as that process unfolded and made public in these pages, the diplomat Richard Holbrooke, ostensibly the president's representative on Afghanistan, decried a process overtaken by, in his words, "pure mil-think."

THE OBAMA ADMINISTRATION also doubled down on the kind of White House power grabs that had frustrated Powell during the Bush administration. From Obama's first days in office, Jones, the national security advisor, pledged to expand the National Security Council's reach. What was disparagingly referred to as "back-channel" communication between the president and cabinet members like the secretary of state would be constrained. Jones's successors, Tom Donilon and Susan Rice, each ratcheted up the level of control, according to senior officials.

Samantha Power, who served as director for multilateral affairs and, later, in Obama's cabinet as US ambassador to the United Nations, conceded that there were "some fair critiques" of the administration's tendency to micromanage. "It *was* often the case," she recalled, that policies made at anything but the highest tiers of the White House's hierarchy, "didn't have the force of law, or a force of direction. People weren't confident it wouldn't get changed once it went up the White House chain." We were holed up in a shadowy, exposed-brick corner of Grendel's Den, a bar near Harvard's Kennedy School of Government, where she was a professor. Power, the one-time bleeding-heart war reporter and professor of human rights law, had won a Pulitzer Prize for her book on America's failure to confront genocide around the world. She had long been a favorite subject of awed, inadvertently sexist journalistic paeans, which often began in the same way. Power "strode across the packed room and took a seat, her long sweep of red hair settling around her like a protective shawl," the *New York Times* offered. She was "ivory-toned, abundantly freckled and wears her thick red hair long," added the *Washington Post*. "Her long red hair," *Vogue* agreed, was "striking against the UN's hopeful sky-blue backdrop." Samantha Power's hair, through little fault of her own, shimmered its way across a decade of profiles until, finally, the feminist blog *Jezebel* pleaded, "Enough With Samantha Power's Flowing Red Hair." Power had a winning earnestness and a tendency toward authentic rambling that had, on occasion, made her a PR liability. She memorably called Hillary Clinton a "monster" during the 2008 presidential campaign. She said "fuck" a lot.

"The bottleneck is too great," she continued, "if even very small aspects of US foreign policy have to get decided at the deputies' and principals' level in order for it to count as policy." Denis McDonough, Donilon's deputy and, later, White House chief of staff, would chastise senior officials who attempted to, as he put it, "color outside the lines," according to two who received such rebukes. Susan Rice, according to one senior official, exerted even tighter control over policy related to virtually every part of the globe except Latin America. Rice pointed out that every administration struggles with questions of White House micromanagement. "That is ever the charge from the agencies," she said, "and I have served more time in the State Department than I have in the White House in my career. I'm very familiar with both ends of the street. Find me an agency that feels like the White House isn't up in their knickers and I'll be amazed and impressed."

But some career State Department officials said the Obama administration had gotten the balancing act wrong more often than previous administrations. Examples abounded. Policymaking on South Sudan, which was elevated to a "principals" level under Obama, often stalled when Secretary of State John Kerry or Secretary of Defense Ash Carter were unavailable to join meetings due to their numerous competing obligations. Lower-level officials were disempowered to fill the void. Meetings would be canceled and rescheduled, and weeks would be lost, with lives hanging in the balance. That, Power conceded, "should have been at best a deputies process, because, given inevitable bandwidth constraints, it was very unlikely to be sustained as a principals' process."

The centralization of power had a withering effect on capacity outside of the White House. "The agencies got habituated to always be coming back and asking for direction or clearance," she reflected, as a waitress slid a plate of curry in front of her. She doused it with a shocking amount of sriracha sauce, which makes sense if you're ordering curry at a bar. "The problem," she continued, "is that central control, over time, generates something like learned helplessness." The defiant, world-striding scholar-stateswoman sounded, for a moment, almost wistful. "I think people in other agencies felt that they couldn't move."

THE KINDS OF WHITE HOUSE CONTROL exerted by Presidents Trump and Obama were, in some ways, worlds apart. Where one administration closely micromanaged agencies, the other simply cut them loose. "In previous administrations," Susan Rice argued, the State Department "struggled in the rough and tumble of the bureaucracy. Now, they're trying to kill it." But the end result was similar: diplomats sitting on the sidelines, with policy being made elsewhere.

The freefall of the Foreign Service has continued through both the Obama and Trump eras. By 2012, 28 percent of overseas Foreign Service officer slots were either vacant or filled by low-level employees working above their level of experience. In 2014, most officers had less than ten years of experience, a decline from even the 1990s. Fewer of them ascended to leadership than before: in 1975, more than half of all officers reached senior positions; by 2013, just a quarter did. A profession which, decades earlier, had drawn the greatest minds from America's universities and the private sector was ailing, if not dying.

Every living former secretary of state went on the record for this book. Many expressed concern about the future of the Foreign Service. "The United States must conduct a global diplomacy," said George P. Shultz, who was ninety-seven by the time we spoke during the Trump administration. The State Department, he argued, was stretched too thin and vulnerable to the changing whims of passing administrations. "It was ironic, as soon as we had the pivot to Asia, the Middle East blew up and Russia went into Ukraine. . . . So you have to conduct a global diplomacy. That means you have to have a strong Foreign Service and people who are there permanently."

Henry Kissinger suggested that the arc of history had emaciated the Foreign Service, skewing the balance further toward military leadership. "The problem is whether the selection of key advisers is too much loaded in one direction," Kissinger mused. "Well, there are many reasons for that. For one thing, there are fewer experienced Foreign Service officers. And secondly, one could argue that if you give an order to the Defense Department there's an 80 percent chance it'll be executed, if you give an order to the State Department there's an 80 percent chance of a discussion." Those imbalances in usefulness are deepened, inevitably, during times of war. "When the country is at war, it shifts to the White House and the Pentagon," Condoleezza Rice told me. "And that, I think, is also natural." Rice reflected a common thinking across multiple administrations: "It's a fast-moving set of circumstances," she argued. "There isn't really time for the bureaucratic processes . . . it doesn't have the same character of the steady process development you see in more normal times."

But, by the time the Trump administration began hacking away at the State Department, it had been nearly twenty years since "normal times" in American foreign policy. This was the new reality with which the United States had to contend. Rice's point—that the aging bureaucracies shaped during the post–World War II era moved too slowly for times of emergency—was often true. But ruthlessly centralizing power to avoid broken bureaucracies, rather than reforming them to do their jobs as intended, conjures up a vicious cycle. With State ever less useful in a world of perpetual emergency; with the money, power and prestige of the Pentagon dwarfing those of any other agency; and with the White House itself filled with former generals, the United States is leaving behind the capacity for diplomatic solutions to even make it into the room.

"I remember Colin Powell once said that there was a reason the occupation of Japan was not carried out by a Foreign Service officer but by a general," Rice remembered. "In those circumstances, you have to tilt more to the Pentagon." But just as the occupation of Japan being carried out by a Foreign Service officer registered as an absurdity, the negotiation of treaties and reconstruction of economies being carried out by uniformed officers was a contradiction, and one with a dubious track record.

THE POINT IS NOT that the old institutions of traditional diplomacy can solve today's crises. The point is that we are witnessing the destruction of those institutions, with little thought to engineering modern replacements. Past secretaries of state diverged on how to solve the problem of America's crumbling diplomatic enterprise. Kissinger, ever the hawk, acknowledged the decline of the State Department but greeted it with a shrug. "I'm certainly uncomfortable with the fact that one can walk through the State Department now and find so many offices empty," he said. Kissinger was ninety-four when we spoke. He slouched on a royal blue couch in his New York office, staring at me from under a brow creased with worry lines. He appeared to regard the problems of the present from immense distance. Even his voice, that deep Bavarian rasp, seemed to echo across the decades, as if recorded in Nixon's Oval Office. "It is true that the State Department is inadequately staffed. It is true that the State Department has not been given what it thought was its due. But that is partly due to the fact that new institutions have arisen." But by the time I interviewed Kissinger, during the Trump administration, there were no new institutions emerging to take the place of the kind of thoughtful, holistic foreign policy analysis, unshackled from military exigencies, that diplomacy had once provided America.

Hillary Clinton, sounding weary about a year after she lost her 2016 presidential campaign, told me she'd seen that shift coming for years. When she took office as secretary of state at the beginning of the Obama administration, "I began calling leaders around the world who I had known in my previous lives as a senator and a first lady, and so many of them were distressed by what they saw as the militarization of foreign policy in the Bush administration and the very narrow focus on the important issues of terrorism and of course the wars in Iraq and Afghanistan. I think now the balance has tipped even further toward militarization across the board on every kind of issue," she said. "Diplomacy," she added, expressing a common sentiment among former secretaries of state, both Republican and Democrat, "is under the gun."

These are not problems of principle. The changes described here are, in real time, producing results that make the world less safe and prosperous. Already, they have plunged the United States deeper into military engagements that might have been avoided. Already, they have exacted a heavy cost in American lives and influence around the world. What follows is an account of a crisis. It tells the story of a life-saving discipline torn apart by political cowardice. It describes my own years as a State Department official in Afghanistan and elsewhere, watching the decline play out, with disastrous results for America, and in the lives of the last, great defenders of the profession. And it looks to modern alliances in every corner of the earth, forged by soldiers and spies, and to the costs of those relationships for the United States.

In short, this is the story of a transformation in the role of the United States among the nations of our world—and of the outmatched public servants inside creaking institutions desperately striving to keep an alternative alive.

PART I

THE LAST DIPLOMATS

■

PAKISTAN, 2010

If you ain't speakin' money language I can't hang
You know your conversation is weak, so it's senseless to speak

—DR. DRE, *EVERYDAY THING* (WITH NAS AND NATURE)

1

AMERICAN MYTHS

THE DIPLOMAT WAS NOT always an endangered species. Those who hold the profession in reverence point out that it once flourished, upheld by larger-than-life, world-striding figures whose accomplishments still form the bedrock of the modern international order. Stories of diplomacy are a part of the American creation myth. Without Benjamin Franklin's negotiations with the French, there would have been no Treaty of Alliance and no naval support to secure American independence. Without Franklin, John Adams and John Jay brokering the Treaty of Paris, there would have been no formal end to war with the British. Had Adams, a Massachusetts Yankee of modest upbringing, not traveled to England and presented his credentials as our first diplomat in the Court of King George III, the new United States might have never stabilized relations with the British after the war. Even in the nineteenth century, when diplomats barely made living wages and Congress saddled the State Department with a slew of domestic responsibilities from maintaining the mint to notarizing official documents, the Department defined the modern map of the United States, brokering the Louisiana Purchase and settling disputes with Britain over the border with Canada. Even after the First World War, as the nation turned inward and grappled with the Great Depression, American secretaries of state orchestrated the Washington Naval Conference on disarmament and the Pact of Paris, renouncing war—forging bonds that were later integral in rallying the allies against the Axis powers.

American politicians have forever exploited a vein of nationalism and isolationism against the work of foreign policy. One late nineteenth-century congressman accused diplomats of "working our ruin by creating a desire for foreign customs and foreign follies. The disease is imported by our returning diplomats and by the foreign ambassadors sent here by monarchs and despots to corrupt and destroy our American ideals." He suggested confining diplomats on their return from assignments, "as we quarantine foreign rags through fear of cholera." But great diplomatic accomplishments always cut through that hostility.

This was never more true than during World War II, when the Department adapted to the challenges of the day and gave rise to the most fruitful period of diplomatic accomplishment in American history. The State Department faced an existential crisis then not unlike the one that unraveled in 2017. "The American nation desperately needs and desperately lacks an adequate State Department at this hour of the shaping of its future," screamed the *St. Louis Post-Dispatch* in 1943 copy that would splice neatly into coverage of Trump's secretaries of state generations later. But the response was a world apart: Between 1940 and 1945, the Department modernized and reformed. It tripled its workforce and doubled its budget. It restructured, creating offices to address long-term planning, postwar reconstruction and public information in an age of fast-changing mass media.

That modernized State Department, led by a new generation of hard-charging diplomats, shaped a new international order. Those years saw the forging of a great wartime alliance between the United States and the United Kingdom, brokered by Winston Churchill and Franklin Roosevelt. The same era brought about the creation of the World

Bank and the International Monetary Fund, negotiated between the United States, Canada, Western Europe, Australia, and Japan. It produced the "containment" doctrine that came to define US engagement with the Soviets for decades to come. Among the prominent architects of this era were six friends, later celebrated as "the Wise Men." Two, George Kennan and Charles Bohlen, were members of the Foreign Service, the, at the time, newly formed professional organization for diplomats. In the postwar years, the Wise Men guided President Truman to what would become the Truman Doctrine, committing the United States to support other nations against the Soviets and to the massive Marshall Plan for international assistance to those nations. The same timeframe yielded the creation of NATO, championed by another member of a rejuvenated State Department, Under Secretary Robert Lovett.

The era of the Wise Men was far from perfect. Some of their most celebrated ideas were also fonts of blunder and misery. Despite Kennan's warnings, for example, containment was appropriated as a rationale for the military escalation and conflict that came to define the Cold War. "As much as I love reading *Present at the Creation*," John Kerry said of Dean Acheson's densely detailed 800-page memoir of his time at the State Department, "Maybe history and some distance tells us that Acheson and Dulles made some mistakes out of a certainty and a view of the world that we paid for a long time, certainly in some places? In my generation, Richard Holbrooke and I both knew that the supposed best and the brightest got plenty of our friends killed in Vietnam."

But the Wise Men had undeniable success and staying power in stabilizing the world. And diplomats of their stature, and the kind of old-school diplomacy they practiced, seem harder to find today than seventy years ago, or fifty, or twenty. "Is it the person or the role or the times?" Kerry wondered. "I see some really first-rate diplomats who have done great work. . . . Maybe we just don't celebrate people in government and at State the way we once did?"

Henry Kissinger argued that a broader shift had taken place: that something had changed not simply in the State Department and its relative bureaucratic influence, but in the philosophy of the American people. It was not lost on me that I was sitting across from someone with a more complicated legacy than even the Wise Men: regarded in some circles as an exemplar of the ferocious diplomat, and in others as a war criminal for his bombing of Cambodia. (It wasn't lost on him either: he attempted to end our interview when I approached subjects of controversy.) This may have been why Kissinger tended towards the general and the philosophical. Tactics, he felt, had triumphed over strategy, and fast reaction over historicized decision-making. "The United States is eternally preoccupied with solving whatever problems emerge at the moment," Kissinger said. "We have an inadequate number of experienced people in the conduct of foreign policy but even more importantly, an inadequate number of people who can think of foreign policy as a historical process."

That was how the last standard bearers of the diplomatic profession found themselves, increasingly, at odds with administrations seeking political expedience and military efficiency. Kissinger pointed to the confrontation between the Obama administration and its representative on Afghanistan and Pakistan, Richard Holbrooke: a struggle to be heard in a policy process overtaken by generals, and to apply the lessons of Vietnam in an administration fixated on innovation. "They wanted to start something new, and he wanted to apply lessons from the past," Kissinger said of Holbrooke. Similar battles were lost by other diplomats before, and more have been lost since. But the story of Richard Holbrooke, and the disintegration of his last mission, and the devastating effect that had on the lives of the diplomats around him, provide a window into what was lost when we turned away from a profession that once saved us. "It's one great American myth," Kissinger added, speaking slowly, "that you can always try something new."

2

LADY TALIBAN

T HE POWER WENT OUT, as it often did in Islamabad, and the room went dark. But the laptop had juice, so the human rights activist I had come to see swung the screen around and told me to watch. A video flickered on screen. It was shaky, surreptitiously captured from a distance. Six young men stumbled through a wooded area, blindfolded, hands bound behind their backs. In typical civilian *kurtas*, they did not look like fighters. Soldiers in Pakistani Army uniforms led the young men to a clearing and lined them up against a stonework wall.

An older, bearded officer, a commander perhaps, approached the young men, one by one. "Do you know the *Kalimas*?" he asked, referring to the Islamic religious phrases sometimes uttered before death. He rejoined more than half a dozen soldiers at the other end of the clearing. They were lining up in the style of an execution squad. "One by one, or together?" asked one. "Together," said the commander. The soldiers raised their rifles—G3s, standard issue equipment in the Pakistani military—took aim, and fired.

The men crumpled to the ground. Several survived, wailing and writhing on the ground. A soldier approached and fired into each body, silencing the men one by one.

For a moment after the video ended, no one said anything. Street traffic rattled through a nearby window. Finally, the human rights activist asked: "What will you do now?"

THE VIDEO WAS SHOCKING, but its existence was no surprise. It was 2010 in Pakistan, home to America's most important counterterrorism partnership. Al-Qaeda's leadership had fled American military operations in Afghanistan, evaporating into the thin mountain air of Pakistan's untamed border country. This was the heart of the war on terror and the hunt for Osama bin Laden. As a rookie recruit to the State Department's Afghanistan and Pakistan team, charged with talking to development and human rights groups, I found that diplomacy in the region had a quality of pantomime. Every conversation, whether about building dams or reforming education, was in fact about counterterrorism: keeping Pakistan happy enough to join the fight and allow our supplies to pass through its borders to American troops in Afghanistan. But often, the Pakistanis were unwilling (according to the Americans) or unable (by their own account) to move against their country's terrorist strongholds.

The previous fall, there had been a rare success—Pakistani forces had staged an offensive in the rural Swat valley, seizing control and capturing Taliban militants. But it wasn't long before rumors began to circulate about what exactly that success had entailed. Public reports were emerging of a new wave of executions in the wake of military operations in Swat. By that summer, Human Rights Watch had investigated 238 alleged executions and found at least 50 were heavily corroborated. As with everything in government, the executions even had an acronym: EJK, for "extrajudicial killings." The issue was complex. In rural Pakistan, courtrooms and prisons were more the stuff of aspiration than reality. Some Pakistani military units viewed summary executions as the only practical way of dealing with extremists they apprehended. But the tactic was also proving useful in disposing of a growing number of dissidents, lawyers, and journalists. Pakistani military personnel, when they could be enticed to acknowledge the issue at all, bitterly pointed out that the United States pressed them to target some bad guys, then complained when they took out others.

The killings were a point of extraordinary sensitivity in the relationship between Pakistan and the United States. For the Pakistanis, they were an embarrassment. For the Americans, they were a fly in the ointment. American taxpayers had bankrolled Pakistan to the tune of $19.7 billion in military and civilian assistance since September 11, 2001. Revelations about the murders raised the specter of unwanted scrutiny.

Inside the State Department, I circulated news of the video, and of mounting calls for a response from human rights watchdogs. The results were Kafkaesque. Officials set to work quashing meetings with the groups behind the reporting. When they acquiesced to a single briefing, in Washington, with Human Rights Watch, it was with the understanding that we would allow no questions of the US government, and that our comments be limited to "very general press guidance." A career bureaucrat with a prim demeanor and a vacant smile responded to my emails on the subject with a cheerful suggestion:

Sent: Monday, March 08, 2010 4:43 PM

Subject: RE: Extrajudicial Executions/HRW Meeting Request

One suggestion: rather than specifically referencing the term *EJK*, we've been trying to work these issues under the umbrella of "gross violations of human rights" (statutory language lifted from Leahy provisions). One advantage of using the Leahy phrasing is that it covers the broad swath of abuses (including EJK) of con-

cern to the USG; another is that it encompasses abuses committed by insurgents as well as those attributed to government forces
and agencies. The bonus is that it helps to insulate "open source"
meetings from the sensitive policy discussions on the high side.

Just a semantic twist in service of diplomacy.

The statute she was referring to—named after its sponsor, Senator
Patrick Leahy of Vermont—banned giving American assistance to foreign military units committing atrocities. I forwarded the exchange to
a colleague. "Oh boy, how Rwanda-press-conferences-circa-1994 is
this!?", I wrote, referring to the "semantic twists" US officials under-
took to avoid using the word "genocide" in the midst of that crisis.

Several months later, I pushed a dossier across a conference table
toward Melanne Verveer, Hillary Clinton's ambassador-at-large for
global women's issues. We were both visiting Islamabad and she'd
asked what human rights groups were saying. I printed up some of
the reporting—nothing classified, just open-source documents. All the
same, I stuck to euphemisms.

"There's a spike in . . . gross violations of human rights."

"And when you say, 'gross violations'? . . ." she said, flipping
through the file.

"Executions."

It was June, Islamabad's hottest month of the year, and the air felt
close in the cramped room at the American embassy in Pakistan. Across
the table from the two of us, a diplomat stationed at the embassy glared
at me. She'd shot me a warning look when the topic came up. Now
her lips were pursed, her eyes boring into me. On the table in front of
her, her knuckles were marble-white. Ambassador Robin Raphel, the
career Foreign Service officer who was overseeing a spike in American
assistance to Pakistan that year, was furious.

LATER THAT WEEK, embassy staff and locals gathered outside the American ambassador's residence in Islamabad's secure "red zone." Nestled at the foot of the densely forested Margalla Hills, the city's wide avenues are lined with eucalyptus and pine trees. By that June in 2010, its parks and lawns were an explosion of white gladiolus and purple amaranthus. At night, the posh districts hummed with intellectual energy. As the war raged nearby, an international set of diplomats, reporters, and aid workers met for golden-haloed cocktail parties, exchanging whispers of palace intrigue.

Robin Raphel had been a fixture at such parties for years, since she began working in Pakistan decades earlier. To many locals, she was simply "Robin."

That night at the ambassador's residence, she was in her element, holding forth for a clutch of party-goers. With high cheekbones and ramrod-straight posture, she had an aristocratic quality, her blond hair pulled into a tight French twist. She spoke with a locked jaw and the clipped, mid-Atlantic cadence of a 1940s movie star. Tossed over one shoulder, she wore, as she so often did, an embroidered pashmina shawl that made her dress suit resemble the flowing *salwar kameez* of the local women.

Since that day in the conference room, Raphel had done her utmost to kneecap the junior diplomat who had responded to the question about human rights. When she couldn't keep me out of meetings, she would cut me off in them, with relish. That night at the party she made little secret of her disapproval. "How *dare* you bring up—" here she lowered her voice conspiratorially, "—*EJK* in a meeting at *this* embassy." Her lip quivered. "You are not of value on that issue."

I wondered how much she was frustrated by my criticism of America's role in Pakistan and how much she just found me personally annoying. I explained, trying to stay deferential, that the State Department had adopted a policy of acknowledging the human rights report-ing, even if we didn't confirm it. "Well, that may be the case in DC," she sniffed. She fingered the loop of pearls at her neck. "This isn't DC. And we do not discuss that issue here."

It would be three years before the gutting of Mahogany Row, but in national security hot spots like this, you could see the power slipping away from diplomats in real time. Pakistan was the perfect illustration of the trend: for decades, the Pentagon and the CIA had bypassed the United States' civilian foreign policy systems to do busi-ness directly with Pakistan's military and intelligence leaders. In the years since September 11, 2001, they'd gained more freedom than ever to do so. Standing in the warm Islamabad summer, I wondered at Robin Raphel, so keen to avoid tough questions about a foreign military and its entanglements with our own. What did she under-stand her role to be, at a time in which so much of that role was being carved away and carted off? When nineteenth-century pundits sug-gested quarantining diplomats, lest they bring back mixed allegiances, was this what they meant? Was this something old or something new?

FOR DECADES, ROBIN RAPHEL embodied a tradition of old-school diplomacy. Born Robin Lynn Johnson, she grew up in a sleepy lumber town in Washington State, tearing through the *National Geo-graphic* magazines her father collected and dreaming of the wider world. At Mark Morris High, she was voted "most likely to succeed." "She seemed to have a worldly sense about her," remembered one classmate. In college, she'd leapt at opportunities to travel, spending a summer in Tehran with a church group, before heading to a junior year abroad at the University of London.

"Are you still religious?" I once asked her. She snorted derisively. This seemed an absurd question to her. "What do you *mean*, 'am I still religious'?" she snapped. When pressed, she waved a hand dismissively.

"I wouldn't say one way or another." If Robin Raphel had time for spirituality, she didn't have time to share it with me. She was all flinty pragmatism. She prided herself on it.

After college, she spent a year studying at Cambridge and found a dazzling set of fellow Americans with their own international dreams and yearbook superlatives. It was the height of the Vietnam War, and the dorms of Oxford and Cambridge filled with debate about an American proxy war gone wrong. There were eerie parallels to another war that would, decades later, have a cataclysmic impact on Robin Raphel's life: another new administration faced with a fatigued public, an uncooperative partner force, and an elusive insurgency with safe havens across a tactically challenging border.

Raphel, then still Johnson, started dating a young Rhodes Scholar and fellow University of Washington graduate, Frank Aller, and befriended his roommates: Strobe Talbott, who would go on to become a journalist and deputy secretary of state, and an aspiring politician named Bill Clinton. In their modest house at 46 Leckford Road in North Oxford, the friends spent hours agonizing over the threat of the draft. Clinton and Aller were both classified as "1-A"—available to be drafted—and both opposed the war. Clinton considered various strategies for avoiding the draft but ultimately decided against them, as he put it, "to maintain my political viability within the system." Aller, on the other hand, stayed in England, on the run from the draft and agonized by the resulting stigma. A year later, he went home to Spokane, put a .22-caliber Smith & Wesson in his mouth, and blew his brains out.

I asked Raphel how Aller's death, so soon after they dated, affected her. "Oh," she said, as if I'd asked her about a fender bender. "I was very upset, needless to say!" She paused, realizing how she'd sounded. "As you've no doubt noticed, I'm passionate about being dispassionate." Robin Raphel wasn't about to let emotion be an obstacle to the life on the world stage she was, even then, beginning to craft. In the following years, her path would wind from Tehran to Islamabad to Tunisia.

OVER THE COURSE of that journey, Raphel's critics would not share her dispassion. By the end of her career, she would be called a traitor, a turncoat, and a terrorist sympathizer. In the Indian press, she was called, with delight, "Lady Taliban." The astonishing nadir would come during the Obama administration. Four years after our run-in in Islamabad, Raphel arrived at her desk on the first floor of the State Department, in a sea of cubicles not far from the cafeteria. She checked her email and took a few routine meetings. It was early afternoon when she saw the missed calls. The first was from Slomin's Home Security; someone had been trying to get into Raphel's house. The next call was from her daughter Alexandra, who was panicked. Raphel had to get home immediately, Alexandra said. Raphel got into her Ford Focus and drove the twenty-minute route to her home in Northwest Washington, DC.

What she arrived, she saw a dozen FBI agents crawling over her modest two-story Cape Cod–style house. Two earnest-looking agents in plainclothes approached her and showed her their badges. Next they handed her a warrant.

It specified that Robin Raphel was being investigated under 18 U.S.C. Section 793(e), a criminal statute that covers the illegal gathering or transmission of national security information:

Espionage.

3

DICK

VIETNAM WAS A SPECTRAL HORROR for the friends at 46
Leckford in the late 1960s, but for other young men, the war had
an almost magnetic pull. Richard Holbrooke, who years later became
close to Strobe Talbott, and through him, Bill Clinton, sought out the
war as a proving ground. His experiences there would echo through
forty years of American warfare. Decades later, he would become one
of the last voices to carry the lessons of Vietnam into the modern conflict in Afghanistan and Pakistan.

Holbrooke was a New Yorker, born to Jewish parents. He was
"Dick" to his friends, until his elegant third wife enforced a transition
to the more genteel "Richard." (His enemies never transitioned.) Dick
Holbrooke was grasping, relentless, wore his ambition on his sleeve—
the kind of person who could go in a revolving door behind you and
come out ahead of you, one friend said. He was oblivious to social
graces in the pursuit of his goals. While making an impassioned point,
he once followed Hillary Clinton into a women's room—in Pakistan, she would stress in the retelling. A former flame recalled waiting
with him, endlessly, for a cab during a torrential storm in Manhattan.

When one finally approached, he kissed her on the cheek and hopped in without a word, leaving her in the downpour. As Pamela Harriman, the socialite-turned-diplomat, once remarked tartly: "He's not entirely housebroken."

He always struck me as vast—not so much taller but somehow more expansive than his six foot, one inch frame. He had pale eyes and a gaze like a bird of prey, but also an irrepressible twinkle, his thin lips always on the verge of a smirk. His eruptions of temper were legendary, but he would just as often go still, dropping his voice to a near whisper. He deployed both tactics in a singular negotiating style he compared to "a combination of chess and mountain climbing"—flattering, bullying, charming, and intimidating his way to persuasion. He wrote voluminously, and had the uncanny ability to speak in crisp, complete paragraphs. As oblivious as he could be to the sensitivities of people around him, he was a detailed observer of the world and indomitable in his excitement about it. In other words, he was the rare asshole who was worth it.

As a child, he idolized scientists: Einstein, Fermi. But his interests turned to the wider world. After his father succumbed to colon cancer, he grew close to the family of his classmate, David Rusk, whose father Dean would soon become Kennedy's secretary of state, and who visited Holbrooke's class at Scarsdale High School to extol the virtues of the Foreign Service. At the time, it was journalism that captivated Holbrooke. He was sports editor at his high school's newspaper, then editor in chief of his college's, the *Brown Daily Herald*, where his analyses of Cold War tensions ran under announcements for cheerleading tryouts. As a sophomore, he convinced his editors to send him to the 1960 Four Powers Summit in Paris, where Western leaders were set to meet with Nikita Khrushchev to try to ease tensions over the division of Berlin. The summit was a spectacular failure. Days before, the Soviets shot down a U-2 spy plane and the ensuing confrontation soon shut down the talks. James "Scotty" Reston of the *New York Times*, whom

Holbrooke idolized and who gave the young student journalist a job fetching drinks for the *Times* team in Paris, told Holbrooke: "Whether you go into journalism or the Foreign Service as a career, you will always be able to say, 'I started my career at *the worst* diplomatic fiasco ever held.'" He was wrong: Holbrooke would see worse. After graduating from Brown, he tried and failed to get a job at the *Times* and decided to take the Foreign Service exam. So it was that newly minted Foreign Service officer Richard Holbrooke arrived at Tan Son Nhut airport in Saigon on a muggy June night in 1963.

VIETNAM WAS THE FIRST modern test of American "counter-insurgency"—the strategy of securing a vulnerable population while winning its loyalty through social programs. During a Foreign Service training course, Holbrooke and his Vietnam-bound contemporaries—including Anthony Lake, who would later become Clinton's national security advisor—whiled away sweltering nights playing a game called "fan ball," which involved throwing a tennis ball at a ceiling fan, then scrambling to chase it as it ricocheted around the room. (They could hardly have designed a more conspicuous Vietnam metaphor if they tried.) At the time of his arrival, twenty-two-year-old Holbrooke was single and could be sent to the rural frontlines to oversee development programs. It gave him an unvarnished view of mounting failures that his superiors in Washington lacked.

He also witnessed the precipitous militarization of policymaking in Vietnam. During a trip with the 9th Marine Regiment in rural Da Nang, Holbrooke watched General Lewis Walt, commander of the Marine Amphibious Force, kneel and push away semicircles of sand in front of him, showing how the Americans would supposedly push out the Vietcong, making way for the South Vietnamese and good governance. A group of Vietnamese children looked on, chattering curiously. Holbrooke, never one to mince words, pointed out: "But the VC will just move in behind you." The general, and Americans across Vietnam, kept on pushing for years. "Despite the hours and days of instruction they had in 'counterinsurgency,' despite all the briefings which emphasized the political nature of the war, they could not understand what was going on or how to deal with it," Holbrooke wrote in one unpublished memo. The insurgents would not give up, and the locals "were not going to switch sides in return for some free soap."

Holbrooke dissented, loudly. During his time in the provinces, he once argued openly with General William Westmoreland, the commander of US forces in Vietnam.

"How old are you?" Westmoreland finally asked, exasperated.

"Twenty-four."

"What makes you think you know so much?"

"I don't know," said Holbrooke, "but I've been here two years and I've spent all of the time in the field."

Westmoreland was reporting back to Washington his conviction that he could break the insurgency through increasing levels of force. As Holbrooke ascended to positions at the White House and State Department, he sent vigorous, often unsolicited memos to his bosses. "I have never seen the Americans in such disarray," he wrote in one when he was just twenty-six. Forty years later, when I was working for him as the military pushed for a troop surge in Afghanistan, Holbrooke unearthed the memo and had me forward it to his Vietnam buddies.

When the Department of Defense launched the top-secret review of Vietnam eventually known as the Pentagon Papers, an official named Leslie Gelb, who went on to become the head of the Council on Foreign Relations and a lifelong friend to Holbrooke, tapped the iconoclastic young diplomat to write one volume. Holbrooke's contributions were scathing. The counterinsurgency was "faultily conceived and clumsily executed." The hawks, he argued, had dangerously commandeered policymaking.

When the legendary diplomat Averell Harriman headed a delegation to negotiate with the North Vietnamese, Holbrooke numbed his bosses into submission hustling for a spot on the team. He believed in the power of negotiation to end the war. "Holbrooke wants to always talk with the other side," said Nicholas Katzenbach, the under secretary of state who was Holbrooke's boss in the late 1960s. "He always thinks there's some negotiation, some middle road." But Paris was an agonizing failure. During a close presidential race, the Nixon campaign, it later emerged, worked to scuttle the talks, encouraging South Vietnam to drag its feet. Famously, the team wasted two months arguing over the shape of the negotiating table, as the war raged.

Shortly after Nixon took office, Holbrooke resigned and left government. "[I]t was neither foreordained nor inevitable that the war should continue, with another twenty-five thousand Americans and countless Vietnamese dead," he later wrote. "A negotiated end to the war in 1968 was possible; the distance to peace was far smaller than most historians realize." He'd seen the United States squander one chance to end a war; he wouldn't let it happen again.

As the war in Afghanistan raged in September 2010, the State Department Historian's Office released the final volume in the government's official history of Vietnam. Richard Holbrooke walked from his office to the State Department's George C. Marshall Conference Center to deliver remarks on the publication, which contained one of his early memos. It was a gray day, and he wore a gray, rumpled suit, and stood in front of a gray drop cloth. The fluorescent lights cast deep shadows under his eyes. He paused a little more often than usual. When an audience member asked about the parallels between Afghanistan and Vietnam, Holbrooke managed a wan smile. "I was wondering how long we could avoid that question."

He spoke carefully. As Holbrooke's contemporaries slipped from power and a new generation took hold, the word "Vietnam" increasingly registered as an unwelcome history lesson. But privately, I had heard him lay out the comparison. In Vietnam, the United States had been defeated by a country adjacent to the conflict, harboring enemy safe havens across a porous border; by our reliance on a corrupt partner government; and by an embrace of a failing counterinsurgency doctrine at the behest of the military establishment. In Afghanistan, he was witnessing echoes of all three dynamics—including yet another administration favoring military voices and missing opportunities for negotiation. "Dick Holbrooke was, of course, a friend of mine," Henry Kissinger said. "It was a fair comparison," he observed of the parallels Holbrooke drew between Vietnam and Afghanistan. In both cases, the United States would find itself applying frameworks that had worked elsewhere in the world with disastrous results. "Vietnam was the attempt to apply the containment principles of Europe to Asia," Kissinger continued, "But, in Europe, containment was applied to societies that had existed for hundreds of years and whose internal structure was relatively stable except for the impact of the war." Vietnam had proved to be another matter entirely. Likewise, in Afghanistan, the question after 9/11 was, "Can we turn Afghanistan into a democratic government which no longer supports such efforts?" as Kissinger put it. "That was the wrong question."

That day at the State Department, Richard Holbrooke was quick to point out that Afghanistan was not Vietnam. The inciting event— an attack on American soil—made the strategic calculus different. "But structurally there are obvious similarities," he said. "And leafing through these books here, they leap out at you. Many of the programs that are being followed, many of the basic doctrines are the same ones that we were trying to apply in Vietnam."

4

THE MANGO CASE

SHORTLY AFTER RICHARD HOLBROOKE left behind the wreckage of Vietnam and resigned from the Nixon administration, Robin Raphel departed Cambridge and returned to Iran, taking a job teaching history at Damavand College for women. Before the fall of the shah, Tehran was cosmopolitan and welcoming. Raphel danced and acted in US-backed theater productions, including one of *Anything Goes*. She fell in love with a handsome, funny Foreign Service officer, Arnold Raphel; "Arnie," to friends. In 1972, they married on the grounds of the American embassy in an interfaith ceremony bringing together his Judaism, her Christianity, and a lot of 1970s velvet.

When he was posted to Pakistan in 1975, Raphel went with him. Pakistan didn't faze her any more than Iran had. Islamabad was a sleepy town, lush and green, with a third of its current population. "It was great," Raphel recalled, lighting up at the memory. "It was up and coming." She joined the Foreign Service and took a job at USAID. The young American couple cut a glamorous profile, throwing cocktail parties and hosting screenings of American movies. She slipped effortlessly into Pakistani high society, developing a network of connections that would serve—and haunt—her in years to come. For Raphel, like generations of Foreign Service officers before her, advancing American influence was about friendship and conversation. "You *need* to be engaged and figure out what makes people tick and what motivates them," she said. "To me that's blindingly obvious." She reflected on this for a moment. "But sometimes we forget. And in this post-9/11, more urgent and demanding time, we fell into finger-wagging demanding."

Just a few years after Raphel's first, golden days in Islamabad, a transformation swept the region. When the secular, American-backed shah of Iran fell to an Islamist revolution in 1979, it cemented America's reliance on Pakistan as a military and intelligence partner. The United States had lost important listening stations in Iran used to monitor the Soviets. The CIA approached Pakistan's Inter-Services Intelligence agency—the ISI—which agreed to build Pakistani facilities to fill the void.

THE CALL OF ISLAMIC REVOLUTION also sounded from Iran to neighboring Afghanistan, where a Soviet-backed Marxist regime had seized control a year earlier. Under the guidance of the KGB, the Marxists had instituted secular reforms, including mandatory girls' education. On propaganda posters, women with red babushkas and red lips held open books under Cyrillic screaming: "IF YOU DON'T READ BOOKS, YOU'LL FORGET THE LETTERS." For conservative Afghans, it was too much. The Afghan army erupted against the communists.

Initially, the Soviets hesitated as the revolt spread. But in Moscow, diplomacy had been sidelined and the KGB's influence had swelled. KGB chief Yuri Andropov neatly bypassed Soviet diplomats voicing caution. On Christmas Eve, transport planes loaded with Soviet troops landed at Kabul airport. The Carter administration saw the invasion as a chance to embarrass Moscow. Carter green-lit a covert war orchestrated through the United States' military alliance with Pakistan. "It is essential that Afghanistan's resistance continues," National Security Advisor Zbigniew Brzezinski wrote. "This means more money as well as arms shipments to the rebels . . . To make this possible, we must both reassure Pakistan and encourage it to help the rebels. This will require a review of our policy toward Pakistan, more guarantees to it, more arms aid, and, alas, a decision that our security policy toward Pakistan cannot be dictated by our nonproliferation policy."

Pakistan had not been a paragon of virtue in the late 1970s. Its military dictator, Mohammed Zia-ul-Haq, hanged the civilian leader he had forced out of office, Zulfikar Ali Bhutto, and canceled elections. Pakistan was aggressively pursuing the atom bomb, resisting American calls to stand down. In the name of war with the Soviets, as was the case in the later war on terror, all those concerns were secondary.

Over the course of Reagan's first term, Congress's approved funding for the covert war swelled from tens to hundreds of millions of dollars a year. Zia insisted that guns purchased with those funds be dispersed entirely on Pakistan's terms. A Top Secret Presidential Finding at the outset of the war called for the CIA to defer to Pakistan. One Islamabad station chief remembered his orders this way: "Take care of the Pakistanis, and make them do whatever you need them to do." When Zia visited Reagan, Secretary of State Shultz wrote a memo advising that, "We must remember, without Zia's support, the Afghan resistance, key to making the Soviets pay a heavy price for their Afghan adventure, is effectively dead." (When I asked Shultz about his advocacy for the Pakistani regime, he was unapologetic. "Zia and President Reagan, they had a relationship. The whole idea was helping the mujahedeen get the Soviet Union out of Afghanistan," he said, using the Arabic word for Muslim fighters engaged in jihad, like those fighting the Soviets. "And we succeeded.") And so, as Zia insisted, weapons would be given to Pakistan's ISI, which would hand-select the mujahedeen who received the spoils. The United States, still stinging from the complexities of managing a proxy war in Vietnam, was happy to leave the details to Pakistan.

AMID THE URGENCY of battle with the Soviets, the partnership's less pleasant realities were easy to overlook. Pakistani officers sold their CIA-supplied weapons on the black market—once, they even sold them back to the CIA. Pakistan continued to brazenly flaunt its nuclear development. In 1985, the Senate passed the so-called Pressler Amendment, requiring the president to certify, on an annual basis, that Pakistan didn't possess nukes. The rule was strict: no certification, no assistance. Zia lied to President Reagan about the Pakistani nuclear program. "There is no question that we had an intelligence basis for not certifying from 1987 on," said one veteran CIA official. But Reagan continued to certify that Pakistan was nonnuclear anyway. Ohio senator John Glenn argued that nuclear proliferation was "a far greater danger to the world than being afraid to cut off the flow of aid to Afghanistan. . . . It's the short-term versus the long-term." But he was a rare voice of dissent.

The covert war also required that the Americans turn a blind eye to the brutality of the jihad being armed across the border. The Pakistanis passed the American arms to the most ruthless of the Islamist hard-liners: radicals like Abdul Sayyaf and Burhanuddin Rabbani and Jalaluddin Haqqani, all with strong ties to terrorist networks. One of the ISI's favored sons was Gulbuddin Hekmatyar, a vicious fundamentalist who reputedly specialized in skinning captured soldiers alive and whose men indiscriminately murdered civilians. A pugnacious CIA agent named Milt Bearden took over the program in the latter half of the 1980s. By his estimate, the Pakistanis gave nearly a quarter of the American spoils to Hekmatyar. "Hekmatyar was a favorite of the Pakistanis, but he certainly wasn't a favorite of mine," he told me. He added flatly: "I really should have shot him when I had the chance."

International Islamists were attracted like moths to the fires of extremism stoked by the Pakistanis and Americans. A wealthy Saudi patron named Osama bin Laden moved to Pakistan in the mid-1980s and drew close to some of the ISI's favored jihadis, including Hekmatyar and Sayyaf. He offered cash stipends to fighters from the ISI's training camps, and eventually established his own, modeled closely after the ISI's.

And it worked. Within a few years, the CIA declared the covert war cost-effective. The true costs became apparent later.

ROBIN AND ARNOLD RAPHEL had moved to Washington, DC, just before the war with the Soviets broke out and "a lot of stuff went south," as she would later put it. This was an accurate description of events in both the US-Pakistani relationship and her own. She wanted children; Arnold didn't. They divorced in the early 1980s. Raphel would have two subsequent marriages, and two daughters. But friends described Arnold as the love of Robin Raphel's life. One sensed she'd sooner jump out of a window than cop to such sentimentality.

Arnold, still a rising star in the Foreign Service, returned to Pakistan as US ambassador. On a hot afternoon in August 1988, he joined President Zia in a stretch of desert near the provincial city of Bahawalpur for a demonstration of the American Abrams tank—the latest offering to be purchased with Pakistan's still-ongoing flood of assistance—and then accepted a last-minute invitation to join Zia in his American-made C-130 Hercules, for the commute back to Islamabad. They were joined by Zia's chief of staff and ISI chief General Akhtar, who had hand-selected the mujahedeen supported by America's covert war, along with General Herbert M. Wassom, who oversaw US military assistance to Pakistan. Exactly five minutes after they took off, the plane plunged into the desert and exploded into a massive fireball. All thirty souls aboard were dead, including Zia-ul-Haq and Arnold Raphel.

The incident is, to this day, one of the great unsolved mysteries of Pakistani history. Although an American ambassador had been killed and the FBI had statutory authority to investigate, Secretary of State Shultz ordered FBI investigators to stay away. Milt Bearden, likewise, kept the CIA away. The only Americans allowed on the site, seven Air Force investigators, ruled out mechanical failure in a secret report. The only possibility was sabotage. A canister containing VX nerve gas or a similar agent could have wiped out the plane, perhaps. A long-standing conspiracy theory held that nerve gas was secreted in a case of mangoes, loaded onboard before takeoff.

For Pakistan, the crash deepened mistrust of the Americans. General Beg, who seized power afterwards, was as committed as Zia to Pakistan's nuclear development and support for terrorist proxies—but less friendly to the United States. For Robin Raphel, the tragedy severed her from those early, hopeful days in Tehran. When I asked about losing Arnold, she gave a small, brittle laugh. "It would be difficult for anyone. But life goes on."

That was the year the last of the Soviets pulled out of Afghanistan. The CIA station in Islamabad's cable relating the news read, simply, "we won." But the lack of broader strategic dialogue between the United States and Pakistan hit hard and fast once the Red Menace subsided.

FOUR MONTHS LATER, when Pakistan's new prime minister, Benazir Bhutto, made her first official trip to the United States, the cracks were already beginning to show. Bhutto, the daughter of Zulfiqar Ali Bhutto, the prime minister over whose hanging Zia had presided, had returned to Pakistan after years of exile. Harvard-educated and just thirty-five years old, she cut a glamorous profile. Wearing a white headscarf, a gold and pink *salwar kameez*, and literally rose-colored aviator glasses, she stood in front of the American flag at a joint session of Congress and quoted Lincoln, Madison, and Kennedy. "Speaking for Pakistan, I can declare that we do not possess nor do we intend to make a nuclear device," she said emphatically.

But days beforehand, Bhutto had sat at Blair House, kitty-corner from the White House, and received an alarming briefing from CIA director William H. Webster. According to one person who was present that day, Webster walked in with a soccer ball converted into a mock-up of the kind of nuclear prototype he now knew Pakistan possessed. Webster told Bhutto that if her country continued the process of converting its gaseous uranium into solid "pits"—the cores of atom bombs—there was no way President Bush could certify that Pakistan was non-nuclear later that year. Before the end of the month, the jig was up. The CIA had irrefutable evidence that Pakistan had machined its uranium into several cores. In 1990, just a year after the Soviets' departure from Afghanistan, George H. W. Bush became the first president to decline to certify that Pakistan remained nonnuclear. Under the terms of the Pressler Amendment, most economic and military assistance was suspended, and F-16 fighter jets ordered and paid for by Pakistan were left to collect dust in Arizona for years. To this day, the F-16s are a point of obsession for every Pakistani military official I've met. They symbolize a betrayal America quickly forgot—and Pakistan never did.

When the military relationship came screeching to a halt, there was little by way of meaningful diplomatic context to soften the blow. Even Milt Bearden, maestro of mujahedeen chaos, lamented the lack of dialogue: "The relationship was always shallow," he remembered. "When the Soviets marched out of Afghanistan in February 1989, within the next year we had sanctioned them and cut off military contacts." It set the tenor for the relationship in the following decade, with Pakistan in the role of jilted lover. "They love to love us," reflected Bearden, "but they really deeply believe that every time the chips are down, we screw 'em."

Absent the urgency of a proxy war, the American foreign policy establishment turned on Pakistan. The country's support for militant Islam, once a convenience, was now a liability. When the Soviets left, the ISI attempted to install Hekmatyar, its favored extremist, into power. But after he lost a bloody fight for Kabul, the Pakistanis turned to a different solution, arming and funding another conservative movement they hoped would serve as a counterbalance to their regional rival, India: the "students of Islam," or Taliban.

Stories of the Taliban's hard-line social policies and brutal repression of women began to reach the Western world. Incoming secretary of state Madeleine Albright was among the ranks of establishment figures who began to rally against the regime for its deepening repression. ("I do not regret not dealing with the Taliban," she said years later. "I am willing, however, to admit that it was very complex in terms of who really was in charge.") That outrage gathered steam as the threat of the terrorists Taliban leaders were harboring became apparent. The 1998 bombings of two US embassies in Africa, and the revelation that their orchestrator, Osama bin Laden, had close ties to the Taliban, sealed the regime's status as an international pariah. Pakistan, as the Taliban's benefactor, shared in that reputation.

ROBIN RAPHEL WAS a lone voice of dissent. When Bill Clinton took office as president in 1993, he had tapped Raphel, his old friend from England, to become assistant secretary of state for South Asian affairs. As relations between Washington and Islamabad chilled over the course of the 1990s, Raphel was a stalwart advocate for the country where she had formed so many relationships earlier in her career. When a senator named Hank Brown introduced legislation to ease restrictions on assistance to Pakistan, she worked with Pakistani diplomats for months lobbying for the bill. Its passage, in 1995, cleared the way for arms exports to Pakistan, despite the country's growing nuclear arsenal. Raphel was also an ardent defender of Benazir Bhutto, who returned to power during Raphel's first year as assistant secretary, and who was covertly authorizing assistance to the Taliban—while lying about it to the Americans. Raphel told me she went into the relationship with eyes open. "I didn't believe Bhutto. I felt we needed to be talking to everyone." Nevertheless, she argued against sanctions and helped secure assistance for Pakistan.

Raphel also campaigned for talks with Taliban leaders. A cable summarizing one of her visits to Kabul in 1996 conveyed a rosy view of the regime, quoting one leader who told Raphel, "We are not bad people," and optimistically describing the Taliban's "growing awareness, previously absent, of their own limitations." Shortly after the Taliban took control of Kabul that year, Raphel called on other countries to embrace the regime at a closed-door session at the United Nations. "They are Afghan, they are indigenous, they have demonstrated staying power," she said. "It is not in the interests of Afghanistan or any of us here that the Taliban be isolated." As one veteran Pakistani diplomat who worked with Raphel for many years put it: "If Robin had lasted another year as assistant secretary, there would be a Taliban embassy in Washington, DC."

Raphel, with her fringe embrace of the Pakistanis and the Taliban, aroused suspicion, both in Washington and in the region. This was the point at which the Indian press began tarring her as "Lady Taliban," a moniker that would stick for decades. "It was silly," she said. "Because I did go and talk to these people. That was my job. But, because I wasn't horrified and didn't want to treat them like pariahs . . . people found it absolutely shocking that I thought it was perfectly normal to talk to them." She sighed. "It was a mistake to demonize the Taliban. That might well have contributed to how they got totally out of hand. Nobody would listen to them . . . we blew them off and thought they were complete Neanderthal ragheads." It was, in her view, the worst kind of mistake: "emotionally driven."

Many in the foreign policy establishment later embraced those same arguments for talking to the Taliban, including Richard Holbrooke. Did Raphel have any regrets about her more isolating and controversial positions, I asked? "No," she told me, with a laugh. "I was ahead of my time!"

At the height of Raphel's efforts to warm relations with Pakistan in 1995, an aide from then–Deputy Secretary of State Strobe Talbott's team knocked on her office door and told her about a troubling development. While surveilling Pakistani officials, intelligence agents had picked up what they took to be an illicit exchange. Raphel, they claimed, was leaking classified information to the Pakistanis, revealing the sensitive details of American intelligence on their nuclear program. Raphel was shaken. She met with the State Department's internal police, the Diplomatic Security Service, whose agents grilled her. Their investigation came up empty. Raphel wasn't cited for any infraction, and the matter was quickly forgotten—though, it would later come to pass, not for good.

RAPHEL ROTATED THROUGH several other roles, serving as ambassador in Tunisia, and vice president of the National Defense University, and coordinating assistance in the early days of the Iraq War. But her story always arced back to Pakistan. When she left Iraq, tired, in 2005, she joined Cassidy & Associates, the glossy K-Street lobbying firm whose client list included the Egyptian intelligence services, and, on occasion, Pakistan. During Raphel's time there, the firm had two Pakistani contracts, prompting the press—especially the Indian press—to call her a "Pakistan lobbyist." ("Lobbyist who tormented New Delhi in the 1990s," screamed the *Times* of India. "Brazenly pro-Pakistan partisan in Washington.") Raphel laughed at this, saying she only worked on one contract "for three weeks" before the deal was canceled when Pakistani strongman Pervez Musharraf suspended the country's constitution in November 2007.

At a cocktail party in 2009, Raphel ran into fellow career Foreign Service officer and then-sitting US ambassador to Pakistan Anne Patterson. Patterson was a small, steely woman from Fort Smith, Arkansas, who spoke in a quiet Southern drawl and didn't mince words. She was a diplomat in the classic tradition, with decades of service from Latin America to the Middle East. In Pakistan, she was confronting a new era in one of the world's most difficult relationships—an era in which Pakistan had once again become essential to the United States. But Americans with deep contacts within Pakistani society were hard to come by. In the modern era, tough posts like Pakistan had become in-and-out assignments for junior officers looking to check a box and get a year or two of hazard pay (a 30 percent premium in Islamabad at the time). Someone with Raphel's grasp of the Gordian knot of Pakistani politics could be indispensable. Patterson asked Raphel if she'd come back for one more assignment, helping to manage assistance in Islamabad.

Raphel had turned sixty-one by then. She'd been married three times—most recently to a British diplomat, a union that lasted just a few years and ended in 2004. She'd raised her two college-age daughters, Anna and Alexandra, mostly by herself. Lobbying had given her a chance to spend more time with them, and with her friends. But her mind, one sensed, was quick to turn back to public service.

She told Anne Patterson that she'd think about it.

5

THE OTHER HAQQANI NETWORK

THE DAY AFTER PRESIDENT CLINTON announced Robin Raphel's nomination as assistant secretary of state in 1993, she'd boarded a flight to Sri Lanka, en route to the funeral of the country's recently assassinated president. Seated near her were Pakistan's prime minister Nawaz Sharif and a thirty-six-year-old Pakistani diplomat named Husain Haqqani. In the years that followed, Haqqani would become a fixture of US-Pakistani relations. His critics would come to know him by some of the same labels ascribed later to Robin Raphel: turncoat, traitor, spy.

Haqqani was urbane and charming and a flatterer. "As you know well," he often said with a feline smile. "As a man of your experience of course understands." He grew up in a lower-middle-class neighborhood in Pakistan's commercial hub, Karachi. His parents were Indian migrants: his mother, a schoolteacher; his father, a lawyer, who arrived in Pakistan with few professional contacts and turned to representing the poor and needy. The Haqqanis lived in a barracks for families uprooted by Pakistan's partition from India. Young Husain was fourteen before he lived in a real house. Like Holbrooke, he wasn't born among elites—he clawed his way up.

He received both a traditional Islamic education and a secular modern one. A quintessentially Pakistani fault line ran through him: between church and state, old and new, East and West. When he enrolled at Karachi University, he became a student leader associated with the Jamaat-e-Islami party, joining a new generation of Muslims sparking change around the region. But he was torn. He spent hours at the American Center in Karachi's US consulate, devouring the books in its library. He soaked in Western perspectives and grew disenchanted with his peers' rising anti-Americanism. When an angry mob enflamed by anti-American sentiment burned down the US embassy in Islamabad in 1979, student leaders in nearby Karachi approached Haqqani and asked him to lead the charge. As he tells the story, he gave a dramatic speech, citing the Quran to dissuade them from further violence. One ulterior motive he didn't tell the angry students about: he wanted to protect his beloved library inside the consulate, and the Western books on its shelves.

Like Holbrooke, Haqqani was drawn to journalism and diplomacy. He wrote for the *Far Eastern Economic Review*, and later worked with Pakistani state-run television, sometimes burnishing the legacy of Zia-ul-Haq's military regime. By his early thirties, Haqqani had built a reputation as a silver-tongued communicator with a knack for moving between Western and Pakistani audiences.

AFTER BENAZIR BHUTTO became prime minister on a progressive, secular platform in 1988, the conservative opposition leader, Nawaz Sharif, tapped Haqqani to develop his media strategy. By Haqqani's own admission, Sharif was exploiting xenophobia and anti-Americanism, but Haqqani felt Sharif "might be able to bring some balance to the country, after almost a decade of military rule."

It wasn't long after Sharif took power (and after, in the conventional cycle of Pakistani politics, Bhutto was ousted on corruption charges) that Haqqani found himself at loggerheads with his boss. In 1992, as the Soviet war faded and the United States became more brazen in its misgivings about Pakistan, the State Department asked Haqqani to help deliver a message to Sharif: The United States knew that Pakistan was providing "material support to groups that have engaged in terrorism" and lying about it. It had to stop, or the US would add Pakistan to its official list of state sponsors of terrorism, triggering crushing sanctions. Sharif gathered his cabinet for a conversation that pitted Islamist generals against progressives like Haqqani. The ISI chief at the time, Lieutenant General Javed Nasir, reflected a traditional Pakistani outlook: the letter was the fault of an "Indo-Zionist" lobby and a Jewish ambassador (that the ambassador, Nicholas Platt, was, in fact, a Protestant was the least of Haqqani's concerns).

As Haqqani told the story, he made the case that Pakistan should reconsider its use of proxy relationships in favor of a greater emphasis on diplomacy. When Sharif sided with the intelligence and military voices, Haqqani threatened to quit. Sharif made him take the ambassadorship to Sri Lanka instead—a way of neutralizing him without negative press. It was the Pakistani equivalent of exile to Siberia. A year later, he resigned.

BUT HAQQANI WAS NOTHING if not resilient. After new elections brought Bhutto back into power, he became her spokesperson. He stood by her after she was, like clockwork, ousted again on corruption charges, and grew more public in his criticism of Pakistan's military and its vice grip on power as civilian leaders came and went.

It won him few fans. In 1999, Pakistani intelligence agents pulled him off a crowded street, threw a blanket over his head, and pushed him into a waiting car. On a cell phone secreted in his pocket, he dialed a friend, who alerted the media. He credits the call with saving his life, though he remained jailed for two and a half months on trumped-up corruption charges. When General Pervez Musharraf seized power, Haqqani realized he couldn't live safely in his homeland during its frequent bouts of military rule. "He didn't look very kindly on my writings at the time," he said of Musharraf. "I felt very pressured, because it was military rule again. So I left. I came to the US." Husain Haqqani Americanized. He took an associate professorship at Boston University, decrying Pakistan's military leadership from a safe distance.

Haqqani and Benazir Bhutto, in the midst of her own exile in Dubai, often talked about the future of Pakistan. She had him draft a paper outlining a new vision for Pakistani foreign policy, should she return to power. He argued that the military-to-military relationship had reinforced Pakistan's sponsorship of terrorism. Pakistan had become a "rentier state: it lived off payments from a superpower for its strategic location and intelligence cooperation" rather than its aligned interests. The flow of easy cash from the United States fueled the disproportionate power of Pakistan's army and intelligence services and blunted the potential for reform. Bhutto liked the paper, and "the idea of a new relationship with the United States that would be strategic rather than tactical."

FOR ONE MOMENT, it looked like she might get a chance to make that vision a reality. After years of diplomatic pressure from the Americans and the British, Musharraf allowed Bhutto to return to seek election. There were plenty of people who wanted her dead, and she asked for more security after narrowly escaping one bombing. Musharraf granted only some of the requested reinforcements. If anything were to happen, she emailed her lobbyist, Mark Siegel, "I wld hold Musharaf responsible."

On December 27, 2007, as shadows lengthened in the late afternoon, Bhutto left Liaqat National Park in Rawalpindi, less than two miles from the headquarters of the Pakistan Army, after a stump speech calling for democracy. Supporters swarmed her white Toyota Land Cruiser. Bhutto, wearing her trademark white headscarf and a purple *kameez* over simple white cotton pants and black flats, climbed onto the backseat, poked her head out of the sunroof, and waved, like Eva Peron on the balcony. Gunfire cracked through the air, accompanied by the deafening explosion of a suicide bomber detonating his payload. A Getty photographer, John Moore, activated his camera's high-speed motor drive, capturing the out-of-focus chaos: an orange fireball; frightened faces, surging through sparks and smoke; survivors staggering among bodies.

Bhutto was dead. Her will passed leadership of her political party to her widower, Asif Ali Zardari, known by critics as "Mr. Ten Percent" as a result of long-standing corruption allegations. Her grieving supporters swept him into the presidency.

During Bhutto's exile, Haqqani had grown almost as close to Zardari as to her. When Zardari and his prime minister, Yousuf Raza Gilani, were looking for a new ambassador to the United States after the election, they asked their old party spokesperson, Husain Haqqani.

He accepted. In June 2008, he headed to Washington and presented his credentials to George W. Bush.

Haqqani was back in power, but many Pakistanis regarded him with suspicion. His switching sides to work for Bhutto—a woman he once campaigned against—was a mark against his loyalty. And some viewed his flight to America as a Rubicon. Days after Bhutto's assassination, Musharraf had anatomized what he viewed as her failure. One all-important rule she broke: "Don't be seen as an extension of the United States." Haqqani, fresh from years of American exile, was picked for the ambassadorship for precisely that unforgivable quality.

Years later, Pakistan's *Express Tribune* opened a profile of Haqqani with George Orwell's description of Squealer in *Animal Farm*: "a brilliant talker, and when he was arguing some difficult point, he had a way of skipping from side to side."

"None of this, of course, is to draw a comparison to the esteemed Mr. Husain Haqqani," the profile continued, "after all, Squealer remained loyal to the pigs throughout."

6

DUPLICITY

RICHARD HOLBROOKE had been a prodigiously young assistant secretary of state for East Asia during the Carter administration before departing to Lehman Brothers during the years of Republican leadership between his diplomatic posts. As in all his roles, he grew close to the journalists around him while working on East Asia. As luck would have it, that included Strobe Talbott, who had, as predicted at Oxford, gone on to a career in journalism, covering foreign affairs for *Time*.

Holbrooke's contacts in the Clinton administration were thin. He had backed Al Gore in the 1988 primary, and sat out the Clinton campaign almost entirely, though not for a lack of trying. He badgered friends from Vietnam with better proximity to Clinton—like Anthony Lake, to whom he sent an unsolicited memo describing the brewing conflict in Bosnia as "the key test of American policy in Europe" and warning of the danger of inaction. Holbrooke watched, frustrated, as plum positions went to Lake and other peers. It was only after lobbying from Talbott, who was appointed deputy secretary of state, that Holbrooke was asked to take the post of ambassador to Germany. And it was only by sheer willpower that he ascended to assistant secretary of state for Europe, and then to the defining role of his career, as the administration's negotiator in the Bosnia conflict.

The ethnic slaughter sparked by the disintegration of Yugoslavia had, for years, been an intractable problem at the periphery of American interests. By 1995, at least 100,000 people—and upwards of 300,000, according to some estimates—had been killed. Faltering efforts at mediation, including one led by Jimmy Carter, had barely interrupted Serbian forces' aggressions against the region's Muslims and Croats. It was only after the massacre of thousands of Muslim men and boys in the town of Srebrenica drew international outrage that the United States shifted from its conviction that the violence was a "European problem" and green-lit a more aggressive diplomatic push.

Holbrooke had always viewed the conflict in grand terms—as a test of NATO with potentially dramatic consequences for the future of Europe and, by extension, American strategic interests. When the Clinton administration was deciding who would lead the new intervention, Holbrooke campaigned for the position, hard. He was disliked, but some saw his maverick style as a positive. "The very qualities for which he was sometimes criticized—aggressiveness, impolitic interaction with adversaries, a penchant for cultivating the media—were exactly what the situation required," Secretary of State Warren Christopher said. The parties to the conflict—Serbian President Slobodan Milošević, Croatian president Franjo Tuđjman, and Bosnia's Alija Izetbegović—were scrappers with a history of underhanded tactics. Richard Holbrooke was a rare figure who could meet them toe to toe. Years later, President Clinton toasted Holbrooke with a gentle jab: "Everyone in the Balkans is crazy and everyone has a giant ego. Who else could you send?"

Over a three-month period in 1995, Holbrooke alternately cajoled and harangued the parties to the conflict. For one month, he all but imprisoned them at Wright-Patterson Air Force Base in Dayton, Ohio—a stage where he could precisely direct the diplomatic theater.

At the negotiations' opening dinner, he seated Milošević under a B-2 bomber—literally in the shadow of Western might. At a low point in the negotiations, he announced that they were over, and had luggage placed outside the Americans' doors. Milošević saw the bags and asked Holbrooke to extend the talks. The showmanship worked—the parties, several of them mortal enemies, signed the Dayton Agreement.

It was an imperfect document. It ceded almost half of Bosnia to Milošević and the Serbian aggressors, essentially rewarding their atrocities. And some felt leaving Milošević in power made the agreement untenable. A few years later, he continued his aggressions in Kosovo and finally provoked NATO airstrikes and his removal from power, to face trial at The Hague. The night before the strikes, Milošević had a final conversation with Holbrooke. "Don't you have anything more to say to me?" he pleaded. To which Holbrooke replied: "Hasta la vista, baby." (Being menaced by a tired Schwarzenegger catchphrase was not the greatest indignity Milošević faced that week.)

But the agreement succeeded in ending three and a half years of bloody war. In a sense, Holbrooke had been preparing for it since his days witnessing the Paris talks with the Vietnamese fall apart, and he worked hard to avoid repeating the same mistakes. Crucial to the success of the talks was his broad grant of power from Washington, free of micromanagement and insulated from domestic political whims. And with NATO strikes authorized, military force was at the ready to back up his diplomacy—not the other way around. Those were elements he would grasp at, and fail to put in place, in his next and final mission.

Dayton made Holbrooke a bona fide foreign policy celebrity. The next year, he received a Nobel Peace Prize nomination. A *Time* magazine political cartoon envisioned him as Tom Cruise in *Mission: Impossible*, dangling on a wire over the region, sweating bullets. But just a year after Dayton, he was passed over as secretary of state in favor of Madeleine Albright. Holbrooke, devastated, accepted a post as US Ambassador to the UN instead. "I know he wanted to be Secretary of State," Albright said. "But I was. It was kind of a surprise to many people but I think [especially] to him." Al Gore later said Holbrooke would have been "first in line" to be secretary of state in a Gore administration in 2000. Circumstance always just managed to snatch away the job he wanted most.

WHEN RICHARD HOLBROOKE PRESIDED over the signing of the Dayton Agreement in 1995, the United States had only just begun slashing away at diplomatic spending and the shift to military and intelligence dominance that took place after 9/11 was years away. In the years between that triumph in Bosnia and Holbrooke's next attempt to end a war, the United States' place in the world would change dramatically. Afghanistan and Pakistan were at the epicenter of those changes.

Before the 9/11 attacks, the CIA had already collaborated with Pakistan in efforts to capture Osama bin Laden. And so it was little surprise that, afterwards, the United States took a narrow, tactical approach, working through Pakistan's military and intelligence agency. By the morning of September 12, 2001, deputy secretary of state Richard Armitage was meeting with General Mehmood Ahmad, the director-general of the ISI, attempting to lock down Pakistan's support for American retaliation in Afghanistan. Mehmood pledged that support—and an end to Pakistani collaboration with the Taliban—to Armitage. Musharraf did the same to Colin Powell. Just like that, Pakistan went from foe to friend again. Sanctions that had accumulated over Pakistan's nuclear program and Musharraf's coup evaporated. "I called President Musharraf after we suggested it was time to make a strategic decision to move away from" support for the Taliban, Powell later said. "And he reversed the direction in which Pakistan was moving."

This was wishful, if not magical, thinking. The ISI had spent the years leading up to 9/11 pumping money, arms, and advisers into Afghanistan to prop up the Taliban and vanquish its enemies—including the coalition of warlords known as the Northern Alliance, which received support from India. When the United States' demands for cooperation rolled in after 9/11, Musharraf assembled his war room—stacked with generals notorious for championing the Taliban and other Islamist militant groups—and decided to "unequivocally accept all US demands, but then later . . . not necessarily agree with all the details," as one attendee recalled. Pakistan was playing a double game, as it had in the past. As had been the case in the midst of cooperation against the Soviets, the United States looked the other way.

The other half of the American response involved arming the Northern Alliance, and the consequences of backing the two opposing factions became apparent almost immediately. As US-backed Northern Alliance fighters toppled the Taliban stronghold of Kunduz, Musharraf made a frantic call to President Bush and asked for a favor: a break in the bombing, and permission to land in Kunduz and airlift out Pakistanis. A series of flights collected men and ferried them into Pakistan, where they promptly disappeared. The operation was kept secret, and American officials lied to conceal it. "Neither Pakistan nor any other country flew planes into Afghanistan to evacuate anybody," then–Secretary of Defense Donald Rumsfeld insisted. Those evacuated were, by most accounts, not innocent bystanders: among them were numerous al-Qaeda loyalists. A CIA agent who worked with the Northern Alliance at the time told me flatly of the incident: "it was a mistake."

The extremists who escaped set up shop in Pakistan, where organized terrorist structures flourished in two safe havens. In Quetta, Mullah Omar built a new Taliban council or *shura* and appointed commanders to lead an insurgency in Afghanistan's southern provinces. In the Federally Administered Tribal Agencies (FATA) in Northwest Pakistan, Jalaluddin Haqqani (no relation to Husain, the ambassador) and Gulbuddin Hekmatyar—both former operatives used by the ISI and CIA against the Soviets—ran their own Taliban-allied movements. The ISI also continued to directly fund and arm the Taliban inside Afghanistan. Pakistan's military and intelligence leadership allowed the extremists to function openly, while brazenly lying to the Americans and denying anything was amiss. This was one of the great ironies of the war on terror—as the United States drew closer to Pakistan to fight the Taliban, it was in effect also ensuring the survival of the Taliban.

Husain Haqqani, who had become ambassador in the final year of the Bush administration, said Pakistani military and intelligence brass repeatedly asked him to lie about the support for terrorists. When Lashkar-e-Taiba (LeT), a group based out of Pakistan and heavily sponsored by the ISI, executed a series of bombings and shootings in Mumbai, India that killed 164 people, ISI director Ahmed Shuja Pasha told Haqqani to inform the Americans that "nobody in Pakistan had any knowledge" of the attack and that none of the perpetrators were Pakistani. "I said, 'But you know, that's an outright lie.' The reason why America and Pakistan have this huge trust deficit is because we tell them bold-faced lies," Haqqani said. "Diplomacy is never 100 percent truth, but it's never 100 percent lies either. I wanted it to be . . ." he paused, a half-smile turning the edges of his lips. "Truth *well told.*"

The Bush administration knew Pakistan was playing a double game but, as a general rule, publicly denied it. CIA director Michael Hayden even said at the time that the United States had "not had a better partner in the war on terrorism than the Pakistanis." Hayden, a retired four-star general, was a compact, energetic man with an affable manner. He spoke quickly, his eyebrows darting up and down over the ovals of his small rimless glasses. When I pressed him on the Bush administration's rosy characterizations of the relationship with Pakistan, he was frank. "If I said that about the Pakistanis," he told me, "it was to balance that which then followed. Which was, this is the ally from hell because, actually, they have made a deal with the devil." He had seen strong cooperation from some divisions of the ISI. But there were others, like the infamously pro–al-Qaeda Directorate S, "whose sole purpose in life was to actually sustain groups who we would identify as terrorist groups," Hayden said. General Pasha, likewise, had been "duplicitous." Pasha declined to respond. "I can not tell half truth," he wrote in an email, "and I do not think I should tell the whole truth!!" (General Pasha corresponded with courtly politeness and a lot of exclamation points, like a Victorian gentleman dictating to a millennial teen.)

Multiple senior Bush administration officials said they seldom, if ever, confronted Pakistan about the support for terrorists, for fear of jeopardizing the counterterrorism alliance. Hayden recalled only one such direct conversation, late in the administration, in which Musharraf "fobbed it off on retired ISI officers. You know, the ones who supported the 'mooj' during the Soviet War." The US had helped create Pakistan's state sponsorship of militant Islam in that era, and now it couldn't put the genie back in the bottle. If it wanted to, Hayden argued, that would take more than the narrow confines of intelligence and military cooperation. "Look, I mean, the director of the CIA is not going to cause the government of Pakistan to change course based upon a conversation he has in either Washington or Islamabad," he said. "That requires a whole government effort of long-term . . . and really powerful sanctions that I saw no evidence that we were prepared to make." He was describing the urgent need for a larger diplomatic effort that would never take place.

The result of Pakistan's double-dealing, and the United States' relative tolerance of it, was a slide into violent turmoil on the Afghan side of the border, with the Taliban steadily resurging over the course of the Bush administration. American and NATO operations offered periodic pushback, but the supply of fighters always replenished from the safe havens in Pakistan. Over the course of Bush's second term, the insurgency gained strength, staging devastating attacks, sometimes with the Pakistani military providing cover from across the border, firing on American and Afghan soldiers. The Taliban's gains allowed them to establish a parallel government in the country's south and then east—complete with governors and judges. By the beginning of the Obama administration, America was losing.

7

THE FRAT HOUSE

A S AFGHANISTAN AND PAKISTAN unraveled, Richard Holbrooke was still chasing the role he felt he was born to play: secretary of state. I first met him as he came close yet again in 2004, throwing his weight behind John Kerry's failed bid for the presidency. Holbrooke was a private citizen then, working as an investment banker again, but still a fixture at United Nations and charity functions. I was working with UNICEF, in New York and several conflict zones. In Sudan, I began cranking out *Wall Street Journal* and *International Herald Tribune* columns about a gathering ethnic cleansing campaign there. For years, Holbrooke was religious about sending appraisals of my stories: "Ronan, this is a splendid, vivid piece. . . . You should try to get lift-off on this issue with State and the UN. I'll send it around." Or, just as often: "Next time, put a bit more emphasis on solutions so that it comes across as more than an anti-UN rant."

He took correspondence seriously. In that 2010 State Department speech marking the release of the Vietnam documents, he lamented that "in all likelihood, the volumes being released now will never be

matched again . . . with emails and video teleconferences, documentation just isn't what it used to be." He was, by the time I knew him,
a practitioner of dying arts. That I was far too young for any of it—a
teenager, when I interned for him during his time advising the Kerry
campaign—never seemed to faze him. It made sense: he himself had
perfected the art of being too young and outspoken for his station. He
let me in, and I was green enough to think nothing of it.

Holbrooke was on the outside then, a role that would become
familiar in the following years. So it was on January 19, 2009, the night
before President Barack Obama's inauguration and the prime moment
for the preinaugural parties that send DC elites into a frenzy of invitation chasing every four years. One such party, hosted by Republican socialite Buffy Cafritz and her husband Bill, had been a venue for
bipartisan schmoozing since the 1980s. Most years, it drew 250 or 300
guests. This year, more than 500 packed the ballroom of The Fairfax
at Embassy Row, humming with excitement. Movie star jostled politician jostled reporter. They huddled, cocktails in hand, necks craning
for marquee names from the new administration. Change was in the
air, and everyone wanted to be a part of it.

You can feel the energy of a crowd of political operators change
when someone worth currying favor with walks in. When Bill and
Hillary Clinton walked in that night—she, defeated on the campaign
trail but lifted by her nomination as Barack Obama's new secretary
of state—the dimly lit ballroom practically tilted. Hillary Clinton
smiled a wide, frozen smile and nodded her way through the crush.
Huma Abedin, Clinton's longtime body woman, trailed behind,
thumbs pounding on her BlackBerry.

Richard Holbrooke had been studying the crowd with undisguised
intensity, eyes darting across the sea of faces as he half paid attention to
our conversation. He was standing at the outskirts of the ballroom in
an ill-fitting charcoal suit and a purple and white tie. At sixty-seven,

he was overweight and graying; a universe and a generation apart from the lanky Foreign Service officer smiling from behind horn-rimmed glasses in photos from the Mekong Delta. But the smirk and the piercing eyes were the same.

We caught up briefly. But Holbrooke's focus never left the crowd. He was "on." This was work. When Clinton entered the scene, he departed with a clipped "We'll talk later," and strode over to her, fast enough to attract a few sideways glances. He and Clinton had been close since her husband's presidency, when Holbrooke was at times a mentor during her early years on the international stage. During the coming administration, she would prove to be his staunchest defender. But he never seemed on sure footing in those years, even with her. Every moment of precious face time counted. "One could not be with him for even the briefest period without knowing how badly he wanted to succeed," the war reporter David Halberstam wrote after becoming close with Holbrooke in Vietnam. That night at the Fairfax was Exhibit A.

IN BACKING HILLARY CLINTON, Holbrooke had, once again, bet on the wrong horse. But he was scrappy as ever, and the moment Clinton lost the 2008 primary, he began a campaign to break into an Obama administration to which he was very much an outsider. He worked the phones, calling anyone he could think of until, finally, friends told him to rein it in. For a time, he held a record for having appeared more often than anyone else on the PBS interview show hosted by Charlie Rose. In an August 2008 appearance, he tried, frantically, to pivot toward Obama.

"I supported Senator Clinton, based on an old and close personal relationship and long-standing commitments. But I—I've read Senator Obama's positions extremely carefully . . . and there was no major position he took which I would disagree on . . ."

"He also brought together a group of thirteen foreign policy people . . . And a lot of people noted that your name—your presence was not there," Rose fired back. Holbrooke never had much of a poker face, and looked, for a moment, almost despairing. "And they were disappointed, frankly," Rose went on, "because they think you are one of the principal spokespeople for foreign policy on the Democratic side of the aisle, because of your wide experience and your—"

"—My frequent appearances on your program." He laughed a little too hard.

"Your frequent appearances on this program. Why weren't you there?"

"I think I was doing a program with you."

"Be candid with me. Tell me why you weren't there and what was the story?"

Holbrooke glanced to the side then said, in a tone that suggested he'd rather douse himself in gasoline and self-immolate on that oak table than admit what he said next: "I wasn't there because I wasn't invited." To which he added quickly: "I don't have any problem. They can have anyone they want at a meeting. Actually, I was out of the city on that day and I couldn't have gone anyway."

Rose asked if he'd spoken to Obama, and Holbrooke instead responded with a list of advisers he had ties to. "We have all worked together, Susan Rice, Tony Blinken for Biden, Greg Craig. I worked closely with all of Senator Obama's current team. I know them well."

But the truth was, Richard Holbrooke had precious little currency with Obama's team. He had indeed worked with Susan Rice, during the Clinton administration. To say they didn't get along would be putting it mildly. During one meeting, the feud got so bad that she flipped him the bird in front of a room full of staffers. Holbrooke allies in turn called her a "pipsqueak" with a "chip on her shoulder" in the press. Officials who worked with both said she felt Holbrooke had trampled over her. ("He *tried* to trample over me," she clarified. "I don't think he succeeded.") Holbrooke's relationship with Blinken, likewise,

wasn't enough to prevent his boss, Vice President Joe Biden, from telling Obama "he's the most egotistical bastard I've ever met." (Though
Biden did admit Holbrooke was "maybe the right guy" to tackle the
war in Afghanistan.) And Greg Craig, whom Holbrooke also listed,
would soon fall out of favor with the Obama camp.

To many Obama loyalists, Richard Holbrooke was the enemy: part
of the old guard of foreign policy elites that had accreted around the
Clintons and dismissed Obama and his inner circle as upstarts. Holbrooke had avoided publicly criticizing the young senator from Illinois,
but he had also leaned into his role as a Hillary loyalist, calling other
foreign policy experts and signaling that support for Obama might
mean throwing away job opportunities in a Clinton presidency (and,
presumably, a Holbrooke State Department). Like much of the Democratic foreign policy establishment, he also wore the scarlet letter of
his initial support for the war in Iraq. Later, he wrote and spoke about
the disastrous repercussions of that invasion, including the neglect of
Afghanistan. But in the eyes of many in the new administration, he
remained exactly what Obama had run against.

There was also a divide of culture. Obama had run on excitement
and change, not history or experience. He would later describe himself
as "probably the first president who is young enough that the Vietnam
War wasn't at the core of my development." When the United States
finally pulled out of Vietnam in 1975, he was just thirteen, "so I grew
up with none of the baggage that arose out of the dispute of the Vietnam War." With a few notable exceptions, he surrounded himself with
young men of the same generational outlook. Perhaps the most sustained and influential voice on foreign policy in the White House, Ben
Rhodes, was given his bespoke role—deputy national security advisor
for communications—at thirty-one. Staffers spent years swatting away
a recurring comparison: White House as "frat house."

In this White House, representatives of the dusty establishment
were out of vogue. After a bruising race, Clinton loyalists were even

less welcome—especially those with outsize personalities. "I think his whirlwind of activity, um, did cause some raised eyebrows in the White House," Hillary Clinton said of Holbrooke. "They thought he was going outside the lines of the orderly policy process, the no-drama White House they were trying to run. And it was very painful for me."

Two days after the election, Richard Holbrooke arrived in Chicago to interview with the president-elect. The meeting, which lasted thirty minutes, was an immediate disaster. According to friends Holbrooke called afterward. Obama greeted him as "Dick"—to which Holbrooke corrected him, saying that his wife, the writer Kati Marton, preferred that he be addressed as "Richard." "That's a joke, right?" Les Gelb, Holbrooke's longtime friend who had involved him in the Pentagon Papers years earlier, recalled telling Holbrooke. "You didn't really say that, did you?" It wasn't. He did. Obama was annoyed—and later told several people so. "For some reason, President Obama thought he"—that is, Holbrooke—"had been treating him with some condescension," Henry Kissinger said. "I do not know whether that's true. But anyway, certainly Holbrooke had a lot more experience than the new people coming in." In a sense, these were all characterizations of something simple: this was a job interview, like any other, and Obama just didn't like the guy.

AMID THE SWEATY SCHMOOZING at the Fairfax on inauguration eve, Holbrooke was laser focused. Hillary Clinton becoming secretary of state was bittersweet, but also a reprieve. He would play a role in the administration. I watched as he and Clinton talked. He whispered in her ear. The two of them laughed. He made sure the assembled crowd saw it.

Clinton was at her most ebullient. The Obamas weren't coming and she was the focus of every glance and whisper. She and I had attended the same law school, where several antediluvian professors spanned both of our enrollments. We'd met a number of times over the years, and she had always been kinder than she needed to be. Clinton had a preternatural knack for social recall, or at least artfully covering for memories she lacked. She professed to have read some of my foreign policy columns, and asked what I was doing next. I said I was deciding whether to go back to the law firm where I'd been a summer associate. She looked at me hard and said: "Talk to Holbrooke."

She and Holbrooke had already begun crafting a new role for him, one she would later describe as, "by many metrics," the most difficult in the administration. "Ever since my experience in Paris in 1968 as a junior member of the Vietnam negotiating team under Averell Harriman and Cyrus Vance," Holbrooke once wrote, "I had wanted to test myself against the most difficult negotiations in the world." He would get his wish.

8

MISSION: IMPOSSIBLE

WHEN HOLBROOKE'S ASSIGNMENT first leaked, the role was framed as "a special envoy for India, Pakistan and Afghanistan." This was not sloppy reporting. Though his mandate was ultimately downsized to include only the latter two countries, Holbrooke had initially envisioned sweeping region-wide negotiations. "Afghanistan's future cannot be secured by a counterinsurgency effort alone," he wrote in 2008. "It will also require regional agreements that give Afghanistan's neighbors a stake in the settlement. That includes Iran—as well as China, India, and Russia. But the most important neighbor is, of course, Pakistan, which can destabilize Afghanistan at will—and has." In Bosnia, Holbrooke had juggled similarly fractious parties: not only Bosnian Muslims, Croats, and Serbs, but also Russia, the European allies, and organizations like the UN and NATO. Here, he again saw a need for a grand, strategic approach.

This ambitious plan for another *Mission: Impossible*–style political settlement built on old-school diplomacy quickly collided with the realities of the new administration. Two days after the parties on inauguration eve, Holbrooke stood in front of a crowd of current and former diplomats in the Benjamin Franklin State Dining Room, the grandest ceremonial chamber on the State Department's eighth floor. The room was renovated in the 1980s in a classical style meant to evoke the great reception halls of continental Europe. Ornate Corinthian pillars, clad in red plaster and painted with faux-marble veins, lined the walls. Portuguese cut-glass chandeliers hung around a ceiling molding of the Great Seal of the United States: a bald eagle, one set of talons grasping a bundle of arrows, the other an olive branch. Holbrooke was flanked by Barack Obama and Hillary Clinton on his right, and Joe Biden and the administration's newly appointed Middle East peace envoy, George Mitchell, on his left.

"It's an extraordinarily moving thing for me to return to this building again, having entered it so many years ago as a junior Foreign Service officer," he began. In Afghanistan, he described a war gone wrong; in Pakistan, a challenge "infinitely complex." He thanked the president for paying tribute to diplomats on his second day in office, and Obama, in turn, stressed his "commitment to the importance of diplomacy" and his recognition "that America's strength comes not just from the might of our arms." Those convictions were tested during his eight years in office.

Holbrooke looked out at his wife, Kati, his sons David and Anthony, and colleagues he'd known across decades. He seemed emotional, his voice wavering. "I see my former roommate in Saigon, John Negroponte here," he said. "We remember those days well, and I hope we will produce a better outcome this time." The audience laughed. Obama was expressionless.

While other regional initiatives being announced by the new administration were headed by "envoys," Holbrooke, in what was to be one of many annoyances for the White House, insisted that he be given a sui generis title: "Special Representative." It was, in his view, a more concrete managerial term than "envoy"—a way to signal that he was building up a sizeable, operational team.

In 1970, a young Holbrooke had written an article in *Foreign Policy*, the upstart publication at which he would later become editor, decrying the sclerotic, siloed bureaucracy of the State Department. Returning decades later, he decided to shake things up. He began assembling a crack team with officials detailed from across the government. There were representatives from USAID and the Department of Agriculture, the Treasury and the Department of Justice, the Pentagon and the CIA and the FBI. Then there were the outsiders—counterculture thinkers drawn from civil society, business, and academia. Vali Nasr, the Iranian-American scholar of Middle East studies, had received a midnight text in December. It was characteristically theatrical: "If you work for anyone else, I will break your knees." And then, anticipating Nasr's preference for an Iran-focused job: "This matters more. This is what the president is focused on. This is where you want to be." Barnett Rubin, a New York University professor and authority on Afghan history and culture, got a call as well. Rina Amiri, an Afghan activist who had worked with the UN and Open Society Institute, recognized Holbrooke on a Delta shuttle from DC to New York and began pressing him about the upcoming Afghan elections. Holbrooke was impressed, and told her he was assembling a team. "I know," she said, "but I'm here to lobby you."

"I'm very efficient," he said. "I just turned your lobbying into a job interview."

My own interview was, likewise, distinctive.

"WHAT SHOULD WE BE DOING DIFFERENTLY?" Holbrooke shouted over the hiss of the shower he was taking in the middle of that job interview. From the next room over, I laughed. I couldn't help it.

It was the culmination of a sprawling, hours-long meeting, which had ranged from his office, to the secretary of state's, to his townhouse in Georgetown. I had followed up on Clinton's advice at the preinaugural party at The Fairfax and begun talking to Holbrooke and his chief of staff, Rosemarie Pauli. A little over a month later, in March 2009, I arrived at the State Department to meet with him in person. He barreled out of his office, lobbing policy questions at me. How would I reinvigorate trade in Central Asia? How would I maximize the impact of assistance to the Pakistanis? Never mind that I was a wet-behind-the-ears lawyer, with a modest foreign policy background in Africa, not Afghanistan. I'd worked with local nongovernmental groups in the developing world, and Holbrooke wanted to ramp up the United States' emphasis on those groups—a change of culture in a war zone where most of the implementation happened through powerful American contractors. He wanted nontraditional answers, unencumbered by government experience.

The State Department, in DC's Foggy Bottom neighborhood, is an imposing slab of stripped classical architecture, clad in limestone and built, in portions, in the 1930s and 1950s. The earliest part of the complex was intended for the growing War Department after World War I, though with the construction of the more ambitious Pentagon, it never actually became the military's headquarters. The looming rear entrance to the building is still known as the War Department—a flourish of irony, for the seat of American peacemaking. The Department is a literal hierarchy, with opulent ceremonial rooms for receiving foreign dignitaries on the eighth floor, the secretary's office on the seventh, and offices of roughly descending importance on the floors beneath. During Holbrooke's prodigious turn as assistant secretary in his mid-thirties, he had occupied an office complex on the sixth floor. Now, he'd been relegated to the first, next to the cafeteria— where Robin Raphel was later deposited, and across the hall from the Department newsstand, where Holbrooke would load up on junk food between meetings.

Our walk-and-talk started in his office and moved into the hallway, then up to the seventh floor and the secretary of state's ornate, wood-paneled office. He moved briskly through the entire conversation, only occasionally making eye contact, aides hurrying after him and handing him papers. He paused my answers frequently to take calls on his BlackBerry. This was not real-life government, where meetings are seated and staid. This was government as dramatized by Aaron Sorkin.

Holbrooke and I, and a veteran CIA officer Holbrooke was also lobbying to join his team, Frank Archibald, met with Clinton briefly in the antechamber outside her office. He outlined a dazzling vision for the roles we'd play. Repackaged and artfully marketed by Holbrooke, every underling was a one-person revolution. Archibald was going to single-handedly heal suspicions between State and the CIA. I was going to realign American assistance to NGOs. Amiri, I heard him say on numerous occasions, had written the Afghan constitution. (As he worked up a particular lather about this at one function, she leaned in and whispered in my ear: "I did *not* write the Afghan constitution.") None of us had any business interviewing with the secretary of state for our jobs, but many of us did, through dint of Holbrooke's willpower. Holbrooke had leaned on the patronage of great men himself, from Scotty Reston at the *Times* to Dean Rusk and Averell Harriman. He wanted to be the man that people would say was that kind of man, and he was.

After meeting with the secretary, we had returned to Holbrooke's office suite on the first floor, where he'd picked up his luggage. He had just returned from a trip and had to go home to change before an afternoon meeting at the White House. He passed me a suitcase and out we went to hail a cab, not interrupting the flow of questions. Would I favor more overt United States branding on USAID assistance in the region? How would I enlist local watchdog groups in ensuring electoral transparency? I had just recovered from several years in a wheelchair, the result of a bone marrow infection left untreated while working in Sudan. Holbrooke was aware of this but characteristically oblivious to it in the moment. I hobbled after him with his luggage. When we arrived at his Georgetown town house, he headed upstairs—not asking, naturally, just carrying on with the conversation. He left the bathroom door ajar and peed. "What about negotiations with the Taliban?" he asked demurely. *"Really?"* I said. *"What?"* he replied innocently from behind the bathroom door, as if this were the most normal thing in the world. And for him, it was— virtually everyone seemed to have a story about Holbrooke meetings in bathrooms. He poked his head out, unbuttoning his shirt. "I'm going to hop in the shower." I stood outside the door. The job interview continued.

Many Holbrooke wooed hesitated. Rina Amiri, worried about her outspoken views on human rights being muted, held out for a month. Barnett Rubin made it a condition that he be allowed to keep his academic perch at NYU part time. I myself wasn't convinced. The State Department wasn't a glamorous career move. "I would go to Davis Polk," one law school classmate wrote to me, referring to the law firm where I had a job offer. "What is the point of these technocratic positions? Do you really want to spend forty years trying to move your way up? If you work really hard you might end up where Holbrooke is himself, which is a whole lot of nowhere, really. Fuck that."

But Holbrooke brought to every job he ever held a visionary quality that transcended practical considerations. He talked openly about changing the world. "If Richard calls you and asks you for something, just say yes," Henry Kissinger said. "If you say no, you'll eventually get to yes, but the journey will be very painful." We all said yes.

By the summer, Holbrooke had assembled his *Ocean's Eleven* heist team—about thirty of us, from different disciplines and agencies, with and without government experience. In the Pakistani press, the colorful additions to the team were watched closely, and generally celebrated. Others took a dimmer view. "He got this strange band of characters around him. Don't attribute that to me," a senior military leader told me. "His efforts to bring into the State Department representatives from all of the agencies that had a kind of stake or contribution to our efforts, I thought was absolutely brilliant," Hillary Clinton said, "and everybody else was fighting tooth and nail."

It was only later, when I worked in the wider State Department bureaucracy as Clinton's director of global youth issues during the Arab Spring, that I realized how singular life was in the Office of the Special Representative for Afghanistan and Pakistan—quickly acronymed, like all things in government, to SRAP. The drab, low-ceilinged office space next to the cafeteria was about as far from the colorful open workspaces of Silicon Valley as you could imagine, but it had the feeling of a start-up. The office was soon graced with cameos from eclectic and unexpected faces. Holbrooke hosted a procession of journalists, to whom he remained as close as he had in previous jobs. Prominent lawmakers visited. He met with Angelina Jolie about refugees and Natalie Portman about microfinance. Holbrooke knew what he was doing was counterculture, and he believed it to be historic. There were reminders of his view of our place in history everywhere. Even his office was a shrine to wars that came before. In framed pictures on the walls, there he was, smiling in the Mekong Delta; there he was with Bill Clinton in East Timor, or in Sarajevo flanked by armed guards. "Are you keeping a journal?" he'd ask me. "One day you'll write about this."

CLINTON HAD TOLD HOLBROOKE he would be the direct civilian counterpart to General David Petraeus, who was then the commander of US Central Command (CENTCOM), the powerful Pentagon division responsible for Iraq and Afghanistan and Pakistan. "He has more airplanes than I have telephones," Holbrooke later grumbled. Petraeus was a small man with a wiry physique honed through a daily, predawn workout regimen that had become catnip for profile writers: five miles of running, followed by twenty chin-ups—a torturous modification involving a full leg-raise until his shoelaces touched the bar—and then a hundred push-ups. At a 2016 meeting of the shadowy Bilderberg Group in Dresden, Petraeus, by then in his sixties, was accosted by twenty-something-year-old reporters shouting questions. He sprinted away. They tried, and failed, to catch him. He had once taken an M-16 shot to the chest during a live fire training exercise and lived to tell the tale. Legend had it that he ate one meal a day and never slept more than four hours. I once had the misfortune to stand in line at a buffet next to him. His eyes flicked down to my plate of mac and cheese. "I'm . . . going for a run later," I offered defensively. He clapped a hand on my shoulder. "Really? Think you can keep up?" (I have never gone for a run in my life.)

Petraeus, like Holbrooke, was a larger-than-life operator who knew how to build a public narrative and use it to his advantage. He too, had the ear of every reporter in Washington, a direct line to the op-ed pages, and a tendency to surround himself with experts who could help propagate his message outside of the government. He was, enraptured profiles noted, a scholar-general, and this was true—he had been an ace student at West Point before receiving a doctorate from Princeton's Woodrow Wilson School of Public and International Affairs. His doctoral dissertation was titled "The American Military and the Lessons of Vietnam: A Study of Military Influence and the Use of Force in the Post-Vietnam Era."

Holbrooke and Petraeus both interrogated America's misadventures in Vietnam, but they came up with diametrically opposed answers. Holbrooke believed counterinsurgency doctrine—or COIN, as it came to be known—was a recipe for quagmire, breeding dependency in local populations. Petraeus believed in the doctrine and built a career championing its revival. In Iraq he relied on a sweeping COIN strategy. Broadly speaking, that meant a large deployment of troops, integrated within Iraqi society over a long period of time, securing communities while getting the bad guys. Petraeus had emerged from that conflict a hero. Critics argued that he benefitted from events outside his control—like al-Qaeda leader Muqtada al-Sadr declaring a unilateral ceasefire. Others contended that his accomplishments fell apart after his departure, or that they were exaggerated to begin with. (That included then-senator Hillary Clinton, who, in a 2007 congressional hearing, accused Petraeus of presenting an overly optimistic assessment of the Iraq troop surge at a time when she was seeking to create distance from her Iraq vote. "I think the reports that you provide to us really require the willing suspension of disbelief," she said.) But in Petraeus's view, COIN had worked in Iraq, and for his many ardent supporters in the Pentagon, it became gospel. In Afghanistan, he intended to put COIN to the test a second time.

Shortly after Hillary Clinton accepted Obama's job offer, she, Petraeus, and Holbrooke sat around the fireplace at her Georgian-style mansion near DC's Embassy Row and shared a bottle of wine. "I worked really hard to make sure Richard had relationships with the generals," Clinton said. "I invited him and Dave Petraeus, who hadn't met each other, to come to my house and to talk about what each of them thought needed to be done." She knew Petraeus—who had just become commander of CENTCOM—would play a defining role in some of her greatest international challenges.

That night at Clinton's home marked the first of a series of dinners and drinks between the two men, and the partnership was often characterized as a strong one in the press. "Richard did share Petraeus's interest in an aggressive counterinsurgency strategy," Clinton recalled, "but focused on increasing the credibility of the government in Kabul and trying to weaken the appeal of the Taliban. Richard wasn't sure that adding more troops would assist that, he thought it would maybe undermine goodwill."

The truth was, Petraeus and Holbrooke were wary of each other. Organized, tightly controlled Petraeus (though, subsequent years of scandal would suggest, not so tightly controlled in some areas) was often uncomfortable with Holbrooke's freewheeling improvisation. *New York Times* reporter Mark Landler later recalled Petraeus arriving for a meeting as he interviewed Holbrooke, and Petraeus's dismay both at Holbrooke's impromptu suggestion that Landler stay on with the two of them, and at Holbrooke's shoeless feet propped on a coffee table. "Richard, why aren't you wearing shoes?" Petraeus asked, horrified. Holbrooke said he was more comfortable that way.

I first met Petraeus at the Kabul headquarters of ISAF—the NATO mission in Afghanistan. I'd presented a PowerPoint (the military loves PowerPoints) on civil society in Afghanistan, and afterwards Holbrooke, in his typical manner of elevating subordinates, introduced me to the general. "So, you're working for my diplomatic wingman," Petraeus said, rising from his seat to shake my hand. Petraeus called Holbrooke his "wingman" a lot, in private and in the press. Holbrooke hated it. He didn't particularly relish being anyone's wingman. And the power imbalance, and what Holbrooke took to be Petraeus's ribbing about it, struck a deeper nerve, running against the grain of Holbrooke's belief that military power should be used to support diplomatic goals. "His job should be to drop the bombs when I tell him to," Holbrooke told our team testily. Petraeus later told me he intended "wingman" to be a show of respect. But he admitted that the relationship was fraught. "He was a difficult partner at various times. I think he had ADD and some other things. Very difficult for him to stay focused," he recalled. "Richard came in thinking, 'I am Richard Holbrooke' and the administration came in thinking, 'I am Barack Obama.' Seriously bright people. But they were supposedly going to be able to do something that nobody else could do."

AS THE NEW ADMINISTRATION ASSEMBLED, Obama ordered a sweeping review of America's role in Afghanistan and Pakistan. The process was so torturous that the journalist Bob Woodward managed to spin an entire book out of disgruntled accounts of it. For ten meetings spanning more than twenty-five hours, the president heard arguments and proposals. Countless more meetings were conducted by lower-ranking officials. The fundamental question: how many troops to deploy and when. The military had already requested a surge of 30,000 troops when Obama began his term, and during the review, military leaders fought tooth and nail for a fully resourced counterinsurgency, with as many troops as possible, as fast as possible, to remain as long as possible. "We cannot achieve our objectives without more troops," Petraeus argued. After the very first National Security Council meeting on the subject, he said he was going to move forward on the pending troop surge. White House Chief of Staff Rahm Emanuel had to rein him in: "Hold on," he said, according to leaked accounts. "General, I appreciate you're doing your job, but I didn't hear the president of the United States give that order."

Holbrooke was nominally the co-chair of the review process, along with retired CIA veteran Bruce Riedel and, according to Riedel, Petraeus as an "unacknowledged third co-chair." But Holbrooke was sidelined—by Riedel, who had greater access to the president, by a series of generals, and by the White House itself. The review threw into sharp relief the generational and cultural chasm between Holbrooke and Obama. In a February 2009 National Security Council meeting, Holbrooke compared the deliberations to those Lyndon Johnson conducted with his advisers during Vietnam. "History should not be forgotten," he said. The room fell silent. Obama muttered: "ghosts." When Holbrooke brought up Vietnam again several months later, the president was less demure. "Richard," he snapped, cutting him off. "Do people really *talk* like that?" Holbrooke had begun tap-ing audio diaries of his experiences, with an eye toward history (and a memoir). "In some of the early NSC meetings with the president, I referred to Vietnam and was told by Hillary that the president did not want any references to Vietnam," he said in one, his voice sounding tired on the scratchy tape. "I was very struck by this, since I thought there were obviously relevant issues." "He was incredibly unhappy with the way he was personally treated," Hillary Clinton reflected. "I was too. Because I thought a lot of what he was offering had real merit and it didn't somehow fit into the worldview that the White House had." Holbrooke had allowed himself to be categorized not as someone to be heard but as someone to be tolerated.

But the more meaningful divide was with the military. Holbrooke was no dove. He had supported the invasion in Iraq, and at the outset of the review, he endorsed an initial deployment of troops in advance of the Afghan elections as a stopgap. But he felt military engagement should be organized around the goal of achieving a political settle-ment. He was alarmed by the force of persuasion the military voices at the NSC table commanded, sometimes crowding out nonmilitary solutions. "I told David Axelrod that we had been dominated much too long by pure mil-think," he said in another tape. "Military think-ing and military domination. And while I had great respect for the military, uh, and Petraeus was brilliant, I liked them as individuals and they were great Americans, they should not dictate political strategy, which is what's happening now."

After one meeting, he emerged, exhausted, and told Vali Nasr something absurd: Secretary of Defense Robert Gates had *bigger folders*. His maps and charts were *more colorful*. The SRAP team had cranked out voluminous policy papers, but they were going unread by many of the president's advisers. "Who can make graphics?" he asked in one meeting. Everyone looked at me. "Ageism," I muttered, and went to work making technicolor PowerPoints out of his policy proposals, which he dictated in minute detail. Often, they focused on political and diplomatic solutions he felt were being given short shrift by the White House. A series of concentric circles showed the complex landscape of global players he felt the United States needed to do more to engage—from international donors, to NATO states, to rising powers like India and China. Triangles linked by arrows illustrated trilateral relations between Pakistan, India and the US. A flow chart, titled "Changing Pakistan's Behavior Toward the Taliban," offered a storybook simplification of his plan for the most difficult bilateral relationship in the world:

1. Focus on entire country with new US-led international assistance and new commitments campaign . . .
2. . . . Which builds pro-US-sentiment . . .
3. . . . Which helps turn the Pakistani government and Pakistani military toward our position . . .
4. . . . Which gets Pakistan's military to take more action against the Taliban and Al Qaeda.

The graphics did little to move the needle. Advocates for a full troop surge were more numerous and had better access than voices of caution. Riedel rode on Air Force One with the president, and briefed him without others present. Secretary of Defense Bob Gates supported his generals and their lobbying for a robust troop surge. Retired General Jim Jones, the national security advisor, did as well. So did his deputy in charge of Afghanistan, Retired Lieutenant General Doug Lute. Hillary Clinton, despite her advocacy for Holbrooke, was fundamentally a hawk. "There's plenty of blame," Ben Rhodes, the deputy national security advisor, later recalled. Holbrooke's "biggest defender was Hillary, and yet she constantly sided with the generals in the policy discussions."

"I was convinced that Richard was right about the need for both a major diplomatic campaign and a civilian surge," Clinton said. "I did disagree with him that additional troops weren't needed to make that work, because I thought, given how the Bush administration had kind of lost interest in Afghanistan because of their hyper-concern about Iraq, that the Taliban was really on the upsurge and that there had to be some demonstration that we'd be willing to push back on them."

Holbrooke had to hold his tongue, but he knew force alone couldn't solve the crisis in Afghanistan. "My position was very precise," he said over a meal with Bob Woodward, who recorded the conversation. "I will support you in any position you take cause you're my boss but you need to know my actual views. I have serious concerns about the fact that our troops are going to be spread too thin and I'm most concerned we're going to get into a mission/resource mismatch. A lot of people thought I was overly influenced by Vietnam. It didn't matter to me. At least I had some experience there."

"I always had such regret about the Holbrooke thing," Rhodes said. "It went wrong and it feels very unnecessary when I look back." It was, he reflected, like "Holbrooke was in a game of musical chairs, and he was the guy without a chair to sit in."

One of the Kafkaesque qualities of the period was the profusion of seemingly duplicative reviews—not just the White House's process led by Riedel, but prior assessments by Petraeus, and one by Stanley McChrystal, the new general in charge of Afghanistan. Just before McChrystal released his recommendations, Holbrooke told our team exactly how the process would play out. There would be three choices. "A 'high-risk' option," he said, gesturing above eyeline, "that is what they always call it, which will call for maybe very few troops. Low troops, high risk. Then there will be a 'low-risk' option," he said, moving his hand down, "which will ask for double the number they are actually looking for. In the middle will be what they want." Holbrooke had seen this movie before. The first recommendation of the final Riedel report was for a "fully resourced" counterinsurgency in

Afghanistan. After months of dithering, the President chose COIN, and a deployment of 30,000 additional troops.

Obama announced the surge with an expiration date: two years later, in mid-2011, withdrawals would begin. Conspicuously absent from either the Riedel report or the president's announcement was any commitment to negotiation, either with Pakistan over the terrorist safe havens, or with the Taliban in Afghanistan. There was "no discussion at all of diplomacy and a political settlement," Vali Nasr recalled. "Holbrooke wanted the president to consider this option, but the White House was not buying it. The military wanted to stay in charge, and going against the military would make the president look weak."

9

WALKING ON GLASS

IT WAS RAMADAN in 2010, and Umar Cheema, a Pakistani journalist, woke up in the middle of the night to spend time with friends
while they waited for *suhoor,* the predawn meal with which observant
Muslims break fast. They hung out at Daman-e-Koh park, which in
the day overlooks spectacular views of Islamabad and at night turns
into a warren of romantic courtyards and gardens, bathed in golden
light. The group left at around 2:30 a.m., crowding into Cheema's car
for a ride to their respective homes. He had dropped off the last of his
friends and was on his way home when he noticed two cars had been
following him. One, a white Toyota Corolla, fell in line behind him.
Another, a black Jeep, pulled in front of him.

As he stopped, three men in police uniform jumped out of the
Jeep. They said, strangely, that he'd run over a man and fled the scene.
Cheema, who wrote for Pakistan's *The News* and had won the Daniel
Pearl Fellowship for foreign journalists and worked for the *New York
Times,* had never been involved in a crime in his life. He had, how-
ever, written a series of hard-hitting articles about the powers that be.

He exposed army controversies, including allegations that court mar-
tialed officers were being denied fair trials. He dug into evidence that
Pakistani intelligence was behind a series of disappearances of civilians.
He reported that intelligence agents were letting suspects in a major
terrorist attack go. He told the officers there'd been a mix-up, but let
them lead him into their car. That's when they blindfolded him and
took away his phone.

When they pulled off his blindfold, Cheema was seated in a bare
room with peeling green cement walls. It was lit by a single, exposed
light bulb. A fan turned slowly in a corner. When he asked where he
was, his captors told him to shut up. In the dim light, he could see
three of them, their faces covered with children's party masks. They
tore off Cheema's clothes, threw him on the floor, and beat him with
wooden rods. They shaved his head and eyebrows, and took pictures
of him cowering. They didn't mince words about their motivations.
"You're here because of the stories," said one. "This will teach you to
be obedient."

"I had been reporting about the missing persons, so that gave me
the idea of the horrifying stories the families had been through," he
told me. "I thought of my son, he was two years old. I realized if I
didn't make it back, my son would grow up alone." Cheema steeled
himself against the pain. "I told myself, 'I am being punished for doing
something good, for being truthful.'" Cheema's captors beat him on
and off for nearly seven hours, then dumped him, naked and bleeding, by the side of the road outside Islamabad. His car had been left
there. They gave him 100 rupees to cover tolls back into the city. The
operation was a well-oiled machine of intimidation; Cheema had the
distinct sense that they'd done it before. His case was unusual solely in
that the intimidation didn't work: he immediately went public.

There was little question, in Cheema's mind, who was behind the
attack. His night from hell was preceded by a series of meetings with

the ISI—which had gotten in touch before and after his stories with ominous "advice." The agency had a history of "dealing with" disobedient people, agents would remind him.. Being a journalist in Pakistan can be a death wish. Reporters there are routinely beaten, and sometimes worse. The year after Umar Cheema's beating, Syed Saleem Shahzad, who had been reporting on links between the ISI and Islamist militant groups, was beaten to death. His corpse was found floating in a canal outside of Islamabad. The CIA later intercepted telephone calls that suggested the killing was directly ordered by the ISI—likely by General Pasha himself. Since 1992, the Committee to Protect Journalists has documented sixty murders of reporters with motives related to their work in Pakistan. Stories about human rights, the war in Afghanistan, and corruption are all dangerous, but the single most deadly beat, comprising 67 percent of deaths, is politics: often, stories about the ISI or the military. Pakistan was a paradox in this respect—the country had a sophisticated twenty-four-hour TV news cycle. It had spirited columnists and commentators. But the military and ISI still ruled with an iron fist. Countless reporters were even on intelligence payroll, paid to write favorable stories and as insurance that they wouldn't write harsh ones.

The plight of the journalists, like the disappearances and extrajudicial killings they sometimes died covering, underscored the waning space for conversation in the US-Pakistan relationship. At the State Department, I found that raising the disappearing reporters and verboten stories was an uphill battle. It was another fight not worth picking at the height of counterterrorism cooperation. Such moral compromise was a familiar—some would say inevitable—feature of national-security-sensitive relationships. But the growing list of subjects that the United States appeared to be powerless to raise was alarming. This was the challenge Richard Holbrooke faced when he stepped into the job: a relationship in which no one talked about anything outside of tactics.

Cheema related his experience to several State Department officials, who were sympathetic, but not interested. "There was literally
no word about these human rights violations, unless there are tensions
going on between ISI and CIA," he told me. "Washington has its own
interests. Why would they bother if there is any problem as long as
the ISI is cooperating with them?" The human rights issues threw the
power imbalances of the American government into sharp relief. The
bilateral relationship with Pakistan was almost entirely run between
intelligence agencies and militaries. But neither of those entities felt it
was within their mandate to raise human rights.

"It never entered into my conversations" with the Pakistanis, General Hayden said of the murders and disappearances. "When I went to
Islamabad, I had very specific asks. I was going for a purpose. 'We
need to go to do this. I need your help to do this. Here's what we're
going to offer. Can I count on your assistance here?'" Hayden sighed.
"We already know that the ISI were apparently killing journalists.
Alright? That may affect my overall view of ISI, but it doesn't affect
my working with ISI to try and capture an al-Qaeda operative in
Wana or Mir Ali." This was a common sentiment among intelligence
and military leaders overseeing the Pakistan relationship. These kinds
of broader conversations were, they felt, someone else's problem. But
because the power within the US policy process was so skewed away
from civilian leadership, it was hard to know who could meaningfully
raise such issues.

Hayden's successor at the CIA, Leon Panetta, found his attempts
to confront these issues frustrating. Panetta was a former politician
and veteran of the executive branch but an outsider to the intelligence
community when President Obama appointed him to the agency job.
He was heavyset and bespectacled, with an avuncular manner and
an easy laugh. He said he was conscious of the legal requirement to
stop assistance to military units engaging in human rights abuses—the
so-called Leahy Law. "When we found out that they were obviously

implementing *extrajudicial approaches*," he said, chuckling at the turn of phrase, "it raised some real concerns. So the approach that we decided on was to, rather than slam them down, try to see if there were ways to improve their own process."

The Pakistanis tended to be less than receptive. "They kind of looked at me with a whimsical look as if to say, 'You know you guys don't get it' "—more laughter—" 'You've got all these nice laws and rules, but the fact is these people are killers, they've killed people, they've killed us, and our history is one of basically dealing with these people on the same basis.' At the same time, you say, 'Well look, you want F16s, you want the latest equipment, do you want to be able to get what we can provide? Then this is something you're going to have to pay attention to . . . ' They were kind of looking at you out of the side of their eye saying, you know, 'We'll play along with this joke but let's not forget it is a joke.' " He laughed again. I have never seen anyone laugh so much during a conversation about extrajudicial killings.

The region's counterterrorism imperatives and Pakistan's nuclear capacity conspired to strip the United States of its power. "No matter how much you would bitch about what they were doing, and the games they were playing, and the difficulty in the relationship, the bottom line was, you were dealing with a nuclear-powered country," Panetta recalled. "As a result of that, there was always the danger that if you got on their wrong side, either because of their own carelessness or just the way they operated . . . that at some point a terrorist group would get their hands on one of these weapons," he added. "You were always walking on glass when you were dealing with the Pakistanis."

And so, the dynamics of the relationship remained unaltered. Bald-faced lies were its bedrock—and within the confines of counterterrorism cooperation, those lies were tolerated, or even encouraged. The entire strategy of drone strikes used to take out al-Qaeda leadership

was premised on a mutual understanding that the Pakistanis would lie
to their people out of political necessity. The culture of deception in
the relationship sometimes felt impossible to roll back. "It was a hard
place to get your head around," Ambassador Anne Patterson later told
me in her subdued Southern drawl. "It was so weird. It was just down-
right nonlinear."

The typical rhythm of the relationship went something like this:
the ISI would plant negative items about the US in the Pakistani media,
including conspiracy theories about Indian operatives in Congress or
the White House. The stories whipped up a frenzy of anti-American
sentiment. Then the ISI would come back to the Americans and insist
that public opinion prevented them from changing their approach to
terrorist safe havens, or to supporting Islamist militias. "Which is actually true," Patterson reflected. "But it's public opinion that they themselves have generated." Patterson had a frank, straightforward manner
and was one of the few diplomats to try to confront the layers of deception head on. In one meeting, she told Zardari: "I come here, Mr.
President, and talk to you, and then there's a press release and it says
something we never even talked about." He looked at Patterson like
she'd lost her mind and said, "Well you really wouldn't want us to put
out what we actually talked about!" A similar cycle was repeated in
other hot spots where the United States relied on difficult foreign militaries, like Egypt.

Panetta said that after his meetings with General Pasha and the ISI,
colleagues would often remark, "You *do* understand he's lying?" Panetta
did. "Oh yeah, it wasn't as if I didn't know. . . . You had a pretty good
sense . . . people often asked me why our operations were classified—
the reason they were classified is because the Pakistanis *wanted* them to
be classified so that they would never have to acknowledge what was
happening!" Panetta was laughing again. General Pasha, in his curiously millennial manner, declined to respond to Panetta's comments.
"Sorry Ronan. I am not in it. Let Leon have his say!!!!"

———

ACCEPTING PAKISTAN'S DOUBLE GAME supposedly safeguarded cooperation, but even at a tactical level, the relationship could be fraught—sometimes for both sides. One Pakistani army commander, who spoke on condition of anonymity as he now serves in a more prominent position in the military, told me that joint operations were rife with deadly miscommunication. He'd lived through one such operation when he was an infantry commander during the initial series of failed counterterrorism efforts in Swat valley in early 2009. It was still winter, and the air in the mountainous valley was freezing. He was leading his unit of thirty-five men through the difficult terrain, pursuing a "very important" terrorist target chosen by the Americans. (How important, he never learned. "When you're operating in the field, commanding a unit, you do not have the ability to figure out if it is a high-value target," the commander reflected. "You're just concerned about taking him out before he takes me out.") Overhead, he could see American drones shadowing him. "Very few people know that we had a US technical team with us, that would have a certain control of Predator drones, flying overhead," he said. "Of course with the consent of Pakistan."

One such American technical team was some distance away from the combat operations in Swat, monitoring through the drones. The Americans' presence was a matter of strict secrecy. Even the men in the commander's own unit weren't informed of the specifics. But the commander had an open line of radio communication with American officers, and was told Predator strikes could be called in as a force multiplier.

According to the commander, on the first night of the operation, his unit closed in on its target, only to watch him escape into a "hostile zone" they had been ordered against entering. The commander radioed the coordinates to the Americans. The drones had been in close proximity for hours. But no strike came.

The following night, another unit, operating about thirty-five miles away, had a similar encounter with a target, and called in a strike. This time, it came—targeting not the terrorists they were pursuing, but the Pakistani unit itself. "Our own soldiers," he told me, planting a fist on the table in front of him, "We lost thirty-one of our men. And it was attributed to operator error. . . . We never called for a drone strike ever again." The Pakistanis told the American technical team they wouldn't cooperate; less than two weeks later, the Americans left.

The story reflected a sentiment that came up often in conversations with Pakistani military brass. "There was an absence of sincerity," the commander said, born of the narrow scope of the relationship and lack of communication. He found it galling how little the Americans seemed to share about the overarching goals of the operations for which he was risking his life. "The United States has never shared with us, in formal terms, its end state in Afghanistan," he grumbled. "That is the classic example of strategic interaction between the United States and Pakistan. We have been working on the operative issues. We have not been talking about the grand strategic issues that the two nations should be talking to each other about." Another Pakistani military official who was present while we spoke nodded vigorously. "Nobody is asking questions of what *makes* Pakistan do what it does," that second official added.

OPINIONS VARIED as to whether the compromises of the relationship were worth it. Anne Patterson was of the opinion that "we had an extraordinary degree of cooperation with ISI on some of these CT issues, really very unique in the world," a sentiment echoed by many other State, Pentagon, and intelligence officials. On the other hand, just as many had serious misgivings. Petraeus, reflecting on his time as CIA director, told me "ISI was not one of the greatest sources of intel . . . the bottom line is that there was a very transactional relationship."

That debate was pressurized each time deficiencies in Pakistan's counterterrorism cooperation were revealed. When a terrorist narrowly failed to detonate a truck bomb in Times Square in 2010, the FBI learned that the culprit, a thirty-three-year-old Pakistani-American named Faisal Shahzad, had trained in one of Pakistan's terrorist safe havens in Waziristan. They quickly realized that the ISI had done nothing to alert them of the threat. Furious White House officials dressed down the Pakistanis and demanded that they share more intelligence, including passenger data from flights out of Pakistan, and that they stop holding up visas for Americans. In a characteristic show of cognitive dissonance, the Pakistanis insisted they were already sharing everything, then refused to hand over the flight data.

The blocking of visas was a particular point of difficulty. When I arrived at State in 2009, the Pakistanis were years into brazenly strangling the flow of travel documents for US officials. The crackdown was a concession to anti-American sentiment within Pakistan, including fears that CIA agents were slipping into the country en masse. The cost to civilian assistance efforts was considerable. Often, State Department officials simply couldn't get into the country. In one case, a day before I was scheduled to depart for a trip to Islamabad, I learned that my months-old visa request was still languishing. As was usually the case with Pakistan, the answer didn't lie with the civilians. Instead, I secured a meeting with the military attaché, Lieutenant General Nazir Ahmed Butt. We met in his large office on the fourth floor of Pakistan's embassy, with a view of China's across the street. Butt, in full uniform with three stars on his collar, was distinguished looking, with a graying chevron moustache and, unusual for a Pakistani, electric blue eyes. He leaned back and listened intently as an assistant poured tea out of a china pot dusted with pink flowers and I spoke about the importance of working with Pakistani civil society, trying my best. An hour later, I walked out of the embassy with a multiple entry visa, good for a year. Not everyone was so lucky. At any given time, hundreds of applications were pending, requiring direct clearance by the Pakistani military or intelligence operatives.

The situation finally became so problematic that Hillary Clinton raised it with Pakistani prime minister Yousuf Raza Gilani. Gilani quietly authorized Husain Haqqani to begin approving visas without going through Islamabad—making him, as Haqqani put it, "visa czar." Over the course of the following year, he approved a wave of American visa requests, keeping the relationship from tilting into hostilities. He was, in his view, "papering over a lot of problems between Pakistan and the US." Haqqani knew his efforts would draw suspicion from the Pakistani political establishment. For him, as was the case with Robin Raphel's misunderstood diplomatic endeavors, talking to the other side was about to become a dangerous game.

10

FARMER HOLBROOKE

UNABLE TO MOVE THE NEEDLE away from what he called "mil-think," Richard Holbrooke set to work around its margins. He still felt that any hope for success depended on broadening America's role, in both Afghanistan and Pakistan, beyond tactics.

On the Afghan side of the border, he proposed a flood of new civilian-led assistance. Prompted by his agitation, the Obama administration requested from Congress $800 million more for reconstruction in 2009 than the Bush administration had the year before. Holbrooke commandeered control of USAID projects, insisting on signing off on many of them personally. He was able to secure that control because USAID reports to the State Department. His outsize influence was a source of bureaucratic rancor—especially when Holbrooke, always a whirling dervish of activity, would leave projects awaiting approval for months, unwilling to relinquish control. But he considered the move necessary. Afghanistan was full of expensive, embarrassing USAID boondoggles—from cobblestone roads that Afghans considered unusable as they hurt camels' feet, to farming projects on land with groundwater too salty to sustain crops, to fertilizer handouts that inadvertently enhanced poppy cultivation and, in turn, Afghanistan's drug economy. When Holbrooke was in Vietnam, USAID had a robust corps of technical specialists in areas like agriculture. By the Obama administration, decades of budget cuts had shrunk the size of the workforce and robbed it of such expertise. The funding USAID did receive was often mismanaged and misspent, with projects going to American megacontractors with high overhead and little understanding of circumstances on the ground. This was one of the symptoms of the imbalance that had bedeviled Holbrooke throughout his career. By the modern war on terror, almost all of the capacity and resources lay instead on the military side.

Holbrooke was convinced that the key was agriculture. The US military, which led many of the counternarcotics efforts in the region, had long contended that lucrative poppy cultivation for heroin sustained the Taliban. So the Bush administration had focused on crop eradication, slashing and burning its way through Afghanistan's fields. Holbrooke was incensed by this. He pointed to intelligence assessments that showed support from Pakistan and the Gulf States was far more central to the Taliban's livelihood. He argued that eradication pushed penniless farmers into the arms of the Taliban—often their only source of employment after their crops were wiped out.

He set out to refocus the United States on supporting Afghan farmers. "They need the kind of soup-to-nuts agricultural support that Roosevelt gave farmers during the great depression," he said. He was a man possessed. Pomegranates, once a lucrative export for the Afghans, were a particular obsession. At Holbrooke's request, I organized dozens of meetings focused on the fruit. Sometimes he'd cut me off in the middle of an unrelated sentence and say, from a faraway place, "Where are we on the pomegranates?" By the end of his first year on the job,

Richard Holbrooke, a man who as far as I was aware had never so much as kept a potted cactus alive, could explain the pomegranate's required levels of moisture, favorable types of soil, and ideal timeline for harvest. Hillary Clinton took to calling him Farmer Holbrooke.

But, despite Holbrooke's efforts, civilian reconstruction remained dwarfed by an order of magnitude by the Pentagon's programs in the same space. In the early years of George W. Bush's administration, State reconstruction spending sometimes outweighed the Pentagon's by a ratio of more than ten to one. By the time Holbrooke came to State, the situation had nearly reversed. The trend lines were hard to miss: From 2008 to 2010, State spending on reconstruction in Afghanistan jumped from $2.2 billion to $4.2 billion, while the Pentagon's budget for similar efforts more than tripled from $3.4 billion to $10.4 billion. This included a sea of development projects conventionally associated with State and USAID, ranging from counternarcotics programs, to education, to the catchall Commander's Emergency Response Program, which was primarily used for road building and repair. The Army Corps of Engineers, likewise, worked on infrastructure projects around the country, and USAID was sometimes the last to know.

Even for the projects underwritten through the new USAID and State Department funding, Holbrooke had trouble disentangling development and military objectives. Counterinsurgency strategy was typically described in three steps: "clear, hold, build"—as in, clear the area of the enemy, hold it with our forces, and begin to build capacity. As the first year of the Obama administration wore on, that COIN language, ripped from Petraeus's counterinsurgency manual, began appearing in USAID development contracts. One request for applications for a community-based development initiative called for USAID's partner charities to "enable COIN-focused, unstable communities to directly implement small-scale community level projects" and "support military . . . efforts in communities by helping to 'hold' areas after they are cleared."

Security and development objectives in an active theater of war are never completely separable, but there had, historically, been an acknowledgment that development should be driven by technical expertise and long term goals, not shackled to tactics. Explicitly militarizing the contract language was new—and, it turned out, tone-deaf. The nongovernmental organizations applying for the contracts revolted. The head of one charity told me its staffers had been targeted for attacks based on their visible identification with the military. Others said it was destroying trust with communities of Afghans who were comfortable with American reconstruction, but not American military might.

Holbrooke correctly judged that the years of narrow, military-driven engagement under the Bush administration had also atrophied relationships with civil society, especially at a local level. Large American companies took equally large commissions, then subcontracted to other groups, which in turn sometimes subcontracted yet again. The result was obvious: massive inefficiency and a lack of accountability.

One of the first problems: The United States simply wasn't aware what groups were on the ground, and where. Holbrooke's response was typically ambitious: he asked me to track every NGO in Afghanistan and Pakistan. I enlisted the one computer science geek I knew—a programmer named Jillian Kozyra, who was snapped up by Google soon after—and we pulled all-nighters in my tiny basement studio on U Street as I designed and she coded. Using the programming language Ruby, she built a scraping application—an automated tool that extracts data from internet sources—married to Google Maps and basic analysis tools that could, for instance, break out a pie chart of different types of civil society activity in a given area. At the end of the process, we had a map of Afghanistan and Pakistan populated with more than a hundred thousand local groups. We put it up on an open, nongovernment URL that I purchased. Holbrooke was delighted by the technology and asked me to present it at the White House, the Pentagon, and our embassies in Afghanistan and Pakistan.

But the project also illustrated, in miniature, the pitfalls of his bull-in-a-china-shop approach. The American contractors were incensed by Holbrooke's push away from them. They began lobbying for his firing and complaining about the focus on local NGOs in the press. And, as in all of Holbrooke's endeavors, the military was an overpowering and not always friendly counterpart. Within two years of the first demonstrations of the NGO tracking technology, both Pentagon and CIA lawyers descended on my office. Where had this mysterious technology come from, they wanted to know? Where was I getting my data? Who was funding it? The answer was, of course, that this was a jury-rigged solution using open-source data and tools, at the cost of a single domain name. Both agencies asserted ownership of the work product, but did nothing with it. When I left government after nearly four years, the United States still lacked the basic database of civil society entities Holbrooke had sought.

Later, I received a large manila envelope from an anonymous P.O. box in Virginia. Inside was an application form for a job interview process to be conducted under a strict veil of secrecy. A timed online test and a series of meetings at hotel bars with unnamed officials followed. They had little interest in my work at State. Would I be willing to depart to work as a lawyer or journalist under nonofficial cover, they asked? "Come on," said one interviewer. "What you're all doing over there is a side show. This is the real work."

Like most things Holbrooke, SRAP was ambitious and exciting and, for many, alienating. Prioritizing outsiders over career Foreign Service officers made the office hated inside the State Department bureaucracy. The interagency convening role he had taken upon himself was the traditional domain of the White House—and this was a particularly controlling White House. These were original sins for which Holbrooke would never fully atone. From the moment we started, the system went to work expelling this peculiar creation, like a body rejecting a transplanted organ. It would cost Holbrooke, and, some would later argue, the country, dearly.

11

A LITTLE LESS CONVERSATION

A WEEK AFTER the ceremony in the Ben Franklin Room announcing Richard Holbrooke's role in January 2009, Holbrooke and Husain Haqqani sat in the Hay-Adams hotel's Lafayette dining room—an airy, light-filled hall with cream-colored walls and wide views of the White House. The property was once home to career diplomat and Secretary of State John Hay, and the legendary salons he and neighbor and political scion Henry Adams hosted for DC's intellectual elites. In the 1920s, their homes had been razed to make way for the elegant, Italian Renaissance complex where Haqqani and Holbrooke now lunched. Holbrooke had passing encounters with Haqqani over the course of their overlapping diplomatic careers. The two had struck up a rapport in 2008, when Haqqani became ambassador to the US and Holbrooke, who was at the time chairman of the Asia Society, began making trips to build up his bona fides in the region. The day his new role was formally announced, he had called Haqqani and suggested they have lunch. Someplace where they'd be seen, he'd said wryly but pointedly. The Hay-Adams was hard to top for visibility. Yet such a consideration also captured Holbrooke as a creature of another era, when being seen at a prominent locale sent a signal, and when there was a clique of interested power brokers and observers ready to receive such a transmission. The truth is, nobody was paying attention.

Holbrooke laid out his goals: he wanted an end to the war in Afghanistan, and a stable Pakistan. He wanted a settlement. As always, he asked incisive questions, many of them about bringing regional parties to the table. "Could the United States be friends with both India and Pakistan at the same time?" he asked. He wanted a more candid discussion of Pakistan's national interests. If there's one thing Haqqani knew from experience, it was that candor would be hard to come by.

"Remember one thing," Haqqani warned Holbrooke. "This is not Yugoslavia." He quoted a passage from Holbrooke's book about Bosnia, *To End a War*: "The leaders of all three sides were willing to let their people die while they argued."

"In the subcontinent," Haqqani went on, "it's not just that. People are unwilling and do not know what compromise means. This is not going to be as easy as you think."

The two men—both, for different reasons, outsiders in their political establishments, and both staring down the hardest foreign policy problem in the world—looked at each other.

Holbrooke observed that the new American president's pivot to the region might make life hard for Haqqani, too. "Increased focus and scrutiny raise questions to which there are no easy answers." He said he didn't envy Haqqani's job. The feeling was mutual. Over the course of the ensuing two years, the two men became close. Holbrooke would jolt Haqqani out of bed at 7 a.m. with calls about his latest diplomatic schemes. They'd take walks together near Holbrooke's Georgetown townhouse. On weekends, when Holbrooke's wife was out of town, they'd go to the movies. In March 2010, they walked to the E Street Cinema to see *The Ghost Writer*, Roman Polanski's thriller about a British prime minister accused of war crimes while working too closely with the Americans, and his wife, who turns out to be a CIA agent. Afterwards, Holbrooke and Haqqani got frozen yogurt.

Pieces of Holbrooke's desired region-wide role had been carted off before he could grab them. The Iran job had been commandeered by the White House, who appointed Dennis Ross to head up dialogue with that state. In an even bigger blow, the Indians, whose meteoric economic rise made them a far greater diplomatic center of gravity than the Pakistanis, pitched a fit at the idea of being included in Holbrooke's war portfolio alongside a rogue state like Pakistan. They successfully lobbied the Obama transition team to nix any India envoy role, and particularly one involving Holbrooke.

Holbrooke told me he intended to address the Indian elephant in the room anyway, and proceeded to regularly include said elephant in his regional diplomacy. And the Indians weren't his only targets. In February 2010, he had his staffers, including myself, assemble a list of his international travel in the job. It was exhausting to behold. In the first two months of 2010 alone, his shuttle diplomacy included trips to twenty cities in nearly as many countries. London, Abu Dhabi, Islamabad, Kabul, New Delhi, Paris, Munich, Doha, Riyadh, Tashkent, Tbilisi, Berlin; the list went on and on. Alongside the list of cities, we noted commitments he had secured from foreign partners, for either Afghanistan or Pakistan. New Delhi pledged continued civilian assistance to and increased trade with Afghanistan, along with a promise to avoid "provocative assistance in the security sector." The Russians, at one point, offered "technical military training" and helicopter maintenance for the Pakistanis. This was a global threat, and Holbrooke intended to build a global solution.

The dream was to bring the Pakistanis and Indians together to defuse the root causes of Pakistan's support for terrorists. He even set up a secret meeting between himself, Haqqani, and former Indian high commissioner to Pakistan, S. K. Lamba. "We met together once," Haqqani admitted. "Holbrooke encouraged me and the Indians to talk." But Haqqani considered his own country inhospitable to any meaningful negotiations. "What will satisfy the Pakistanis," he mused, "short of India stopping to exist?" The India-Pakistan problem required a fundamental shift in the posture of the negotiating parties—the kind that Holbrooke achieved in Dayton only with the robust backing of the White House and the threat of military strikes he could meaningfully direct. In this case, he barely had a mandate to talk to the Indians, and frequently had to do so in secret to avoid irritating not only the Pakistanis but also the White House. Here, the military was driving engagement. Here, he would have to work around the limitations of his job description.

ANOTHER GREAT CHALLENGE was simply talking to the Pakistanis. Years of conversation conducted between intelligence agencies, with blinders on to any broader dialogue, had worked during the war with the Soviets. But during that conflict, the Pakistanis and the Americans had been on the same side. Both needed the invading forces out of the region, each for their own reasons. The relationship was already fraught with deception in other areas, like Pakistan's nuclear development. But there was at least a strategic alignment. There wasn't broader dialogue, but there didn't need to be.

In the Global War on Terrorism, the Americans attempted to rebuild the same relationship, but there was an essential difference that was almost impossible to overcome: this time, Pakistan was on the other side. Now we wanted al-Qaeda–aligned militants out of the region. But Pakistan had kept right on using them as a proxy force, just like we taught them to do. However often the Pakistanis appeared to accede to American demands for cooperation, they always had goals opposed to those of the United States. If Pakistan was going to reconsider its basic priorities, there needed to be a broader and more honest conversation. To succeed, Holbrooke would have to turn the uneasy

transactions of proxy war into a true diplomatic alliance—or something closer to it.

Holbrooke knew that coaxing the Pakistanis into broader dialogue
would require a show of commitment from the United States in areas
other than military assistance. He needed action—or at least money.
In April 2009, he gathered many of the countries on his international
engagement list for a donor's conference in Tokyo, where he wooed
them into $5 billion of pledges to Pakistan. "That is a respectable
IPO," he joked. Was it enough, a reporter asked? "Pakistan needs $50
billion," Holbrooke said, "not $5 billion."

Back home, he and David Petraeus followed up with a frenzy of
lobbying. "Richard and I worked that very hard on the Hill," Petraeus
told me. "I remember the two of us worked that together." It was the
zenith of Holbrooke's BlackBerry jujitsu, as he worked every connec-
tion he had in every legislator's office. In September 2009, the Senate unanimously authorized $7.5 billion in new assistance to Pakistan
over five years. The legislation was named Kerry-Lugar-Berman for
its sponsors. It was the first long-term civilian aid package to Pakistan
born of a deliberate effort to roll back the almost exclusively military-
to-military nature of the relationship. "That was a grand strategic
attempt to address the perception that the US was only engaging with
the Pakistani military and didn't care about democracy or the Pakistani
people," recalled Alan Kronstadt, the Congressional Research Service's analyst on Pakistan assistance. But changing those perceptions
proved more difficult than any of the Americans had bargained for.

The day the Kerry-Lugar-Berman Act passed, Mark Siegel,
Benazir Bhutto's lobbyist, held a party at his house. He had brought
his Pakistan account to his firm at the time, Locke Lord, and a large
crowd of employees, Pakistani diplomats, and politicians toasted the
achievement. Less than twenty-four hours later, the fallout began.
Mohsin Kamal, a young Pakistani lobbyist, had joined Siegel's firm

the day of the party. He expected to capitalize on an apparent thaw
in the relationship. Instead, his first job was frantic damage control.
Items began appearing in Pakistani outlets excoriating the bill. It
was "degrading," with "vicious designs on Pakistan's sovereignty,"
raged *The Nation*. "An affront to the country in the eyes of its people," opined diplomat Maleeha Lodhi in *The News*. Even the Pakistani army chief, General Kayani, expressed outrage and privately
harangued US officials.

At issue was a requirement that the US secretary of state annually
certify that Pakistan was meeting basic thresholds for good behavior to keep security assistance flowing. That included cooperation
on ensuring nuclear weapons stayed out of terrorists' hands; ceasing
support for extremist and terrorist groups, and helping to confront
the safe havens in FATA and Quetta. It was, in fact, a pretty modest nod to accountability. The certification requirements only applied
to security-related assistance, and even then, could be waived freely
for any national security reason. In practice, this was a no-strings-
attached gift. Few legislators in America had considered the possibility
that it would actually threaten to burn down the entire relationship.
But in Pakistan, paranoia is a national pastime. This episode, like just
about everything else, prompted two reactions. Some were convinced
it was evidence of Indian meddling. And some were convinced it was
Husain Haqqani's fault. "Husain Haqqani did something very stupid,"
was Mohsin Kamal's straightforward reading of events. "He put those
provisions in."

As the furor grew, Holbrooke gathered staffers in his office for a
crisis session. He paced back and forth in his socks. Holbrooke's chosen
response, seeded to any reporter who would listen, was to insist that
the assistance came with "no conditions"—which he jokingly referred
to as "the c word." John Kerry, whose name the legislation bore, was
dispatched to Islamabad to try to pacify the Pakistanis. "We did a whole

apology tour with Kerry-Lugar-Berman where we met with Nawaz and the whole gang over there," remembered one senior official. On one occasion, Kerry sat for five hours with General Kayani over dinner. "We want to give you this money, we want to change the nature of our relationship," Kerry told him. "But to be able to do that, you guys have to be sensitive to how you're going to be perceived if you continue to do some of the bad things that you've been doing." "Look, I'm a politician too," replied Kayani. "I understand your politics. I know how difficult this is." As was so often the case, the Pakistanis had one message for their people and another for the Americans.

I wondered, for a moment, what an outside observer might make of this madness: a supposed ally convulsed with rage over a $7.5-billion handout, and a world power bending over backward to deny that said handout contained any accountability. The situation held a mirror to the deep problems in the relationship. Holbrooke had tried to buy a broader conversation. But Pakistan had been a proxy for America's military interests for too many years. While the conversations between spy chiefs and generals flourished, the untended broader relationship had become a petri dish for paranoia and suspicion. $7.5 billion couldn't buy it back.

ROBIN RAPHEL SAID YES to the job offer from Anne Patterson, the US ambassador to Pakistan at the time. The month before the Kerry-Lugar-Berman Act passed the House and Senate in September 2009, she packed up her things and moved to Islamabad one more time. She settled into life in a two-story, stucco house in Islamabad's comfortable, leafy F-6 sector, right next to the Margalla Hills. She got a refurbished Toyota and drove herself to parties and functions. During my trips to Islamabad, I saw her working her way through house parties thrown by Russian diplomats and British charity heads, always thronged by Pakistanis. Robin Raphel was back among the Islamabad elites she'd known since her twenties. The task of spending the new flood of money that Holbrooke and Petraeus had fought for on the Hill fell to her.

"I believed at the time, and still do, it was a good idea to do Kerry-Lugar-Berman, to make a grand gesture . . . to help raise the standard of living overall for the people and not just the military," she told me. But spending the money proved just as fraught as announcing it. This, too, was partly an echo of the long history of transactional rapport— the relationship simply wasn't set up to accommodate $1.5 billion a year in civilian assistance. It quickly became apparent that there was more money authorized than USAID could spend effectively. The result was, in the eyes of many Pakistanis, yet another broken promise—a hyped-up number that, after all the furor, never became a reality.

As in Afghanistan, there was a lack of technical expertise. In certain areas, like water infrastructure, there just wasn't anyone qualified at USAID. I began pulling in outside groups and linking them up with the Pakistani government and USAID. But no amount of outside expertise could get the machine of US assistance moving fast enough to fit the timeline set by the wartime legislation. "The fact is, we weren't doing much," admitted Raphel, "because it takes a very long time to get going on stuff. So there was this huge expectation buildup and there was no way we could meet it."

The same broken system that blighted Holbrooke's efforts in Afghanistan frustrated Raphel's struggle to get projects through the pipeline faster. Despite the quest to identify local NGOs, much of the Kerry-Lugar-Berman money went through hulking American contractors using layers of subcontracts. "We pissed away most of that money to contractors," Raphel said flatly. And there wasn't enough time to fix the issues. Five years are the blink of an eye in the context of infrastructure projects, and shorter than that, in terms of the long-term relationship change Holbrooke sought to effect. "I didn't realize right at the beginning that it should have been a ten-year program, not a five-year program," Raphel told me later, "because we couldn't figure out quickly enough how to spend the money well." Yet again, timelines dictated by military exigencies and domestic political pressures didn't fit with the realities of diplomacy and development.

Then there was the pushback from the groups responsible for implementing the assistance—who, just like in Afghanistan, had little desire to be identified as a part of the American war effort. Holbrooke and Petraeus sold Kerry-Lugar-Berman on simple logic: we'd spend a lot of money on dams and schools, Pakistanis would see all those American dollars flowing and—hey presto!—Pakistan would transform from an avatar of the CIA in shadowy counterterrorism operations to a friend of the United States. Meetings about assistance to Pakistan often devolved into senior officials making increasingly desperate pleas for highly visible "signature projects" that could bring about this fabled winning of hearts and minds.

Holbrooke wanted that as much as anyone. In a picture taken at a refugee camp in Northwest Pakistan, he slouches next to a bearded Pakistani refugee, who sits lotus style with his young daughter in his lap. Holbrooke has taken off his sunglasses and sincere sympathy is written on his face, along with intense focus. Tufts of his graying hair stick out from underneath a khaki-colored hat emblazoned with "USAID" and then underneath, its slogan: "from the American people." He took to wearing it a lot. "Seems like Pakistani press is taking particular interest in RCH"—Holbrooke's initials—"baseball cap," Vali Nasr wrote in an email to Holbrooke and his chief of staff, Rosemarie Pauli. "Does that have deeper meaning, Dr Freud?" Holbrooke wrote back. "It was practically the only sign, however temporary, that there was a US civilian effort. . . . Every other country's aid here, even Iran's, is better branded than us. Only our helicopters are visible. China's field hospital (which I drove by in Thatta), Turkey, Saudi Arabia (I visited their refugee camp, where they are building a mosque), Australia (field hospital in Multan), Switzerland, UK, etc. While we hide and the NGO partners refuse to admit that we fund them."

Holbrooke was right—in sensitive areas of Pakistan rife with violent anti-American sentiment, nongovernmental groups often tried to minimize the stars and stripes, fearing they could trigger attacks on workers. In the most volatile areas, the US even permitted the complete scrubbing of flags and USAID logos through waivers. This had long been a gentleman's agreement. But Holbrooke began agitating, publicly and privately. He forwarded the exchange to Clinton aide Jake Sullivan, who forwarded it to Clinton. Days later, she raised the issue publicly, saying "we have to fight to get the US Government's label on our material because a lot of our aid workers and our NGO partners are afraid to have association with the US Government."

Suddenly, we were at war, with the groups responsible for much of the assistance at the heart of the Afghanistan-Pakistan strategy. "We're aiding Pakistan. Don't put a target on our backs," blared the headline of a *Washington Post* op-ed written by the head of the NGO coalition InterAction. "In countries such as Liberia or Congo, US NGOs that get funding from the US government routinely promote the fact that they are delivering help 'from the American people,' wrote Sam Worthington. "But in Pakistan, where aid workers' lives are more often at stake, an enforced branding campaign could . . . put the lives of Americans and their Pakistani colleagues at risk." I was dispatched to quiet the storm, bringing the groups into the State Department and heading to a summit of NGOs to make the case against a boycott.

Both sides dug in. Judith McHale, the former Discovery Channel executive serving as Clinton's undersecretary of state for public diplomacy, emailed the op-ed to Clinton, saying, "As you know I believe passionately that it is not in our national interests to continue to provide billions of dollars in aid and assistance without the very people we are helping knowing we are the ones providing the assistance." Clinton replied: "Thx—I love working w you—I feel sometimes we were separated at birth!" Jake Sullivan chimed in, in an email to McHale: "Surely they shouldn't hide their support, offering it covertly?" He added, using the one-letter abbreviation for the secretary of state: "S believes we should expand this beyond Pakistan—make the case for displaying the support of the American people throughout the world."

As the crisis-management email chains ballooned, I was pulled in to help draft an op-ed that would run under the byline of Rajiv Shah, the head of USAID.

I was, absurdly, given my junior rank, the only person actively communicating with the groups threatening to pull out. It struck me that there was a thoughtful solution here—a more specific conversation not about whether American branding should be used, but about when and where and how—essentially an adjustment of the waiver policy that was already in place. Other changes, like working with local groups that had expressed a willingness to use the American flag, even in difficult areas, could have a greater impact than focusing on strong-arming Western groups that already faced controversy in Pakistan.

In a series of memos to Holbrooke and emails to the group, I tried to gently make the case. Holbrooke hit the roof. He called me into his office one night, after a reply I'd sent to the group suggesting a public acknowledgment of the waivers already available for unsafe areas. His face was slick with perspiration and he looked exhausted. He was, by then, facing off against an unfriendly White House almost daily. "Have you taken leave of your senses?" he thundered. He snatched the memo I'd brought him with such force it tore in half. I looked at the jagged half page in my hand and then at a vein standing out on Holbrooke's forehead. "I know you think you're special," he raged on. "I know you think you have a *destiny*. That you'll do great things. That you'll make a difference for your country. I know you've felt sure of it ever since you were young—" even at the time, it was hard to avoid the feeling he'd stopped himself from saying "since you were in Vietnam." A picture of young Holbrooke smiling from behind Coke-bottle glasses in the sunlight of the Mekong Delta stared at us from a nearby wall. "—But you have *got* to know your place. To pick your battles. To realize that even the best point isn't a good point if no one wants to hear it. And right now, no one wants to hear—DONNA?!" His assistant, a mild-mannered Southern grandmother named Donna Dejban, was standing outside his office door, gaping at us, weeping openly. "Donna. STOP. CRYING!" he bellowed.

The op-ed from Rajiv Shah ran in the *Huffington Post*, with a brief mention of waivers. None of the major implementers pulled out, and the assistance continued. But the dream of a sweeping new civilian assistance agenda in Pakistan never quite materialized. Much of the funding was never even appropriated by Congress. In some cases, acts of god interfered. US responses to flooding and a refugee crisis had to be bankrolled with the authorized funds. "Humanitarian aid siphoned off a lot of that," said Kronstadt, the congressional researcher. More significantly, changes were afoot that would dramatically alter the stakes of the relationship—and with those changes came dramatically smaller appropriations.

IN MARCH 2010, Clinton and Pakistani foreign minister Shah Mehmood Qureshi sat at the head of a series of long tables arranged in a rectangle in the Ben Franklin Room. Behind them stood alternating US and Pakistani flags: red, white, and blue juxtaposing white crescents on green. A Pakistani delegation sat on Qureshi's side and the Americans on Clinton's, with Holbrooke around the corner from her. Even with the odds arrayed against him in his civilian funding surges in Afghanistan and Pakistan, Holbrooke forged ahead trying to bring the players to the table. He convinced Clinton that Pakistan—like weightier allies India and China—should receive an annual "strategic dialogue": a high-level, ceremonial talk on the most pressing issues in a relationship.

Little of substance was discussed at that first meeting, and the commitments Qureshi did secure were all in the traditional arena of counterterrorism cooperation ("We've agreed to fast-track our requests that have been pending for months and years on the transfer of military equipment to Pakistan," he gushed to reporters.) But the mere fact that it had occurred, after so many mishaps, was a small miracle. After the talks, Clinton stood with Qureshi in front of the blue walls and Corinthian pillars of the State Department Treaty Room and thanked Pakistan for its friendship. Holbrooke framed the talks as the beginning of a new kind of relationship: "Pakistan is important in its own right. We don't view it simply as a function of its giant neighbor to the east or its war-torn neighbor to the west." It was more aspiration than reality, but it was a start.

Holbrooke made the most of the opening. He championed additional, trilateral talks with Afghanistan. Working groups were spun out to address specific issues. Those were sometimes his best chance to tackle big challenges that exceeded his mandate, like restrictions on trade that were driven by animosity between Pakistan and India and strangled Pakistan's economy. He couldn't bring India to the table, but he pushed aggressively on trilateral talks with the United States, Pakistan, and Afghanistan, culminating in the signing of an agreement to open up trade. It was the first breakthrough in a negotiating process that had been stalled, literally, since 1965. In 2015, even India began to signal its willingness to enter the trade pact.

Another trilateral working group's focus—water policy—became a fixation for Holbrooke. In a little-publicized view, he came to believe mounting tensions over water issues could trigger a complete collapse of the uneasy peace between India and Pakistan. The Indus River basin fed both countries, running through India and disputed Kashmir on its way to Pakistan. A 1960 treaty, negotiated by the World Bank, split the various Indus rivers between the two countries. But climate change was putting stress on the tenuous arrangement. Floods threatened farmland on both sides of the border, increasing the risk of turf wars. Drought could trigger a similar effect, and was already a visible trend. One study predicted that shrinking glaciers would reduce the flows of the Indus by 8 percent by 2050. "If we ignore this," Holbrooke told me, "it could very well precipitate World War III." I gave him an incredulous look. He stayed absolutely serious.

Holbrooke raised the water dimension of the regional struggle in a National Security Council session, hoping he could expand his effort with higher level support. White House officials were incredulous and asked whether he was kidding. If there were any laughs to be had, Holbrooke's would be the last—in 2016, the Indians began making ominous threats to pull out of the Indus Waters Treaty.

Realizing he was being frozen out, Holbrooke fought to have another official—Under Secretary of State Maria Otero—serve in a sort of informal water envoy role. (As usual, he was never confident that anyone who wasn't him could do a job. "Is she okay?" he asked me after one of his briefing sessions with her. "Is she smart enough for this? This is important.") And he kept pushing on talks. I spent months traipsing around the world with the water working group, to make sure they were integrating outside experts that could help them prepare for a potential crisis. A refrigerator magnet inexplicably given to me by the Pakistani government shows me, a handful of Department of Agriculture officials, and a Pakistani minister giving a thumbs-up next to equipment used for testing groundwater levels. At one point, we sat at the garish Ritz-Carlton in Doha trying to jumpstart a come-to-Jesus conversation between India, Pakistan, and Afghanistan on the subject. Bearded Afghans sat next to artificial lagoons declining piña coladas. It felt like a waste of time. India refused to send an official envoy.

But Holbrooke didn't think he was tilting at windmills. Conversations between regional players, however halting, were happening—to an extent that hadn't been seen in years. And the Pakistanis were moving against terrorists within their own borders to an extent they'd never managed before. "There was a period in 2009 where we thought, 'This thing is really working,'" Petraeus told me. "And that was the period in which they did Swat, Bajaur, Mohmand, Khyber, Orakzai, South Waziristan. . . . We were providing fair amounts of financial, intel, training, infrastructure and logistics assistance, and we felt it was going very well." Holbrooke seemed buoyed. Despite the obstacles, he told me, he was edging toward something important.

12

A-ROD

JUST AFTER THANKSGIVING in 2010, a sleek Falcon 900EX triple-engine jet touched down at the snow-blanketed Munich Airport. The jet belonged to the *Bundesnachrichtendienst*—Germany's CIA—and had taken off from Qatar. Onboard was a man named Syed Tayyab Agha. He was in his late thirties, with youthful features and a neat black beard. He spoke English, choosing his words carefully, with a calm, measured demeanor. Agha was a longtime aide to Taliban leader Mullah Omar and had served in the regime's embassy in Pakistan. He had been involved in years of sputtering efforts to start talks with the outside world, including an approach to the Afghans in 2008. His flight to Germany was the culmination of a year of careful negotiation led by Holbrooke's German counterpart, Michael Steiner. Steiner, a thin, distinguished-looking man with craggy features and stooped shoulders, had also been Holbrooke's German counterpart during Bosnia. He had a similar reputation for aggressive negotiating tactics and larger-than-life theatrics. (During a later stint as ambassador to India, he and his wife staged a reenactment of a popular Bollywood movie, complete with Steiner lip-syncing his way through song-and-dance numbers, that surely ranks as one of the strangest YouTube videos ever uploaded by the German Foreign Office.) He also shared Holbrooke's belief that talks were the only way out of Afghanistan. German agents had communicated with Agha only indirectly, through intermediaries who kept his location secret. He confirmed his identity to the Germans by posting specific, agreed upon messages on official Taliban websites.

Agha was whisked away to a German intelligence safe house in an upscale village in the Bavarian countryside, not far from the city. Security was tight, with the area surrounding the safe house locked down. The next day, two Americans trudged through the cold to the house. One was a White House staffer named Jeff Hayes. The other was our deputy on Holbrooke's team, Frank Ruggiero, who had served as the civilian adviser to the military in the Taliban stronghold of Kandahar. They joined Steiner, a Qatari prince who attended at Agha's insistence as a guarantor of safety, and Agha. It was the first time in a decade the United States had talked to the Taliban.

For Agha, the stakes were high. He was on German and American terrorist watch lists, and came only on commitments from both countries that he wouldn't be arrested. Should al-Qaeda, or the al-Qaeda–friendly factions within Pakistan's ISI, discover the talks, he risked a more gruesome fate. There was risk for the Americans, too. Just a year before, a supposed double agent informing on al-Qaeda to the Jordanian intelligence agency had been welcomed onto a base in Khost, Afghanistan. He turned out to be a triple agent, detonating a bomb and killing seven CIA officers. The memory was still fresh for everyone working on Afghanistan. German intelligence promised the Americans Agha had been vetted and searched.

The group was together for eleven hours. Several were devoted to sightseeing (the Taliban official was excited to see traditional German castles). Six hours were spent talking. Agha outlined the Taliban's main concerns: its leaders wanted to be clearly distinguished from al-Qaeda, asked that Taliban names be removed from a UN sanctions list, and sought permission to open a political office in Qatar, not just in Pakistan where they currently operated. There was one more, almost obsessive focus: they wanted the release of Taliban prisoners held by the US in Afghanistan and at Guantánamo Bay. The Americans outlined their conditions: that the Taliban lay down arms, renounce al-Qaeda, and accept the Afghan constitution and its protections for women. And the United States had its own prisoner request: it wanted the release of Sergeant Bowe Bergdahl, who had been captured by the Taliban after deserting from the Army a year before.

After Agha left, the negotiators were elated. Holbrooke, who had been obsessively monitoring the talks from afar, met Ruggiero's flight back the next day at Dulles. At Harry's Tap Room on Concourse B, Holbrooke ordered a cheeseburger and Ruggiero briefed him on every detail. This was not an intensive negotiation—not yet. But Agha hadn't balked at the American conditions. It was the most important break to date in Western efforts to drive a wedge between al-Qaeda and the Taliban.

"REMEMBER THIS MOMENT," Holbrooke had told Ruggiero when he tapped him to make the trip a month earlier. "We may be on the verge of making history." It was a Sunday afternoon in October 2010, and Ruggiero was driving over the Benjamin Franklin Bridge in Philadelphia with his seven-year-old daughter when he got the call. As instructed, he never forgot. For a variety of reasons—to avoid public scrutiny; to avoid the fallout should the contact prove to be a fake; to skirt the perils of his fraught relationship with the White House—Holbrooke had decided against attending the first meeting himself. But the expectation was that he would take charge of any further negotiations.

Holbrooke had first heard about Agha during one of his whirlwind international rallying efforts in Cairo in the fall of 2009. The Egyptians told him that Taliban leaders, including an aide to Mullah Omar, had visited them. Steiner and the German diplomats, who had also made contact, felt Agha was authentic. And, tantalizingly, he was willing to talk to the Americans. Clinton, who had initially been skeptical of high-level talks, told Holbrooke to begin exploring the prospect under a strict veil of secrecy. Holbrooke's love of the Yankees had solidified at age fifteen, when his father refused to let him cut class to see Game 5 of the World Series and what turned out to be Don Larsen's historic perfect game. He took to referring to Agha as "A-Rod," to keep a lid on leaks.

A negotiated settlement with the Taliban had, to that point, been the white whale to Holbrooke's Ahab. Barney Rubin, whose desk sat not far from mine in our State Department suite, had been hired expressly because he was the foremost expert on the Taliban in the Western world. Just before Holbrooke scooped him up in early 2009, Rubin had met with Taliban intermediaries in Kabul and Saudi Arabia. During these exploratory trips, he had probed what conditions had to be met for talks to proceed and hit upon the same priorities A-Rod later raised. Rubin believed talks were a real possibility. The day Holbrooke was sworn into his job, he met with Rubin about his trip and the prospects for negotiation. "If this thing works," Holbrooke said, "it may be the only way we will get out." Holbrooke didn't consider the decision to deploy more troops to be at odds with the possibility of a political settlement. Quite the opposite: he often talked about using the period of greatest military pressure as leverage to bring parties to the table. It was a tactic he had used, to great effect, in the Balkans.

There were two schools of thought on talking to the Taliban. The modest approach was to peel off and reintegrate low-level fighters—

the kind in it for a living wage rather than an ideological fight to the death—from the bottom up. The more ambitious approach—the one Holbrooke and Rubin were discussing—was to bring Taliban leadership to the table to attempt reconciliation. The exhaustive policy review led by Bruce Riedel had endorsed reintegrating low-level fighters, but flatly rejected a peace process. Taliban leaders "are not reconcilable and we cannot make a deal that includes them," that report concluded. The very idea of such talks ran counter to a basic ethos that had calcified during the Bush years: you don't talk to terrorists. For much of the first two years of the Obama administration, we were forbidden from so much as referencing the idea in unclassified communications. Reconciliation, Vali Nasr later said, was "a taboo word . . . the military would say, well, you're talking to the Taliban, you're already throwing in the towel."

Holbrooke longed to make his case to the president and lobbied for a meeting, but he never got one. Instead, he argued for a diplomatic approach with any one else in the administration he could get to. The toughest nut to crack was the military. Much of the leadership, including Petraeus in his seat at CENTCOM, felt talking to the Taliban would interfere with their case for military escalation. But Petraeus's commander in Kabul, McChrystal, began to come around to the idea. He and Holbrooke didn't have an easy relationship, but I saw him listen closely when Holbrooke worked up a lather—unlike Petraeus, who could be more visibly dismissive. An Army colonel under McChrystal named Christopher Kolenda, who had been working on reintegration efforts for insurgents at a local level, came to believe the Taliban was growing more moderate in some ways, and to share Holbrooke's view that negotiation held promise. McChrystal was intrigued and contacted Holbrooke, and the two began discussing the pros and cons of reconciliation, and how it might fit with the United States' military campaign. In early June, McChrystal notified his staff that he was "on board" with Taliban negotiations, and even began preparing a briefing for Karzai on the subject.

A few weeks later, Holbrooke woke up to the sound of his Black-Berry ringing. It was 2:30 a.m. and we were all staying at the US embassy in Kabul—he in one of the proper visitor's suites, I in my "hooch"—a white Conex shipping container outfitted with a bunk bed, a mini-fridge, and a tiny sink. "Remember to wash your hands! :)" read a peeling laminated sign to the left of the sink. "ROCKET ATTACK INSTRUCTIONS," read a notice to the right. One of said instructions was to hide under the bed, which didn't inspire much confidence. The day before, Holbrooke had been in Marja, a tactically important town that had been reclaimed from the Taliban a few months prior. As he made his approach, Taliban fighters opened fire on his V-22 Osprey—a futuristic but troubled combat aircraft with swiveling "tiltrotors" that allow it to act as either a helicopter or a plane. He'd descended safely and laughed off the incident to assembled reporters. ("I've been shot at in other countries," he said with his usual bravado. "A lot of other countries, actually.") But the gunfire continued during his brief visit, and moments after he took off again, three suicide bombers detonated themselves nearby. It was a violent reminder of how ephemeral military victories in Afghanistan were proving to be. I'd stayed behind at the embassy, eating greasy food at the commissary and taking meetings. Holbrooke returned looking spent. By 2:30 a.m. he was fast asleep.

The wake-up call was from Stan McChrystal, across town at ISAF headquarters. Holbrooke was annoyed. What was possibly urgent enough for this? "There's a *Rolling Stone* story coming out," McChrystal said. "And I said some embarrassing things in it." "Stan, don't worry about it," said Holbrooke. McChrystal, of course, was right to worry. Michael Hastings's story, "The Runaway General," had captured McChrystal and his staffers taking a blowtorch to just about everyone in the administration. "The Boss says he's like a wounded animal," one member of his team had said of Holbrooke. "Holbrooke keeps hearing rumors that he's going to get fired, so that makes him dangerous. He's a brilliant guy, but he just comes in, pulls on a lever, whatever he can grasp onto. But this is COIN, and you can't just have someone yanking on shit." Another memorable moment saw McChrystal looking at his BlackBerry and groaning. "Oh, not another email from Holbrooke. I don't even want to open it." Two days later, President Obama accepted McChrystal's resignation. Military support for reconciliation departed with him.

In McChrystal's stead, Obama installed Petraeus in Afghanistan. This was technically a demotion for Petraeus, since McChrystal had reported to him. But it elevated Petraeus to a far more direct role in shaping policy for the war. And he did not share McChrystal's openness to negotiation. "I just don't think it was negotiable," Petraeus told me. "We certainly tried and our forces supported the movement and security of potential interlocutors. But I doubted that we could get the right Taliban to come to the table and truly deal. Their nonnegotiable redlines were totally unacceptable to the Afghans and to us. And if you couldn't get the true Taliban leaders, you certainly couldn't get the 'Haqqani Taliban' leaders, or those of the Islamic Movement of Uzbekistan or al-Qaeda," he said, referring to the more extreme elements across Afghanistan's borders. "The leaders of all the groups were sitting in sanctuaries and it was clear that the Pakistanis, at that time, were not willing or capable of going after them." He found the incessant calls for negotiations, from Holbrooke and the State Department, to be an unhelpful distraction. "There was a belief that if we just tried a little harder, we could get a negotiated settlement," he said. The message given to the military was that "we're just not trying hard enough. Just put our shoulder to the wheel. You guys are obstacles. You don't want it enough." Years later, Petraeus was still defensive on this point: he argued that he did "all humanly possible," including "reintegrating" tens of thousands of low-level Taliban within Afghanistan. "But we could never bring pressure on the leaders of the groups outside Afghanistan and they had little incentive to negotiate when they knew they just needed to wait us out given the announced drawdown date." In October 2010, as Holbrooke closed in on the A-Rod talks, he tried to approach Petraeus. "Dave, we need to talk about reconciliation," he said.

"Richard, that's a fifteen-second conversation," Petraeus shot back. "Yes, eventually. But no. Not now."

THAT THOSE FIRST, SECRET TALKS in Munich even happened was a monument to Holbrooke's relentlessness. Time and time again, he had pushed on the subject and been rebuffed. The White House was even more strenuous in its opposition than the military—to the idea of talks, and, even more so, to the idea of Holbrooke leading them. In July 2009, the Saudis notified President Obama that their intelligence service was in contact with Taliban officials and they sensed an opening for talks. They asked the Americans to send a representative to meet with them. Holbrooke pushed the request with the White House, but they wouldn't act on it. Later, he fought to have some Taliban names removed from the UN blacklist—as it turned out, one of A-Rod's first requests in Munich. This, too, was flatly rejected by the White House, the military, and the CIA. Even raising negotiations in conversations with the Afghans was verboten—Holbrooke's lobbying to put Taliban talks on the president's agenda during one of Karzai's trips to the United States dead-ended.

But Holbrooke kept pressing, sending SRAP members to explain the merits of reconciliation to Clinton and gradually wearing down her skepticism. The White House even began to come around. In early 2010, Lieutenant General Lute, the president's Afghanistan adviser, began pushing a plan for reconciliation, led not by Holbrooke but by Algerian United Nations diplomat Lakhdar Brahimi. It was a deliberate slight aimed squarely at Holbrooke. Clinton hit the roof. "We don't outsource our foreign policy," she told our team. Holbrooke "would say often, 'You don't make peace with your friends,' and we had to be open with talking to and exploring the Taliban," Clinton remembered. "But it was a constant uphill struggle."

The struggle wasn't just a product of ideological division on negotiating with the enemy—it was also born of petty personal politics. What began as whispers of malcontent from Obama's inner circle about Holbrooke's antics eventually turned into a three-ring circus of humiliation. General Jim Jones, the national security advisor, along with Lute, were both used to the military calling the shots in theaters of war, and were working in a White House that had aggressively marshalled other national-security-sensitive policies under its own roof. Jones and Lute were furious that Holbrooke had maintained control of the Afghanistan and Pakistan operation.

Every Monday afternoon, in a moodily lit, wood-paneled conference room on the State Department's seventh floor, Holbrooke held an interagency meeting on the region—called, in a nod to the local term for consultations, "the shura." The meeting was a Holbrooke invention, but in a concession to the ongoing tensions with the White House, it was nominally led by Lute as well. Each week, we'd watch the two men take their seats at the head of the table, backed by a world map and digital clocks displaying the time in major capitals and in the secretary of state's current location. You could have refrigerated a steak in the chill between them. "I'm pleased to have General Lute here co-hosting with me," Holbrooke told the group, kicking off one early meeting. Lute leapt in quickly. "I'm so pleased Ambassador Holbrooke could join. To co-host with *me*."

Jones and Lute compiled a dossier of Holbrooke's supposed misdeeds. They kept him off the plane for the president's first trip to Afghanistan—a trip he didn't even learn about until Obama was en

route. Rather than supporting Holbrooke during tense discussions
with President Karzai in Afghanistan, White House officials sought
to drive a wedge between the diplomat and the Afghan president as
part of their lobbying to fire Holbrooke. During one of Karzai's visits
to the United States, they cut Holbrooke from the list of attendees at
the Afghan president's Oval Office meeting, and drafted talking points
for President Obama specifically designed to undermine Holbrooke—
noting that only those in the room had the president's trust. Clinton
intervened and insisted Holbrooke attend.

On another occasion, in a moment of government slapstick that
became the stuff of State Department legend, Jones sent a note to the
US ambassador in Kabul, Retired Lieutenant General Karl Eikenberry,
promising Holbrooke would soon be fired. Eikenberry had a similarly
dim view of Holbrooke, and Jones knew he was a safe confidante for
the message. Unfortunately, he accidentally sent the note as an official
White House correspondence, automatically copying every agency
involved in Afghanistan policy. Jones moved fast, calling Holbrooke
in for a meeting at the White House in which he dressed the diplomat
down and told him he should plan his exit strategy from government.
Hillary Clinton once again interceded, compiling her own dossier on
Holbrooke's accomplishments and going directly to President Obama
to stop the plot to fire him. "White House aides told me point blank
to get rid of Richard," she recalled. "They said, 'You need to fire him,'
and I said, 'I'm not going to do it. . . . If the White House wants to fire
him they need to tell him themselves.'" Holbrooke wasn't fired, which
left him in a state of purgatory: inside, with everyone wanting him out.

Lute "hated Holbrooke, actually hated him," one of his staffers
told me. When the firing campaign later leaked into the press, Lute
sounded sheepish, saying, "I'm not driven by hatred of anyone or anything," but admitting that "it was a very personal experience for me
and I'm still to a large extent unpacking it. But I think the tensions
became at some point a bit personalized."

Holbrooke's pariah status was partly or largely of his own making, depending on whom you asked. He had earned the nickname "the
Bulldozer" during the Clinton administration for a reason, and here
again he took a high-handed manner, including with Lute. "He'd, you
know, make his own appointment, he'd come in, he'd close the door,
typically put his feet up on the desk," Lute later recalled, bristling at the
memory. "You know, he was confident edging on arrogance, he knew
where he was going and no one should get in his way." Always, there
was a sense that Holbrooke was out of step with the era. "You know
very candidly," Lute went on, "I'll tell you that he had more of a free
rein in the Clinton administration and perhaps expected that same free
rein under Obama."

Nothing illustrated that tension better than Holbrooke's relationship with the press, which he had used to great effect to amplify his
negotiating tactics in Bosnia. A frequent fixture in Jones's and Lute's
case against Holbrooke was the allegation that he was the source of a
series of leaks of cables early in the administration. This was untrue.
Reporters on the Holbrooke beat, including the *Washington Post*'s Rajiv
Chandrasekaran and the *New York Times*'s Mark Landler, later wrote
that Holbrooke was not a leaker. But he did like talking to reporters he
respected, and I heard his end of countless background conversations,
in which he never leaked secrets, but provided garrulous commentary.
Heartbreakingly, those background calls tended to be studiously politic about the administration; indeed, as his position in it became more
tenuous, he appeared to overcorrect, sounding at times like the world's
most cheerful team player.

But the conversations widened the yawning chasm between Holbrooke and the Obama team. For Holbrooke, the media was a stage,
a space to theatrically curry favor with or squeeze the weak points
of opponents. Those tactics were galling for the "no drama Obama"
White House, which prided itself on keeping internal arguments out
of the press and wanted the focus on the boss. (Or at least, on the cho-

sen allies of the president—as the administration wore on, virtually all of Obama's core staffers pursued showboating profiles.) A September 2009 story by George Packer in *The New Yorker* threw a hand grenade into the already tense relationship with the White House just as Holbrooke was getting started. Packer, an incisive journalist with a narrative flair, had turned what Holbrooke had hoped would be a celebration of his Afghanistan and Pakistan policy and his fight for Taliban negotiations into a sweeping biographical piece, replete with pictures of Holbrooke in Vietnam. As the scope of the story became apparent, Holbrooke tried to slam the brakes. He refused to sit for a photo shoot. (*The New Yorker* used an existing photo, a moody portrait by celebrity photographer Brigitte Lacombe.) His wife, Kati Marton, called *New Yorker* editor David Remnick and pleaded with him to rein in the piece. "Kati," he said, "you shouldn't be making this call."

When the magazine contacted the State Department to fact-check the story, alarm spread through the administration. "Importance: High," read the email from P. J. Crowley to Clinton aides Jake Sullivan, Huma Abedin, Cheryl Mills, and Philippe Reines. "Obviously Richard strayed shall we say from discussion of our strategy. It ends up being a semi-profile on Richard. I'll alert the WH." Holbrooke had already warned Clinton. "I know more about this if you wish to discuss," she responded to Mills. The episode confirmed what advisers inside the Obama White House believed about Holbrooke: that the rest of us were just characters in his story.

"That *New Yorker* profile doomed him for this administration," Marton said. "They didn't want anybody in those early years to steal the president's thunder." She told her husband not to worry, that he was part of the team and Obama's inner circle would surely see any positive press as a boon. "You don't understand how they are," he told her. She didn't.

13

PROMISE ME YOU'LL
END THE WAR

WE ARRIVED AT FORT MCNAIR at 7 a.m. sharp. It was
September 2010, and Holbrooke was set to co-chair a
civilian-military review of Pakistan policy with Petraeus's successor
at CENTCOM—one General James "Mad Dog" Mattis, future secretary of defense. More than 225 participants were due, including
Holbrooke's British, German, and French counterparts, and the British ambassador to Pakistan. The guests filed into the National Defense
University's George C. Marshall Hall, a hulking brick and concrete
structure built in the style of a megachurch, with taupe stonework and
a yawning, multistory atrium. Like the rest of the NDU campus, it
was set on a narrow peninsula extending south of Washington, DC,
at the meeting of the Potomac and Anacostia rivers. Mattis seemed
receptive to Holbrooke's agenda, listening intently as I ran through
my NGO-tracking technology, and suggesting that I brief his team at
CENTCOM in Tampa. Holbrooke was distracted. His conflict with
the White House had reached its very public nadir, with a steady
drumbeat of leaks suggesting his days were numbered. But against
all odds, he felt he had momentum. The month before, Marton had

caught him with what she described as a "faraway look" and asked what he was thinking about. "I think I've got it," he told her. "I think I can see how all the pieces can fit together." Marton and Holbrooke shared a flair for crafting a narrative, in this case the notion that what was missing was an answer, a way to put together this puzzle, as opposed to a bunch of incredibly hard and complicated problems that would never cleave neatly, that required less a grand solution than grinding work. Nevertheless, in the following weeks, he began putting together a memo for Hillary Clinton forcefully articulating what had gone wrong with America's relationships in Afghanistan and Pakistan, and how to set them right. It was, he told me, to be a document of record; the fullest statement of his views that had often been muzzled over the course of the administration.

Sending documents through the government bureaucracy is a special kind of hell. Memos for the secretary of state go through "The Line," a corps of gatekeepers who ensure documents are "cleared" by any offices with equities before reaching the boss's desk. In this case that meant embassies and the White House—the bureaucratic rivals engineering Holbrooke's removal. He wanted to get his message directly to Clinton, and he didn't want a digital record of it. His original, trusted staff assistants had been replaced by new officers he feared were more loyal to the system than to him. In a sign of how profound his bureaucratic isolation had become, he asked if I would help him put together the memo and pass it to Hillary Clinton. Despite Holbrooke's around-the-clock love affair with the BlackBerry, I never saw him use a word processor. He didn't even have a computer on his office desk. So the day before our trip to Fort McNair, he had dictated a first draft to me. The next morning, he stepped out of his sessions with Mattis to scrawl notes and corrections in the margins. It was, he said, "eyes only," a handling instruction intended to ensure only Clinton saw it—but, by dint of Holbrooke's own effort to skirt the system, it was never formally classi-

fied. Still, I texted a friend at the time that I felt antsy walking around
with it.

"TO: HRC, FROM: RCH," the memo began. "SUBJECT: AT
THE CROSSROADS." Over nine, single-spaced Times New Roman
pages, Holbrooke made his case in stark terms. "I still believe that the
importance to our national security of Afghanistan, Pakistan, and the
region remains as high as ever," he wrote. "But our current strategy
will not succeed." The Afghan government, populated with warlords
we had used as Cold War–style proxy forces in the wake of 9/11, was
buckling under the weight of corruption and exhibiting few signs of
strategic alignment with the United States. "Whatever happens in
counter-insurgency, our policies are in peril for a basic reason: the
lack of a credible and reliable partner who shares our goals . . . ," he
went on, listing a litany of instances of Karzai's government engaging
in double-dealing and corruption. "I know of no strategic partner in
the history of American foreign relations who has behaved in such an
extraordinary manner. Yet we have tolerated it, made allowances and
excuses for it, and generally given him the sense that he can get away
with almost anything."

Though accounts of the Afghanistan review process from Bob
Woodward and others have broadly characterized Holbrooke's perspectives on troop deployments, he was always meticulous about withholding his views publicly and in documents disseminated through normal
channels in the administration. "During the debate last year," he wrote,
"I shared my recommendations only with you and Tom Donilon, who
says he shared them with the president. They never became public."
The memo contains perhaps the only frank summary of those recommendations in his own words. "I recommended at that time a strategy
that would have given McChrystal a somewhat lower troop level with
a significantly different configuration—about 20–25,000, 'composed
of only one combat brigade and its enablers (about 10,000 troops), and

about 10,000–15,000 trainers, advisors and their support.' My view was that this would cause less American and civilian casualties, be less provocative to the Pakistanis (who had opposed the larger number), and perhaps buy more time from the American public. It would also have been about $15–20 billion cheaper per year." He also took issue with Obama's addition of a July 2011 deadline for beginning troop withdrawals, which "was introduced at the last moment, almost as an afterthought, and far too late for us to consider its full implications." Among those implications was, he told me, a squandering of American leverage in any negotiations with the Taliban, which now knew it could wait the Americans out.

Using the Pakistanis as a proxy for American counterterrorism objectives was also failing. He urged broader diplomacy, including yet another stab at bringing India to the table. Obama was scheduled to travel to India the following month, and Holbrooke made the case for a Pakistan stop. Integrating Pakistan in Presidential trips had always been a thorny matter, since it risked annoying the Indians—and potentially the Pakistanis, too, as they invariably received a briefer and less celebratory visit. But Holbrooke suggested now was the moment to take that leap.

> [T]his would be an obvious time for such a trip, since overflying the stricken area without a stop could provoke criticism. In these unique circumstances, I think the perennial issue of balancing relations and visits to the two countries, which President Clinton managed successfully in 2000, can be finessed.

In the end, the president visited only India, as planned. Holbrooke suggested that the failure to transition Pakistan from a transactional, military-to-military relationship to a broader partnership left the United States with little prospect of permanently addressing the terrorist safe havens in the border region. In the end, he could see only one way forward. Holbrooke bolded the following passage, drawing on lessons from Vietnam that the administration seemed to have little desire to hear about:

In the end, however, the insurgents win in a guerilla war if they don't lose. Moreover, there is one constant about counter-insurgency: it does not succeed against an enemy with a safe sanctuary. Yet we cannot convince Pakistan to make its strategic interests symmetrical with ours because of its obsession with India and the military domination of its strategic policies. For these reasons, we should explore whether there is a basis for a political settlement with the Taliban that falls within our red lines. Nothing is less appealing than the idea of dealing with the Taliban, but it would be irresponsible to continue to ignore this area.

In addition to the upcoming effort with A-Rod, which he told Clinton he'd brief her on, he suggested the United States publicly announce support for low-level talks between the Karzai government and any forces who renounced al-Qaeda. He urged a continuation of the kind of thinking behind the Kerry-Lugar-Berman Act, with "a major new effort to help the people of Pakistan," undertaken "with due attention to India." And he threw his weight behind a slower draw-down of troops, with a three- to five-year timeline for transferring authority to Afghan forces (of whose capacity he painted a bleak picture) and a pledge to maintain at least some American military presence "as long as needed to go after those terrorist groups which directly threaten the United States."

In the memo, Holbrooke argued that the United States had missed critical openings for diplomacy, and pointed the finger squarely at the systematic military domination of the policy process. It topped his list of challenges:

> 1. Military domination of the review process must be ended. Even though everyone paid lip service to the proposition that "counter-insurgency" required a mixed civilian-military strategy, last year the military dominated and defined the choices. And even though everyone agreed the war would not end in a purely military outcome, State was never able to make a detailed presentation to the full NSC on the civilian-political process or the need to look for a political solution to a war. Unlike the military, we never had a meeting alone with the President, with the important exception of your weekly private session on all issues with the President, which I attended once. In the coming debate, we should seek to redress this imbalance.

The military, he said, had been "grading themselves," crowding out room for a "frank assessment" of progress on the ground. It was a direct echo of his earliest memos from Vietnam. Contrary to the military's assessment that they just needed more time, more troops, Holbrooke felt COIN was fundamentally untenable in Afghanistan, for many of the same reasons it had been untenable in Vietnam. "'[C]lassic COIN,' a phrase used repeatedly by Petraeus and McChrystal in last year's review, is just that—something out of the past which, where it succeeded, was primarily a colonial concept that involved a great deal of coercive force," Holbrooke wrote. "And COIN cannot succeed when insurgents have a safe sanctuary." In this case, withdrawing US and NATO troops on the timetable dictated by domestic political concerns would require a self-sufficient government in Afghanistan, with an autonomous security force. It was, Holbrooke said simply, "unrealistic."

The lack of space for civilian voices, including his own painful freeze-out, had led to an unwillingness to step outside of that military thinking. That, in turn, had led to a failure to pursue broad-based strategic relationships at the moment the United States had exercised maximum leverage. The result was a bleak prognosis. "The *best* we can achieve in an acceptable period of time is a murky outcome, in which local violence continues but at a much reduced level." But he still felt he could secure Pakistani buy-in to a regional agreement, and he still felt a deal with the Taliban was realistic—even "one that still protects women from a return to the worst parts of 'the black years.'" He was sober. The administration had lost important opportunities. But he wasn't giving up.

THAT FALL HAD an ominous feeling. As animosity with the White House reached a fever pitch, every day seemed to herald Holbrooke's departure. When Holbrooke called for an "all-hands-on-deck" staff meeting at the end of November, several staffers confided that they thought it was the end. And then there was Holbrooke himself, who looked increasingly drawn and tired. He stopped and stood still more often than usual. He fell silent on occasion, as if out of breath. In the memo to Clinton, he had outlined a relentless schedule of shuttle diplomacy, and the constant travel seemed to be taking its toll. At a previous all-hands-on-deck meeting, earlier in the year, Holbrooke had risen, his voice wavering with emotion, to announce that he would have to cancel a major trip to Afghanistan due to test results that had revealed a heart ailment in need of urgent treatment. Then, strangely, the trip was back on. Further tests had cleared him, he said.

But many of us around him remained concerned. Frank Wisner, another veteran diplomat with whom Holbrooke had forged a friendship in Vietnam, later told a reporter how, over lunch that fall, Holbrooke had nicked his nose with a cherrystone clam (he was not a delicate eater) and begun to bleed profusely. "What the hell's wrong with you?" Wisner asked. Holbrooke said he was taking large doses of the blood thinner Coumadin for ongoing heart problems. "Today was a difficult day, because I woke up in the morning feeling quite uncomfortable and realized I was back in atrial fibrillation," Holbrooke said in one of his nightly recordings for his memoirs. He over-enunciated "uncomfortable" in his distinctive almost-an-accent drawl, hitting each syllable crisply. "Did not do the kind of work I should have done over the weekend, but that's par for the course. One can just feel the growing tension and pressure in every direction. I certainly can feel it." Wisner was one of several friends who began to counsel Holbrooke to quit. "There wasn't a week that went by that I didn't tell him to leave," said Les Gelb.

Holbrooke was in the professional fight of his life. He was watching another mission go awry, as it had in Vietnam, and now, as then, he felt he was the only one capable of giving an honest assessment of the harsh realities. But beneath the sweep of history was a small human struggle, of ego and age and fear. Departure would be an admission of just how far his star had fallen. Clinton had protected Holbrooke from being fired, but not from being sidelined. He too was an insurgent with a sanctuary. Perhaps he too could win by not losing.

"He was always hoping that tomorrow there would be a miracle and Obama would like him," Gelb went on, "and everything would be fine."

IT WAS DURING THIS PERIOD that Holbrooke and I had our knock-down-drag-out session that left poor Donna Dejban in tears. Our communications had been perfunctory in the weeks since. This kind of chill was routine for those of us who worked for Richard Holbrooke year after year—I'd counseled his closest assistants through tearful low points in his equally volatile relationships with them. In the final days of November, as the first conversation with A-Rod came together, I ran into Holbrooke in the hallway near the cafeteria. "You're not leaving us, are you?" he asked. I'd just been sworn into the New York bar, which I'd been studying for at night during my first year at State. "Don't practice. That's a whole lot of nothing." He smiled at me, deep lines creasing around his blue eyes. "Anyway, you're just getting warmed up." On December 8, he called in a favor. His friend James Hoge, the longtime editor of *Foreign Affairs*, was being honored at an event that night. He planned to roast him. Could I find an article from "some time in the 1970s" making fun of him for being too hand-some? His memory was, as usual, preternatural—after several hours of hassling staffers at the Library of Congress, I tracked down an *Esquire* profile of Hoge from September 1979 entitled "The Dangers of Being Too Good-Looking." I passed a copy to Holbrooke just before he got on the shuttle to New York. "Terrific work, Ronan!" he emailed me. "I knew if anyone could do it, 'twas you. Thanks, it is just what I needed." It was the last email I got from him.

On a cold morning two days later, Holbrooke and Husain Haqqani sat down for breakfast at the Four Seasons hotel in Georgetown. Both men were frustrated. Holbrooke was preparing to make one more push to meet with the president and make the same case for a political settle-ment that he had made to Clinton. Haqqani was, increasingly, taking heat from the ISI. His close relationship with the Americans had been a source of controversy in each of his incarnations over the years. After the visa freeze subsided and he began letting in more Americans, that controversy had reached new heights, with some whispering that he was letting in spies to undermine Pakistani interests.

"I have all these problems with the ISI and you have all these prob-lems with the NSC, how long are we going to do it?" Haqqani asked.

"Husain," Holbrooke replied. "We are going to do this for as long as we can make a difference."

Holbrooke's very next meeting was at the White House, where he made a final impassioned push for an audience with the president to

Obama's close adviser David Axelrod. Clinton had delivered a memo to Obama on Taliban talks, and Holbrooke thought he could sell the president on his plan to use them as a way out of Afghanistan, given the chance. "Hillary has delivered the all-important memo to the president seeking negotiating routes out of this thing," he said in one of his recordings. "Finally the president is focused on it. Maybe we'll look back on it as one of the most important memos we wrote, but that remains to be seen." Axelrod said he'd see about the meeting. Holbrooke looked flushed and seemed out of breath— Axelrod's assistant offered him a glass of water.

He ran long at the White House, and arrived late to his next meeting with Hillary Clinton, Jake Sullivan and Frank Ruggiero—their first major strategy session on Taliban talks after the secret meeting with A-Rod. She was waiting in her outer office, a spacious room paneled in white and gilt wood, with tasseled blue and pink curtains and an array of colorfully upholstered chairs and couches. In my time reporting to her later, I only ever saw Clinton take the couch, with guests of honor in the large chair kitty-corner to her. She'd left it open for him that day. "He came rushing in. . . . " Clinton later said. "And, you know, he was saying 'oh I'm so sorry, I'm so sorry.'" He sat down heavily and shrugged off his coat, rattling off a litany of his latest meetings, including his stop-in at the White House. "That was typical Richard. It was, like, 'I'm doing a million things and I'm trying to keep all the balls in the air,'" she remembered. As he was talking, a "scarlet red" flush went up his face, according to Clinton. He pressed his hands over his eyes, his chest heaving.

"Richard, what's the matter?" Clinton asked.

"Something horrible is happening," he said.

A few minutes later, Holbrooke was in an ambulance, strapped to a gurney, headed to nearby George Washington University Hospital, where Clinton had told her own internist to prepare the emergency room. In his typically brash style, he'd demanded that the ambulance take him to the more distant Sibley Memorial Hospital. Clinton overruled him. One of our deputies on the SRAP team, Dan Feldman, rode with him and held his hand. Feldman didn't have his BlackBerry, so he scrawled notes on a State Department expense form for a dinner at Meiwah Restaurant as Holbrooke dictated messages and a doctor assessed him. The notes are a nonlinear stream of Holbrooke's indomitable personality, slashed through with medical realities. "Call Eric in Axelrod's office," the first read. Nearby: "aortic dissection—type A . . . operation risk @ > 50 percent"—that would be chance of death. A series of messages for people in his life, again interrupted by his deteriorating condition: "S"—Secretary Clinton—"why always together for medical crises?" (The year before, he'd been with Clinton when she fell to the concrete floor of the State Department garage, fracturing her elbow.) "Kids—how much love them + stepkids" . . . "best staff ever" . . . "don't let him die here" . . . "vascular surgery" . . . "no flow, no feeling legs" . . . "clot" . . . and then, again: "don't let him die here want to die at home w/ his fam." The seriousness of the situation fully dawning on him, Holbrooke turned to job succession: "Tell Frank"—Ruggiero—"he's acting." And finally: "I love so many people . . . I have a lot left to do . . . my career in public service is over."

Holbrooke cracked wise until they put him under for surgery. "Get me anything you need," he demanded. "A pig's heart. Dan's heart."

When they told him about the risky nature of the procedure, he said, "I feel better. Now I know you're not BS-ing me." When one of his doctors, Jehan El-Bayoumi, made him promise to relax, he quipped, "You have to promise me that you're going to end the war in Afghanistan." Variations of the quote received so much coverage that P. J. Crowley, the State Department's spokesperson, had to take to the podium in the press room and clarify that Holbrooke was joking. But the joke was only that he'd ever ask anybody else to do it.

THREE NIGHTS LATER, hundreds of guests packed the Ben Franklin Room as Hillary Clinton stood at the lectern where, two years earlier, she'd announced Richard Holbrooke's role. Foreign ambassadors to the United States were there, along with six members of Obama's cabinet. "Ambassador Richard Holbrooke has been a giant of the diplomatic corps for almost fifty years," she began. "And this week, his doctors are learning what diplomats and dictators around the world have long known: There's nobody tougher than Richard Holbrooke. He's a fierce negotiator. I'm sure there are some shoulders here tonight that are still a little bit sore from his arm-twisting." She paid somber tribute to Holbrooke's staff, and to the dignitaries in attendance. "Now, in a moment," she said, her voice rising festively, "You will be treated to another holiday delight, a musical performance from the incomparable Marvin Hamlisch and J. Mark McVey!" She stepped aside, revealing a shiny black grand piano behind her. Hamlisch and McVey began to perform an upbeat rendition of "Deck the Halls." The World Children's Choir joined in. Bright, TV-style lights set up around the stage cast an antiseptic glare on the proceedings. Someone had decided that the most appropriate way to handle the annual State Department Christmas party for foreign ambassadors was to merge it with a Holbrooke tribute event. Standing there listening to the carols, I wasn't sure.

The president arrived to briefly bop his head to the carols then say a few words. After a laugh line about Clinton's bipartisan appeal outshining his own (a common observation at the time), he moved on to "our friend and partner Richard Holbrooke. Richard Holbrooke has been serving this nation with distinction for nearly fifty years. . . . He never stops, he never quits. Because he's always believed that if we stay focused, if we act on our mutual interests, that progress is possible. Wars can end, peace can be forged." He called out our dazed team, assembled in the crowd. "The SRAP team, where are they? Richard recruited them, he mentored them, and I want you to know that, in our meetings, he consistently gave you guys unbelievable credit. He was so proud, and is so proud, of the work that you do." The foreign ambassadors applauded, murmuring appreciatively in several languages. We

stared at the president. Holbrooke would have burst his aorta volun-
tarily if he'd known it would conjure up these fond recollections.

"America is more secure and the world is a safer place because of
the work of Ambassador Richard Holbrooke," Obama went on. "He
is a tough son of a gun so we are confident that as hard as this is he is
going to be putting up a tremendous fight." He moved on, looking a
little relieved, to a joke about Clinton's travel schedule.

Three blocks away, Richard Holbrooke lay in an induced coma
with his chest cut open. After twenty hours of surgery, he was, the doctors said vaguely, "hanging in there." The day before the party, they'd
performed an additional surgery to restore circulation to his lower
extremities. They'd registered a faint pulse in his feet. The condition
of his most celebrated attribute, his brain, was completely unknown.

Because they'd kept his chest open, no one was allowed in the
room with him, but the team had spent the past three days by the door
anyway. We divided hospital duties into two-hour shifts, each taken
on by a pair of staffers. The pair on duty would greet the eye-popping
luminaries who began arriving to pay tribute. I'd shown in Joe Biden,
and John and Teresa Heinz Kerry, and Judy Woodruff. I sat with future
treasury secretary Jack Lew and Clinton's chief of staff, Cheryl Mills, as
they tried not to look horrified at doctors' sketches of the torn aorta on
a nearby table. People talked in vague terms about Holbrooke "feeling"
the "positive energy." But it felt like a wake.

I had passed my tolerance for grim Christmas carols and returned
to my desk on the first floor when Rina Amiri ran in and flung herself
across the couch, sobbing. They were taking him off life support. I
trudged through the night back to the hospital with Rosemarie Pauli,
Holbrooke's tough-as-nails chief of staff, with whom he'd worked since
Bosnia. It was bitterly cold, and a high wind had picked up. "Afghans,"
Rosemarie muttered, pulling her coat tight and leaning into the wind.
"So dramatic." (It's true: Afghan grieving is unlike anything I've experienced elsewhere, with a customary forty-day mourning window.)

Street signs rattled. We arrived at the hospital and stood in the lobby as they unplugged him.

Hillary Clinton had been on her way from the State Department party to a dinner at the White House when she got the call. She redirected quickly and arrived in time to be with him at the end. Still wearing a double-breasted, silver-and-gold striped jacket with a flouncy Peter Pan collar that made her look like she was gift-wrapped, she stood under the hospital lights and pulled together the weeping team. I handed out tissues. "There's our NGO guy, always helping," she managed. "He was the closest thing to a father I had," I said quietly, surprising myself. She hugged me. For a woman who'd just lost a friend of many years, Clinton was generous. "Well, I don't know about you," she told the group, "but I'm going to the nearest bar."

AS SNOW STARTED FALLING outside, we crowded into the nearby lobby bar of the Ritz-Carlton hotel. We were joined by a growing group of mourners. Maureen White, the wife of financier and Obama adviser Steven Rattner, opened a tab. Clinton held court. And everyone exchanged stories about the inimitable Richard Holbrooke. At the time of Holbrooke's death, the US government was poised to release the first "Quadrennial Diplomacy and Development Review" (or QDDR), a long-term plan to reorganize the State Department and USAID to be more efficient and more in sync with broader changes in national security objectives. (For example, the first process elevated counterterrorism within the bureaucracy.) The aspirations of the project hearkened back to young Holbrooke's essay in the first issue of *Foreign Policy*, calling for a reorganization of the State Department bureaucracy he described as "the machine that fails." The reality of the initiative, on the other hand, was of the kind of unwieldy and inefficient bureaucracy Holbrooke had decried all those years ago, with

years of infighting leading to mostly subtle organizational changes.
"Oh, the QDDR," Clinton said wistfully. "He hated that document.
We should dedicate it to him." And she did.

"I really believed that if Richard had lived, we would have been
able to present to the administration some kind of peace deal," Clinton
told me. "I really believe that. I'm not sure they would have accepted
it, but with all the work he did, that Frank Ruggiero did, the meetings
that were underway. . . . I was very hopeful that, with the meeting
we'd have at Lisbon, the NATO conference, we'd be able to build on
the peace efforts that Richard was leading. And obviously that didn't
happen because of what, terribly, happened to him that December."
And perhaps that's true.

As we filed out into the night at around 2 a.m., a lone, drunk
woman with lank, graying hair called at me from a nearby table. "I
know who you are," she slurred, leering at us. "I know who you all are."

"Have a good night," I said, turning to leave.

"Don't take it too hard, sweetheart," she called after me. I glanced
over my shoulder. She was grinning wide, showing a row of blood-
red, wine-stained teeth. "Everything ends."

14

THE WHEELS COME
OFF THE BUS

THE MONTH AFTER Richard Holbrooke died, a white Honda Civic pulled up to an intersection in Lahore, Pakistan and stopped at a red light. Known as the Mozang Chungi stop, the intersection marked the start of Ferozepur Road, a trade route that ran to the town of the same name in India. A short drive away, the crumbling arches of the ancient Walled City reflected Lahore's history as a seat of power of the Mughal Empire. But the intersection embodied a more modern side of Lahore: crowded urban sprawl, fueled by a fast-expanding business sector. It was afternoon, and a pollution haze hung over the dense traffic of bikes, rickshaws, and beat-up cars from different eras.

Inside the Honda was a barrel-chested, broad-shouldered American. His salt-and-pepper hair was thinning, and he had a day of stubble on his chin. He wore a plaid work shirt over a white tee. Raised in the fading coal town of Big Stone Gap, Virginia, he had wrestled at Powell Valley High, where friends remembered him as "solid muscle" and "an American Rambo." He had served in the Army

Special Forces. A career as a private security contractor followed. "Nobody here remembers the guy," his commander at Fort Bragg, North Carolina, later told a reporter. "You could put him in a crowd of 50 people and he wouldn't stand out," echoed a former football coach at Powell Valley High. A few years later, even the high school was sold to a bank and torn down, another casualty of an American dream that had left coal towns like Big Stone Gap behind. At thirty-six, Raymond Davis never left much of a mark anywhere, until that afternoon in Lahore.

As Davis stopped, a black motorbike carrying two young Pakistani men approached from the opposite direction and swerved in front of the Honda. The rear passenger was carrying a gun. Davis pulled out a 9mm semiautomatic Glock and took aim from his seat behind the wheel. He fired five times, blowing a cluster of holes through the windshield and sending spidery fractals across the safety glass. The bullets hit one of the two men, nineteen-year-old street criminal Mohammed Faheem, in the stomach and arms. He hit the ground, dead. The second man, Faizan Haider, ran. He made it about thirty feet before Davis got out of the car and shot him several times in the back, killing him, too. Davis used a radio in the car to call for help, then took pictures of the bodies with his cell phone. "He was very peaceful and confident," one onlooker said. "I was wondering how he could be like that after killing two people."

Minutes later, a Toyota Land Cruiser barreled down the crowded street in the wrong direction, killing one pedestrian and scattering others. By the time the Land Cruiser reached the intersection, Davis was gone. The American driver waved a rifle at onlookers, ordering them to get out of the way, and made his way back to the US consulate. Davis, it turned out, had fled, making it about two miles before Pakistani police stopped him.

Grainy video shows Davis being questioned at Lahore's Kot Lakh-

pat jail. "I just—I need to tell the embassy where I'm at," he told officers in a light Southern accent, handing over a walkie-talkie from his
pocket. "You're from America?" one of the officers asked.

"Yes," said Davis, stabbing a finger at an ID hanging from a lanyard
around his neck. "USA." He told them he worked at the consulate.

"As a . . . ?" the officer asked.

"Uh, I just work as a consultant there," he replied.

For a consultant, Raymond Davis had remarkably good aim.
The debris left behind at the intersection—ammunition, knives and
gloves, a blindfold—suggested something else. As did Davis's phone,
which was full of surreptitiously taken photos of Pakistani military
sites. Raymond Davis was, very clearly, a spy—more specifically, it
came to pass, a CIA contractor. The realization dawned on the Pakistani public almost as quickly as it did on the ISI. From virtually the
moment Davis was spirited away from the crowded intersection to
Kot Lakhpat jail, the nation was convulsed, from street protests to
searing, around-the-clock media coverage.

Two weeks later, President Obama, outraged, described Davis as
"our diplomat" and called for his release under the "very simple principle" laid out in the Vienna Convention: "if our diplomats are in another
country, then they are not subject to that country's local prosecution."
Privately, Leon Panetta delivered a similar message to General Pasha
and the ISI. When Pasha asked point-blank if Davis was a CIA agent,
Panetta said: "No, he's not one of ours." Panetta didn't comment on
the specifics of that conversation, but said that, in general, "If we have
to play both sides of the streets with these guys in order to make sure
that, in the end, we are protecting our people, that's what we're going
to do." If the Pakistanis were going to lie to him, he, apparently, wasn't
above doing so back.

————

THE NEXT DAY, Mohsin Kamal, the lobbyist Mark Siegel had hired as the Kerry-Lugar-Berman imbroglio began, was in DC's Chinatown neighborhood at their lobbying firm, Locke Lord. Kamal had a standard associate's office with anonymous furnishings and a depressing view of the Verizon Center. It was just after 11 a.m. when the phone rang. It was General Butt, whom I'd schmoozed for my visa the year before. The two men had met years earlier when Kamal served in the army, and had an easy rapport. "Hey, where are you?" Butt asked. Kamal already knew what it was about—the Raymond Davis scandal had been making headlines in both the American and Pakistani press for the past twenty-four hours.

An hour later he was in Butt's office on the fourth floor of the Pakistani embassy. An assistant poured tea. Kamal took his with milk and sugar. "You have to say very clearly to Congress that he does not have immunity," Butt was saying. "He was a contractor and a CIA guy." The incident had stung Pakistan deeply, tapping into existential insecurities about sovereignty. Maybe, Butt suggested, they could use the mess as an opportunity to push back against the CIA's demands for more access. He told Kamal he was worried about Husain Haqqani, who in unclogging the flow of visas, had incurred more suspicion than ever. Had he been responsible for letting in Davis, and perhaps scores of other Raymond Davises? And would he try to help the Americans spirit out their spy?

"What role will Husain play in this?" Butt asked.

"A role none of us can guess," replied Kamal. "He is a most unpredictable man."

Kamal and Mark Siegel fanned out across Washington disseminating Pakistani outrage and dispensing lurid details from the ISI's investigation. Davis had been living in a safe house with other spies. The American agents had referred to it as "La Whore House," Kamal and Siegel told shocked staffers on the Hill. The CIA was risking the entire relationship with an important ally, they argued. A deal would have to be cut with the Pakistanis.

John Kerry was dispatched to Lahore to try to do just that. Before he left, Siegel gave one of Kerry's aides, Jonah Blank, a full download of the Pakistani perspective. Kerry performed exactly as the Pakistani lobbyists had hoped. Massaging from him and the US ambassador to Pakistan, Cameron Munter, brought General Pasha around to a deal. Husain Haqqani, as Butt had predicted, helped the Americans devise the solution: the CIA would pay $2.3 million to the families of those killed in the Davis incident. Two senior Pakistani intelligence officers told me that there was another assurance made by the Americans; one that was never made public. The United States would severely curtail the CIA's activities in Pakistan, for good. Mohsin Kamal said that's how Butt described the deal to him. No American would confirm that there was an explicit commitment made. Whether it was part of a deal or a natural consequence of the strain the incident had put on the relationship, the agency quietly began pulling dozens of its undercover operatives out of Pakistan.

"THE WHEELS JUST CAME OFF the bus of the relationship at that point in time, coming after problems created by the WikiLeaks issues and unkind assessments of the Pakistanis in a book by Bob Woodward," Petraeus told me. The Obama administration froze all high-level talks, including Holbrooke's hard-fought Strategic Dialogue and trilateral working groups with Afghanistan. Clinton canceled a meeting with Foreign Minister Qureshi.

In the months that followed, the dominoes kept crashing down. Just after 11:00 p.m. one night in early May 2011, two Black Hawk helicopters, outfitted with brand new stealth technology to avoid radar detection, took off from Jalalabad, in Eastern Afghanistan. Two larger Chinooks followed in case the Black Hawks' mission went awry. Collectively, the aircraft contained seventy-nine American commandos and a dog. (Name: Cairo. Breed: Belgian Malinois.) The rest is history: a team of Navy SEALs descended on the Pakistani town of Abbottabad, used C4 charges to blow through the gates of a walled residential compound, and shot Osama bin Laden in the head and chest. The Americans spirited away the body, and a backup sample of bone marrow, into the night. A single Black Hawk that had crashed during their initial descent was destroyed to keep its technology from the Pakistanis, leaving behind a smoldering helicopter tail and a lot of questions.

If the Raymond Davis incident brought the US-Pakistan relationship to its knees, this slammed it, face first, to the curb. The most wanted man in the world had been discovered not in a lawless safe haven on Pakistan's border, but in a suburban town full of the summer homes of Islamabad's elites. Bin Laden's compound was just a few hundred yards from the military academy in Kakul—essentially Pakistan's West Point. Either the Pakistanis were incompetent, or they knew he was there. The raid had happened without Pakistan's consent, and they weren't notified beforehand, at least at a leadership level. "We are still talking with the Pakistanis and trying to understand what they did know and what they didn't know," Under Secretary of Defense Michele Flournoy said a few days later. It's a debate that continues to this day. During the political maelstrom that ensued in Pakistan, General Pasha pled ignorance, standing before the country's parliament and offering his resignation—which was, ultimately, not accepted. Petraeus, who took over the CIA a few months later, tended to buy Pasha's claims. "It's very possible some low-level guy knew, but I doubt even that," he said. "People just don't understand Pakistan or big walls or that people don't know all their neighbors. It's possible to hide somebody there." But the ISI is a multifaceted organization, and how much its more obscure chapters, like the pro–al-Qaeda Directorate

S, knew was anyone's guess, according to several CIA analysts who worked the bin Laden case.

The Pakistanis, as usual, offered muted resignation in private and saber-rattling in public. Minutes after the raid was declared a success, Panetta had watched Chairman of the Joint Chiefs Admiral Mike Mullen call Pakistani army chief General Kayani outside the Situation Room. "The one moment they were most honest with us," Panetta told me, "was the night of the raid, because they knew damn well what had happened. . . . General [Kayani] basically said, 'I understand what's happened here and you'd better announce it to the world.' That was probably the frankest moment of that relationship. After that, politics took over and they were doing everything they could to make it appear that it wasn't their fault that he was living where he was living."

Publicly, Kayani loudly ordered the US military to scale back its presence in the country to the "minimum essential" and warned them against future raids. The White House gathered to debate how to get tougher with the Pakistanis. Pakistan remained important in the broader fight against extremism, but bin Laden had totemic significance. Without him, there was a shift in attitude, palpable even at State. We needed Pakistan, but how much? "People say, 'Boy that bin Laden raid, that really queered your relationship with the ISI,'" General Hayden reflected. "It didn't at all, it just pulled the veil back into how difficult the relationship was."

The month after the raid, the president sent Panetta and National Security Advisor Jim Jones to Islamabad to deliver a searing condemnation of Pakistan's double game. Panetta knew that elements within the ISI had been tipping off al-Qaeda fighters before American operations—and now there was political will to confront it. "It was something. Steve Kappes, who was my deputy at the time, had gone through this before, and laid out the intelligence we had on some of the double-dealings that were going on, and they said they would act to correct it but never did. So the president thought it was important to go to the highest levels . . . sit down and lay this out. Because I think he was very concerned about the United States being in a position where we were ignoring a lot of the behavior that they were engaged in, and he thought that if that ever got out—that we were simply ignoring it or accepting that kind of behavior—that it would undermine the position of the United States in that region."

"Was he angry about it?" I asked.

"Yeah. I think you could say he was *pissed*," Panetta said with another belly laugh.

Obama wasn't alone. Admiral Mullen had invested years in building rapport with Kayani, and often counseled conciliation from his position as chairman of the joint chiefs. Sitting before a room of congressional representatives a month after Panetta's explosive session with Pasha, he issued the United States' most naked public condemnation yet. The militant Haqqani network "acts as a veritable arm of Pakistan's Inter-Services Intelligence agency," he said. "The support of terrorism is part of their national strategy."

The hits kept coming. In the cold, small hours of November 26, 2011, American air support called in by Afghans conducting an operation against the Taliban opened fire on Pakistani troops stationed on the border between the two countries. General John Allen, who succeeded Petraeus as commander in Afghanistan, was one of the first to be notified. "We ended up killing twenty-four of their kids overnight," he recalled. "Now lots of fingers are being pointed, I don't want to get into that, but the bottom line is my people defended themselves, and twenty-four Pakistani border troops got killed." The recriminations were vicious and swift. Two days later, Pakistan shut down the all-important "Ground Lines of Communication," or GLOCs—the NATO routes used to deliver 80 percent of the supplies for US forces in Afghanistan. "Imagine a 150,000-person theater, with another 100,000 civilians, having 80 percent of my supplies cut off in one day," Allen remembered. He was left with just sixty days of supplies and a problem with no elegant solution.

The incident was a stark reminder of the strategic realities that made Pakistan such an important proxy force to begin with. But it also illustrated the extent to which US attitudes were changing. With the relationship on ice, Allen simply worked around the Pakistanis. "I had to shift everything to air or coming out of central Asia from the North. . . . It was a Berlin Airlift–scale resupply by air. . . . No country other than the United States could do that. But we did it." The maneuver cost the United States $100 million a month, but it worked. Ultimately, an apology from Hillary Clinton pacified the Pakistanis. The day she cleared the air with them, she emailed Under Secretary of State Wendy Sherman: "How do you spell 'relief'? 'GLOCS' . . ." Never one to under-use a good line, she emailed Deputy Secretary Bill Burns twenty minutes later: "How do you spell 'relief'? 'GLOCS' . . ."

Allen said that nadir in US-Pakistan relations was a lost strategic opportunity that could never be regained. "We had no relationship with Pakistan after that for nine months . . . and in that period of time my numbers were coming down," he said, referring to the dwindling count of American boots on the ground. "Our ability to have the Pakistanis on one side and us on the other side and have a real decisive effect on the safe havens was lost during those nine months. And looking back on how much we could have accomplished to get after the safe havens, it's a sad state of affairs, frankly."

Congress, which had little appetite for assistance to Pakistan after the bin Laden raid, refused to reimburse the Pakistani military for its activities during the long months the ground lines stood closed. It put the biggest dent in Holbrooke's ambitious five-year assistance plan yet. A year after he went to his grave, the relationship he had desperately fought to transform followed him. Clinton cheerfully reflected in her campaign season State Department memoir that "the negotiations and eventual agreement over the supply lines offer lessons for how the United States and Pakistan can work together in the future to pursue shared interests." One could just as reasonably conclude that the lesson was about the perils of leaning on a military junta with no strategic alignment with the United States.

IN FEBRUARY 2011, I'd watched Clinton take to the stage at the Asia Society, an organization with which Richard Holbrooke had a long history, and formally announce US support for a political settlement in Afghanistan, including talks with the Taliban. Frank Ruggiero was dispatched for a series of further meetings with A-Rod, the secret Taliban contact. As a confidence-building measure, the United States pressed the UN to separate the Taliban from al-Qaeda on its terrorist blacklists—another Holbrooke proposal. But Karzai's government in Kabul derailed the attempted talks. A Taliban political office in Qatar, one of A-Rod's first requests, opened in 2013, then shut down a month later after it put up a flag for the "Islamic Emirate of Afghanistan"—presenting the Taliban as a government in exile rather than a political faction. Karzai once again hit the roof. Talks were iced for years. It wasn't until 2016 and 2017 that they once again began to show fitful signs of life, with the Afghans in the lead and at least one US official shadowing meetings. The future remains uncertain.

Several Obama administration officials sympathetic to Holbrooke said they felt that antipathy toward him and his campaign for diplomacy may have squandered the United States' period of maximum potential in the region. When US troop deployments were high, both the Taliban and the Pakistanis had incentives to come to the table and respond to tough talk. Once we were leaving, there was little reason to cooperate. The lack of White House support for Holbrooke's diplomatic overtures to Pakistan had, likewise, wasted openings to steel the relationship for the complete collapse that followed. Richard Olson, who took over as ambassador to Pakistan in 2012, called the year after Holbrooke's death an "annus horribilis." We lost the war, and this is when it happened.

15

THE MEMO

HUSAIN HAQQANI was trying to make a habit of not checking his phone first thing in the morning, "otherwise things would go bad." Waking up early in the residential suite of the Pakistani embassy on October 10, 2011, he got dressed in the dawn light, then moved into the study next to his bedroom, which he had lined with books. Haqqani had a lot of those; he was a professor, after all. He sat down in an oversized office chair and thumbed through the papers. As he made his way through the salmon pink broadsheet of the *Financial Times,* an op-ed column caught his eye: "Time to take on Pakistan's jihadist spies," read the headline. It was by an acquaintance of his named Mansoor Ijaz.

"A week after U.S. Special Forces stormed the hideout of Osama bin Laden and killed him," the column began, "a senior Pakistani diplomat telephoned me with an urgent request." Ijaz claimed that the diplomat wanted to pass a message from Pakistan's president, Zardari, to Admiral Mullen, the chairman of the joint chiefs—without the ISI finding out. "The embarrassment of bin Laden being found on Pakistani soil had humiliated Mr Zardari's weak civilian government to such an extent that the president feared a military takeover was imminent," Ijaz wrote. "He needed an American fist on his army chief's desk to end any misguided notions of a coup—and fast." Ijaz claimed that he drafted a memo according to the diplomat's specifications, over the course of a series of phone calls. Its request: that the United States order Pakistan's army chief, General Kayani, to "stand down the Pakistani military-intelligence establishment." There was more: President Zardari was supposedly assembling a new national security team to take power and eliminate hardline elements within the ISI. Whatever its provenance, Ijaz did write a memo, and sent it to recently departed National Security Advisor Jim Jones, who passed it to Mullen.

The Raymond Davis incident and the bin Laden raid had revived whispers about Haqqani's loyalties. The previous year, he had been responsible for unstopping the flow of visas. Now, as stories of uninvited spies and Navy SEALs roiled Pakistan, fingers pointed at him. "One of the things that the ISI held against me was that the people on the ground who had helped on the raid had probably been given visas by me behind their back," Haqqani told me. "That's how they thought, because they are so conspiratorial." The narrative favored by the conspiracy theorists—that Haqqani colluded with the Americans to let in a secret network of spies—continues to have life in Pakistan. In March 2017, a copy of a letter from the prime minister's office authorizing Haqqani to issue visas without notifying Islamabad surfaced in the press, giving credence to Haqqani's claim that he wasn't acting unilaterally. But that was swiftly followed by another leak, this time of a letter from the Ministry of Foreign Affairs, allegedly warning Haqqani not to approve visas for CIA agents. In the eyes of some in the military establishment, Haqqani was a turncoat; the man who had opened up Pakistan's borders to the interlopers.

Haqqani realized how the *Financial Times* op-ed would look to anyone with that view. It was hard to think of another "senior Pakistani diplomat" who so closely fit the pro-civilian, pro-American ideology described in the memo. When he got to the bottom of the column, Haqqani picked up his BlackBerry for the first time that morning and called Mansoor Ijaz on his London-area-code cell phone.

"What's happening?" Haqqani asked.

"You're not the only Pakistani official I know," Ijaz replied, as both men remembered the conversation. Haqqani said that Ijaz laughed as he said it.

"This could provoke some sort of political crisis," Haqqani said, less amused.

"Nah, I don't think that's going to happen," Ijaz said, according to Haqqani's recollection. "The rest of the article's more important."

Haqqani shook his head at the memory. "The man was completely out of his depth," he told me. Ijaz said there was another beat in the conversation: Haqqani telling him, shortly before hanging up: "You have just killed me."

MANSOOR IJAZ WAS on his yacht when, according to his telling, he got the call from Husain Haqqani and flew into action to draft the memo. Ijaz had the biography of a supporting character in an Agatha Christie novel. Perhaps he planned it that way. A Pakistani-American businessman who made his fortune as a hedge-fund manager, he flitted around the French Riviera. He emphasized his rags-to-riches story when talking to the press: he was born in Florida; raised on a farm in Floyd County, Virginia; covered his tuition at UVA through a weight-lifting scholarship. He gave plenty of attention to the riches part too. "God gave me so much in this world, but if all I left in the world was a jet on the runway, a yacht in the harbor, 10 homes around the world, and my wife's 5,000 pairs of shoes, I will not have done my job," he told the *Washington Post* during the scandal. Ijaz's father told him, "God gave you a great brain but a shit personality. You have to get into politics to teach you humility." When Ijaz hit pay dirt in finance, he began donating hundreds of thousands of dollars to the Democrats and built up as many contacts as possible. He wrote op-eds. He started projecting himself into international conflicts. In the 1990s, he approached the Clinton administration, saying he was negotiating with Sudan to secure the arrest of Osama bin Laden, who was sheltering there at the time. Clinton officials dismissed him as a "Walter Mitty" type, "living out a personal fantasy," according to one report. Later, he surfaced as a *Fox News* commentator and made sensational claims that radical Iranian mullahs were smuggling chemical weapons into Iraq. He later admitted this was "erroneous." A string of assertions, on air and in op-eds, were similarly colorful—and suspect.

But none had precipitated an international incident like this latest claim. A few days after the *Financial Times* op-ed ran, the first items began appearing in the Pakistani press. Zardari had made a deal with the devil, critics crowed. The civilian government was in cahoots with the Americans. Haqqani got a call from President Zardari. "What happened? The army is taking this seriously." Haqqani, not explicitly named in the initial op-ed, became a fixture in subsequent coverage after the politician Imran Khan named him as the culprit. The ISI launched an investigation, with General Pasha rendezvousing with Ijaz in London and downloading evidence from his BlackBerry. Logs of his calls and messages later presented in court showed a flurry of exchanges between the two men, though the calls were brief and the messages often came from Ijaz, not Haqqani. Haqqani said he was a victim of his own politeness, and that perfunctory "thank you very much for sending" messages were being used against him. Two months after the op-ed ran, Zardari called again and ordered Haqqani back to Pakistan, where the ISI, and the public, wanted blood.

Haqqani fielded a flurry of warning calls from Americans: Holbrooke's successor, Marc Grossman; one of Doug Lute's staffers; Deputy CIA Director Mike Morell. "Don't go," Haqqani remembered

Morell saying. "The boys at the ISI have it in for you." Haqqani was already boarding a flight to Doha, en route to Islamabad. "I had struggled too long for civilian government to let it fall on the basis of a false allegation against me," he said. "I wasn't going to let the military topple the elected government." He told his wife and kids that, if he didn't return, it would be because he paid the ultimate price for his beliefs. On his flight, they were playing a film about Harry Houdini. Haqqani decided this would be his frame of reference for his final showdown with the ISI: "They can tie me up, they can do anything, I'll be Houdini and get out of it. Screw that, I'm going."

On arrival, Haqqani's passport was confiscated and he was whisked to the president's palace, where Zardari had guaranteed his safety. He had packed three days of clothes. He ended up being there for more than two months. Kayani and Pasha, the all-powerful heads of Pakistan's army and intelligence agency, questioned him.

"What do you say to all of this?" said Kayani.

"It's all nonsense," Haqqani replied. He had Admiral Mullen on speed dial, he pointed out. Why would he use a businessman in the Riviera as a go-between? Haqqani's exchange with Kayani and Pasha was gleefully rendered by the media as a multihour interrogation. "What the fuck, I'm here," Haqqani muttered to himself, watching the gruesome reports. But as the months wore on, he grew more worried. His case was handed not to the Parliament, which had pro-civilian voices, but to the Supreme Court, which was under the military's thumb. The court issued a travel ban. At one point, Zardari suffered a stroke and was flown to Dubai. His protector gone, Haqqani was moved to the prime minister's house, which is guarded by the army. In the middle of the night, he heard shuffling boots and thought, for a moment, that they might have finally decided to take him out. It turned out to be a routine changing of the guard.

His anxiety peaked when, one Friday night in late January, the Supreme Court announced a sudden hearing for the following Monday. Hearings were never announced at night. There was a knock at the door. A businessman, whom Haqqani and others involved declined to name, gave him instructions: The Supreme Court would open briefly in the morning, despite it being a Saturday. Haqqani was to file an application to leave the country. Then he was to depart immediately, before the hearing. With Haqqani gone, the court proceeded ex parte, issuing a report based only on the testimony of Ijaz, who continued to point the finger at Haqqani. In an allegation later revived by Pakistani authorities in 2018, Haqqani was also accused of paying off Americans using a Pakistani slush fund and failing to report back home on the particulars. But, since Haqqani wasn't present, there was no formal legal judgment. It was classic Pakistani political theater. The military and intelligence powers got the optics of acting against an American stooge, without any of the consequences.

Haqqani had his suspicions that Ijaz may have cooked up the memo at the behest of the ISI. But he conceded it was more likely that a serial fantasist got in over his head—and the ISI and the military seized the opportunity to eliminate an enemy. Mansoor Ijaz maintained that Haqqani had dictated the memo to him but otherwise declined to comment. "There are material inaccuracies in this recantation," he said of Haqqani's version of events, "too many, I'm afraid, to take a lot of time to fix them."

A FEW YEARS LATER, I caught up with Haqqani in his small office at the Hudson Institute, the conservative think tank. A narrow window overlooked gray buildings on Pennsylvania Avenue. On the walls hung photographs of Haqqani shaking hands with George W. Bush and Barack Obama. In one picture, he was arm-in-arm with Richard Holbrooke. Haqqani sat at a table stacked with loose paper. It was 2017, and he was in a familiar position: under fire in the Pakistani press. In a *Washington Post* op-ed, he had defended Donald Trump's contacts with the Russians, comparing them to his own entrees to the Obama administration. He suggested his outreach during Obama's transition later helped the United States stage the bin Laden raid. It was true, indirectly. It ultimately fell to him to approve visas for Joint Special Operations commander Admiral McRaven and others involved in planning the operation. By the time the column reached Pakistan, it had been inflated into a long-awaited confirmation that Husain Haqqani built a network of CIA agents right under his bosses' noses. "The veracity of concerns about his role in the entire issue also stands confirmed," read a gleeful tweet from a Pakistan Army spokesperson.

In a sense, Haqqani had chosen this life as a pariah. But he never stopped wishing his homeland would understand his belief in dialogue, and his skepticism of a bilateral relationship built on transactions between generals. He handed me one document after another chronicling in minute detail the "memogate" controversy, which still loomed large in his imagination. Wearing a loose gray suit and a cyan tie dusted with white tridents, he looked tired. "Look, it's taken an adjustment," he said heavily. "In the view of many people in Pakistan, I'm not a patriot."

"You've spent your whole life working for your government," I said. "That must be painful."

"Yeah. For my country, for democracy in my country. So it hurts me."

He still wondered if he should go back, but he always had second thoughts. "What if someone really thinks I am a traitor and shoots me?" he pondered. Exile was bittersweet. Haqqani survived, but his life's work—his fight to transform the relationship between the two countries, to build something more sustainable and less transactional— was done. In his final conversation with Richard Holbrooke at the Four Seasons, both men had pledged to keep going in their respective fights against entrenched military thinking until they couldn't. A year after Holbrooke's fight ended, so did Haqqani's.

16

THE REAL THING

THAT AWFUL DAY IN 2014, Robin Raphel stood on her porch and stared at the warrant, and the espionage statute listed on it. The two young FBI agents looked at her. One asked: "Do you know any foreigners?" Raphel goggled. "A thousand," she said. "I'm a diplomat." The agents asked her about Pakistanis. She named Husain Haqqani and his successor as ambassador to the United States, Jalil Abbas Jilani. The agents glanced at each other.

"Do you have any classified material in the house?" the other agent pressed on.

"No," said Raphel, "of course not."

They handed her several State Department cables marked "CLASSIFIED" and dated back to her time as assistant secretary. They'd found them in a filing cabinet in Raphel's basement. Raphel smacked a palm to her forehead remembering the moment later. Cleaning out her office years before, she had taken a number of items home and neglected to remove the cables. They "shouldn't have been there," she was quick to admit. "But it was just a case of me, when I left the office, not having the time to kind of look through everything." She knew dozens of prominent officials with worse habits. We all did.

As the agents' questioning grew more intense, Raphel tried to convince them there'd been a misunderstanding. "I mean, I was just such an idiot, complete idiot. Because I thought, 'Oh, I can just explain!'" It was nearly two hours before she realized she needed a lawyer. She called one she knew—a government contracts specialist she met while lobbying at Cassidy & Associates.

A few hours later, she and her daughter Alexandra sat at DeCarlo's, a nearby Italian restaurant with bread sticks on the tables and faded green carpeting that her kids had always called a "mafioso spot." It was a frequent meeting place for CIA agents, according to neighborhood lore. They were joined by two lawyers: the one she'd called and a younger associate who'd raced over in an Uber to get there more quickly. Alexandra, a short, feisty redhead, was distraught. "How could you possibly have documents in the house," she wailed. "What were you thinking?" Raphel tried to process what had happened. She ordered a glass of wine. "The truth is, I was in shock," she later told me. "In medical terms."

The next day, Diplomatic Security arrived at the house to confiscate her BlackBerry and work ID. She was summoned by State Department Human Resources and informed that her security clearance was suspended and her contract, which was up for renewal, would be allowed to lapse. It was the first time she had walked into State without Department ID in years. When the guard at the C Street entrance saw the name on her driver's license, Raphel recalled him trembling visibly. Days later, the story hit the front page of the *New York Times*: "FBI Is Investigating Retired U.S. diplomat." A State Department spokesperson told reporters only that the Department was cooperating with law enforcement. "Ms. Raphel's appointment expired," the spokesperson added. "She is no longer a Department employee." Robin Raphel was never allowed back into her office. FBI agents scoured her desk, then sealed the doors.

A few weeks earlier, Raphel had arrived in Islamabad with a mission from Dan Feldman, from whom Holbrooke had jokingly requested a heart and who had recently assumed the special representative for Afghanistan and Pakistan job. Protesters were taking to the streets across Pakistan, railing against alleged vote rigging that, in 2013, propelled Nawaz Sharif back into power. Some commentators argued that a "soft coup" was under way, with Sharif quietly surrendering control to the military. Robin Raphel, with her peerless Rolodex in Islamabad, was there to ferret out information on whether the government would actually fall. She set to work, attending dinner parties and making notes about gossip she heard, which she reported back to Feldman and the ambassador in Islamabad, Richard Olson. "What she was doing," Olson told me, "was diplomacy." In the three years since the "annus horribilis" of 2011, the relationship between countries had remained icy. Colleagues at State viewed Raphel as a vanishing asset: someone the Pakistanis still talked to.

She had no way of knowing that her every move during that trip to Islamabad was being watched by the FBI. Raphel's brand of old-school diplomacy was struggling to find purchase alongside not only the military domination of foreign policy but also the surveillance state that had evolved since 9/11. Face-to-face conversations had been steadily eclipsed by "signals intelligence" or intercepted communications. In early 2013, NSA analysts listening in on Pakistani politicians' phone calls began to focus on an American in the conversations: Robin Raphel. She seemed to be discussing sensitive matters—drone strikes, coups. They sent an "811 referral"—indicating suspected chatter about classified material—to the FBI. The two agents Raphel later met on her porch were selected to lead the investigation for their focus on "65 work"—spy cases. They began to look at Raphel's contacts, her personnel files at the State Department, her personal life. After a few months, they obtained a Foreign Intelligence Surveillance Court warrant to monitor her Skypes and calls with Pakistani officials.

It had been a year since Edward Snowden's whistleblowing, and the bureau was looking for moles and leakers. With Raphel, they hoped they'd hit pay dirt. Her background seemed to have all the hallmarks: decades spent largely abroad, her status as a registered lobbyist, her brazen sympathies with dubious Pakistan, of all places. ("Oh totally," she told me when I asked if she felt that sentiment prejudiced the investigation. "Everybody hated Pakistan, so of course.") The Pakistanis she spoke with sometimes went on to refer to her as a "source" and tout how informative she had been. And digging revealed further flags: she'd been cited for a handful of minor infractions related to the handling of classified material; leaving documents out or computers unlocked. And then there were the documents in the filing cabinet in her basement—which could carry a criminal charge, separate from the more serious espionage charges.

But the FBI investigation also flowed from multiple layers of misunderstanding. The intelligence and law-enforcement agencies searching for moles had little knowledge of the peculiar rituals of diplomacy in Pakistan. Anyone who had ever spent five minutes at a dinner party in Islamabad knew that the nominally "classified" topics Raphel had been discussing, like drone strikes, were an unavoidable matter of public debate. Bragging about Americans being sources of information was, similarly, a typically Pakistani expression of bravado.

Raphel was also up against a more general kind of confusion. The old-fashioned schmoozing and relationship-building she had built her career around was out of vogue and foreign for a generation raised in the surveillance age. Holbrooke's SRAP team, which she had joined— with its interagency staff, all aimed at broadening rather than narrowing the conversations in the region—was particularly out of step with the times. "People didn't understand the SRAP office, which I'm sure doesn't surprise you," Raphel recalled. "They didn't understand the bureaucratic structure. Who were all these people? Who did they report to, what were they doing there? What was their scope of work?" The value of all this talk wasn't self-evident. How could it be? In places like Pakistan, conversation had long been an afterthought to the business of generals and spies.

ONE EVENING about a week before Donald Trump's inauguration in 2017, Robin Raphel came in from the Washington, DC, winter and took off her coat. We were at Garden Cafe, a quiet bistro around the corner from the State Department with peach walls decorated with bland paintings of flowers. Jazz played faintly. As always, her personal style reflected her years in Pakistan. She wore a taupe pashmina with silver embroidery thrown over one shoulder of a gray jacket, and her blond hair was swept into a French twist. She ordered a sauvignon blanc. "I look back on it now and I see the *humor* in it," she said, with a tone that suggested she didn't see the humor in it at all, "but it was . . . you know, anyway you slice it, it is profoundly wrong to do that to somebody." She seemed unchanged: lips tightly pursed; chin held high; the same haughty delivery. But in fact, just about everything had changed for Robin Raphel.

As the FBI dug deeper, their case lost steam. Circling Raphel over the course of months, investigators had avoided talking to her coworkers at the State Department, not wanting to tip her off and lose a chance to catch her in the act. Once they began speaking with officials familiar with her work, they started to understand that Raphel's incriminating behavior was in fact simply old-school, relationship-driven diplomacy. In early 2015, the US Attorney's office overseeing the case told Raphel's lawyer that it was dropping the espionage charges. Prosecutors still seemed to want to extract something to save face, like a plea in the lesser charge related to the classified material. Raphel wouldn't budge—she knew those infractions were common and not grounds for significant criminal proceedings. In March 2016, prosecutors finally dropped the case entirely. It had been seventeen months since the raid on her house. She had spent more than $100,000 in legal fees. Friends banded together to help cover them, but she was still decimated financially and out of a job.

"I haven't worked in two years," she told me, "and I have significant responsibility still for my children, and legal bills, and stuff like that." She laughed coldly. "It's just beyond imagination that you spend forty years working hard, and this is what happens." She was looking for work, but the cloud of suspicion made it difficult. "Nobody is going to hire you when the FBI has accused you of being a spy on the front page of the *New York Times*, above the fold." The investigation's announcement was a circus. Its resolution barely registered a blip. Later she took odd consulting jobs, part time—anything she could find to make ends meet.

Life on the outside was hard to adjust to. Raphel's work had, for as long as she could remember, been her life. "I'm a working woman," she said. "I'm not a homemaker. I mean I can cook and do various things, but I've never been a homebody." She struggled to hold on to some semblance of her old world. Every day, she woke up early, sat at her dining room table in front of an aging laptop, and put out feelers for work. She advised nongovernmental groups on the subject of reconciliation in Afghanistan, a project the United States government had once again left for dead. She read copiously, especially about politics and Pakistan. She went to every think-tank and foreign policy event she could, especially anything about South Asia. In early 2016, I interviewed Pakistani filmmaker Sharmeen Obaid-Chinoy about her documentary on honor killings in front of a small audience at the United States Institute of Peace. There was Robin Raphel in the front row, taking notes. A few attendees glanced at her curiously and exchanged whispers.

Her family had to adjust. Alexandra continued to feel "mortified . . . it was a real body blow to her," Raphel said. She was engaged to be married and explaining the scandal to her in-laws became a family crisis. "She was afraid people wouldn't come [to the wedding], that everyone would be thinking about this embarrassing thing. . . . " she recalled. Raphel took the bus to New York and met with the bridegroom's parents, a successful investment banker and his polished, yoga-going wife. "I'm not a spy," she told them. "Oh," they replied.

THAT NIGHT AT THE GARDEN CAFE, Raphel raked her red-lacquered nails across the white tablecloth with a "*snnk*" sound. "If anybody put these guys onto this," she said, "it would have been an American."

"An American who felt you were too close," I said.

"Yep. And you know," she said under her breath, leaning in conspiratorially, "The intelligence community is chock *full* of Indian Americans who have a huge chip on their shoulder about Pakistan. They're there for their language skills. You see these people coming in from INR"—The State Department intelligence bureau—"to brief and they're clueless. They have an attitude. They don't know anything!" She leaned back and picked up her sauvignon blanc with a slosh. I spoke with more than a dozen of Raphel's colleagues about the investigation. None thought she was a spy. Several questioned her coziness with a treacherous regime. The term "clientitis" sometimes came up. Robin Raphel was a loyal, even patriotic American public servant. But she had internalized Pakistani attitudes—right down to the tendency to blame India, even Americans of Indian descent.

Raphel's approach was imperfect. Unlike Richard Holbrooke, who used diplomacy to transform the strategic orientation of the relationships he tackled, she followed the rules. She used diplomacy to maintain the status quo, and for decades, the status quo in Pakistan had been holding things together just enough for military and intelligence cooperation to continue. Sometimes, that could look like appeasement. Empowered diplomacy, used as a frontline tool as Richard Holbrooke had urged, might have looked very different.

But Raphel was a believer in an old-fashioned diplomatic maxim: you never stop talking. Dating back to her advocacy for the Taliban, she had been an extreme embodiment of that ethos. Now, in an era where diplomacy of any kind was being sidelined in America's most sensitive relationships, that behavior was more than unusual—it even looked criminal. "She was trying to work on the US national interest, doing things we all thought were important," one senior official told me, on condition of anonymity since the investigation was still a sore point with law enforcement. "And by doing that she looked to someone like a spy. The danger of the whole thing was criminalizing diplomacy."

When the *Wall Street Journal* profiled the Raphel case, it headlined the resulting article, "The Last Diplomat." As Raphel rose from our table, she shook her head at the characterization. "Ronan, can we please get this straight? I have had foreign policy people come up and say, 'You were doing the old-fashioned thing and now there's a new thing.'" She fixed her blue eyes on me. "I wasn't doing the wrong thing. I wasn't doing the out of date thing. I was doing the real thing." Robin Raphel pulled on her coat and stepped back out into the cold.

PART II

SHOOT FIRST,
ASK QUESTIONS NEVER

■

SYRIA, 2016

AFGHANISTAN, 2002

THE HORN OF AFRICA, 2006

EGYPT, 2013

COLOMBIA, 2006

Do not be deceived: Bad company ruins good morals.

—1 CORINTHIANS 15:33

17

GENERAL RULE

S EVEN YEARS AFTER Richard Holbrooke died, I walked by the
front door of what had once been the office of the special representative for Afghanistan and Pakistan. The hospital-white paint job on
the wall was the same, and the wooden door with the honey-colored
stain. The sign was new: "Special Presidential Envoy for the Global
Coalition to Counter ISIL," it read. The SRAP team, and Holbrooke's
dream of negotiating with the Taliban, had been quietly shuttered over
the course of Donald Trump's first year in office, and its last employees
let go. In the first days of 2018, Trump's first secretary of state, Rex
Tillerson, told me he hadn't yet made a final decision on the office's
future, but it was obvious that he didn't think much of it. "Whether
we need an SRAP or not, we're considering that," he said. Tillerson argued that the conventional roles responsible for Afghanistan and
Pakistan—the ambassadors to those countries, and the assistant secretary for South and Central Asia— were "much better than an SRAP.
Much better." But by early 2018, the South and Central Asia Bureau
still didn't have a permanent assistant secretary. If someone was actively
championing diplomatic solutions for the region, it wasn't apparent.

The fears of militarization Holbrooke had expressed in his final, desperate memos, had come to pass on a scale he could have never anticipated. President Trump had concentrated ever more power in the Pentagon, granting it nearly unilateral authority in areas of policy once orchestrated across multiple agencies, including the State Department. In Iraq and Syria, the White House quietly delegated more decisions on troop deployments to the military. In Yemen and Somalia, field commanders were given authority to launch raids without White House approval. In Afghanistan, Trump granted the secretary of defense, General James Mattis, sweeping authority to set troop levels. In public statements, the White House downplayed the move, saying the Pentagon still had to adhere to the broad strokes of policies set by the White House. But in practice, the fate of thousands of troops in a diplomatic tinderbox of a conflict had, for the first time in recent history, been placed solely in military hands. Diplomats were no longer losing the argument on Afghanistan: they weren't in it. In early 2018, the military began publicly rolling out a new surge: in the following months, up to a thousand new troops would join the fourteen thousand already in place.

Back home, the White House itself was crowded with military voices. A few months into the Trump administration, at least ten of twenty-five senior leadership positions on the president's National Security Council were held by current or retired military officials. As the churn of firings and hirings continued, that number grew to include the White House chief of staff, a position given to former general John Kelly. At the same time, the White House ended the practice of "detailing" State Department officers to the National Security Council. There would now be fewer diplomatic voices in the policy process, by design.

America's relationships around the world, too, took on a distinctly military flavor. In early 2018, the Trump administration leaked its plans for a "Buy American" strategy that would give State Department diplomats around the world a new mandate: drumming up arms sales for defense contractors. American arms sales had already been climbing over the preceding five years. But a spate of new deals under the Trump administration suggested a widening gulf between such sales and any diplomacy that might provide context and direction for them. During a diplomatic crisis between Qatar and other Gulf States in 2017, as Trump excoriated the Qatari government for its ties to terrorists, the Pentagon announced it was selling $12 billion in F-15 fighters to the nation. Secretary of Defense Mattis met with his counterpart, the Qatari defense minister, to seal the deal. State Department officials were barely involved, according to several Pentagon staffers.

Military exigencies trumped concerns that had been obstacles to such deals in prior administrations. In the midst of a human rights crackdown in Bahrain—including murder and torture by government forces—the State Department announced that it would resume the sale of F-16 fighter jets to that country's monarchy without any attendant human rights conditions. At the State Department in late May 2017, a reporter asked Acting Assistant Secretary of State Stuart E. Jones—a career Foreign Service officer in a post to which no permanent appointee had been nominated—how the administration reconciled a record-setting $110-billion arms deal with Saudi Arabia with that regime's abysmal human rights record. Jones sighed heavily. "Um. Um . . ." he muttered, glancing around, knitting and re-knitting his fingers. Then he froze for twenty seconds, his face slackened into a thousand-yard stare. He offered a few halting sentences about fighting extremism and another interminable pause before hurrying offstage, head down, like he'd realized he was naked in a dream.

AGAIN AND AGAIN, President Trump called authoritarian strongmen to sing their praises. Abdel Fattah el-Sisi of Egypt, as he presided over one of the worst human rights crackdowns in the country's history, was "fantastic" and "we are very much behind [him]." The Philippines' Rodrigo Duterte, who admitted to murdering opponents and cheerfully encouraged his troops to rape women, was doing an "unbelievable" and "great" job. Trump personally invited both to the White House, breaking with the previous administration. Of all of the living secretaries of state, only one, James Baker, wholeheartedly endorsed the closer rapport. "Egypt, the Philippines and Turkey are all historic partners of the United States and it is important that we deal with those leaders," Baker said. "An observation often attributed to President Franklin D. Roosevelt puts this phenomenon in the proper perspective. 'He may be an SOB,' President Roosevelt said of a Latin American dictator, 'but he's our SOB.' " John Kerry evinced a more typical perspective: "I don't understand," he said, "what this president aims to achieve by going so far as to hold up as positives or describe as 'strong' things which violate international norms and certainly are unprecedented coming out of the mouth of an American president of any party." The diplomats once charged with managing these delicate relationships were as surprised as anyone: repeatedly, they weren't informed.

"If anyone's seen the increasing militarization of foreign policy, it's definitely me," said Chris LaVine, a career official who had been one of Holbrooke's special assistants on the SRAP team and was working on Syria policy at State when news of the cuts and firings hit. Stationed in a series of assignments focused on the Islamic State, he witnessed two dynamics that helped to plunge America's Syria policy into chaos. The first was inside the State Department. The new sign on what was once Holbrooke's door was not incidental. Counter-ISIL activities had become a whirlpool, pulling in more and more of the Department's resources and activities. Brett McGurk, the special envoy on combatting ISIL, had become one of the most powerful officials in the building. The second change had come from outside. The Department had yielded more and more of its power to the military. "We ceded a lot of policy ground to the folks doing counter-ISIL, in the Pentagon, in

Tampa, and in the building at State," he said, referring to the Penta-gon's Central Command headquarters in Florida, CENTCOM. "Hard underlying parts of the diplomacy were absolutely ceded, and progress on other policy issues such as human rights concerns, economics, and the bilateral relationship [with Turkey] were largely sacrificed."

With no centralized dialogue led by diplomats, and the White House—beginning with Obama and continuing under Trump—vacillating between different half measures, the CIA and the Pentagon essentially built the United States' Syria policy. This proved prob-lematic as the two agencies set about creating separate and sometimes conflicting relationships with forces on the ground. The CIA covertly armed and trained the loose coalition of so-called "moderate" rebels in the Free Syrian Army (FSA). The Pentagon set up and began arm-ing a coalition called the Syrian Democratic Forces, dominated by the Kurdish YPG (*Yekîneyên Parastina Gel* or "People's Protection Units").

Both relationships proved problematic. FSA arms ended up in the hands of terrorist groups like Jabhat al-Nusra. And the YPG was inex-tricably entwined with the Kurdistan Worker's Party or PKK (*Partiya Karkerên Kurdistanê*)—a revolutionary group labeled a terrorist organi-zation by the United States. "They play shell games with their organiza-tions' names," said LaVine. "These guys are one and the same as PKK." The Pentagon's unbridled relationship with the YPG also presented a further wrinkle: the Kurds are the mortal enemy of the Turks. "Due to our singular focus on eliminating the immediate threat of ISIL, we've exacerbated a thirty-five-year conflict between Turkish security forces and the PKK, which is likely to rage for much longer," he continued.

From the barrel-bombed husk that was once the city of Aleppo, an FSA commander named Abdullah Al-Mousa was more blunt: "American policy with the SDF will make a civil war in the future between Arabs and Kurds . . . the US do a very big mistake." That very big mistake was already apparent on the ground: at several times, the Kurds, Turks, and Syrian rebels were all locked in battle, all undergirded by the United States' arms and air support. One hot, summery Saturday in August 2016, rockets hit two Turkish tanks in northern Syria, killing one of Turkey's soldiers and unraveling a delicate web of alliances for the United States. Turkey quickly blamed the YPG, and struck back hard, killing twenty-five Kurdish YPG fighters the next day, according to Turkish state-run media—in addition to twenty civilians. The FSA announced the capture of ten Kurdish villages the same day. Videos circulated online showed US-backed FSA fighters brutally beating US-backed YPG soldiers.

A month later, Abdullah Al-Mousa, the FSA commander, sheltered in an encampment outside of Aleppo, the shelling audible even through his closed windows, even late at night. "It's really a chaos," he said. "When the United States is supporting those groups like the Kurd groups, which don't fight [Syrian President Bashar] al-Assad, and just want to make their country, it's really a very big mistake." Unsurprisingly, he viewed his own FSA forces as a more suitable partner—though he conceded fighting the Syrian regime was his first concern, before combatting ISIL at the behest of the United States.

Free Syrian Army lawyer Osama Abu Zaid said the United States' presence in the Syrian conflict inspired confusion, with the CIA backing the FSA and the Pentagon backing the SDF and its Kurdish subsidiaries. "There is no direct communication between Pentagon and Free Syrian Army," he said. The divisions between US agencies led to strange situations within joint command and training centers, with Pentagon officials refusing to talk to confused FSA commanders being armed by the CIA. Abu Zaid said sometimes the Americans seemed to relish the tension. "Sometimes the CIA people here, they were happy, because the Pentagon program is false." This was what tactics without strategy looked like: deadly farce.

During the first half of 2017, the Trump administration chose its side, first reauthorizing Pentagon support for the Kurds over the objections of the Turks, then shutting down the CIA's covert support for rebel elements. The Pentagon seizing control effectively shut the State Department out of what should have been an important mandate: maintaining relations with Turkey, a necessary but difficult regional ally. Military proxy wars replacing diplomacy in the region had been "completely corrosive" from a strategic standpoint, said LaVine. "I worked on managing the Turkey relationship, and the US arming the YPG so overtly has competed with and eroded our bilateral relationship. Turkey perceives the YPG as we would if they were based in Texas and arming the Sinaloa cartel." It undercut civilian efforts to talk to the Turks on a range of issues. "We had to restrain ourselves on issues of mutual concern we should have been able to address: human rights in Turkey, the clamping down on civil society, and mass purges related to the July 2016 coup attempt, and making progress on bilateral issues with a NATO ally," LaVine added. "Instead, cooperating with the Syrian Kurds dominated the conversation and limited our ability to conduct diplomacy."

Hillary Clinton bridled at the suggestion that she had ever been absent from policymaking on Syria. She had backed her military and intelligence counterparts' case for more muscular intervention. "I thought we needed to do more to support the legitimate opposition to Bashar al-Assad," she explained. "I got the CIA and the Defense Department on board with that." But at a working level, multiple officials said the State Department had surrendered so much power that there was little counterbalance from civilian voices—at least those who didn't fall into lockstep with the requests of the Pentagon or Langley. "You have mostly mil-mil contacts," at this point, said LaVine. "This is the Pentagon talking to their counterparts. State felt like the fourth or fifth most important agency in foreign policy." And back on Mahogany Row, there was no alternative perspective left. The most powerful voices in the building were "aligned with the commanders prosecuting the Counter-ISIL campaign at the expense of the longer-term US foreign policy objectives in the region. For State, it's become impossible to have an honest policy disagreement with the uniform, or you risk being sidelined from the discussion at all."

LaVine, "a kid from Brooklyn, who witnessed September 11 and wanted to serve," had initially intended to leave State in 2010, after his Afghanistan and Pakistan assignment ended. He'd remained there after promising Holbrooke, not long before his death, that he'd stay to fight another day. LaVine left amid the budget cuts and firings in mid-2017, after more than ten years at the Department. "It was clear," he said, "that we were creating more problems through systemic indecision and inaction, rather than solving them."

LEANING ON FOREIGN FORCES and strongmen, a mainstay of the Cold War, was in the midst of a renaissance. It had been for nearly two decades, since the very first days after September 11, 2001. Some of these relationships were born under George W. Bush's leadership, in a moment of urgency immediately after the attacks. But many were continued and expanded upon over the course of the Obama administration. Ironically, it was Obama's noninterventionist, "don't do stupid shit" approach to foreign policy that prompted a double down on these tactics. His was an administration intent on a legacy of low-footprint intervention, and, along with drones, alliances with foreign militaries and militias were at the heart of that legacy. In 2014, he stood at the United States Military Academy in West Point, New York, and described to more than a thousand graduating cadets, clad in traditional gray, his vision for a new era of American engagement in the world. At the center of that vision was proxy war: over and over again, he used the word "partner," referring to foreign militaries or militias doing the bidding of the United States. Why send American sons and daughters to do work that Yemenis and Pakistanis could be paid to do for us? While the motivations changed from administration to administration, all three presidents since 2001 doubled down on that principle.

But these relationships invariably carry with them the acute compromises, to human rights and to broader strategic interests, that LaVine witnessed in the United States' Syria policy. We don't have to speculate about the effects of those compromises: the trend has already proved disastrous for America's trajectory in conflicts the world over. Sidelining diplomacy in favor of direct dealings between our military and local warlords was at the heart of America's declining fortunes in Afghanistan. Similar choices contributed to the unleashing of new terrorist threats in the Horn of Africa. And a policy built around strongmen left us flat footed when revolution struck Egypt, and powerless to stop atrocities thereafter. There were also exceptions: a precious few military-to-military alliances with a more balanced approach integrating diplomatic interests, as was the case with the United States' interventions in Latin America's Cocaine Triangle.

That cautionary tale seemed largely lost on the Trump administration as it set about its tilt to military-led foreign policy. But it was inescapable for many diplomats who found their work increasingly overtaken by military alliances—including those who worked in Afghanistan. For some of us, that realization began with a warlord, and an unsolved murder.

18

DOSTUM: HE IS TELLING
THE TRUTH AND
DISCOURAGING ALL LIES

YOU CAN SMELL A MASS GRAVE before you see it. Jennifer Leaning had her knitted scarf, the black and blue and red one she always traveled with, pulled tight around her neck. Her black Marmot jacket was too big for her, concealing her slight frame and letting her pass for a man at a distance; a small safeguard on a dangerous mission. She brought a hat, too, but she'd given that to her local interpreter. He was just a kid, maybe eighteen, and jittery—partly from the cold and partly because he was scared of where they were headed. It was midday and not freezing, as Afghanistan could be in January, but a wind had whipped up. A foul smell carried: the garbage odor of death etched in Leaning's consciousness from her time as a physician in conflict zones from Kosovo to Somalia. It came from no specific direction. It was like the ground was rotten. Leaning, small under a vast gray sky, felt exposed. The desert here was flat, horizon to horizon; no place to hide. She edged forward, cautious, knowing the ground might be mined. The scene was unmistakable: against the surrounding desert, freshly churned soil stood out, dark and damp and crisscrossed with heavy tire marks. It was dotted with a strange harvest: tufts of black and white and cheerful red. It took Leaning a moment to realize what they were: turbans, clothes, and between them, flip-flops and prayer beads. She stopped cold: "There were fragments of skull. There were pieces of rib cage. Human bones." By her side, another investigator, John Heffernan, took a picture.

It was the beginning of 2002, in the remote north of Afghanistan. Leaning and Heffernan had been dispatched by the watchdog group Physicians for Human Rights to investigate the treatment of the prisoners of the new war on terror. Instead, they had stumbled into a deeper and more dangerous mystery, one which would fuel more than a decade of recrimination, land on the desks of some of the most powerful people in the world, and trigger a cover-up spanning two administrations. The investigators were staring down one of the earliest illustrations of the costs of a strain of post-9/11 foreign policy led not by diplomats, but by soldiers and spies. The unmarked grave was in part the product of American relationships with warlords that filled the void created by the sidelining of diplomats. The consequences were about more than human rights: in Afghanistan, American support for provincial despots would reshape the country, helping to create the conditions for the longest war in American history.

The investigators had no idea of any of that as they sought to measure the scale of the grave. War-crimes experts are trained not to eyeball body counts from afar, but it was clear that this was a large site: body after body, stretching as wide as a football field. As Heffernan took pictures, Leaning got out her notebook. She carried the black-and-white marbled kind favored by middle-school students. The stiff covers made them easy to balance on a knee in the field, and her messy handwriting fit in the wide lines. She didn't have much time for notes. They had only been there ten minutes when they saw the dust cloud on the horizon, and, emerging from it, the dark vehicles. There were four or five covered Jeeps or Toyota Land Cruisers, Leaning guessed at a distance, and they were heading their way fast.

Leaning and Heffernan scrambled back into their own weather-beaten Toyota. The interpreter looked ashen. Their driver, a grizzled man in his fifties, revved the engine. He, too, had been afraid of this part of the desert—he'd spent the drive there nervously glancing in his side mirrors, scanning the horizon. Now he slammed on his accelerator as the Jeeps gave chase, tailing the investigators as they crossed the barren half mile back to the provincial capital, Sheberghan. They didn't stop until they had put Sheberghan behind them, continuing east toward the larger regional hub of Mazar-i-Sharif. Leaning and Heffernan sat in tense silence during the drive. Everyone in the car suspected they'd dodged a bullet—or several.

The grave was within visual range of the stronghold of one of the most feared and mythologized warlords in modern Afghan history: a horseback-riding, sword-wielding Uzbek warrior named General Abdul Rashid Dostum. He had been an ally and a traitor to every side in the Cold War. In the months following the September 11 attacks, he was at the heart of the United States' new strategy in Afghanistan. Armed by the Americans and shadowed by special forces, his horse-back fighters toppled Taliban strongholds across the country's north. The prisoners the Physicians for Human Rights investigators were tracking had surrendered in Dostum's battles. And the Jeeps had pulled out from behind his gates.

FOURTEEN YEARS LATER, I stood in General Dostum's court, and stared at his reindeer, and tried not to act surprised. The reindeer seemed confused as to why he was there, and I must have seemed confused as to why the reindeer was there. But there he was, at least 200 pounds, one antler broken, thrashing against the rope around his face. I stepped out of the way to avoid getting impaled by an antler. As an attendant struggled to hold onto the other end of the rope, Dostum indicated to the deer with both hands, like Vanna White presenting a *Wheel of Fortune* prize. He beamed at the deer and then at me—a magnanimous smile that said "see, I brought a reindeer," as if this was the most normal way in the world to arrive at an interview. I pursed my lips for a moment. He was waiting for a response. "That's a beautiful animal, General," I said. You choose your words carefully in the courts of warlords, especially when they're flanked by men with M4 carbines slung across their chests. Plus, the antlers.

It was August 2016. General Dostum had by then gone from anti-American warlord, to American proxy fighter, to vice president of Afghanistan. He was a living embodiment of the militarization of American foreign policy: a warlord, who had, off the back of collaboration with the Americans, ascended to the very top of the new power structures created in his country by the United States. That night in 2016, we were in the Vice Presidential Palace in Kabul, which was like a cross between a James Bond villain's lair and Liberace's dressing room. Dostum had carpeted the entire place in live grass, and, as far as I could tell, wherever one could possibly fit a plant, he had attempted to do so. Hundreds of trees and bushes in mismatched terra-cotta planters crowded the place. Festooning every branch was a wild array of Christmas-tree lights, like someone had cleared out a section of Home Depot. There were the big bulbs that flashed in sequence, and the fake icicles that illuminated in a dripping pattern, and, everywhere, yards of rainbow rope light. You had to push through the foliage and lights to reach the seating area in the center, a dais with a mismatched collection of rattan patio chairs and leatherette La-Z-Boy recliners. Vases of fake flowers and Hummel-style porcelain statuettes of horseback soldiers stood on Louis XIV–style end tables. In a wicker cage, a fat chukar partridge clucked mournfully. There was, of course, a giant tank full of sharks. This was warlord chic.

Here is how one journalist described General Dostum: "Over six feet tall with bulging biceps . . . a bear of a man with a gruff laugh, which, some Uzbeks swear, has on occasion frightened people to death." (That reporter, Rashid Ahmed, claimed that shortly before he visited Dostum's stronghold in Northern Afghanistan, Dostum tied a soldier who had been caught stealing to the tracks of a Russian tank and drove him around until his body was reduced to a meat slurry, a charge Dostum later denied.) But Dostum was also, he reminded me frequently, an animal lover. "When people bring some birds, or some sheep, or some animals to be slaughtered, to eat, I tell them 'please take it away, take it. I don't want to kill this bird, this sheep, or this goat . . . ,'" he said, visibly moved. General Dostum was not an animal lover in the way you or I might be a cat person or a dog person. He was an animal lover as only a powerful Uzbek warlord could be, with a menagerie of hundreds of deer and horses and game birds. On at least one occasion on each day I spent with him, he would mention a horse or a deer being injured, and his eyes would fill with tears, and his lower lip would jut, like a child who had just been told the family hamster went on to a better place.

"It is very rare that I agree to give any interview for a journalist," General Dostum said in Uzbek through an adviser-slash-translator doing his best. A lot of the Uzbek language is formed in the back of the throat, and Dostum's delivery was particularly deep and throaty. He spoke in a lazy, slightly slurred drawl, like a tape played at half speed. "I have friends who are saying to do interview and so far I never agree to," he continued. His comments to the press had been limited to rare quotes given over the phone, and he'd sat down only with academics and adventurers who transcribed his legends into rapt panegyrics. "You're a good fellow from a friendly country, therefore I agreed to accept you here today," Dostum said, his eyes flicking up and down my person, regarding me with some suspicion.

But I had not come to tell the tale of General Dostum, or at least not in the way General Dostum seemed terrifyingly assured I would. I had come to Dostum's grass-carpeted palace in Kabul to ask about an unmarked grave at the ends of the earth.

ORIGINALLY, DOSTUM WAS JUST ABDUL RASHID, one of nine siblings, born to Uzbek peasants in the desert plains of Afghanistan's Jowzjan Province. The nom de guerre "Dostum"—literally, "my friend" in Uzbek—came later, as he marshaled power as a military commander. His family owned a simple, clay-brick home: three rooms, dirt floor, no electricity. Surviving in the desolation of Northern Afghanistan was a feat, and Dostum showed particular resilience. He claimed that, as an infant, he was once swept away by a flash flood of melting snow water, and clung to a branch, and survived, alone in the icy water. A villager eventually spotted his tiny hand above the waves and pulled him out. "What is this?!" Dostum intoned, theatrically channeling his rescuer. "Oh it is a hand of some baby!" The villager took him to a nearby mosque and held him upside down against a mud wall until water poured out and he regained consciousness.

Other childhood legends speak to a different quiddity: his constant flair for violence, starting with schoolyard scraps. "I was always fighting with the other kids," he conceded. "And still, I'm the same person." He paused, sounding, for a moment, a little rueful. "But, never in my life I attacked anyone else. When they attacked me, I defended myself."

His favorite pastime, then and since, was the ancestral Central Asian game of *buzkashi*, or "goat grabbing," in which fifteen horsemen brawl for control of a headless goat corpse they have to maneuver from a pole at one end of the field to a circle of chalk at the other. The game was famously violent and chaotic, with terrified stallions galloping and whinnying as players whipped, punched, and trampled each other. It was not unusual for referees to carry rifles to keep rowdy players in line. *Buzkashi* required "strong horses for a strong man," Dostum explained. Plus, he said, "I love horses. I have very good memories of horses." Once again, his eyes misted over. I said he'd have to teach me to play. He withheld his appraisal of my competitive prospects. The skeptical once-over he gave me didn't bode well. (Like Petraeus, Dostum correctly surmised my athletic prowess.) But he invited me to Sheberghan to watch. He warned gravely that his team had grown strong enough to best him on occasion. In his prime, Dostum was unbeatable.

Dostum spent brief stretches as an oil refinery worker, a plumber, and a wrestler, but war was his true discipline. He was conscripted into army service as a teenager and rose through the ranks, effortlessly mastering the low-tech cavalry combat of his ancestors. Later, he joined the Afghan army, staying aligned with them, and the Soviets, even as the anti-Soviet mujahedeen gained strength.

Those anti-Soviet fighters were, over the course of the 1980s, flooded with American money and guns. Ronald Reagan dubbed them "freedom fighters," and they became a cause célèbre for Americans gripped by red panic. A Texas socialite named Joanne Herring—all fake lashes and big hair and scriptural quotations—managed to goad her lover at the time, a louche alcoholic congressman named Charlie Wilson, into drumming up support on the Hill. At the peak of the pro-mujahedeen frenzy, Congress was allocating more money to the fighters than the CIA wanted. That many of the anti-Soviet mujahedeen were radical hard-liners was, at the time, a feature, not a bug. By the mid-1980s, the CIA was even commissioning local-language translations of the Quran, and paying to distribute them by the thousand behind Soviet lines. Milt Bearden, the CIA handler who brokered some of the relationships with the mujahedeen, defended that thinking years later. "Let's be clear about one thing: moderates never won anything," he told me. "Moderates. Don't. Win. Wars." The CIA was more concerned with small-scale tactical challenges. "You had to make things 'mooj proof,'" Bearden recalled of the equipment being dispersed. "So he couldn't put the pink wire on the green post and then screw it down and then BAM it blows him up!" He laughed thunderously. "A couple of guys got blown up, but they weren't suicides." Not then, anyway.

This was history that would echo uncannily after 9/11, when the United States again banked on the enemy's enemy to turn the tide. Even Joanne Herring cropped up again in that later era, bursting into the State Department in a cloud of perfume and hairspray during my time there. She was eighty, taut and tweaked and still "saving" Afghanistan, this time by soliciting hundreds of millions of dollars for a coalition of development groups she ran, dubbed the Marshall Plan Charities. She took me by the hand, and called me a "blessing," and had the diplomats of the South and Central Asia bureau join hands and pray before a meeting. Eyes pressed shut, she delivered an impassioned prayer to the Lord, and to the Commanders' Emergency Response Program funds she wanted. After she left, Holbrooke shook his head in disbelief and called her something too colorful to repeat here. When I asked Herring about her role in propping up the mujahedeen—in the view of some, laying the foundations for 9/11—she grew testy, saying the Stinger missiles provided to the fighters had a limited shelf life and her legacy ended with those.

When Aaron Sorkin's original script to *Charlie Wilson's War*, the Hollywood film of Herring's and Wilson's fight to rally support for the mujahedeen, ended on a shot of smoke coming out of the Pentagon on 9/11, Herring was reported to have had her lawyer saber rattle until it was changed. But the film still ends on a cautionary note: As the Soviets withdraw and Wilson celebrates, the CIA agent Gust Avrakotos tells the story of a Zen master who sees a young boy being given a horse and his village celebrating the blessing. "We'll see," says the Zen master. When the boy falls off the horse and breaks his leg, and the villagers declare the horse a curse, the master only offers another, "We'll see." Later, when war breaks out and the boy avoids conscription due to his injuries, the village celebrates the horse as a gift again. "We'll see," the Master says again. As Wilson takes in the implications, we hear a plane roar by overhead.

DOSTUM WAS NO RADICAL. But by the end of the Cold War, he had proved himself dangerous in other ways. His religion was survival, which he ensured through a dizzying succession of crosses and double-crosses. Even during his years commanding the most powerful unit in the Soviet-aligned army, he kept contact with the mujahedeen commanders on the other side of the battlefield, and mused openly about defecting to their cause. The pragmatism paid off—as the Soviet grip on Afghanistan weakened, Ahmed Shah Massoud, the favored son of the Americans among the mujahedeen, passed word to Dostum that the Soviet regime felt threatened by Dostum's growing popularity and was planning to force him out. Dostum crossed Moscow before Moscow could cross him, joining his 40,000 soldiers with the Islamist mujahedeen he had been fighting for years on the battlefield. The move proved decisive in tilting the balance of power against the Soviets.

After the Soviets pulled out, the former freedom fighters descended on Kabul and drenched it in blood. Dostum was on the frontlines—his militias were reported to be behind a campaign of rapes and executions. But when a new government began to take shape, he found himself frozen out. As ministerial positions were doled out to the other commanders, Dostum retreated to his fiefdom in the north, where his power diminished as the Taliban encroached. When his second-in-command betrayed him and defected to the Taliban in 1997, he fled the country altogether, to Turkey. By early 2001, though, Dostum was back, arraying his tattered forces against the Taliban. He would soon become an expedient solution to the United States' latest problem in Afghanistan.

AMERICA'S LIMITED OPTIONS in the region after 9/11, and the resulting decision to arm Dostum and his fellow warlords, were a direct result of a vacuum of diplomacy. By some combination of ideological opposition, inertia, and inattention, no one had sought a meaningful conversation for years with the medieval Taliban regime that had harbored bin Laden in Afghanistan. American officials did take a number of meetings with the Taliban over the course of the 1990s, but all were either perfunctory or focused on the narrow demand that the Taliban turn over bin Laden. Despite advocacy from supporters of dialogue like Robin Raphel, those meetings never evolved into anything resembling real negotiations. In early 2001, as the threat from the region became more dire, the United States did champion UN Security Council sanctions, entailing an arms ban and a freeze of Taliban assets. But it was all sticks, no carrots. Sanctions were not an attempt to bring the Taliban to the table; this was about breaking a brutal regime.

In the late 1990s, the United Nations briefly pushed broader regional dialogue that showed promise. Lakhdar Brahimi, the Algerian UN envoy to Afghanistan, maintained civil contact with the Taliban's second-in-command, Mullah Mohammed Rabbani, who was skeptical of his group's growing dependence on al-Qaeda and deepening bond with Osama bin Laden. A Taliban official even joined as an observer at 1999 talks in Tashkent, Uzbekistan between the Americans, Russians, and Afghanistan's six regional neighbors, to discuss a peaceful resolution to the country's civil conflict. But these efforts were swiftly overpowered by the United States' military alliance of choice in the region, with Pakistan. Just days after the countries at Tashkent agreed to stop arming the parties to the Afghan conflict, Pakistan worked with the Taliban to launch a major offensive against opposing military commanders.

After the September 11 attacks, opportunities for negotiated settlements were dismissed or undermined. When General Dostum's forces, working with the Americans, surrounded the Taliban stronghold of Kunduz, there was a three-day negotiation process, involving Dostum and more than a dozen American Special Forces officers and intelligence agents. Taliban who had peacefully surrendered were offered a generous deal: they could return to their villages safely in exchange for laying down arms, with the exception of targets of high intelligence value chosen by the Americans. In exchange, Dostum promised two Taliban generals, Mohammad Fazl and Nurullah Nuri, amnesty, which he publicly announced as a sign of wider reconciliation to come. But both commanders soon wound up at Guantánamo Bay. It was, for years, a subject of mystery and consternation for those following Afghanistan's descent into chaos. "Fazl and Nuri were by your side and you were promising them amnesty, then they end up in Guantánamo," I started to ask Dostum. He grunted. "Short question. I don't feel good."

"Did the Americans pressure you to turn them over?" I pressed.

Dostum laughed mightily. "I didn't surrender them to the United States forces. But they didn't take by force. They came to take them, and I told them, 'Listen, they're Taliban, they are Muslim. I am also Muslim, you are not Muslim. If I surrender them, if I give them to you I will be blamed. *'General Dostum is a Muslim but he gave the Taliban to the Americans. . . . '* It would damage my credibility. . . . Bush was talking on the TV about how to approach prisoners . . . " he said, referring to early comments about respecting the Geneva Conventions. "Then the military people came and said, 'Listen, we have to implement the order, I don't care what Bush says. If I want to take them, I will take them.'" Dostum shrugged. He was wiggling his knees, restless. "I

Junior political officer Thomas Countryman reviews cables (and models an
early prototype of his celebrated mullet) at his desk at the US embassy in
Belgrade in 1985. (COURTESY OF THOMAS COUNTRYMAN)

Countryman, then principal deputy assistant secretary of state for political-military affairs, surveys landmine removal efforts in Afghanistan in May 2010. (STATE DEPARTMENT PHOTO)

Robin Raphel—then Robin Lynn Johnson—shares a moment with two of her students at Damavand College for Women, around 1971. (COURTESY OF ROBIN RAPHEL)

Raphel boards a Pakistani army helicopter after a visit to the site of a planned dam in Gilgit–Baltistan, Pakistan, in October 2010. (COURTESY OF JONATHAN PECCIA)

Raphel takes notes as Richard Holbrooke has a pensive moment during a breakfast with Pakistani parliamentarians at the Serena Hotel in Islamabad in 2010. "He's a classic bully," Raphel recalled of Holbrooke. "But I liked him because he wanted to get something done and was right-minded and wasn't a wuss." (COURTESY OF MORGAN J. O'BRIEN III)

Richard Holbrooke, as was so often the case, with a book in hand, during his early years as a Foreign Service officer in southeast Asia in 1963. (COURTESY OF KATI MARTON)

From left: Christopher Hill, who would later go on to lead North Korea talks; Secretary of State Warren Christopher; Holbrooke; President of Bosnia and Herzegovina Alija Izetbegovic; and Serbian President Slobodan Miloševic pore over maps of disputed territory in Holbrooke's quarters at Wright-Patterson Air Force Base during the Dayton negotiations in 1995. (COURTESY OF KATI MARTON)

Richard Holbrooke and his Office of the Special Representative for Afghanistan and Pakistan (SRAP) team in the courtyard of the State Department in 2009. To his immediate right are me, communications director Ashley Bommer, and scholars Barnett Rubin and Vali Nasr. (COURTESY OF MORGAN J. O'BRIEN III)

From left: Holbrooke, SRAP military liaisons Colonel Doug Rose and Colonel Brian Lamson, and I meet with General William B. Caldwell (pictured from behind), the commander of the NATO training mission for Afghan forces, in Kabul in 2010. (COURTESY OF MORGAN J. O'BRIEN III)

Husain Haqqani, at the time the spokesperson for Pakistani Prime Minister Benazir Bhutto, looks on as Bhutto delivers remarks in Islamabad in 1994, in a photo she later signed for him. (COURTESY OF HUSAIN HAQQANI)

Haqqani whispers in Richard Holbrooke's ear as Secretary of State Hillary Clinton announces aid projects at Pakistan's foreign ministry, in Islamabad, in 2010. "He was frustrated," Haqqani recalled of Holbrooke's outlook that year. "He was frustrated with the fact that for some people, it was less important to get things done, and more important who did them." (B.K. BANGASH / AP / REX / SHUTTERSTOCK)

Human bones litter the freshly bulldozed earth in a photo taken by John Heffernan minutes after he and fellow Physicians for Human Rights investigator Dr. Jennifer Leaning discovered the mass grave in Afghanistan's Dasht-i-Leili desert in January 2002. The area, Leaning recalled, smelled "rotten, messy, foul," like "disturbed garbage." (JOHN HEFFERNAN / PHYSICIANS FOR HUMAN RIGHTS)

Dr. Jennifer Leaning interviews detainees at Sheberghan prison in northern Afghanistan in January 2002. "They were very sick," she said, "very thin."
(JOHN HEFFERNAN / PHYSICIANS FOR HUMAN RIGHTS)

General Abdul Rashid Dostum and US Special Forces meet with surrendered Taliban and al-Qaeda detainees at Sheberghan prison on December 1, 2001. (COPYRIGHT ROBERT YOUNG PELTON)

General Dostum looks on as one of his beloved deer thrashes in the receiving hall of the Vice Presidential Palace in Kabul, in August 2016. (PHOTO BY RONAN FARROW)

General Dostum (right) prepares to host a match of *kurash*, a Central Asian martial art, at the Vice Presidential Palace in Kabul in August 2016. I take notes (centre), wearing a traditional Uzbek *chapan*, or cloak, for the occasion at Dostum's request. (COURTESY OF THE OFFICE OF VICE PRESIDENT DOSTUM)

Thomas Evans (left, then sixteen years old), his mother Sally (centre), and his brother Micheal (right, then fourteen) pose for a picture at Trafalgar Square in London in 2006, long before Thomas left home. Thomas was "very caring," Sally remembered. "I've no idea how he became that person he became."
(COURTESY OF MICHEAL EVANS)

After delivering a speech on youth and democracy in February 2012, Hillary Clinton looks out at the Mediterranean from a Tunisia newly roiled by revolution and skeptical of American alliances in the region. (PHOTO BY RONAN FARROW)

Protestors hold up a tear gas canister manufactured by Jamestown, Pennsylvania–based Combined Systems Inc. and used by Egyptian security forces against crowds of civilians during the Rabaa massacre in Cairo in August 2013. (COPYRIGHT TEO BUTTURINI)

Freddy Torres prepares for another long haul in the cab of the Chevrolet Isuzu FRR he uses to transport fruit, including *tamarillos* and *lulos*, across Colombia in 2018. (COURTESY OF FREDDY TORRES)

Secretary of State Rex Tillerson (centre) talks to former Secretaries George P. Shultz (right) and Condoleezza Rice (left) at an event at Stanford University in January 2018. (STATE DEPARTMENT PHOTO)

Christopher Hill (left) and Richard Holbrooke (right) pal around on one of their many flights to Belgrade as they worked toward a negotiated end to the Bosnian War in September 1995. Hill recalled "learning the trade from Holbrooke, like an apprentice watching a master carpenter."(COURTESY OF CHRISTOPHER HILL)

Christopher Hill dons a hazardous materials suit and enters the Yongbyon nuclear power plant in North Korea in the fall of 2007. The regime in Pyongyang had begun deactivating and dismantling the plant, abiding by the terms of the six-party talks that Hill led. (COURTESY OF CHRISTOPHER HILL)

Secretary of State John Kerry and the team of American diplomats behind the Iran deal (left) negotiate with Foreign Minister Mohammed Javad Zarif and the Iranians (right) in the Palais Coburg's Blue Salon in Vienna in 2015. (STATE DEPARTMENT PHOTO)

said 'OK, whatever you want.'" In the early months of the war in Afghanistan, that same dynamic played out repeatedly, including in Kandahar, where Hamid Karzai's attempts at reconciliation were overruled by Donald Rumsfeld, who bristled at the thought of dealing with the Taliban.

That the United States shunned negotiation with the Taliban in favor of military action in the immediate aftermath of the attacks was little surprise. To suggest diplomacy over force in dealing with the regime that harbored the perpetrators of the 9/11 attack was akin politically to proposing a national program of cannibalism in public schools. But that recalcitrance continued long after the Taliban had been thwarted on the battlefield. There was never a concerted effort to embed military gains in a larger strategic context, and, for years, there was no political space to acknowledge what had become obvious: that the total defeat and elimination of the Taliban was not possible and that, barring that, peace would only come through diplomacy.

Instead, in the weeks after the terrorists plunged hijacked planes into America's centers of power and its consciousness, the debate over how to respond took place almost entirely within the military and intelligence community. There were those, like the CIA station chief in Islamabad at the time, who wanted to continue to work solely through the United States' military alliance with Pakistan, using the Pakistanis to pressure the Taliban regime they had for years supported to surrender Osama bin Laden. Others, back in the CIA's Counterterrorism Center in Washington, had a simpler suggestion: give American guns to anyone who could fight the Taliban. Before any coherent policy could be developed across the US government, that latter faction began quietly executing its proposal. And "anyone who could fight the Taliban" meant the warlords and brigands of the Northern Alliance.

Robin Raphel, who had fought long and hard for negotiation with the Taliban, despaired at the choice. "We didn't need to be fighting [the Taliban] . . . they realized who we were and the power that we had. They wanted to go home. And we wouldn't have it . . . we were the tough guys, right?" She rolled her eyes. "And we rode in with the Northern Alliance on donkeys . . . it was such nonsense. Sorry, but it was."

In December, 2001, the United Nations led a halfhearted attempt to build a new Afghan government, culminating in talks in Bonn, Germany. The Taliban—the vanquished party and an indispensable part of any sustainable political settlement—was absent from the talks. The conference was instead dominated by the Northern Alliance fighters the Americans had chosen to rely on in their initial military offensives. For the diplomats who had pushed for dialogue, it was an elementary failure. "I said from the beginning, that they"—the Taliban— "should've been at Bonn," Raphel later told me. "That was our biggest mistake." Barnett Rubin, who was part of the UN team that organized the talks and had a desk near mine in Holbrooke's State Department offices, often told me that exclusion had far-reaching repercussions. "The Bonn Agreement did make Afghan government and politics more inclusive, but it could not overcome US counterterrorism policy, which dictated the exclusion of the Taliban," he later wrote.

Immediately after the talks concluded, Taliban leaders even reached out to newly installed Afghan interim president Hamid Karzai to offer a truce in exchange for amnesty—an offer that was immediately overruled by Donald Rumsfeld and the Americans. Taliban leaders who swore fealty to the new central government and returned to their villages were hunted down and captured, often by Northern Alliance warlords.

These new foot soldiers in America's war on terror made for an unpleasant rogue's gallery. Abdul Sayyaf, a former mentor to Osama bin Laden, had helped establish the training camps in Pakistan and Afghanistan that formed the bedrock of modern Islamist terrorism and was behind a bloody massacre of Shiite Hazaras during the struggle for Kabul after the Cold War. Burhanuddin Rabbani's forces, working with Sayyaf's, were accused of slaughtering the elderly, children, even dogs during that siege. Mohammad Mohaqiq and his men were implicated in murders, rapes, and systematic looting in the months after 9/11. His militias' trademark: kidnapping young girls and forcing them into marriage. Atta Mohammed Noor's militias were behind a campaign of looting and rapes targeting ethnic Pashtuns in the same period. And then there was Atta's rival in countless bloody skirmishes: Abdul Rashid Dostum.

WHEN AND HOW Dostum started working with the Americans was a matter of some dispute. Hank Crumpton, the CIA official who, as head of the agency's newly formed Special Activities Division, oversaw the initial response to September 11, later told me that the agency had been developing its relationship with the warlord for some time before 9/11, working through an Uzbek-fluent agent named Dave Tyson. Dostum insisted that Tyson only got in touch after the attacks. What's not disputed is that a CIA team came, and then a unit of Green Berets from the Army's 5th Special Forces Group, code-named "595." It was a peculiar union. "Dust kind of settles. And out of the dust comes the sand people," Team Sergeant Paul Evans recalled. "[Y]ou see a man with an AK who's dressed just like your enemy, and you've gotta walk over to him and basically ask him, 'Hey, how ya doing?' and you have no idea whether he's gonna put out his hand or shoot you." One of those "sand people" was General Dostum. "General Dostum and his advanced security party come ridin' up," said Captain Mark Nutsch. "He jumps down off the horse and—"

"Hell the horse was still moving and he jumps off! He's like 'heyyyy,'" interjected Chief Warrant Officer Bob Pennington, making an expansive gesture.

"—General Dostum agreed to take my team members and I up to his forward command post," Nutsch went on. "So we would mount horses for the first time in combat."

An Air Force controller who joined several days later to coordinate strikes from Lockheed AC-130 gunships and asked to be identified only by his first name, Bart, said the effect was like a time machine. "You're like, 'What year am I in?!' You just got off a twenty-first-century helicopter, sophisticated avionics and everything else on it, and now we've gone back in time." He and the other Americans rode horses while supplies were strapped to donkeys led by Afghans. They slept in a series of frozen mountain caves, with only candles and flashlights to cut through the pitch black, so far from any city lights. "When you rode a horse through the mountains, the stars felt like they were right there in your face," Bart went on. "You were riding into the stars. It was something else." Most of all, he remembered Dostum's stature, both in his literal physical size, and in terms of the reverence he commanded. "Ohhh, he was *the man*," he told me. "He was *the* leader. . . . Those Northern Alliance guys would set his tent up and he would have these pillow beds in there. . . . They carried those on donkey for him. . . . He was laying in comfort. We were laying in a ditch."

The Americans air-dropped supplies, chief among them hundreds of guns. Not the sophisticated weaponry carried by the Americans, but aging Russian Kalashnikovs. Cash came, but, Dostum sniffed, less than he needed. He was most offended when the Americans air-dropped food for his horses and the bags turned out to contain chaff. It was theoretically edible for livestock, but his horses refused to touch it. "United States is such a great country," Dostum said, chuckling. "Such a great people, but why is it so hard for them to give money?"

There were more consequential challenges born of working with the warlords. Bart and the other Americans pulled watches to make sure they were always guarding their own. And there were headaches back at Langley. "David [Tyson, the CIA operative] was with Dostum but we also had Atta [Mohammed Noor] and one of the challenges we had was keeping those guys from killing each other," conceded Hank Crumpton wearily. "These guys are warriors. They've been killing people all their lives, in one of the worst places on the planet." Still, most of the Americans were won over. "He had almost a boyish charm to him," Crumpton said of Dostum. "Had a good sense of humor which I know masked a pretty ruthless capability. But I honestly enjoyed the conversation with him." Mostly, he said, he felt thankful "for his partnership and for his leadership and what he and Atta and others accomplished on the battlefield."

WHAT THEY ACCOMPLISHED on the battlefield was, in immediate, tactical terms, an overwhelming success. Bombing began in October, and over the course of November, the Northern Alliance warlords routed the Taliban from Mazar-i-Sharif, in Afghanistan's north, and then Kabul, and then Kunduz in the northeast, where the Taliban surrendered after a twelve-day siege. With each success came more prisoners of war. Some of these men were hardened fighters who had traveled from Pakistan and the Gulf States to join Osama bin Laden. But many others were ordinary Afghan men and boys; foot soldiers for a regime that had medieval values but little interest in the global jihad of the Saudi rich-kid zealot it safeguarded. In late November, General Dostum and the Americans in Nutsch's unit toppled Kunduz, a last redoubt for thousands of Taliban fighters. As many as 3,500 surrendered peacefully, by one US military estimate. The full count of prisoners was rumored to be twice that.

The detainees were peeled off into separate groups. According to Bart, the Air Force controller, some were taken to a black site, "another location which I can't talk about." The vast majority were taken west by Dostum's forces. Some were sent directly from a surrender point in the desert outside Kunduz to the prison at Dostum's headquarters in Sheberghan. Others were sent to a different prison, a nineteenth-century fortress called Qala-i-Jangi, to be interrogated by the Americans. Qala-i-Jangi's high, muddied battlements had overlooked centuries of conflicts involving occupying forces, from the British to the Soviets. It was about to become the site of America's first casualty in the new war on terror.

The prisoners at the fort rose up in a spectacular ambush, overpowering their American interrogators and killing one CIA agent, Mike Spann. A bloody three-day siege followed. Dostum, who had been at Kunduz, returned along with Mark Nutsch and the other members of Team 595 to find an apocalyptic tableau of twisted metal and shredded bodies. "The bodies. . . . " Dostum recalled, shaking his head. "They couldn't recognize who was my soldier, who was al-Qaeda, who was Taliban." Both the Americans and the Northern Alliance fighters were shaken by the loss of life and bitterly angry at the Taliban prisoners. "I was crying for my horses," Dostum went on, his voice breaking. Later, when Red Cross workers discovered one of those horses alive, "I was just crying from happiness. . . . And I ordered my people to take him right away to the hospital for treatment." He named the horse *K'okcha,* or blueish, and eventually took to riding it in battle himself. For the Americans, the first US casualty of the new war made for "a very painful realization [of] the price we paid for going very fast with very few people on the ground," said Crumpton, the CIA official. "Also it opens up a question of who has responsibility for prisoners of war." That question was tested almost immediately, as Dostum's men loaded the survivors from Qala-i-Jangi into trucks and transported them west again, to join the rest of the prisoners in Sheberghan.

By January 2002, questions about the fate of these detainees were bleeding across Afghanistan's borders and into international headlines. When Jennifer Leaning and John Heffernan arrived that month, even the Red Cross—generally a vault about anything they've witnessed to maintain impartiality and access to prisoners in need—seemed to be raising flags. "Go north," a Red Cross lawyer in Kabul urged them. Leaning pressed her: "You mean the prisoners from Kunduz?" The lawyer nodded. "That was all we got, but it was enough," recalled Heffernan. The investigators made their way to the prison, a squat fort with peeling white paint on its clay brick walls and rusted metal bars securing its windows. International visitors had not, thus far, been welcome at the site. One early attempt to gain access by the Red Cross was barred by two American military officers, according to multiple accounts given to Leaning and Heffernan. But they were able to build rapport with a warden who was troubled by what he was witnessing inside the prison's weather-beaten walls and quietly let them in.

They quickly found confirmation of the rumors they had already heard. Through Pakistani translators, prisoners told anguished stories of starvation, overcrowding, and a mounting death toll. They pleaded for food, water, and medical attention. But Leaning and Heffernan noticed something else: the numbers didn't add up. "The number of people held in the prison at Sheberghan was not the number of people we heard were captured in Kunduz," she told me. "As many as seven to eight thousand had supposedly been captured. We saw perhaps three thousand being held. The question was, 'Where are the rest?.'" It was that question that led the investigators to the Dasht-i-Leili desert the next day, and to the corpses, possibly thousands.

What happened to the missing prisoners? How did these men and boys end up in such a tomb, in such a place? And, a question no one inside the US government wanted to touch for more than a decade after: What did Americans on the ground know and see as the earth was moved and the grave was filled with body after body? We made a deal with Dostum for the territory he could take for us, for the blood he could spill of enemies we shared. What was the price? What did we give up when we shook his hand? How did all the talk of smaller footprints and partner forces hold up against a femur sticking out of the dirt? These were familiar ethical quandaries in America's national-security-sensitive alliances. But, like the smell in the desert, they had become unusually hard to ignore here.

IN THE YEARS AFTER the investigators discovered the grave in the desert, the alliances with warlords reshaped Afghanistan. Anti-Soviet mujahedeen fighters armed by the Americans, who had turned into Northern Alliance commanders armed by the Americans, finally turned into governors and ministers installed by the Americans—or at least with their tacit assent and minimal grumbling. Atta Moham-med Noor, as governor of Balkh province, handed out parcels of land to loyalists and grew fabulously wealthy taking cuts of the province's customs revenue. His militias were implicated in sundry thuggery from murder to kidnapping to extortion. Ismael Khan, who became governor of Herat and then minister of water and energy, was accused of harassing ethnic Pashtuns and withholding provincial revenue from the government. A commander named Mir Alam became chief of police in the Baghlan province and developed a reputation for his spectacular corruption and support for drug mafias. A 2006 US embassy cable concluded that Alam and another commander "contin-ued to act as mujahedin commanders rather than professional police officers . . . abus[ing] their positions of authority to engage in a broad range of criminal activity, including extortion, bribery and drug traf-ficking." The governor of Nangahar province, Gul Agha Sherzai, wreaked similar havoc there—from murder, to drug trafficking, to corruption benefiting his tribe.

And then there was General Dostum, who served as deputy

defense minister before eventually becoming vice president. Robert
Finn, the first US ambassador in Kabul after 9/11, struggled with the
warlords, especially Dostum and Atta, who were frequently at each
other's throats. It made for a stark parable: the two warlords were sitting on oil reserves that had produced hundreds of millions of dollars
in revenues during the Soviet era and could easily have been exploited
for Afghan reconstruction better, and earlier. "I tried to talk Dostum
and Atta into becoming rich people. . . . " Finn recalled. "But they'd
rather kill each other over cows." So it went with opportunities to
rebuild Afghanistan.

Many of these men had been paid by the Americans for decades.
Some traded tattered fatigues for slick suits as they grew rich off of drug
deals, but most continued to behave as they always had: as warlords.
Only now, they were warlords ruling with the imprimatur of a central
government backed by the United States, and a steady stream of lucrative
international contracts to skim from. Finn came to believe the warlords
were at the heart of many of Afghanistan's broader problems. "Ministries
were initially handed out to different warlords and they started running
them as their fiefdoms, so that was a problem," he told me.

But the warlords were hard to shake, in some cases because of their
tenacious grip on local power structures, and in some cases because
there had never been a serious effort to empower alternatives. Often,
the choice the Americans were left with was rule by warlord or complete chaos. Atta, for instance, led one of the most stable provinces
in the country—pushing him out was the last thing on the minds
of the Americans. "I think we should have worked ourselves away
from them," Finn reflected years later. "I understand what happened.
We went in and said, 'Okay who can we get to help us?' . . . but that
doesn't mean you stick with them forever. I think we have stuck with
them too long. Once they're there it's difficult to get rid of them."

The United States' inability to reshape its relationships in
Afghanistan—to forge a new set of bonds with civilian politicians who

might counterbalance the entrenched culture of warlordism—reflected a deeper ill. America's objectives in Afghanistan had turned from conquest to development. But the diplomatic muscle had atrophied. The consequences of shuttered embassies and a withered Foreign Service around the world had come to a head in America's most important war: there weren't enough diplomats, and those in service didn't have the resources or the experience needed to tackle Afghanistan. "There wasn't the background of experience," Finn said. "Diplomats were all there for a very short period, so they learn anew every year. The people that were there over time"—people like Dostum and the other warlords—"they know how to use the Americans. They know exactly what to say and what the Americans would want them to say."

THE WARLORDS' FOOTHOLDS in those American-backed power structures bedeviled efforts to create accountability. The mystery of Dostum's missing prisoners was a prime example. Two successive American presidents effectively evaded questions about the matter. The Bush administration quashed at least three efforts to investigate the grave, across multiple agencies. An FBI agent at Guantánamo Bay began hearing stories about a mass killing from other Taliban prisoners who had survived, but was told to stand down and leave the matter to the military. The Pentagon, in turn, conducted only a brief "informal inquiry," asking members of Team 595 if they had seen anything, then issuing a blanket denial. There was, one senior Pentagon official recalled later, "little appetite for this matter within parts of DOD." At the State Department, Colin Powell assigned the investigation to Ambassador at Large for War Crimes Pierre Prosper, who quickly saw opposition from both Afghan and American officials. "They would say, 'We have had decades of war crimes. Where do you start?'" he recalled. His office later dropped the inquiry.

When President Obama entered office, there was renewed hope.

During a CNN interview in 2009, he went off script to promise an investigation. "It seems clear that the Bush administration resisted efforts to pursue investigations of an Afghan warlord named General Dostum, who was on the CIA payroll. It's now come out, there were hundreds of Taliban prisoners under his care who got killed . . . " Anderson Cooper began gamely. "Right," said President Obama. Cooper mentioned the mystery of the mass grave and asked if Obama would call for an investigation into possible war crimes.

"Yeah," said the president. "The indications that this had not been properly investigated just recently was brought to my attention. So what I've asked my national security team to do is to collect the facts for me that are known. And we'll probably make a decision in terms of how to approach it once we have all the facts gathered up."

"But you wouldn't resist categorically an investigation?" Cooper pressed.

"I think that, you know, there are responsibilities that all nations have even in war. And if it appears that our conduct in some way supported violations of the laws of war, then I think that, you know, we have to know about that."

But no one at the Obama White House wanted to touch the issue either. As the State Department official charged with communicating with nongovernmental groups, I was on the receiving end of some of the calls from groups like Physicians for Human Rights. Again and again I pressed White House staff to disclose something, anything; to allow me to convene a meeting about the grave and at least listen, if not talk. The response was always the same: no comment, no meetings. "I spent all day on the phone with the NSC having them tell me to stall meetings we had set up with human rights groups because they're afraid of questions about the Dasht-i-Leili massacre and don't want to cop to the fact that we've completely abandoned POTUS's promise to investigate," I wrote to Holbrooke's communications director, Ashley Bommer, in March 2010. In a briefing document prepared the same month, there was a bullet point under my outreach to human rights groups: "Dasht-i-Leili w/ Physicians for Human Rights (working with NSC to formulate a clearer position)." In another memo I filed ten months later, the sentence had not changed.

Frustrated with the executive branch's obstructions, human rights groups tried turning to Congress. In early 2010, another Physicians for Human Rights investigator, Nathaniel Raymond, received testimony from a former translator for American forces at Kunduz and Qala-i-Jangi who had gone on to secure asylum in the United States. He claimed to have witnessed what happened to the prisoners—and whether Americans were present. Raymond brought the information to the Senate Foreign Relations Committee and its lead investigator at the time, former CIA agent John Kiriakou, who was later sentenced to thirty months in prison for disclosing the identity of a fellow CIA officer (he has maintained that this was a principled act of whistleblowing on the government's use of torture in the Global War on Terrorism). He considered the story about the grave to be explosive. According to Kiriakou, the reaction from his superiors, including committee chair John Kerry, was explosive too—and not what he expected. "The Staff Director at the time, Frank [Lowenstein], got wind of it and called me into his office and said 'cease and desist immediately.'" Stunned, Kiriakou claimed he took the matter to Kerry directly. "Kerry came down to the office afterwards and said, 'What is this I'm hearing about Afghanistan?'" said Kiriakou. "I told him . . . and he said, 'You've spoken to Frank?' And I said, 'Yeah, Frank called me in and said to kill it.' He said, 'Ok.' I got up and said, 'So what do I do?' And he said, 'You kill it.' I said, 'Alright, I'll kill it.' And that was the end of it."

Kiriakou saw it as a pragmatic call on Kerry's and Lowenstein's part. "Frank devoted his life to protecting John Kerry, and John Kerry wanted nothing more in the world than to be secretary of state. And so, we just couldn't risk any kerfuffle, even if it was historical in nature, anything controversial, so he killed it. It was a shame. I was very disappointed." Kerry said, "I've never heard anything about this—ever," and maintained that he "never pulled punches" on Afghan human rights during his time on the committee. Frank Lowenstein at first similarly denied having any recollection of the conversations with Kiriakou, then later suggested that "[Kiriakou] might have interpreted . . . or he might have come away from our conversation with the impression that that wasn't something that I was particularly interested in pursuing, but I certainly never would have told him to kill it."

In that interview in 2009, President Obama had pledged to open a new inquiry into the massacre. Four years later, after intermittent refusals to comment to reporters, the White House quietly acknowledged that an investigation had been completed, but would remain sealed. A spokesperson mentioned a finding that no US personnel were involved. The White House otherwise declined to elaborate. "It's cowardice," Raymond told me. "I was interviewed by the NSC as part of the investigation. It went nowhere because it wasn't what they wanted to hear."

Physicians for Human Rights, through sheer tenacity, did eventually secure a handful of meetings with senior officials. The group also sent more than a dozen letters to officials across the government. Neither tack produced clarity. The consequences were real and specific: after an initial series of forensic missions, and before additional teams could return for a full excavation, the mass grave disappeared. In 2008, a UN team found, where the site had been, a series of large holes—and none of the bodies that had been previously documented. It was exactly the eventuality human rights advocates had been fighting to prevent. "From square one," said Susannah Sirkin of Physicians for Human Rights, "we realized if anything leaked the site would very likely be destroyed." It did leak, and world powers did nothing to protect the evidence. "There is now a second layer of violation," Sirkin told me. "The literal obstruction of investigation and suppression of information by [the US government]." My inability to cut through that indifference weighed on me. When I set out for Kabul, years later, I was determined to come back with answers.

FOR ALMOST FIFTEEN YEARS, General Dostum never sat for a detailed interview on the missing prisoners and the mass grave. But after months of conversation, he warmed to the idea of an audience with me. Securing an interview with General Dostum involves a lot of waiting. There was a year of conversations with his advisers who travel on his behalf in New York and Washington, all of them loyal Uzbek Afghans, some of them younger men from Dostum's Sheberghan stronghold, who grew up steeped in legends of his heroism. There were introductions to his young sons, Batur, who was being groomed for a career in politics, and Babur, who was in the Afghan Air Force. And then there was a sudden call. Could I be on a flight to Kabul the next day? General Dostum would see me. I agreed, then crafted an email to a dear friend whose wedding the next night I'd have to miss as a result. Diplomacy in that region is ongoing.

Arriving in Kabul on the appointed day, General Dostum did not see me. General Dostum was tired. General Dostum, an adviser informed me gravely, *had a cold*. I waited, like Gay Talese at a nightclub. I strolled the dusty streets of Kabul. I drove through security checkpoints to the bunker-like US embassy for meetings with American officials. I sipped coffee with Dostum's advisers in the gardens of Kabul's Serena hotel, in sweltering late August heat. Eventually, they asked if I would join a meeting between General Dostum and women's rights activists from across Afghanistan. This was central to what Dostum wished to communicate to me and, by extension, the Western world. He, unlike some of the other holdovers from the Cold War, had a more progressive view of women. "I'm probably among the very limited people in Afghanistan who are strongly committed to the rights of women, to protect women," Dostum later told me.

This conviction appeared to be sincere, and he repeated it often over several days of interviews. But General Dostum did not show up for the meeting with the women's activists, either. An adviser presented me instead. A dozen formidable women had gathered in a cavernous government meeting hall, under a mural inscribed with a verse from the Quran: "Never will Allah change the condition of a people until they change it themselves." Each had a personal appeal, from the teacher who begged for better wages to the lawyer who called for more women in government. At the first mention of the vice president's absence, whispers of surprise and disappointment ran through the room. A doctor, who had traveled several hours from the Logar province, left in tears.

By the time I finally got the call telling me that General Dostum was ready, it was late at night. Once I had made my way through the layers of barricades and armed guards to the golden gates of the Vice Presidential Palace, there was another hour of waiting in his strange, grass-carpeted parlor. When General Dostum entered the room, it was 10 p.m.

The feared warrior was now in his sixties. His hair had thinned and whitened, and his gut had expanded prodigiously. But he was still imposing: a slab of a man, built like a refrigerator. His attire—Western jackets over flowing Uzbek robes, accentuated his size. He lumbered into the room and slumped into an ornate throne with a high, carved-wood back and gold upholstery dusted with fleurs-de-lis. Dostum's eyes, narrow under Asian epicanthic folds, reflected his ancestry, which he claimed could be traced back to Genghis Khan, who got around after all.

Dostum rubbed his eyes and yawned. The much-discussed cold may well have been real, but others, including a former American ambassador to Afghanistan, said the general's late starts were attributable to something else. "He continues to have an extremely violent temper, he's an alcoholic, he is nonfunctional," that ambassador alleged. "He needs to leave the country to dry out more than he can be here." Through several of our meetings, Dostum nursed an undisclosed beverage out of an ostentatious designer mug stamped with a gold and rhinestone–crusted Chanel logo. I wondered if his previous meeting had been with the Kardashians or something.

"I don't know why sometimes the media don't express the reality," Dostum was grumbling. I had hit "record" on my phone, and a handler had immediately asked that I stop. A minor fuss had ensued when I'd insisted I continue. Dostum glanced at the phone unhappily. "Unfortunately, nowadays, sometimes journalists, *New York Times*, they wrote so many things." He frowned, that same wounded look crossing his face. "'*He massacred, human rights, he killed Taliban prisoners, he did this or that.*' My American friends from the CIA and other people, they came to my house and they said, 'Listen, they are portraying you in the United States this way, but we know you are a different person.'"

General Dostum was not wrong about his portrayal in the Western press. Human rights groups had brought well-documented charges of mass atrocities and murders against Dostum dating back to the 1990s. Press reports blamed him for violent reprisals against political rivals and their families—and even, on occasion, allies who strayed from loyalty. Human Rights Watch had, just days before I sat down with Dostum, accused his Junbish militias of murdering and assaulting civilians under the guise of anti-Taliban operations. Even Afghan president Ashraf Ghani—who selected Dostum as his running mate to exploit his status as a "vote bank," commanding enduring popularity among Afghanistan's ethnic Uzbeks—once called Dostum a "known killer." The US State Department had echoed Ghani, calling Dostum "the quintessential warlord," and then went a step further and denied him a visa to travel to the United States.

The root of the criticism, he insisted, was political. "Our opponents . . . they fabricate a lot of things against us to give a wrong picture to the American public," he said. The charge that he had assaulted political rivals was, he added, "a very unfair allegation. It's a political motivation. The reason why is first, I have risen from a very deprived ethnic group. The second, I was from a poor family. Third, I had a vision for Afghanistan. I wanted justice, decentralized system, federalized system, all the people in Afghanistan including my people should have the same rights. So therefore they started blaming me unfairly." The same, he said, was true of the alleged rampages of his forces. "I went to the northern part of Afghanistan and we fought alongside Afghan security forces to provide security for the provinces. People were so happy, we've done so many good things for the people!" He frowned again. "But instead of appreciating and saying thank you . . . they started again these political allegations. . . . I believe that even Human Rights Watch and other human rights organizations are not just pure human rights organizations, they are also political . . . they fabricate what they want against you."

The visa denial seemed to have stung on a personal level for Dostum, who still regarded the Americans who armed him against the Taliban as blood brothers. "I believe I have been betrayed by my American friends . . . we fought together, and after all these things, it's a betrayal. But still the United States does not have another strong friend like Dostum, they don't have it." The Americans, he felt, had used him, "like tissue paper." Indignant, he rattled off a list of friends who still stood by him, which included various military officials, an NYPD commissioner, Arnold Schwarzenegger, and Hillary Clinton, with whom he claimed to have bonded over women's rights. "Ms. Clinton, by then she was senator, she visited Kabul, they invited me. . . . I told the story of that American lady who was coordinating the air force operation in Kunduz, then she laughed and said you should come to the United States and you should share this story with female pilots there." He paused, eyeing me again. "So she also invited me to visit the United States," he repeated, in case I hadn't gotten that part. (When Clinton came to Kabul for Hamid Karzai's inauguration, Richard Holbrooke had swooped in to prevent her from shaking

Dostum's hand.) In any case, the father of a slain CIA agent had given him a key to the city of Winfield, Alabama. "I don't need any visa," Dostum sniffed. "I have the key, I can go anytime I want!"

Still, Dostum appeared to realize that his image was in need of renovation. "It's our fault we couldn't tell the American public what kind of good friend to the United States we are." He sighed. For him, the real story had always been simple. "You have a strong, bad enemy like al-Qaeda who is terrorizing your people and also you have a strong and good friend like Dostum, who is ready to fight against your enemy and avenge the blood of your people who innocently were killed in the United States." Dostum, like an Afghan Bob Dole, referred to himself in third person a lot. "We're partners," he went on. "We fought against the same enemy for a good cause."

This was General Dostum as seen by himself, or at least how he hoped reporters like me would see him: a misunderstood champion of his people. He was an animal lover who wept over injured deer. A warlord with a heart of gold. The people's warlord! He was even, briefly, a fitness guru, responsible for "Fitness for All"—the Kabul equivalent of Michelle Obama's "Let's Move!" "When he needed to fight he did that, but now we need peace and he is doing this," a security guard at the palace told reporters when the program rolled out. "It will encourage the young to start doing sports when they see the vice president exercising every morning." Behind him, General Dostum, clad in athleisure, did jumping jacks. Photos of Dostum huffing and puffing his way through aerobics sessions, overlaid with Dari slogans, were "liked" by thousands of loyal followers on his official Facebook page. "Exercise: today's willpower, tomorrow's show of vigor!" one was captioned. "Sports attire is the attire of virtue!" added another.

"Do you resent the term warlord?" I asked Dostum.

"The war was imposed on me," he said. "If any enemy comes to your home, what should you do? You have to defend yourself." He thought for a moment.

"Not warlord," he decided. "I would say *peacelord*."

At this, the eyebrows of General Dostum's loyal translator shot up.

WHEN I ASKED HIM about the mass grave at Dasht-i-Leili, Dostum initially gave the same answer the Americans had given for years. "There are so many graves," he said, shaking his head. "So many bodies." These, he swore, were from other periods—from when he was in exile in Turkey, before 9/11, and his second-in-command betrayed him. It was that commander, Malek, he said, who was responsible for most of the bodies in the desert. "But *specifically*," I pressed, "the prisoners from Kunduz after the uprising at Qala-i-Jangi."

Dostum grunted wearily. He'd been waiting for this. "The fact is, they took the prisoners in Kunduz on the open lorry car, sent to Sheberghan." Dostum said he, personally, had seen to it that the prisoners were loaded. It was an ugly process. "Some of them run, some were hiding," he conceded. But they were, when he was there, in open trucks. This was very possibly true, as far as that particular leg of the journey went.

But according to multiple eyewitness accounts, the convoy from Kunduz didn't go directly to Sheberghan. Instead, it, and, eventually, surviving prisoners from the uprising at Qala-i-Jangi, stopped at a fort called Qala-i-Zeini. One driver who talked to the press in 2002 said he had been hired to drive a closed container truck—the kind with a sealable metal enclosure for freight, generally about forty feet by eight—to the site. According to him, other drivers, and surviving prisoners, Dostum's men herded screaming detainees into the containers. In some cases, they hogtied prisoners and threw them in. Ten prisoners who survived and made it to Guantánamo Bay told an FBI official they were "stacked like cordwood," hundreds to a truck, before the doors were slammed and locked. A villager told reporters that those who didn't move fast were beaten viciously. "The only purpose" of the operation, he said, "was to

kill the prisoners." The horror stories that survivors told are what followed Dostum most forcefully all those years. They spoke of screaming
and beating the walls, of licking sweat and urine to stave off death by
dehydration, of gnawing each other's limbs, from hunger or madness.

It was a well-worn method of execution in the Afghan desert—
locking prisoners in containers and allowing them to burn alive or suf-
focate, depending on the season. That November, the cold air would
have made suffocation and dehydration the method of killing. Dostum's men allegedly carried out the entire operation. Each driver was
joined by at least one soldier in the cab of the truck. When drivers tried
to punch holes in the containers for ventilation or to discretely pass
in water bottles, they claimed they were beaten by Dostum's forces.
Survivors claimed that in some cases those soldiers even opened fire
directly into the trucks, silencing the screams. The drivers who talked
said the convoys continued for days. A top secret cable sent by the State
Department's Bureau of Intelligence and Research concluded that
"we believe the number of Taliban deaths during transport to Sheberghan prison may have been higher than the widely reported 1,000."
A three-letter US intelligence agency, redacted in the version of the
cable released through a Freedom of Information Act request, "puts the
number at least 1,500, and the actual number may approach 2,000."

Dostum sighed when I raised the allegations. In the past, one of his
spokespeople had said only that there were accidental deaths from preex-
isting injuries. Dostum told me a different story. "The road," he explained,
"It was closed. Chimtal road and also Balkh road was closed because the
Taliban was there, revolting." Most of the prisoners, he insisted, stayed in
open cars. "But in probably one container there is Taliban."

"*One* container?" I asked. This would allow for perhaps one sixth
of the count given by even the most conservative eyewitness estimates.

"In one container," Dostum's translator said confidently. As he
spoke, Dostum began tilting his head back and forth, jutting out his
lower lip, reconsidering.

"Probably two or three containers," he conceded.

"Who put them in the containers?" I asked.

"This commander, the local commanders who were supposed to transfer them, probably they were scared because of revolt in Qala-i-Jangi. The road was blocked in Chimtal and Balkh. They thought they might also escape and they will attack them, and they put them in two to three containers."

I asked for a name. Dostum was impatiently wiggling his knees again. "The commander, his name was Kamal Khan, he was one of them, yeah." Dostum ran a hand down one side of his face. "Plus one commander, his name was Hazarat Chunta, he probably opened fire." Dostum and his aides didn't suggest that either commander had faced repercussions for the incident, and said they were unsure of where they were, years later.

Dostum sidestepped questions as to exactly how much of this he had ordered. The fact that prisoners had died, he said, was a surprise. According to his version of events, he was eating lunch at Kunduz when an aide arrived to inform him. " 'Some Taliban prisoner were killed in container,' " the aide told him, "And I asked them, 'Have you showed them to Red Cross?' They said 'no.' Then [I] was very upset with him: 'Why didn't you show it to the Red Cross?! You are just trying to undermine my credibility. My enemies will use it against me. I'm trying to be fair in this war. . . you had to show to the Red Cross." But according to the Physicians for Human Rights investigators, the Red Cross didn't gain access until weeks later, when the killing was done and the secrets buried. I struggled to envision Dostum telling anyone to call the Red Cross, ever.

Whatever Dostum's knowledge of the deaths, the available evidence suggests that he was involved in the subsequent cover-up. The declassified State Department intelligence cables said more needed to be done to protect witnesses, who were disappearing. Dostum and one of his commanders had "been implicated in abuses perpetrated against several witnesses connected with the events surrounding the Dasht-e-Leili site. One eyewitness reported to have operated a bulldozer used at the site to bury bodies was killed and his body discovered in the desert. At least three Afghans who worked on issues involving the mass grave have been beaten or are missing." The UN concluded that still another witness was imprisoned by Dostum's forces and had been tortured.

I had to ask Dostum twice about the disappearing witnesses. Finally, I handed him a copy of the cable itself. He eyed it with no discernable reaction then handed it to an aide. "Is it possible," I asked, "this accusation that witnesses were killed and intimidated afterwards?"

He shrugged. "I don't know. I don't recall."

Thornier still was the question of how much the Americans saw. The witness whose testimony Nathaniel Raymond brought to John Kerry and the Senate Foreign Relations Committee had been a translator for American forces at Kunduz and Qala-i-Jangi. He claimed to have been present during the transfer of prisoners into containers—and to have witnessed two Americans, in blue jeans, speaking English, at the site, watching the proceedings. "Who's going to be at Dasht-i-Leili on November 30th and December 1st, 2001, speaking English and wearing blue jeans?" Raymond said.

"When I left Qala-i-Jangi . . . all the time, American colleagues accompanied me," Dostum told me. He was adamant about this, a point of personal pride for him as he defended his faltering relationship with the nation that had used him to achieve victory, and now seemed intent on turning its back on him. He said that Mark Nutsch, the captain of Special Forces Team 595, had been by his side almost constantly, an assertion Nutsch said was generally accurate: "Yeah . . . ," he recalled, "we worked very closely with [Dostum] nearly every day."

"Were any of the Americans assigned to Qala-i-Zeini [where the containers were loaded]?" I asked Dostum.

"All of them was with me," he replied, tapping his foot impatiently. "They wrongly accused," he added, referring to suggestions in the human rights community that Americans may have been involved in the slaughter. "They say 'oh, Dostum he killed, Americans were firing.' It's not true." Dostum offered this exoneration as evidence of his loyalty to the Americans. But his conviction that the Americans were by his side during the incident raised another set of difficult questions about whether the Special Forces and CIA personnel witnessed any of the communications between Dostum and his commanders about the murders, and failed to either stop them, or report them after the fact.

Nutsch told me he knew of no abuses. "My team has been investigated multiple times over this," he said. "We did not witness, nor observe, anything." Just as Dostum considered the American special forces blood brothers, the camaraderie was apparent on Nutsch's side. "I saw him as a charismatic leader. Led from the front. Took care of his guys," he added. In a celebratory Hollywood rendition of 595's collaboration with Dostum called 12 Strong, Nutsch was portrayed, with exaggerated brawn and smolder, by Chris Hemsworth, the actor who played the superhero Thor. Nutsch grew testy when I asked a series of questions about the more complicated realities of the story. "Dostum's enemies are the ones accusing him of these things," he said. When I told him Dostum had admitted the killings may have occurred, and suggested two of his commanders may have been involved, Nutsch paused, then replied, "I don't have a reaction to that."

As I pressed Dostum on how much the Americans knew or should have known, he grew restless. He had a cold, he reminded me. At one point, he stopped me mid-question. "Listen, every school has a break after one hour," he growled, and changed the subject. "You should have some [questions about] women, children," an aide offered hurriedly. When I turned to the Americans again, Dostum narrowed his eyes at me. "You are asking so many questions. . . . I'm curious, the way you are asking questions, it's not for the book, not for creating a scenario . . . why in so much detail, asking this questions?" The warm air in the Vice Presidential Palace was heavy. Dostum seemed to be reaching his limit. "I was always very truthful, committed to my friendship, I never betrayed," he said at one point. His eyes darted to his son Babur, who stood at attention, M4 in hand. "But I hope you will not do the same to me." I debated how to respond to this. Then Dostum roared with laughter. "You asked for only thirty more minutes!" he explained. I laughed, relieved. "I'm over time! I've betrayed your schedule!" General Dostum knew a good warlord joke.

As we wound down our last night of interviews, soft gymnasium mats were being laid out in the hall of the palace, in anticipation of a match of *kurash*, a traditional Central Asian martial art. Soon, about fifty boys and men in blue and white Adidas judo robes filed in, pairing off, circling each other, jabbing and sparring until one slammed to the ground. It was, Dostum remarked with pride, completely intertribal: Uzbeks against Pashtun, Hazara against Tajik. The men hailed from nine provinces. After each fight, the combatants kissed. But it was hard to say whether this looked more like reconciliation or war: the audible snaps of twisted limbs sounded through the hall late into the night, and some of the boys limped away, wincing. As the fights began, a *dombra*, a traditional Turkic lute, sounded spare notes, and the assembled spectators broke into song, in Uzbek:

> *Let's be strong*
> *Let's live like a man*
> *Like Dostum,*
>
> *Let's serve our country*
> *Let's respect each other*
> *Like Dostum*
>
> *Be born like a man*
> *Live like a man*
> *Be truthful, loyal*
> *Don't betray each other*

And be friends
Like Dostum

Mosquitoes darted in the hot air. Dostum, draped in a traditional
Uzbek cape of shiny blue silk, sat on his throne, clutching his Chanel
mug. As he watched, his eyes filled with tears.

A FEW MONTHS AFTER I LEFT Dostum's palace, he stood in a
blizzard in Sheberghan, listening to another song. He was attending
a game of *buzkashi*, and before the goat was slaughtered, local musi-
cians broke into a tribute to martyrs in the fight against the Taliban.
The lyrics struck a personal chord: A month earlier, the Taliban had
ambushed his convoy, injuring him and killing several members of his
Junbish militias. In a video of the match, Dostum can be seen on the
sidelines, eyes pressed shut, lips trembling, taking silent, heaving sobs.
Fat snowflakes swirled as he took out a white handkerchief and wiped
both eyes.

As the match began—fifteen horses surging into the fray, the intricate scoring rules passed on from Genghis Khan's era incomprehensible
to any casual observer—another fight broke out in the stands. Dostum
swung a punch at a longtime political rival, Ahmad Ishchi. It got much
worse from there: The vice president toppled Ischi and ground a heel
into his neck as more than a thousand attendees watched. "I can kill
you right now, and no one will ask," Ischi later claimed Dostum told
him. Witnesses said they saw Dostum's men drag Ischi's bloodied body
into a truck and drive away with him. Ischi later claimed Dostum
and his men held him captive for five days, beating him mercilessly
and raping him with a Kalashnikov. Forensic evidence provided to
the press seemed to back up Ischi's claims that he suffered severe internal injuries. General Dostum said the allegations were a conspiracy to
remove him from power. He had responded the same way when an

eerily similar charge of physical abuse was brought by another political rival eight years earlier.

Dostum's grip on power had been slipping for some time. Months earlier, he groused to me that "the Doctors"—President Ashraf Ghani and Chief Executive Abdullah Abdullah—ignored him. The year before that, he had burst into tears at a meeting of the Afghan National Security Council. "No one returns my calls!" he howled. The new allegations plunged him into political crisis. "For the Afghan government nobody is above the law. Rule of law and accountability begins in the government itself and we are committed to it," said a government spokesperson, as they announced a criminal investigation.

A six-month standoff ensued, revealing yet again the perils of installing warlords to senior government posts. At one point, soldiers and policemen surrounded the Vice Presidential Palace, attempting to arrest Dostum and his aides. But Dostum commanded his own independent militia, and so police feared the entire neighborhood in Kabul might turn into a war zone. They left empty-handed. Later, when President Ghani left Afghanistan to attend a security conference in Europe, Dostum and a coterie of armed guards arrived at the presidential compound and unilaterally announced that he was serving as acting president in Ghani's absence, to the alarm of the international community. Ghani returned before Dostum could act on that threat.

Across Afghanistan in 2017, the wobbly structures of the American-brokered post-9/11 government were straining against the warlords, popping rivets. In Takhar province, a warlord associated with one prominent Islamist party, Commander Bashir Qanet, created his own police state, opening fire on supporters of the central government. In Mazar-i-Sharif, a provincial councilman named Asif Mohmand got into a social-media fight with Atta Mohammed Noor, threatening to "pump 30 bullets into your head and then help myself to you" in a Facebook post. When Atta sent his forces to arrest Mohmand,

he found Mohmand had his own militias protecting him. The ensuing firefight killed two and wounded seventeen people and plunged
Mazar-i-Sharif International Airport into bloody chaos. The Taliban
was in resurgence as well. And its forces were joined by another rising
threat still more troubling to the Americans: an ISIL affiliate called the
Islamic State of Iraq and the Levant, Khorasan Province. The group
was smaller than al-Qaeda, but, by 2017, proving similarly resilient in
grinding battles of attrition in the Afghan mountains.

Back in America, Donald Trump had, as a candidate, preached the
virtues of withdrawal. "We should leave Afghanistan immediately,"
he had said. The war was "wasting our money," "a total and complete
disaster." But, once in office, Donald Trump, and a national security
team dominated by generals, pressed for escalation. Richard Holbrooke had spent his final days alarmed at the dominance of generals in
Obama's Afghanistan review, but Trump expanded this phenomenon
almost to the point of parody. General Mattis as secretary of defense,
General H. R. McMaster as national security advisor, and retired general John F. Kelly formed the backbone of the Trump administration's
Afghanistan review. In front of a room full of servicemen and women
at Fort Myer Army Base, in Arlington, Virginia, backed by the flags
of the branches of the US military, Trump announced that America
would double down in Afghanistan. A month later, General Mattis
ordered the first of thousands of new American troops into the country.
It was a foregone conclusion: the year before Trump entered office, the
military had already begun quietly testing public messaging, informing the public that America would be in Afghanistan for decades, not
years. After the announcement, the same language cropped up again,
this time from Trump surrogates who compared the commitment not
to other counterterrorism operations, but to America's troop commitments in Korea, Germany, and Japan. "We are with you in this fight,"
the top general in Afghanistan, John Nicholson, Jr., told an audience of
Afghans. "We will stay with you."

Where Obama had proposed a "civilian surge" and at least gestured toward the importance of amplifying American diplomacy in the region, Trump simply acknowledged that the Pentagon would be setting policy. He mentioned negotiation, but more as a distant mirage than a reality. "Someday, after an effective military effort, perhaps it will be possible to have a political settlement that includes elements of the Taliban in Afghanistan," he told the officers at Fort Myer. "But nobody knows if or when that will ever happen." In light of the situation at Foggy Bottom—with the office of the special representative for Afghanistan and Pakistan shuttered, and no permanent assistant secretary for South and Central Asia—this seemed a fair characterization.

Meanwhile, America's longest war continued without end, without even the hope of an end. I was reminded of something General Dostum had told me, in that grassy hall, under winking Christmas-tree lights, with a tank full of sharks burbling absurdly in the background.

He'd been so rowdy as a small child that his mother, he said, had finally tied a rope to his hand. "Don't go away," she admonished him. Dostum had slipped his rope and wandered off almost immediately.

"Are you still hard to control?" I asked.

"Of course," he said. "Childhood is childhood. But when it comes to reality . . . if something is right, I support. If it's the right thing, it has logic . . . but if it's unjust, does not have the logic, if it's not true, no one can control me."

He spread his legs wide and thrust his chin forward. "In the end," he said with an impish smile, like we were both in on the joke, "you should title the book *Dostum: He Is Telling the Truth and Discouraging All Lies.*" In a way, he was right. Abdul Rashid Dostum and his legacy did reveal hard truths: about the United States, and how it wound up in an infinite war at the ends of the earth.

19

WHITE BEAST

SOME OF THE BEARDS were henna red, some white or black, but all of the men had them. They sat in the late afternoon sun, in patterned headscarves and prayer caps, sipping tea. When I saw them, the men were huddled around metal coffee tables in a walled garden near the Embasoira Hotel in Asmara, Eritrea. It was the first days of 2008 and, in the midst of a Horn of Africa plunged into chaos, Asmara was a mirage of calm. Its wide boulevards were shaded by low palm trees and acacias and lined by immaculately preserved architectural jewels in a collision of styles—romanesque, deco, baroque, cubist—left behind from decades of Italian colonial rule. Even the name Asmara, meaning "they made them unite" in Tigrinya, was a beautiful deception for a city that was, at that moment, teeming with warring elements, cast out of the maelstrom of nearby Somalia. The men sipping tea at the Embasoira were among them. My interpreter leaned in and whispered conspiratorially: "There they are!"

"Who?" I asked.

He shook his head—a shake that said, so far as I could tell, that this meant trouble—and replied: "The men from the Islamic Courts."

In Somalia, the loose coalition of Shari'a courts known as the Islamic Courts Union (ICU) had once served as the sole alternative to that country's normal state of chaos: a roiling cauldron of warlords, crossing and double-crossing without end. The courts were retrograde but largely without violent ambition. Nevertheless, the United States, gripped with fear that Somalia might become the next Afghanistan, threw its weight behind a succession of local fighting forces with the intention of ousting the ICU. Not long after the decision to arm Dostum and his fellow commanders, the CIA set to work building a similar set of alliances with Somalia's warlords. Later, when those alliances backfired spectacularly and galvanized support for the ICU, the Pentagon turned to the Ethiopian military, backing an invasion that scattered the leaders of the courts to cities like Asmara, leaving behind radical elements and hastening the rise of the terror group al-Shabaab. By that afternoon just over a year later, when I saw the exiled ICU officials outside of the Embasoira, that transformation was already under way. The Americans had taken a local nuisance and turned it into a terrifying new threat to international security.

In the Horn of Africa, as in Afghanistan, a struggle for control of American foreign policy was playing out in the formative years after 9/11. In both cases, military and intelligence solutions won out. In both cases, the United States actively sabotaged opportunities for diplomacy. And in both cases, the destabilizing effect was felt continents and cultures away.

IT IS DIFFICULT TO IMAGINE a place farther from Somalia than Wooburn Green, in Buckinghamshire, England, a working-class suburb of London. And it was difficult to imagine a person less likely to be affected by the chaos of the Horn of Africa than Sally Evans, whom I first saw in the narrow kitchenette of one of Wooburn Green's low brick houses in 2016. Evans was fifty-eight, with graying hair cropped in a no-nonsense pageboy bob, and sensible shoes. She was pottering around, offering me a cup of instant coffee. "We're just ordinary people," she said, looking out at the hedge-lined street outside her window. "I never thought it would happen. No." But Sally Evans carried with her a secret utterly alien to the rest of the mothers on her street in Wooburn Green.

Evans's sons, Thomas and Micheal, grew up together. In home videos, they are interchangeable: carefree, skinny boys laughing and playing, with identical, tousled brown hair. "We kinda did everything together," Micheal told me. "We had the same group of friends growin' up." Thomas was nineteen when that began to change. When he converted to Islam, Sally said, she took it as a positive, a sign that he was looking for more moral structure in his life. But that was before Thomas moved to a hard-line conservative mosque. After that, she recalled, "Little things began to change. Like his appearance, he grew the beard. Stopped listening to music. And he wouldn't eat my food anymore. What I cooked wasn't right for him anymore because it wasn't halal meat. He just isolated himself from us." Some of the developments had an air of absurdity. Thomas wouldn't be in the living room as long as a Christmas tree was up during the holidays.

He began to spend more and more time behind closed doors, at his computer. "He was always upstairs in the bedroom," Sally recalled. "I can't believe he sat on there just, you know, browsing Facebook or whatever," Micheal added. "He was on there specifically to look at—" he paused. "Look at things he was told to look at."

Then Thomas began trying to leave the country. In February 2011, he was stopped by counterterrorism police at Heathrow, on the verge of flying to Kenya. A few months later, he successfully boarded a flight to Egypt. Initially, he told his mother he was traveling to study Arabic. But Evans disappeared for months, and, when he reemerged, calling Sally in January 2012, it was to say he was in Somalia. He had joined al-Shabaab. "He told us, didn't he?" she said, turning to Micheal. "To go online and look at them. See who they were. And that's when I realized what he'd become." Sally pleaded with her son to come home. She told him that what he was doing "wasn't right." Thomas just kept invoking Allah. "I said, 'No, no, no,'" she told me. "'No god would guide you to this.'"

Over the ensuing year, mother and son fell into a strange rhythm. Thomas, who changed his name to Abdul Hakim and earned the nom de guerre "White Beast," would call home every few weeks. The updates on the life of the White Beast—a persona in which she struggled to see the son she had raised—became increasingly alien. In one call, he told her he had married a thirteen- or fourteen-year-old girl who spoke no English. In others, he talked around the violence of his new life. Sally Evans chronicled some of the conversations in a series of journals. "Thomas rang," she wrote in one in 2012. "I asked him if he'd hurt anybody, and he didn't answer."

A YEAR AFTER THOMAS LEFT HOME, I stooped to the ground in a Nairobi alley and picked up an empty bullet shell. Behind me, the plaster façade of the Westgate shopping mall was still pockmarked from recent gunfire. I was there, with a television crew, reporting on a recent attack that gave an unambiguous answer to the question Sally Evans had posed: If her son was not hurting anyone, his fellow recruits certainly were.

A succession of survivors of al-Shabaab's most elaborate attack yet, just weeks earlier, joined me in the bullet-strewn alley and shared memories that were still raw and painful. Preeyam Sehmi, an artist, had kissed her fiancée goodbye, run an errand, and met a friend for coffee at the upscale mall, not far from her home. She and the friend had bantered for an hour about Sehmi's work as a local artist before she rose to pay their bill at around 12:30 p.m. She was waiting for change when a deafening blast rocked the building. She had no idea what was happening. "I just saw people flying off their chairs and over tables," she recalled. Then "everyone was on the floor," some crawling for safety, others now still and lifeless. She remembered the scene in slow motion, "like being in a movie." Sehmi took shelter in a nearby clothing store, and waited, covering her ears for wave after wave of gunshots and screams.

Young men with machine guns, most in plain clothes, some wearing headscarves, were ripping through the mall, hurling grenades and shredding men, women, and children with bullets. Those who survived the initial attacks were taken hostage and subjected to grisly torture and mutilations. The attackers held the mall for three days against attempted interventions by Kenyan authorities. Sehmi was one of the lucky ones to escape, spirited away by police officers after six tense hours in hiding. By the conclusion of the raid, seventy-two people had been killed, sixty-one of them civilians.

Al-Shabaab quickly claimed responsibility, saying it was counteracting foreign meddling in Somalia. The group had successfully launched attacks outside of Somalia before, including bombings in Uganda in 2010 that left seventy-six dead. The mall shooting was a stark reminder of its international aspirations. The United States saw the shooting as "a direct threat," and dispatched FBI agents to the scene of the wreckage to search for clues.

Thomas Evans claimed, to his family, that he wasn't directly involved in the mall attack. But he cheered it on from afar. This, he said, was the reason he had joined al-Shabaab. "Spoke to Thomas 14th Nov 2013, not a good phone call," Sally Evans wrote in a diary entry shortly after the incident. "We rowed about that shopping mall siege in Kenya. Selfishly, I'm relieved he wasn't involved but very angry with him because he thinks it's okay to murder innocent men women and children out shopping."

THE DESTRUCTION OF SALLY EVANS'S FAMILY, and the violence wrought by the group Thomas Evans and other young men around the world flocked to join in that period, were tied to a long cycle of US foreign policy. The parallels between America's alliances in Afghanistan and Somalia, it turned out, reached back decades. For years, the Soviet Union and the Americans attempted to buy the loyalty of Somalia's authoritarian strongman, Siad Barre, hoping to gain control of the strategically placed country. After Barre was overthrown, the country descended into pandemonium, livened by guns from the United States and other foreign backers, like Libya's Muammar Gaddafi and nearby Ethiopia. International attempts to protect humanitarian interests ended in grisly failure. For most Americans, the word "Somalia" evokes the phrase "Black Hawk Down," the title of Mark Bowden's book and the Hollywood film chronicling the 1993 Battle of Mogadishu, which took the lives of several American servicemen. Western forces withdrew and left the country to rule by warlord.

Over the ensuing decade, only one alternative to the warlords emerged: the Shari'a courts, which gained strength and became increasingly formalized in the early 2000s. Funded and armed by Ethiopia's regional rival, Eritrea, the courts began to band together, and twelve united under a shared banner, as the ICU, in 2004.

In the wake of the 1998 bombings of US embassies in Kenya and Tanzania—and, more acutely, the 9/11 attacks—the ICU became a point of obsession for American leaders. But there was a problem: according to Africa experts fluent in the region's complex dynamics, there was little basis for making Somalia a focal point in America's newfound war on terror. "There was a feeling here after 9/11 that Somalia might become the next Afghanistan. That it would become

a terrorist training ground, a new source of support for global terrorism," Princeton Lyman, who held two ambassadorships in Africa
and was President Obama's special envoy to Sudan, told me. "Really,
Somalia didn't lend itself to that." In 2002, analyst Ken Menkhaus,
who served as a counterterrorism consultant at the State Department
and the UN, estimated that fewer than a dozen Somali nationals had
"significant links" to al-Qaeda. "There's no need to be rushing into
Somalia," one retired American diplomat, David Shinn, agreed.

The ICU even appeared to have a stabilizing effect. The courts
could be brutally conservative, amputating the limbs of thieves, stoning adulterers to death, and declaring sports illegal acts of Satanism.
But they also evinced little extremist ambition beyond maintaining
Islamic law within Somalia. Clerics with broader aspirations of jihad
were a minority without much influence. Of the ninety-seven courts,
just nine were under al-Shabaab control. Under ICU rule, ports and
airports were opened for the first time in years. Even American diplomatic cables at the time acknowledged gains made in humanitarian
access under court rule.

BUT THE UNITED STATES military and intelligence communities
became bent on toppling the courts. Direct intervention was a political
nonstarter, in the shadow of the Black Hawk incident. And so, another
covert proxy war took form. By 2004, the CIA was quietly approaching warlords perceived to be secular and offering them alliances in
exchange for counterterrorism cooperation. For the next two years,
the agency financed clan leaders and warlords across Somalia. Run out
of the CIA station in Nairobi, the operation was a small-scale proxy
war. Pockets lined with US dollars, the warlords were expected to battle the ICU and suspected militants—regardless of whether or not they
truly had ties to al-Qaeda. The operation broadened until "eventually

there was a group of about a dozen militia leaders who came together with United States support," recalled Matthew Bryden, who headed a United Nations group monitoring the flow of arms in the region. The US-backed warlords were even given a PR-friendly title: The Alliance for the Restoration of Peace and Counter-Terrorism, with an acronym unwieldy enough to make any government bureaucracy proud, ARPCT. The strategy was much the same as the agency's embrace of Northern Alliance warlords in Afghanistan: These, ostensibly, were the better guys, if not the good guys. If they weren't secular, at least they were more secular than the alternative.

To say the Somali warlords came with complications would be an understatement. Ironically, many of them had fought American forces in the streets of Mogadishu in 1993. Some, like Yusuf Mohammed Siad—known on the battlefield as "White Eyes," or, for those who recalled his reign of terror capturing swaths of Somalia in the 1990s, "The Butcher"—were for years closely allied with al-Qaeda. When Fazul Abdullah Mohammed, the notorious terrorist behind the 1998 bombings in Tanzania and Kenya, sought refuge from the CIA, it was White Eyes who gave him safe haven. After 9/11, he became a voluble source of anti-American sentiment. Nevertheless, he has claimed, in press interviews, that the CIA approached him during that very same period. "They offered me money, they offered me funding for the region I was controlling," he said in 2011. At the time, he refused.

Other advances were successful, however. Mohamed Afrah Qanyare was approached in late 2002 by CIA agents seeking the benefits of his private airport near Mogadishu, and his 1,500-strong militia. American military and intelligence officials sealed the deal in 2003, kicking off a series of regular meetings and a pricey friendship—by Qanyare's estimation, $100,000 to $150,000 a month, for the use of the airport and, ostensibly, the loyalty of his men. Qanyare was among several warlords who, either at the behest of CIA officials or with their tacit understanding, began undertaking capture-and-kill operations of supposed Islamic terrorists. Sometimes, the targets of the warlords' operations were simply executed. Other times, they were rendered into US custody, as in the case of Suleiman Ahmed Hemed Salim, who was transferred from Somalia to a series of prisons in Afghanistan.

The CIA's relationship with the warlords destabilized Somalia. Warlord rule had, by the mid-2000s, become deeply unpopular across the country. The capture-and-kill operations—often targeting imams and local prayer leaders without apparent links to international terrorist concerns—enflamed Islamist sentiment. "It's a time bomb," the mayor of Mogadishu said of American support for the warlords. "They are waiting, they want to weaken the government, and they are waiting any time that the government falls, so that each one will grab an area." When a tenuous new transitional government for Somalia was installed in 2004 to try to counteract the warlords, its president, Abdullahi Yusuf Ahmed "wondered aloud why the US would want to start an open war in Mogadishu" during a meeting with the American ambassador.

The warlord alliances, in the years after, became an albatross. Jendayi Frazer, assistant secretary of state for African affairs during the second George W. Bush administration, told me that the Department had inherited the policy from the CIA with little opportunity for input. "CIA action in Somalia in 2002 through 2005 was in a restricted channel and not subject to very much interagency discussion or debate," she said. When the relationships finally did arise in conversations outside of the CIA, through Richard A. Clarke's Counter-Terrorism Security Group at the White House, it was "very much a surprise to everyone in the interagency other than the agency." Frazer felt that the CIA wanted to check the box of notifying America's diplomats without actually doing so. "Just to be blunt with you," she told me, "I think they raised it to that NSC group in a way that ensured no one knew what they were talking about. So they could claim we knew."

Still, once Frazer and others in the diplomatic chain of command became aware of the alliances with the warlords, they began defending them. Diplomatic cables from 2006 describe a policy of using "non-traditional liaison partners (e.g., militia leaders)" in Somalia to "locat[e] and nullif[y] high value targets." Diplomats who pushed back on the use of the warlords were quashed quickly. Michael Zorick, a political officer at the US embassy in Nairobi, filed a dissent cable on the subject and was promptly reassigned to Chad, a move that was widely perceived as punishment for asking too many questions.

WHEN A DIPLOMATIC OPTION materialized, it was greeted as an inconvenience, something to be nipped in the bud. In 2004, Somalia's neighbors came together in an intensive diplomatic effort to create an alternative to either the warlords or the courts. Somalia's new transitional government presented a glimmer of hope. But it had little control beyond a few blocks of Mogadishu, and little ability to counteract the strongmen the US had empowered. And so, the members of the Intergovernmental Authority on Development (IGAD)—a regional trade bloc that included Ethiopia, Djibouti, Eritrea, Sudan, Kenya, and Uganda—met in October 2004 and issued a unanimous call for African troops to deploy to Somalia, to ensure that the fledgling government stayed intact. Two months later, representatives from the transitional government, UN, African Union, European Union, and Arab states met in Kenya to discuss a plan for the mission. By the early months of 2005, the AU was on board, with heads of state adopting a resolution welcoming a "peace support mission." The UN Security Council formally backed it by the end of the year.

Tekeda Alemu, a veteran Ethiopian diplomat who was involved

in the negotiations, felt that a regional peacekeeping force could have averted disaster. "I was the head of the Ethiopian delegation," he told me. "And we accepted the proposal unanimously." He noted with a raised eyebrow that even Ethiopia's bitter regional rival, Eritrea, cooperated. (Ethiopia and Eritrea signing on to a shared peacekeeping initiative was like Israel and Hamas doing the same. It was an extraordinary development.) Alemu cut a distinguished profile, with short-cropped, graying hair, professorial spectacles, and just a hint of African new money bling: a chunky gold ring; an outsize watch with Swarovski crystals around the edge. When I spoke to him, he was sitting in his run-down office at the Ethiopian mission in midtown Manhattan, a world away from the Horn. We were on ample suede couches, the kind you'd get at a bargain furniture retailer like Raymour & Flanigan. A plastic ficus drooped behind him. "At that point, it was no problem with the US," he told me with a sigh. "The problem would come later."

The "problem" was that, by the time the African nations began their effort to protect the transitional government from the warlords, the United States had already bet on the other side. The CIA and the Pentagon were fixated on the singular goal of destroying the Islamist threat, perceived or actual. Broader diplomatic initiatives in the region were a fly in the ointment, or, worse, a potential source of opposition to the factions with which the United States was working. Nominally, the American policy—articulated by State Department officials like Frazer—was noncommittal. But behind closed doors, the United States began waging a diplomatic battle to sabotage the deployment of peacekeepers.

In early 2005, the international peacekeeping force was, after months of intense negotiation, essentially ready to go. The United States quietly pushed back—often through State Department officials, but enforcing policy that was, at its root, designed by the intelligence community. In February 2005, diplomat Marc Meznar, who represented the Population Refugees and Migration bureau at the American embassy in Brussels, met with an EU official, Mark Boucey, to make it clear that the United States would oppose the peacekeeping effort. At the time, an EU team was in Nairobi conducting fact-finding in support of the initiative, and was scheduled to travel to Mogadishu to help advance the international force several days later. Shortly after the meeting with Boucey, the EU team canceled the Mogadishu trip. The Pentagon worked its relationships as well: US deputy assistant secretary of defense for Africa Theresa Whelan met with an EU official named Matthew Reece, who subsequently declared the peacekeeping initiative the EU had once backed a "wildcat plan." Several weeks later, when officials from individual EU allies began to offer their support for the peacekeepers, Tom Countryman—at the time the minister-counselor for political affairs at the US embassy in Rome—was dispatched to meet with Italian officials to try to ward them off.

In the end, when international support for the operation had largely coalesced, all that remained was for an arms embargo on Somalia, imposed in 1992, to be lifted to allow the peacekeeping force to train soldiers. At the eleventh hour, the United States threw a wrench in the proceedings, sending a terse statement to the Council of Ministers from the regional players about to commit forces. "We do not plan to fund the deployment of IGAD troops in Somalia and are not prepared to support a UN Security Council mandate for IGAD deployment," it read. Later, the United States publicly threatened to veto any initiative to bring peacekeepers to Somalia. The effort, finally, foundered.

Colonel Rick Orth, the US defense attaché at the time, explained the US opposition plainly: "We didn't want to divert into this tertiary sideshow." Since at least a few of the ICU leaders had historic ties to al-Qaeda, "the agency was running ops to go after selected individuals . . . it was not an effort to have a broader solution, we were just going after more pointed targets."

Tekeda Alemu, the Ethiopian diplomat, said US opposition to the plan was palpable from the beginning. "It was very clear," he recalled. "They didn't even want to look at whether the plan we had would work or not, was good or not. It was not given an opportunity." An aide placed a porcelain cup of Ethiopian black coffee in front of him. He picked it up, frowned, and then put it down, reflecting on the failed diplomatic effort. "Apparently they had some plan," he said of the Americans, "to capture a few people in Mogadishu [using] war-lords who had cooperated with them. Therefore, they didn't want anybody to spoil that. . . . They had the project that they embraced, and didn't want to be adversely affected in any way." He picked up his coffee again. "And that's how superpowers behave." Alemu took a sip and smiled.

US officials argued that there were legitimate reasons for their opposition. Lack of capacity among the African troop contributors was mentioned, as was cost. Above all, they argued that sending in so-called "frontline states"—direct neighbors to Somalia, such as Ethiopia— would enflame regional tensions. It was a canard: the plan already required that troops come from non-neighboring countries. But the Americans argued that even indirect support from the Ethiopians would be viewed within Somalia as a power grab from larger, stronger coun-tries, and worsen the violence. It was a position that would soon after prove hauntingly hypocritical.

WITH NO PEACEKEEPING FORCE in place to oppose the warlords, only the Islamic Courts Union served as a counterbalance. Predictably, the courts grew more popular and powerful, taking control of ter-ritories across Somalia between 2004 and 2006. Finally, after several months of brutal fighting, they wrested control of Mogadishu from the US-backed militias. "People started—the Mogadishu people— admiring this Islamic Court," explained Tekeda. "They were able to defeat a group of people, those warlords, who had been supported by a big power. And the Islamic Court began to be lionized. That's how they became very inflated, totally uncontrollable."

Shortly after the defeat of the CIA-allied warlords, the Pentagon began devising another plan to force out the ICU. Still allergic to direct intervention, the Americans turned to their long-standing ally—and Somalia's regional rival—Ethiopia. The United States was Ethiopia's largest donor. Thanks largely to American support, the country's military was the most powerful in the region.

US statements over the course of 2006 were careful to maintain distance from Ethiopia and its role leading what was increasingly perceived to be an American proxy war. "It's not like we had big NSC meetings saying, 'Hey, why don't we get the Ethiopian—' No, we didn't. The Ethiopians did this," General Hayden, the CIA director at the time, offered haltingly when I asked about the United States' role in the invasion. He shrugged. "They had their reasons for doing it." But even he conceded the move fit neatly with American objectives. "Given the chaos that was Somalia at the time," he said, "this was certainly a near-term palliative that was very welcome."

Many disputed the idea that the Ethiopian invasion simply fell into the Pentagon's and the CIA's laps. Simiyu Werunga, a former Kenyan military official and counterterrorism expert, said that "the dismantling of the Islamic Union would not have taken place without the support and resources of the American government. That is the general feeling in the region." Supporting that narrative was a backdrop of covert collaboration between the two nations: after 9/11, the CIA and the FBI had interrogated alleged terrorist suspects from nineteen countries in secret Ethiopian prisons notorious for the abuse, torture, and unexplained deaths of inmates.

Evidence of the American role in the operation mounted over the course of 2006. The US began publicly emphasizing the ICU's human rights abuses and defending the idea of an Ethiopian intervention. Classified State Department memoranda from the period suggest a decision to back the invasion had already been made, with one noting that the US intended to "rally with Ethiopia if the 'Jihadist[s]' took over." It further clarified: "Any Ethiopian action in Somalia would have Washington's blessing."

When Ethiopia did strike in December 2006, pouring thousands of troops into Somalia, it had more than an American blessing. US Special Forces covertly accompanied the Ethiopian troops, serving as advisers and trainers. The US Navy amassed on the coast to offer additional support, and American air strikes complemented those from Ethiopia's own aircraft. "The US position is, 'Find out from the Ethiopians what they want, and we'll provide,' " one senior defense official, who spoke on condition of anonymity because of the secrecy of the operation, said. "A lot of it was intelligence and special operation support. . . . I was told that they were in more than an advisory capacity and they essentially teamed up with Ethiopian special forces."

The operation, in tactical terms, was a success. The combined might of Ethiopian troops and American support left the ICU splintered and in flight from Mogadishu by the new year. At a January 2007 dinner, Abu Dhabi crown prince Sheikh Mohammed bin Zayed al Nahyan offered a casual compliment to US Central Command boss General John Abizaid: "The Somalia job was fantastic."

BUT, WHILE THE INVASION successfully leveled the ICU's formal structure, it also managed to give the Islamists a new lease on life. Protests against the newly installed Ethiopian forces began almost immediately. The invasion fit easily within the long-standing history of Somali animosity toward Ethiopia—a sentiment extremist elements moved to exploit. "The invasion legitimized the cause of al-Shabaab and won them a network of support both inside Somalia and outside in the diaspora, because they were able to claim a legitimate jihad" against the occupying forces, Bryden explained. Even Frazer conceded that "from a propaganda perspective, the invasion was quite helpful [to al-Shabaab], sure."

Further playing into al-Shabaab's hand, the Ethiopian invasion had caused much of the moderate majority leadership of the ICU to flee Somalia. Those left behind tended to be hard-liners willing to stay and fight, including al-Shabaab leadership. Over the year following the invasion, al-Shabaab transformed from a fringe element with limited influence to a tactically relevant outfit with ambitions beyond Somalia's borders—a group that would recruit around the world, with a bloody message that would reach a troubled, angry young man in a suburb of London and resonate with a brokenness in him that his family would never understand.

Al-Shabaab was also deft at exploiting anti-American sentiment, claiming in one statement that "Jews" in the United States had sent Ethiopia to "defile" Somalia. Al-Qaeda, recognizing the strength of that narrative, fortified its support for the Somali extremist group. Recruitment rates soared. The period following the invasion from 2007 to 2009 was "al-Shabaab's period of greatest growth," Bryden recalled, "because they were an insurgency."

In 2008, the United States designated al-Shabaab a terrorist organization. A few years later, the group announced a formal affiliation with al-Qaeda, completing its shift in focus from Somali politics to global jihad.

IRONICALLY, TO EXTRICATE SOMALIA from the pincers of al-Shabaab, the United States was forced to turn to what looked very much like the peacekeeping solution it had shunned in 2004. Starting in 2007, an international force—the African Union Mission in Somalia, or AMISOM—emerged as the sole potential antidote to the chaos. As the peacekeeping operation grew more robust, it "created the space . . . for the Ethiopians to have a less visible role," recalled Frazer, and eventually "to say that they were leaving, which then denied Shabaab that anti-occupation propaganda to the degree that it mattered."

The United States threw its support behind the new force over the ensuing years. In February 2012, it dispatched Marines to Uganda to train AMISOM combat engineers, now kitted out with American equipment from mine detectors to flak jackets. That effort was augmented by training from private contractors on America's payroll. After so many years of resistance to the idea, the United States embraced a multinational peacekeeping force born of regional diplomacy, bringing the first signs of stability in years. The number of children killed or maimed in the fight between al-Shabaab and government forces declined. Elections resumed.

Yet, as in Afghanistan, the scars of American misadventure remained and the warlords proved entrenched. Some, like White Eyes, went on to occupy high-ranking government ministry posts. And even the best-placed efforts to support the international peacekeepers at times backfired: According to a United Nations report, at one point up to half of the US-supplied weapons delivered to the African Union in Somalia ended up in al-Shabaab's hands.

The threat of al-Shabaab proved hard to roll back. In some ways, it was weakened and quelled. But Bryden, the former United Nations monitor, said the group had changed more than diminished. In response to its dwindling territory in Somalia, al-Shabaab was "abandoning guerilla tactics and returning to [its] roots as a largely clandestine terrorist organization," focused on assassinations and IED attacks. "Its capabilities and tactics have become more sophisticated," he explained. In the decade after I saw the exiled Islamic Courts leaders, sipping tea and plotting their next steps in Asmara, al-Shabaab added to its fatality list with each passing year. In September 2017, an attack on a Somali military base near the port town of Kismayo left more than twenty Somali military personnel dead. The United States remained in steady conflict with a group partly of its own making, launching a fresh spate of air strikes in the last months of that year.

Opinions vary on al-Shabaab's international reach. Anders Folk, a former FBI agent who served on a taskforce focused on the group, called the prospect of a successful attack in the United States "possible." He added: "Do they have the aspiration to conduct violent terrorist attacks against innocents in the United States? Their rhetoric tells us absolutely."

FOR SOME, THE GROUP'S INTERNATIONAL REACH had been clear for years. On the evening of June 14, 2015, Sally Evans was alone in her living room when she got the worst phone call of her life. "It was twenty-five to ten on a Sunday night," she remembered. "And it was a reporter, asking me about how I felt about the death of my son." She told the reporter he wasn't dead. "And I could hear he was backtracking," she said. "Thinking 'I've told her something she doesn't know.'" An hour later, Micheal, her other son, got home. "I walked in the front door. And as I come in here my mom was sat at the living room table. And I could just tell something wasn't right straightaway." Micheal got on Twitter. At first, he thought to search for Thomas Evans. Then he typed in his new name, the name of a man they never felt they truly knew, Abdul Hakim. "And that's the first thing to come up, was a picture from the Kenyan army. And it had all the bodies laid out in the street and laying in the dirt. And it was obvious it was him." Obvious, but, for Sally, hard to reconcile with the man she had raised. "I was devastated to see my son lying on the ground like he was. And he was," she paused, collecting herself, "he looked so skinny. Just didn't look like my Thomas."

A video, shot by Thomas and released shortly after his death by al-Shabaab as propaganda, showed the final moments of the suburban jihadi's life. Earlier that month, under cover of darkness, he and his fellow terrorists had launched an attack on a military base in Northern Kenya. The video shows the quiet night shattering into explosions of gunfire and sparks, red and pink and blue. Evans, finally, is hit, the camera tumbling to the ground. "I have to admit, yes I have watched that," Sally Evans said. "No mother should have to see that. That was awful. And it wasn't— it was just hearing—hearing the final moments, as a mom, and there was nothing I could do."

Thomas's death was an emotional paradox for his family. "I hope God will forgive me," Sally Evans said, "but I am relieved that Hakim is gone. 'Cause he can't do that anymore. Can't inflict pain on anybody anymore." His pictures were still all over her home. She laughed, flipping through albums with Micheal, looking at childhood photos of two spindly, pale boys with toothy smiles. "They had him 99 percent, but there was that 1 percent that he was still my son," she said. "I can't let that go." Even when he became Abdul Hakim, "He always said, 'I love you, Mom.'"

When she finally had to catch the bus to work, Sally Evans walked me to the door and let me out onto the street in Wooburn Green. I thanked her for her time and expressed sympathy for her loss. With some effort, she smiled. "It never goes away," she said, "does it?"

20

THE SHORTEST SPRING

THE SECURITY OFFICERS REVERSED HARD, pulling away as protesters gave chase, swarming their armored Humvee. In an explosion of dust and debris, the vehicle hit a barrier on the edge of Cairo's 6th October Bridge, uprooting a light post and sending it over the edge to shatter on the concrete fifty feet below. The Humvee teetered and then plunged. It landed on its roof, hard. Blood stained the ground. The crowd below closed around the wreckage, throwing stones and shouting. It was August 14, 2013, and the bridge was filled with protesters against Egypt's military regime. For them, that hole in the barrier was a symbol of hope: a punch, delivered to the military and its escalating crackdowns.

Teo Butturini, an Italian photographer, had woken early that morning to a call from another journalist, warning him that police were storming a massive protest at Rabaa al-Adawiya Square. Demonstrators there and at al-Nahda in Giza had taken to the streets after the military overthrow of the country's democratically elected Muslim Brotherhood president, Mohammed Morsi, six weeks earlier. The protests had gradually evolved into semi-permanent encampments, stoking ever more ire from the military regime. The resulting crackdown had been anticipated. The government would later emphasize that the protesters had been warned.

By the time Butturini and the group of thousands moving with him reached the bridge, police had surrounded the area. He heard the boom of the Humvee crashing to the ground, and saw the protesters surging. That's when Egyptian security forces opened fire on the crowd. "The army start to shoot at us," he recalled. "And people start to fall down close to me." Butturini took cover behind a pylon under the bridge. It wasn't until forces started hurling tear gas that he felt he had to run—making a dash toward the cover of nearby buildings. He didn't make it far. "I heard five bullets passing close to me, and hitting me on the left side," he remembered. Butturini struggled through the streets, bleeding, waving his hands at passing cars. Finally, one stopped and took him to a hospital.

Emergency room doctors saved his life by removing most of a bullet-shredded kidney. The rest was a daze. His strongest memory was of the bodies: dozens piled in the back of military trucks, and more overwhelming the hospital. "I tried to scream," he said, "but I'm not sure any sound came out." Butturini, a meticulous photojournalist who had kept snapping pictures through other violent crises, retained few images from that day. His memory card, stashed in a boot as he arrived at the hospital, disappeared as Egyptian security officers swarmed the premises, taking surviving protesters into custody.

This was, many who lived to tell the tale remarked, Egypt's "Tiananmen Square." Reports suggested eight hundred seventeen people were killed at Rabaa al-Adawiya Square alone. By most counts more than one thousand were likely killed in crackdowns across Egypt that day. Human Rights Watch, after a yearlong, exhaustive investigation, concluded that Egyptian "police and army forces systematically and intentionally used excessive lethal force . . . resulting in killings of protesters at a scale unprecedented in Egypt." Snipers were placed on rooftops to fire on protesters. Soldiers were stationed to block exits as people desperately tried to escape.

THE UNITED STATES KNEW the massacre was coming. "It wasn't a secret that the government was going to go in there with overwhelming force," said Anne Patterson, whom I had encountered in Pakistan and who was, by August 2013, the American ambassador in Cairo. "That had been our concern for weeks prior to this." During those weeks, the United States scrambled for a diplomatic solution, both from State Department officials like Patterson and from congressional leaders. Secretary of State John Kerry sent his deputy, Bill Burns, to work out an agreement that would limit the scope and size of the Brotherhood's protests. Congress dispatched its top two foreign policy hawks—Senators John McCain and Lindsey Graham—the week before the massacre to press for a return to calm and to civilian control. The senators pleaded with Egypt's top general, Abdel Fattah el-Sisi, interim vice president Mohamed ElBaradei, interim prime minister Hazem el-Beblawi and others, before the Egyptian cabinet sat down to debate intervention.

Graham later told the press the effort never inspired optimism. "You could tell people were itching for a fight. The prime minister was a disaster," he said, describing Beblawi's approach to the growing ranks of protesters. "He kept preaching to me: 'You can't negotiate with these people. They've got to get out of the streets and respect the rule of law.'" Sisi, meanwhile, seemed "intoxicated by power," as Graham recalled. "We talked to the military endlessly by that time," Patterson, the ambassador, explained. "They had gotten calls from Washington, from me. There just didn't seem to be anything else to be done at that point. I talked to Sisi the day before. They said they were going to exercise restraint."

Even Pentagon leadership eventually stepped in, with then–Secretary of Defense Chuck Hagel calling General Sisi again and again, sometimes as often as every other day, for weeks on end. John Kerry was among the officials who told me the military-to-military rapport that has long anchored US-Egyptian relations was the most potent channel for defusing such crises. "The US investment over decades in building up the Egyptian military . . . made a difference when Mubarak was considering firing on the protesters" during the earlier flash point in Tahrir Square, Kerry said. In that case, "there were back-channel mil-to-mil conversations that I promise you factored into the Egyptian military telling Mubarak they would not follow his orders if he wanted them to go kill ten thousand kids in the square." But in the case of the Rabaa massacre under Sisi's leadership a few years later, those same pleas from American military leaders fell on deaf ears. None of it registered in Cairo.

"Did you make an angry call after it started?" I asked Patterson.

"I don't think so," she said. "Because I think we'd said everything we had to say at that point."

IN THE DAYS BEFORE THE MASSACRE, the Egyptian cabinet huddled in a government building in Tahrir Square to discuss what to do about the protesters. The exertions of the Americans had little bearing on the conversation. "I met McCain and Graham but I felt that they were not able to understand how important [it was] for a transition government . . . to assure they can protect the security of the people," said Beblawi, the interim prime minister. "The security of the people cannot be accepted and believed in," he continued, "if you feel somebody is staking out territory by force, in the middle of the capital." Beblawi told me he had taken calls from Ambassador Patterson and heard her out, but that, ultimately, "I didn't feel any pressure."

Beblawi was in his office at the International Monetary Fund in

Washington, DC, slouching in a green chair that swallowed up his small form. A mantle of dandruff dusted his shoulders. Three years had passed since the Rabaa massacre. "I have no regrets," he said. "I feel very sorry this happened. I don't know how it ended this way, but I think if the situation would have been reversed, it might be even worse." He furrowed his salt-and-pepper eyebrows. "The cost was high, no one expected it to be as much. Also there was a lot of exaggeration and many numbers were brought from outside," he said skeptically. Beblawi's response, like those of most officials behind the crackdown, was a thicket. The loss of life was regrettable, but also not so bad as all that. The decision was the right one, but also out of their hands. The police and military, he later told me tartly, "are not controllable all the time." In any case, he felt, the protesters started it. "Of course, they are challenging the authority, challenging it by force, and actually in both Rabaa and Enada, the first bullet was coming from among the Muslim Brothers. This is for sure, the starting of the using fire was on them." I pointed out to Beblawi that most international human rights assessments disputed that narrative. He shrugged. "They asked for this." When I asked him if American influence had any effect, he said, simply, "No."

Interim Vice President ElBaradei—who had been leading negotiations with the Brotherhood protesters and served as one of the main liaisons with Graham and McCain—pushed back against armed intervention, arguing that a deal with the demonstrators was possible, according to several sources present at the time. Fahmy, the interim foreign minister, reportedly took his side, though he refused to confirm his position on the matter to me. "The decision to do Rabaa was a cabinet decision," Fahmy said, declining to elaborate on the breakdown of perspectives in those final, critical days. After the fact, Fahmy, like Beblawi, has struck a defensive posture, assigning blame to the protesters. "They had blocked all the streets," he told me, shaking his head.

"And this area, by the way, is a heavily inhabited area." The largely unarmed protesters, he sugested, were a menace to public safety. This was the influence America's most muscular diplomatic intervention—and an annual military assistance package totaling $1.3 billion—had purchased: at best, a few extra words, behind closed doors, shortly before the slaughter.

A YEAR AND A HALF BEFORE, on a hot Saturday in February 2012, I'd watched as Hillary Clinton filed into a palace in Tunisia overlooking the Mediterranean, to deliver a speech about the future of democracy in the region. After Richard Holbrooke's death, I had put together a small team of Foreign Service officers to focus on the global implications of the youth unrest I'd seen vividly in Afghanistan and that then unfolded across North Africa and the Middle East. That February in Tunisia, Clinton was announcing my role as part of an initiative focused on youth outreach and public diplomacy.

There was a placard on the podium with a map of the world showing a glowing gradient centered on the Middle East. This was meant to suggest a spreading wave of democratic enlightenment, but it looked more like a blast radius. Clinton appeared small behind the podium, in a vaulted chamber at the heart of the palace, a blue and white jewel of a building called Nejma Ezzohara (Arabic for "Star of Venus"), constructed in the 1920s by an heir to a French banking fortune, Baron Rodolphe d'Erlanger.

A sea of upturned faces—the kind of optimistic, educated, and generally nonrepresentative youths rounded up by American embassies for photo ops—looked on as Clinton preached the virtues of democracy. "You were fearless on the front lines of the revolution, enduring tear gas and beatings. It takes a different kind of courage to be guardians of your new democracy," she told them. "Transitions can be derailed and detoured to new autocracies," she continued. "The victors of revolutions can become their victims. It is up to you to resist the calls of demagogues, to build coalitions, to keep faith in the system even when your candidates lose at the polls. . . . That means not just talking about tolerance and pluralism—it means living it."

On the way out, Clinton, hair pulled back ballerina-tight, black and blue jacket billowing, paused on one of Nejma Ezzohara's spectacular terraces. Squinting into the sun, she extended an arm toward the brilliant blue of the Mediterranean. "Things are changing," she mused.

BUT THE TRUTH WAS that those changes had caught the United States flat-footed and robbed it of credibility on the themes of Clinton's speech. American administrations had chosen to stand shoulder-to-shoulder with the Middle East's autocratic strongmen for decades. When those autocrats' regimes crumbled and the alliances with them became a liability, the United States was slow to adapt. In the Middle East, as in Central Asia, military-to-military deals had eclipsed diplomacy for so long, we barely knew how to do anything else. Egypt was Exhibit A.

Throughout the Cold War, Soviet sponsorship of Egypt's military and constant conflict with Israel were at the heart of the US–Egypt relationship. Bloody skirmishes over land—including the attempt to reclaim the Sinai after which the 6th October Bridge was named—continued into the 1970s. But Egypt's new leader at that time, Anwar Sadat, was dogged in his reorientation of Egypt toward two radical new goals: a peace deal with Israel, and closer ties to the United States. Above all, he wanted the Sinai back in Egyptian hands, and felt peace was the way to achieve this.

In the United States, newly elected president Jimmy Carter seized on the moment, bringing together Egypt and Israel at Camp David for an iconic thirteen-day negotiation. One of its outcomes, a peace treaty signed six months later, forged the modern relationship between Israel, Egypt, and the United States. Israel agreed to withdraw from the Sinai and return it to Egypt. In exchange, diplomatic relations were restored between the two countries, and Israel was guaranteed free passage through the Suez Canal. The diplomatic achievement was secured with military funds, an arrangement that would blight the relationship for decades after. Under the agreement, the United States would commit to bankrolling Egypt.

Since 1987, that assistance has held steady at $1.3 billion per year. The bullets that ripped through protesters during the Rabaa massacre were almost certainly purchased with American funds. US military aid covers the cost of as much as 80 percent of Egypt's weapons. By 2011, the word "Egypt" appeared 13,500 times in the Pentagon's database of military contracts.

That arrangement reflected one of the oldest assumptions in foreign policy: that you can buy security. For a generation, Egypt appeared to be a proof point for that thinking. The country's repressive leaders—for most of those years, the Mubarak regime—helped secure American equities in the region. But, from the revolts of 2011 to the Rabaa massacre in 2013, when change swept the region, it betrayed fatal flaws in that conventional American wisdom. Buying security wasn't enough. Years of neglected diplomacy meant that Washington lacked other, essential tools of persuasion when conflict broke out.

THE CRACKS BEGAN TO SHOW in January 2011. Revolution was spreading—from neighboring Tunisia to Alexandria, and then to Cairo. That month, thousands of protesters in Tahrir Square rallied around an array of frustrations with Mubarak and his regime: from mass unemployment to corruption to heavy-handed policing.

The protesters sweeping the Arab world looked askance at the

United States' reliance on Egypt's repressive military regime as a sur-
rogate. But the US was slow on the uptake: as violence began to spark,
then–secretary of state Hillary Clinton proclaimed the regime "stable."
She deployed Frank Wisner, Richard Holbrooke's old friend and a veteran diplomat who had long been sympathetic to the Mubaraks, who
informed the public that "the president must stay in office." The State
Department was forced to disavow its own envoy's remarks. It called
for Mubarak to step down, too late and to little effect. In just seventeen
days, the uprising ended fifty-nine years of military rule. Mubarak was
removed, and America's relationship with Egypt was unmoored.

A committee of generals known as the Supreme Council of the
Armed Forces (SCAF) stepped in as a caretaker government while
preparations were made for the first free elections in Egyptian history, and promptly began a series of vicious crackdowns on civil society. In one December 2011 incident, employees from ten NGOs were
banned from leaving the country—among them Sam LaHood, son of
then–US transportation secretary Ray LaHood. The military leadership was thumbing its nose at the Americans.

Anne Patterson, who arrived as the new US ambassador to Egypt
in the first months of SCAF's leadership, called that period "really,
really disruptive . . . There were some Americans at the embassy; it
took weeks to get them out, maybe longer. We basically paid bail and
then they jumped bail—that was the deal. That got the relationship off
on a really bad foot."

WHEN THE ELECTIONS TOOK PLACE, the Islamist Muslim Brotherhood party swept the Parliament, with its leader, Mohamed Morsi,
securing the presidency. It was yet another shift in gravity for which
the United States was ill-prepared. The Brotherhood quickly proved
more problematic than the SCAF. Worst of all, from the perspective of the American foreign policy establishment, Morsi threw into

doubt the core tenet of the US-Egyptian alliance: support for Israel. The politician had, years earlier, described Zionists as "bloodsuckers" and "war-mongers," and complained that "futile [Israeli-Palestinian] negotiations are a waste of time and opportunities." Domestically, the Brotherhood's harsh social policies on issues such as women's rights and alcohol consumption alienated much of Egypt's largely secular population. A hastily constructed and fraudulently ratified constitution with terms favorable to the Brotherhood further infuriated Egyptians. After just one year in power, Morsi faced street protests as large as those that had ousted Mubarak.

As protests became more violent, the military—led by then–defense minister Abdel Fattah el-Sisi—forced Morsi from power and placed him on trial. Sisi was, in some ways, a return to the status quo ante: a strongman who would hold the line on Israel.

"I knew Sisi very well, and I knew it wasn't going to be great, don't get me wrong," said Patterson. "But frankly he's proven a lot more brutal than I ever would have predicted." Sisi's security forces clashed with protesters who took to the streets, enraged at the ouster of the democratically elected Muslim Brotherhood regime. Tensions mounted as the sit-ins and rallies grew, finally culminating in the bloody massacres of August 2013, at Rabaa, and elsewhere. In the years since, crackdowns have continued unabated. In the first year after the 2013 coup, under Sisi's rule, at least 2,500 civilians were killed and 17,000 wounded by the police or military. By March 2015, security forces had arrested more than 40,000 people, the majority of them on grounds of suspected support for the Muslim Brotherhood, although leftist activists, journalists, and university students were also detained. Hundreds of Egyptians were "disappeared." The repression, according to Human Rights Watch, was "on a scale unprecedented in Egypt's modern history."

Most of the targeted individuals were thrown in jail on sham charges—or on none whatsoever. As one prisoner recalled of his time at

Azouli, an isolated military jail: "There is no documentation that says you are there. If you die at Azouli, no one would know." In April 2014, 529 Brotherhood members were sentenced to death, one of the largest ever mass death sentences anywhere in the world. The attorneys of the accused were denied access to the "evidence" and those who protested were threatened.

The following year, the same court sentenced Morsi for his alleged role in the 2011 uprising. The former president faced public execution, by hanging, with more than 100 others sentenced alongside him. Morsi's coconspirators included one man who has been in jail since the 1990s and two who had already died.

"I would say it's the worst of anywhere I've ever seen outside of a war zone," said Frank Lowenstein, the longtime adviser to John Kerry. Tony Blinken, the deputy national security advisor at the time, offered a bleak prognosis of Sisi's impact: "Over time and almost inevitably if he continues to repress a significant minority of his own population . . . liberals, secularists, moderates, journalists, you name it, all have their voice taken away and many of them get thrown in jail, and thrown in jail where they're mixed with genuine radicals, that is a recipe for radicalizing a lot more people. And we can't forget that al-Qaeda was born in an Egyptian jail."

GROWING CONCERN OVER THE SISI REGIME and its use of American weapons did, at least, spark a debate over accountability. After Morsi's removal, questions arose over whether to abide by the so-called "coup clause" in US appropriations law—mandating a halt to direct assistance to "any country whose duly elected head of government is deposed by military coup d'état" until democracy is restored. President Morsi, though divisive, was by any account "duly elected." His removal was widely called a coup because, well, what else could you call it? Sisi's military regime had made no pretense of democracy.

But with $1.3 billion in annual military assistance at stake, the Obama administration refused to use the word. It first resorted to what the Associated Press called "difficult contortions" of language to avoid the term. Then, finally, senior State Department official Bill Burns was dispatched to inform lawmakers of the administration's formal decision: this coup would not be called a coup. The most militarized corners of American foreign policy were also among the most constrained, so much so that one of the most obvious coups in recent history could never be called what it was. Those constraints were tightened by the lack of alternatives: there was no diplomatic strategy to confront the disruption that would follow enforcing such a legislative provision.

Congress added to its appropriations a requirement that the secretary of state certify the Egyptian government was introducing democratic reforms, holding elections, defending women's rights and safeguarding free expression. But the conditions were toothless: the new requirements had a national security exemption large enough to fit an Apache helicopter, or several. Citing extremist activity in the Sinai, the administration soon resumed deliveries of just such helicopters, even during escalating crackdowns.

Shortly after the massacre at Rabaa in 2013, the Obama administration quietly, temporarily froze the transfer of several weapons systems. Planned deliveries of helicopters, F-16 aircraft, M1A1 tanks, and Harpoon missiles were placed on hold. It was all larger-scale equipment, rather than the tear gas and small arms being deployed in the regime's urban crackdowns. And other military support, like training operations and the delivery of many other kinds of spare parts for weapons, would continue. In March 2015, President Obama announced a full resumption of assistance. "By that time," Anne Patterson recalled, "the Sinai stuff had flared up . . . And the judgment was, 'yes they needed helicopters.'"

The posturing on Capitol Hill was just that. In fact, there was little leeway to change the relationship. "The problem we would have . . . is that the aid is already committed," said Sarah Leah Whitson of Human

Rights Watch. "Everything's pre-sold." It was a machine that couldn't be turned off. The Obama administration quietly attempted a more modest reform, signing off on an end to "cash flow financing"—a preferential system granted to Egypt and Israel that lets them purchase military equipment of their choice on credit, obligating corresponding appropriations of US assistance, potentially for years to come. "They lost a really important element," with that change, said Patterson. "They'll be forced to buy stuff that we think will be useful for them to buy." It was a slim ration of accountability—and didn't offer any control over what was actually done with the equipment. A scathing 2016 audit by the Government Accountability Office concluded that neither the State Department nor the Pentagon had any functional systems for monitoring how American weapons were being used in Egypt.

IN THE END, the halting reform efforts have been harsh reminders of the resistance to change in significant military alliances. Like Pakistan, Egypt was simply too big to fail, in its own eyes, and in the eyes of American policymakers.

A new array of threats, including the rise of ISIL in the country's Sinai Peninsula, have reinforced that leverage. Competition has played a role in immobilizing the relationship, too. Saudi Arabia, Kuwait, and the United Arab Emirates have pledged billions of dollars of economic support to Egypt, sometimes offering more than the United States, with fewer conditions. Saudi Arabia, in particular, has developed a cozy relationship with Sisi. Russia, too, has stepped into the fray, with meetings between Putin and Sisi and growing assistance packages.

"We certainly have influence," Kerry reflected. "But our leverage is not as simple a formula as some people assume. We are far from the only actor. . . . And leverage is a two-way street—we needed Egypt's help on a set of issues including ISIL and Israel." As a result, said Frank Lowenstein, "their attitude about it is, 'What the fuck are you really

going to do about it? You can't afford to have me fail.' That's the ultimate leverage that Sisi has: that he will fail. And that is an extraordinarily powerful form of leverage."

Meanwhile, years of dependence on military assistance had convinced both sides that arms and equipment sales were the only currency that could purchase influence, and that diplomatic overtures
were essentially cosmetic. As a result, precious little has changed in
the US–Egypt relationship since the Rabaa massacre. Security wasn't
simply the first priority, it was often the only one. And Washington
policymakers reverted to the traditional tools of arms and military
financing to enforce it, in part because they had forged few meaningful alternatives.

Egyptians suffered the consequences as the United States gave Sisi
its endorsement and support. "He's been . . . 'ruthless' is a good word.
Death penalties. Mass arrests of journalists. Shutting out NGOs,"
said General Hayden, the former CIA director, reflecting the common thinking about Sisi among American officials. But when I asked
Hayden if there was a point at which that should trigger an easing of
military assistance, he darkened. "I'm not prepared to say that," he said.
He steepled his hands, peering over his rimless glasses at me. "We make
our compromises," he mused. "We may incur a debt for the future."

Samantha Power, the US ambassador to the United Nations during
the Rabaa massacre, was critical of the American response to that crisis,
and since. "We should have completely revamped the relationship given
who Sisi was and made it purely transactional," she explained, exasperated. Instead, after brief pauses, US assistance inevitably resumed, and
the relationship "looked largely the same as before the massacre."

Power knew that cutting off the $1.3-billion aid package to Egypt
wasn't politically or strategically realistic, but was among the officials
who felt those funds could be allocated more cautiously. "Now the
Camp David rationale is over because [Israel's] Bibi [Netanyahu] and
Sisi have the relationship they need," so much of the logic of giving

the Egyptians whatever equipment they wanted was over, she said. "I argued for giving a huge share of that money to Tunisia. We should be rewarding countries who are struggling to progress in the direction we want them to."

Moral and ethical dilemmas like this were nothing new in geopolitics. But the particular intimacy between Washington and Cairo made the compromises feel closer to home. Of all the dictators who enthralled Donald Trump once he took office, Sisi appeared to earn the most attention and flattery. Trump reversed the Obama administration's decision to withhold invitations to the White House from Sisi and his top brass. Some of the Egyptians who witnessed the Obama-era relationship were optimistic about the shift. "With Trump," said Nabil Fahmy, the former interim foreign minister, "you finally have the two presidents talking to each other."

But for better or worse, even the sputtering attempts at accountability were receding in the rearview mirror. "Sisi is still getting support from the USA," Teo Butturini, the Italian photographer, said, shaking his head. "At the same time he is the person who actually ruled to go shoot at the people in Rabaa. He's the person who . . . made the antiprotest law. He is the person who is jailing a lot of journalists." One of the few photographs Butturini retained from his harrowing day in the midst of the maelstrom was of a tear gas canister, one of many picked up off the bloodied concrete by numb survivors. Several appeared to be American-made. One he photographed bore the logo of CTS—Combined Tactical Systems—a Jamestown, Pennsylvania–based arms manufacturer. It even had a support contact number, with a Pennsylvania area code that, presumedly, an Egyptian would have to call during business hours to lodge a complaint. Butturini never forgot the shouts of the protesters around him, brandishing the empty canisters: "They're shooting at us, the tear gas, and the tear gas comes from the USA."

21

MIDNIGHT AT THE RANCH

WAKING UP IN THE BED OF A WHITE CHEVY TRUCK trundling through the moorlands of central Colombia, Freddy Torres began to suspect that his evening had gone terribly wrong. The mild fall weather had given way to a cold wind; the forested highlands replaced by a low, flat heath. Scattered homes dotted the landscape, and the early dawn was silent. Most worrying were the burlap sacks that bumped against his outstretched legs and the empty bottles of *aguardiente*: they were filled with rifles. Torres—a young man in his twenties, born and raised in the village of Cabrera, Cundinamarca, an afternoon's drive south from Bogota—hadn't meant to end up here, hungover, confused, and hours from home. The truck ride was the final stop on a liquor-fueled twelve-hour bender. Now, three strange men with strange names—*Paisa*, a common nickname for people from Medellin, *Costeño*, meaning "coast," and another man who, improbably, was also named Freddy—had led him to what felt like the end of the world.

It was the early hours of September 17, 2006, and Torres was about to come face-to-face with the secret costs of the United States' most expensive military alliance in Latin America. In the coked-out frenzy of that region's war on drugs, many of the same dynamics evident in Afghanistan, Somalia, and Egypt have plagued the United States' alliances. Colombia, where the costliest of the region's relationships has played out in the form of the multibillion-dollar Plan Colombia military-and-development assistance package, throws into relief some of the worst pitfalls of America's Faustian pacts with foreign militaries. For years, the Colombian relationship served chiefly as a cautionary tale of the human rights abuses, rampant corruption, and explosion of drugs that sprang from America's military interventions in Latin America and its insistence on prioritizing guns over negotiations. But Colombia, in recent years, has also become what US officials described as a success story, a model of how to put civilian assistance front and center in a national-security-sensitive relationship dominated by generals talking to generals.

That night in September 2006 had started quietly for Freddy Torres. Walking home from a job—he often pulled days-long trucking shifts that took him to the far reaches of the country—he bumped into his cousin Elvir at a *rocola,* a neighborhood joint serving as half bodega, half bar. Elvir—always gregarious and fun-loving, never short of friends—was with an acquaintance, the man also named Freddy, and the three ordered rounds of beer. They joked around, calmly whiling away the hours, half-watching children kick a soccer ball around in the park nearby.

As evening fell, the young men grew restless. Several drinks in, their new friend Freddy suggested that the cousins accompany him to a bar in Fusa, a bigger city several hours away. After their friend offered to pay for the trip, the cousins agreed to come with him, on a lark. Their friend left the store to make a phone call—of which Torres caught one phrase: "I'm bringing two people"—and returned fifteen minutes later, telling Elvir to go find a car to rent.

The three packed into an early 1980s Renault and set out for

Fusa, picking up two men—Paisa and Costeño—on the way. A drive that would normally take only two or three hours stretched through the night, as the men stopped in forgettable bar after forgettable bar, in small town after small town. Just as often, they'd swap cars—a detail that an increasingly intoxicated Torres paid little attention to. Around midnight, after a delay at a checkpoint, the drunk men made it to Fusa, and after several boozy hours at the La Curva strip club and a meal of street empanadas, arepas, and shish kabobs, Freddy, Paisa, and Costeño suggested the cousins join them at a nearby ranch—owned by a friend, but long abandoned—to sleep off the drinks before returning home. Dawn was approaching and neither thought twice before accepting. Clambering into the bed of the Chevy—their fourth car of the evening—Torres and Elvir promptly fell asleep.

It was upon waking that Torres noticed the guns.

After a long, tense drive, the men parked the car and handed Torres and his cousin black sweatshirts to change into. The new friends that Torres felt increasingly convinced weren't friends led them to an isolated two-room ranch house, seemingly empty and abandoned, and told them to wait in the bedroom while the other men looked for supplies.

Torres slipped out of the house to urinate. That's when he noticed fresh footprints in the earth around the house—odd, for a supposedly abandoned property. He had been unnerved since their arrival, and he took the footprints as confirmation of his fears: that they were being set up, possibly by more men than the ones they'd been drinking with. Deciding not to wait to learn if he was right, Torres hurried back inside and told his cousin it was time to leave. The two had almost made it out of the house when their drinking buddies opened fire. Dodging the deadly spray, Torres leapt out the back window and ran for a nearby forest, where he hid for nearly ten hours, as his would-be killers scoured the hills for him. When the sun began to fall, he walked to the nearest town and called the police and his family.

Torres survived. Elvir was killed.

This was only the beginning of Freddy Torres's strange saga. To his surprise, the military falsely pronounced Elvir a guerrilla combatant in the civil war, and reported his death as a combat kill. Torres launched a campaign to clear his brother's name, which drew death threats. Eventually, an unseen shooter fired through his windshield as he sat parked near his home in Bogota in February 2007. He escaped injury, but, after the assassination attempt, Torres uprooted his family and adopted a peripatetic life, changing cell numbers and houses every few months. The authorities, he said, were unresponsive to his pleas for protection. ("They don't help anyone," he told me, "because they don't want to have problems with the state.") Torres was convinced that Elvir's murder and the subsequent intimidation efforts could only have come from power players within the Colombian military. Eventually, his suspicions bore out, when an army colonel who had encouraged his soldiers to kill civilians was indicted for Elvir's murder. The men who went by "Freddy," "Paisa," and "Costeño" were never found, let alone arrested.

Torres's story matched thousands of others from bystanders to Colombia's "victorious" war on terror. Elvir was a casualty of the phenomenon of "false positives": the Colombian military's long-unacknowledged practice of extrajudicial killings. Under pressure from their commanders to create the appearance of success in the war against the guerrillas, members of the armed forces lured in unsuspecting civilians, killed them, and dressed the bodies up as FARC rebels. The deaths were used to inflate the military's batting average. Those who carried out the false positive killings were rewarded with vacation time, promotions, and medals. Victims included farmers, children, homeless people, drug users, the mentally disabled, and petty criminals. Rarely—if ever—were victims card-carrying FARC guerrillas.

Until 2008, most Colombian policymakers could pretend the false positives were merely a rumor, but that September, the so-called "Soa-

cha scandal" pulled the curtain back. Prosecutors learned the fates of
twenty-two impoverished young men from the slums of Bogota, who
had been promised well-paying jobs, transported out of the city, and
then murdered and dressed up as FARC members. General Mario
Montoya, commander of the Colombian Army, resigned on November
4, 2008. Prosecutors went on to investigate more than 3,000 alleged
false positives by militia personnel in the 2000s. In 2015, the UN refugee agency UNHCR reported that the total number of victims of false
positives could be as high as 5,000.

Colombia was no stranger to civilian executions, but the practice
soared in the final stage of its decades-long civil war, in the early 2000s.
The army took on FARC rebels with renewed fury, and was eager to
demonstrate progress to a frustrated public, and to its American finan-
ciers. Defense Minister Camilo Ospina de facto endorsed the practice
in 2005 when he issued the so-called Directive #29, which authorized
"the payment of rewards for the capture or killing of ringleaders of
the illegal armed groups." The reward was set at $1,500 per kill—a
little less than half what the average Colombian took home each year.
Civilian executions doubled the following year. How far up the scandal went was unclear, but the practice was common and not limited to
any unit or region. UN special rapporteur Philip Alston, after carrying
out an investigation into the practice, found "no evidence to suggest
that these killings were carried out as a matter of official Government
policy, or that they were directed by, or carried out with the knowledge of, the President or successive Defense Ministers."

FOR WASHINGTON, DC, the false positive killings might have just
been a tragic blip in another country's history, but for one fact: many
of the worst offenders were US-trained and funded. Researchers found
that Colombian army brigades that received more US assistance had
been associated with significantly more executions. In Washington's

race to support its Colombian partners in their mission to secure the country from so-called terrorists, US military officials and other policymakers often failed to take a close look at the fighters they were preparing for battle. Nearly half of Colombian commanders trained at the Western Hemisphere Institute for Security Cooperation at Fort Benning have been charged with a serious crime or commanded units whose members had committed extrajudicial killings. Commanders like General Jaime Lasprilla—a former instructor at Fort Benning who sanctioned or encouraged hundreds of killings under his command—were commonplace.

Even before the Soacha scandal broke, reports of extrajudicial killings were whispered within the United States' intelligence, military, and diplomatic corps. A 1994 cable from the US ambassador in Bogota warned of "body count mentalities," explaining that "field officers who cannot show track records of aggressive anti-guerrilla activity (wherein the majority of the military's human rights abuses occur) disadvantage themselves at promotion time." A CIA intelligence report from the same year was even more explicit, stating that the Colombian security forces "employ death squad tactics in their counterinsurgency campaign" and had "a history of assassinating leftwing civilians in guerrilla areas, cooperating with narcotics-related paramilitary groups in attacks against suspected guerrilla sympathizers, and killing captured combatants." The Pentagon came to a similar conclusion, reporting in 1997 on a "body count syndrome" in the Army that "tends to fuel human rights abuses by well-meaning soldiers trying to get their quota to impress superiors" and a "cavalier, or at least passive, approach when it comes to allowing the paramilitaries to serve as proxies . . . for the COLAR [Colombian Army] in contributing to the guerrilla body count." But the Colombians—and by extension, the Americans—were fighting a war. Often, the brass didn't have the time to police their soldiers, or the interest in doing so.

On October 28, 1998, Colombia's new president, Andres Pastrana Arango, stood in the Rose Garden next to President Clinton and became a participant in one of the strangest political press conferences on record. The goal was to discuss the deepening ties between the two nations that would eventually take the form of a watershed new assistance package. "This was the first stage of Plan Colombia," Pastrana told me. "The first time we really, really talked about Colombia," at such a high level.

The reporters in attendance had other topics in mind. "The first question in the press conference," Pastrana recalled, "was 'How are you going to explain to Chelsea the scandal?!'" In fact, the question was several deep into the conference, but his recollection was, otherwise, correct. The transcript of the press conference reads like a layer cake—Clinton valiantly attempting to redirect toward foreign policy, the press corps hammering him about the sex scandal involving a White House intern and engulfing his presidency.

Clinton, Pastrana recalled, was stressed. "He offered me a Diet Coke. You could tell he was a human being, for the first time you saw the human side." The surreal juxtaposition continued. Around the margins of the press conference, Pastrana asked for ten minutes with Clinton, in the Oval Office. As Pastrana recalled, Clinton went to his desk and pulled out a map of Colombia, and the two men looked at areas that Pastrana intended to demilitarize. Then, Pastrana said, "He asked me what I thought of his answer to the first question," referring to Monica Lewinsky. Pastrana told Clinton he'd done all right. He chuckled at the memory. "It was strange," he said. The two men got along. "It was good chemistry." The conversations continued and, over the following year, evolved into the plan that would define Clinton's legacy in Latin America. "I proposed what I called a Marshall Plan for Colombia," Pastrana said. The result was a ten-billion dollar aid, development, and military assistance infusion.

In selling the expensive plan, Clinton appealed to an American public obsessed with drugs. Gallup polls from 2001 show that overwhelming majorities of US citizens expressed a "great deal" of concern about drug use. Since 90 percent of America's cocaine was coming from Colombia at that point, it made sense that much attention was directed at the Latin American nation. Clinton had an easy sell: "Colombia's drug traffickers directly threaten America's security," he told the public. Plan Colombia "would enable Colombia's counter-drug program to inflict serious damage on the rapidly expanding drug production activity in areas now dominated by guerrillas or paramilitary groups." Anne Patterson, who had been US ambassador to Pakistan during Holbrooke's stint in the region and in Egypt after, was also the ambassador to Colombia for the first three years of the new assistance plan. "The strategy is to give the Colombian government the tools to combat terrorism and narco-trafficking, two struggles that have become one," she told me. "To fight against narco-trafficking and terrorism, it is necessary to attack all links of the chain simultaneously."

President Clinton decided to waive human rights provisions in the funding legislation, arguing that security came first. In justifying the waiver, the president explained that "our assistance package is crucial to maintaining our counterdrug efforts and helping the Colombian government and people to preserve Colombia's democracy."

Initially, Colombia wanted a 70–30 social-military split; the United States wanted the reverse. The final plan was written in large part by a Colombian—by Jaime Ruiz, one of Pastrana's closest aides, in Pastrana's and Ruiz's telling—but it bore the obvious marks of those American priorities. It set aside $1.3 billion a year for a decade to combat "narco-terrorism." The first year, more than 70 percent of the funds went to military and police assistance—including everything from Black Hawks to communications equipment to trainers to chemical warfare technology. As the former US ambassador Robert White put it: "[Colombia] comes and asks for bread and you give them stones." But the remainder of the American money went to economic development, judicial reforms, and aid for displaced people. And the greatest successes of the deal came only as the balance of military and civilian assistance evened, and US and Colombian officials began to recognize the value of rebuilding the country's long-suffering institutions.

THE UNITED STATES' ENTANGLEMENT in Colombia was shaped by the same anti-communist zeal that propelled American involvement from Vietnam to Afghanistan. Concerns over drugs would come later. Seeds of the trends that would explode under President Trump—the devaluing and de-prioritization of diplomacy, the rise of generals in policymaking—were planted in this earlier period, amid the military adventures of the Cold War. Hundreds of thousands of innocents would become casualties of those interventions.

The Colombian intervention began with a Special Warfare trip to Bogota in 1962, headed by Lieutenant General William Yarborough, commander of the US Army Special Warfare Center, who proposed one of the era's classic proxy wars, using locals "to perform counter-agent and counter-propaganda functions and as necessary execute paramilitary, sabotage, and/or terrorist activities against known communist proponents."

Based on his findings, the US helped the Colombian government formulate Plan Lazo, a counterinsurgency strategy modeled on the Phoenix Program in Vietnam. Formally adopted by the Colombian military on July 1, 1962, Plan Lazo was sold to the Colombians as a "hearts and mind" strategy. In fact, it was an American plot to wipe out communists, aided by civilian informants. Plan Lazo was reinforced by a Colombian presidential order called Decree 3398 that stated, "all Colombians, men and women . . . will be used by the government in

activities and work that contribute to the reestablishment of order"—
in effect allowing Colombian authorities to organize ordinary citizens
into militia groups. Together with the US-backed Plan Lazo, Decree
3398 created civilian "self-defense units" and "hunter-killer teams"
instructed and authorized to kill armed or unarmed peasants.

The US Army and the CIA began instructing Colombian troops
in the same techniques being introduced in Vietnam. As part of a CIA
program, USAID provided training to Colombian police at the agency's "bomb school" in Los Fresnos, where the curriculum included
courses like "Terrorist Devices," "Incendiaries," and "Assassination
Weapons."

The United States wasn't just teaching the Colombian army to fight
the communists—it was underwriting that fight. Beginning in the
1960s, Colombian forces used US-supplied vehicles, communications
equipment, and arms to destroy rebel communities across the country. The counterinsurgency campaign against communist campesinos—
most were peasants—began in earnest on May 18, 1964, when the
Colombian army sent one-third of its troops to destroy the left-leaning
village of Marquetalia, defended by a few dozen fighters. The operation
was undertaken at the request of the United States, with American assistance. US military advisers were there for the planning and the execution. After that first assault, the Colombian government began attacking
other self-governing leftist rural communities.

That the Colombian initiatives were corrupt and mismanaged—
and that they encouraged more bloodshed—was no secret in Foggy
Bottom. Secretary of State Dean Rusk and UN ambassador Adlai Ste-
venson admitted to the moral contradiction, writing in cables that US
funding was encouraging rural violence and economic dislocation.
And the State Department would be hard-pressed to argue that the
prolonged fighting between the leftists and the US-backed Colombian military did much to improve the lot of most Colombians: the

underlying class struggle that sparked the conflict persisted, as the landless remained disenfranchised and the urban elite grew rich from the chaos. US investment and loans surged during this time, leading President Alberto Lleras Camargo to remark drily, "blood and capital accumulation went together."

THE REVOLUTIONARY ARMED FORCES of Colombia (FARC) rose up soon after, in direct response to the US-backed attacks on leftists in Colombia. After the obliteration of Marquetalia, the few remaining leftists from the area fled to the mountains, where they banded with other rebel groups, who together pledged to fight for better conditions for people in the countryside and to defend their followers from military abuses.

Their organization swelled rapidly. FARC became not just a guerrilla force struggling for more land, but a political movement pushing socialist reorganization of the country. Rural peasants, indigenous people, Afro-Colombians, landless laborers, unionists, teachers, intellectuals—people "of the soil"—joined the fight. FARC began to organize schools, medical centers, and social projects, essentially running a parallel state.

But the group was still, at its core, a fighting force. Soon after organizing, FARC leaders began training militias in rural areas to carry out attacks. FARC relied on a campaign of terrorism, not only bombing police stations and military bases, but also hospitals, churches, and schools. Kidnapping for ransom provided revenues—until the late 1970s, when the group began trafficking in cocaine.

During Reagan's first term, Colombia accounted for almost eighty percent of both cocaine and marijuana that reached the United States. FARC's newfound drug fortune allowed it to attract support from Colombians who were unhappy with the staggering poverty facing much of the country. By 1980, FARC's numbers had grown sixfold to some three thousand fighters spread across the country. Revenues soared, eventually topping billions. And the violence worsened. FARC's reign of terror targeted priests, politicians, military officers, and even prominent right-wing civilians, often simply to incite fear.

In turn, elite landowners hired right-wing fighting forces, many of which traced their roots to the US-backed groups under Plan Lazo. These groups aggressively targeted anyone hostile to their employers. The paramilitaries were everywhere: at their peak, they counted thirty thousand people in their ranks and operated in two-thirds of the country. Some were armed by the government and legally sanctioned. And they were brutal: one group, the AUC, killed more than nineteen thousand people in its first two years of operation.

The paramilitary death squads over time gained the support of the government, military, traffickers—and even the United States. The White House refused to support any peace dialogue between the government and the leftists, which it decried as "narco-guerrillas." In some cases, Reagan's White House went as far as to directly support right-wing paramilitaries as informants or assassins.

In the eighties, in one of the more ill-fated partnerships in America's transnational war against drugs, the Colombian army and the twenty largest cocaine traffickers teamed up to establish a national counterterrorism training school, supported by US intelligence. The group was known as MAC, or *Muerte a Secuestradores* ("Death to Kidnappers") and had, ostensibly, a simple mission: to thwart FARC's tactic of abducting politicians and the wealthy. Traffickers were required to put down thirty-five thousand US dollars as an initial fee. Generals contracted Israeli and British mercenaries to do the training; CIA and US intelligence agencies participated.

The group was successful in the sense that it was deadly; eventually, it grew into another paramilitary, criminal extension of the army, doing the government's dirty work in the war against FARC, with little, if any, focus on stopping kidnappers. MAC would go on to arrest the peace process led by President Bentancur in the 1980s by murdering over seven hundred FARC members who entered the political process as part of the Unión Patriótica, a leftist political party. In an ironic twist, many of these paramilitary organizations got into the drug business too, and US dollars sent to Colombia to combat the war against drugs found their way into traffickers' pockets.

The result was an Escheresque tesselation of faction and violence. In 1999, Columbia experienced thousands of acts of terror and kidnappings. The homicide rate was a staggering sixty per one hundred thousand. Nearly twenty-thousand FARC fighters were holed up around the country, netting millions from kidnappings. A full half of Colombia's territory lacked a security presence; FARC essentially governed the entire south, where the government did not dare enter. More than 700,000 Colombians left the country from 1995 to 2000. The violence had grown more grisly, too: the AUC massacred civilians by the dozen, making a name for itself with macabre tactics like playing soccer with severed heads and cutting their victims apart with chain saws.

Clinton's drug czar, General Barry McCaffrey, remembered the violence vividly. "You couldn't drive anywhere in country without risking being kidnapped. It was sort of like dialing for dollars: The FARC checkpoint would search your name, get your worth, and you'd end up either kidnapped or dead in jungle." It was a "vile situation."

By the end of the century, Colombians had decided it was time for a permanent peace. Thirteen million people showed up at the "*No mas*" nationwide protest of the war in October 1999, in a country of forty million. Later that month, ten million voted for peace in a symbolic referendum that served as a wake-up call for Colombian politicians. No official political election had ever seen such a high turnout.

Andres Pastrana, who was president at the time and had himself once been kidnapped by the Medellín Cartel, said he immediately understood the ramifications of that vote. "No presidential candidate has ever received that many votes," he said. So, after he was elected president, he "decided the first thing I should do was try and achieve peace." Pastrana attempted tactics never seen before. He met with top FARC leaders, even going as far as travelling into the mountains to personally speak with the rebel commanders. He granted FARC a demilitarized zone as a show of goodwill. He began official peace talks in his first six months on the job. And, of course, he and Clinton, after that strange encounter in the Rose Garden, brokered Plan Colombia.

NEARLY TWO DECADES LATER, that Plan Colombia was considered a success story spoke to just how grim the situation had been before. The costs of the deal were astronomical in both financial and human terms. The United States had spent $10 billion propping up Colombia's security forces, economy, and political institutions. Only Israel and Egypt received more aid. From 2005 to 2014, more than one hundred and seventy thousand political assassinations targeting leftists had reportedly been carried out. The false positives scandal claimed the lives of thousands. Human rights abuses, some of them enmeshed in American assistance, were frequent: US-made smart bombs were used in the mid-2000s to wipe out FARC leaders outside of Colombia's borders, which often led to the deaths of civilians.

Incidents of "secret state terror" were common. Most famous was the destruction of the town of San Vicente del Caguán in February 2002—an attack that echoed the joint US-Colombian attack on Marquetalia forty years earlier. Government forces, under US pressure, invaded San Vicente, in the prosperous, largely self-governing southern territory colloquially referred to as "Farclandia." San Vicente was a successful community, with its own police force, new highways and bridges, widespread electricity, quality schools and a health care system. But after a round of peace talks abruptly broke off, Pastrana ordered the military to invade. US-supplied A-37s and A-47s dropped bombs. Thirteen thousand US-trained troops circled the village. The government declared victory, telling the media they had wiped out the supposed FARC camps in the area. And they had—along with a number of civilians, including children and the elderly.

Victims of the war seldom saw justice. Militants were "incarcerated" on farms and in villas, after which they could emerge with their wealth and networks intact, immune from further prosecution or extradition. US-extradited paramilitary leaders tended to receive light sentences—just seven years, a little more than half what street-level dealers arrested for selling less than an ounce of cocaine would serve.

Nearly two decades after Plan Colombia was launched—and nearly seventy years after US intervention in Colombia began—the question remained: Did Washington's insistence on achieving its military and security aims come at too high a human cost? And could stronger civilian influences at the decision-making table have prevented deaths like Elvir's? When I asked General McCaffrey, the Clinton administration drug czar, whether the United States bore any responsibility for the civilian deaths throughout the civil war, he was fiercely dismissive. The idea of US complicity was "complete illogical poppycock of the worst sort. Just utter nonsense."

"Why would that be the case?" he asked, referring to the data suggesting a correlation between US support and Colombian units committing abuses. "Why would oversight by US Foreign Service officers and military officers . . . increase EJK and mayhem? It's just complete nonsense. More likely those units were just more involved in counterinsurgency . . . some may well have been involved in more action which may have included human rights violations. But [blaming the US] is such poppycock it's beyond belief."

"It was a bloody war, there were some bloody things that happened," he conceded. "But basically [the Colombian Army] was the most trusted institution in Colombian society."And indeed, the militaries were often the most trusted institutions in countries marked by these American proxy wars. The uncomfortable question US officials seldom confronted was the extent to which American support elevated those militaries to their status as the only lasting structures in their lands.

WHATEVER ITS COSTS, Plan Colombia—unlike later efforts in, for instance, Pakistan—eventually rebalanced toward civilian assistance, and laid the foundations for peace. In the plan's first decade, the national police expanded into all of the country's municipalities, helping knock kidnappings down from three thousand a year to just over two hundred. Killings were cut nearly in half, as was the size of FARC's forces. By 2006, Colombia had achieved the voluntary demobilization of more than thirty thousand combatants, put an end to much of the paramilitary violence, and launched peace talks with AUC commanders, many of whom agreed to prosecution in exchange for lighter prison sentences.

In the relationship with Colombia, unlike so many other similar alliances, there was a holistic development plan surrounding the arms and the human rights waivers. The nonmilitary and military components of the deal reinforced one another. "We tried to get Congress to do a Free Trade Agreement with Colombia, we supported [Colombian president] Uribe in his democratic security efforts to rebuild institutions in Colombia," Condoleezza Rice recalled. "But the FARC had to be defeated. The reason you have reasonable peace negotiations now is the FARC couldn't hold Cartagena and Bogota hostage any longer." That more balanced integration of diplomatic and security strategy was at the heart of what ultimately brought peace to an embattled nation. At the end of the day, McCaffrey said, "We're talking about the most successful policy intervention by the US since World War II."

The United States' military alliances around the world present a record of tragedy and chaos, but there are also lessons to be learned. "If you look at Plan Colombia," Rice said, "diplomacy led." But in the years that followed, the Trump administration would struggle to apply elsewhere the lessons that had made Colombia an atypical model of success. As sweeping budget cuts made the kind of comprehensive, integrated development assistance that had anchored Plan Colombia scarce, and a new wave of arms deals and calls to strongmen appeared to unmoor American foreign policy from human rights concerns, there was little indication those lessons had registered at all.

PART III

PRESENT AT THE DESTRUCTION

■

WASHINGTON, DC, 2017

NORTH KOREA, 2007

There ain't no truce or negotiatin' with thug lords
Tried conversatin' but he won't listen

—2PAC, *GRAB THE MIC*

22

THE STATE OF THE SECRETARY

R EX TILLERSON'S TEAM was fighting again. "So, who's going to go in with him?" Margaret Peterlin, his chief of staff, was saying. She looked me up and down with an expression that suggested she'd discovered a pest in the house. We were standing on Mahogany Row, at the wide double doors into the secretary of state's office. Under Secretary of State for Public Diplomacy Steven Goldstein folded his arms and stared daggers at Peterlin. "Well, I guess I won't be," he told her. "Heather can go." He tilted his head toward Tillerson's spokesperson, the former *Fox News* anchor Heather Nauert. Peterlin narrowed her eyes at Goldstein. "Are you *sure*?" she said, with theatrical displeasure. Goldstein didn't reply. Tillerson strode up to the door, cutting the tension.

Such discord often simmered just under the surface in the months before Tillerson's unceremonious firing in March 2018, according to multiple members of his embattled inner circle. Often it emanated from Peterlin, a formidable attorney and former congressional staffer who helped draft the Patriot Act after the September 11 attacks and guided Tillerson through his confirmation process. When she was passed a note indicating I'd arrived that day, she'd given the rest of the team an ultimatum: from the public relations staff, only Goldstein would be permitted in the interview. Goldstein had pointed out that Nauert, as spokesperson, would be the one responsible for answering ensuing public questions. Peterlin had insisted there was simply no room. Two staffers said there was another motivation: Peterlin had been lobbying to get Nauert fired. The standoff hadn't been resolved by the time I was ushered in to see Tillerson, nor as I left, when a second contretemps ensued over who would stay behind with the secretary. (Goldstein again insisted on Nauert, visibly vexing Peterlin.)

This squabbling barely qualified as drama, but it was unusual behavior to display so openly in front of a reporter, and at odds with the kind of tightly organized messaging prized by most of Tillerson's predecessors. It provided a small window into a State Department that appeared to be plunged into chaos at every level. As the Trump administration ceded policy authority to the Pentagon and the growing number of generals within the White House, this was the sole counterbalance: an enfeebled State Department, led by secretaries seemingly drafted into the job based on their willingness to serve as diplomacy's executioners—and, in Tillerson's case, fired just as quickly for their failure to do so.

WHEN WE MET IN JANUARY 2018, Tillerson was wearing a charcoal suit and a canary yellow tie, patterned with horseshoes. He was sitting, legs crossed, relaxed, in one of the blue-and-gold upholstered chairs in the secretary's office, a few feet from the spot where Richard Holbrooke's heart had burst seven years before. The office looked much as it had that day, except for the art: when Tillerson first set up shop, he'd replaced the portraits of dead diplomats with scenes of the American West. Tillerson got compared to a cowboy a lot, and between the decor and the horseshoes, appeared to be leaning into it. The name helped: Rex Wayne Tillerson, after Rex Allen and John Wayne, the actors behind some of Hollywood's most indelible swaggering cowboys.

Tillerson was born in Wichita Falls, Texas, and was raised there and in neighboring Oklahoma by parents of modest means. His father "drove a truck selling bread at grocery stores," his mother raised the kids. The couple had met through the Boy Scouts, when his mother visited her brother at the camp where Tillerson's father worked. Tillerson honored that legacy by remaining active in Boy Scouts leadership for much of his career. His biography was marked by earnest overachievement: he was an Eagle Scout, and then a member of his high school band, in which he played the kettle and snare drums, and which yielded a marching band scholarship to the University of Texas at Austin. Over the course of more than forty years at ExxonMobil, culminating in his decade-long tenure as CEO, he'd amassed a personal fortune of at least three hundred million dollars—not including the roughly one hundred and eighty million dollar retirement package he received upon his departure from the firm to enter government. The call to serve in the Trump administration had thrown into disarray plans for retirement, to his wife Renda and two horse and cattle ranches in Texas. "I didn't want this job," he said. "My wife told me I'm supposed to do this. . . . I was going to go to the ranch to be with my grandkids." When I asked if, a year in, he thought he'd made the right call taking the job, he laughed. Peterlin shot him a warning look. "Yeah," he said. "It's been" —he furrowed his brow, appearing to search for the word— "*interesting.*"

WHEN TRUMP NOMINATED TILLERSON to the job, his experience running one of the largest multinational corporations in the world inspired optimism among career officials. Maybe, several said, he'd be a fierce defender of the Department. Maybe he'd bring to the job a private sector knack for institutional growth—or at least savvy, targeted trimming. And Tillerson's first remarks to his workforce—

about ten minutes of them, standing on the stairs of the packed State Department lobby—had been well received. "I'm the new guy," he'd affably informed the crowd. He'd mentioned the walls at either end of the lobby, where the names of hundreds of Foreign Service officers killed in the line of duty are engraved in marble. "The buzz was okay," recalled Erin Clancy, the Foreign Service officer who narrowly avoided firing during the Mahogany Row massacre, shortly after Tillerson was confirmed. "Things were blue skies. His business record was promising." A source close to the Trump White House echoed that sentiment. "What a different choice," that individual recalled thinking when first consulted about Tillerson. "What a cool guy."

The problems mounted quickly. After arriving at State, Tillerson disappeared. He granted few interviews and throttled press access to an unprecedented extent. For his first Asia trip, he ruffled feathers in the press corps by bringing only a lone writer from a conservative website. Former secretary of state Condoleezza Rice, who'd championed Tillerson's nomination, was among many who expressed dismay. "You have to take the press on the plane," several individuals close to her recalled her saying. "It's called a democracy. That's what we advocate for when we travel on government-funded planes as secretary of state. Why isn't he taking the press on the plane?" When I asked Rice about her views on Tillerson, she was more politic. "I can't assess what's going on inside," she said. "I hear news stories and I know the tendency when they're unhappy to put out a version. I just know Rex Tillerson is a very strong person and a good manager and I think he's a good leader but I can't speak to the specifics of how he's running it."

Tillerson and his aides readily admitted to having a messaging problem. "I don't play the game outside the house, it's not what I do," Tillerson said. "That probably is from my forty-one-and-a-half years in the private sector. I'm just disciplined that way. That's how I do things, and it's frustrated a lot of people, I get it." He laughed. "But I'm not going to change!" But Tillerson's reticence to talk exacted a cost.

The source close to the White House who initially expressed optimism about Tillerson put it bluntly: "They alienated the press." Gossip items began to make the rounds in DC, portraying him as aloof and insulated from the Department. Some were exaggerated, like the *Washington Post*'s claim that Margaret Peterlin had told career diplomats not to make eye contact with the secretary of state. Several sources, including one on Tillerson's security detail, disputed the idea that she'd enforced such a rule. But Peterlin did guard Tillerson so fiercely that many officers agreed with public reports describing her as a "bottleneck." Even peers, like Condoleezza Rice, were reportedly unable to reach him without first going through Peterlin. "I can't get through," Rice remarked in frustration, according to the recollections of one of the individuals close to her. "Margaret screened my call."

More consequential was Tillerson's inaccessibility inside the Department. After the remarks on his first day, he didn't speak to the workforce again until an initial town hall in May—unusually late in an administration for a new secretary of state. With his contained, stoic body language—small, confident gestures, no movement above the elbows—he'd given employees an overview of the basics of world conflicts. Some found it condescending. "It was an exercise in, 'I can read a map,'" recalled one Foreign Service officer in attendance. When Tillerson told a story about attending a Model UN session and telling a twelve-year-old participant how much the Foreign Service inspired him, a middle-aged officer began feverishly muttering, "You don't know us!" at a decibel level audible to three rows of the auditorium. "The fact is that Mr. Tillerson is not witting of everything going on in the Department and he can't be if he's just relying on his little political cabal that's around him," Colin Powell said. "And they seem to spend their time making sure he doesn't get anything from the State Department."

Several staffers said Tillerson's inaccessibility extended to foreign counterparts. "He is not a proactive seeker of conversations or outreach," an officer in the State Department's Operations Center, who spent months connecting Tillerson's calls, told me. "The vast majority of the calls we managed with the secretary while I was there were with people in the administration. . . . It felt like a lot of internal navel-gazing." The existence of those internal calls wasn't unusual. But the ratio of internal to external conversations was, according to officers who worked in Operations under multiple secretaries of state. When new secretaries are sworn in, for instance, they typically receive a flood of courtesy calls from foreign ministers and heads of state around the world. More than sixty came into the Operations Center for Tillerson. He declined to take more than three a day.

Later, when the United States initiated strikes on Syria, the administration entirely skipped the conventional step of notifying NATO allies. Tillerson received a flood of calls. "When news broke, alarmed allies, including the Czechs—who are our protecting power in Syria—were calling, saying 'I would like to speak to Secretary Tillerson,'" the Operations officer told me. It was early on a Sunday afternoon, and Tillerson was in Washington and unoccupied. "We were told that the secretary had a long weekend so he was going to go home and have dinner with his wife and call it a night." No calls. The man was, career officers marveled, committed to work-life balance. But the decision also baffled some. "We just bombed Syria without telling our allies," said the Operations officer, exasperated. "You *might* have to do some phone calls, even from home. That floored me."

Tillerson appeared unwilling to fill the perceived vacuum of leadership by leaning on others inside the Department. Instead, rumors mounted about the sidelining of career experts and their opinions. Aides described Tillerson as an intensive researcher, who prepped deeply for meetings. But his ruthless efficiency also raised eyebrows. "I do read all these memos that come to me . . . " Tillerson had said at that first, long-awaited town hall. "I appreciate those of you that get them on one page, because I'm not a fast reader." He wasn't kidding. Under Tillerson, the formal guidelines for memos bore an all-red, boldfaced warning: "there is a two-page limit." Informally, several officials said, a one-page limit was being enforced. Every secretary of state enforces different guidelines for the kind of briefing papers they like to see. Preventing bloated paperwork was, in theory, a rational goal. But several senior officials said that, in this case, they felt unable to properly convey nuance to a secretary with little background on the intricate relationships he was now tasked with overseeing. Even the brief papers permitted to reach the secretary's office were often withheld for long stretches of time, languishing, awaiting Peterlin's review. According to two officials, special assistants in the secretary's office postdated some memos to reduce the risk of public scandal associated with the backlog.

The source close to the White House was one of many in Tillerson's orbit who struggled to reconcile his peerless track record of private-sector management with his approach to the State Department. "Forty years at Exxon, in the God Pod, telling people to jump based on how high the price of oil is up," the source said, using the pet term for Tillerson's office suite within ExxonMobil. "I'm not trying to be shitty, but, you know, there's a way to run that company." Government, where no man is god except the president, was something else. "At first I thought 'uh oh, this is growing pains; a private-sector guy, realizing how hard Washington is,'" the source close to the White House continued. "And just, what I started to see, week after week, month after month, was someone who, not only didn't get it, but there was just no self-reflection."

UNTIL TILLERSON WAS FINALLY FIRED in March 2018, rumors of his demise were relentless. Former CIA director Mike Pompeo, who ultimately replaced him, was one popularly cited replacement. Trump's ambassador to the United Nations, Nikki Haley, whose potential ascendancy to Tillerson's job was the subject of aggressive strategic leaks from the Trump White House, was another. The perceived rivalry with Haley appeared to be a source of particular vexation for Tillerson and his team. The day I arrived to meet with the secretary, they were still reeling from an announcement Haley had made on the withholding of funding for UNRWA, the UN agency for Palestinian Refugees. Tillerson hadn't been consulted. In a series of tense emails, Haley's press office told Tillerson staffers that it had checked with the White House directly, rather than work through the secretary of state. Several weeks later, when Tillerson delivered well-received, tough remarks on Syria, Haley put out her own statement on the same subject at virtually the same time, prompting grumbling from Tillerson's team that Haley was publicly undermining him. Tensions between secretaries of state and US ambassadors to the United Nations were nothing new, but this particular enmity seemed to run deeper. "Holy shit," the source close to the White House said, "I've never seen anything like the way he's treated her . . . it's shocking." Multiple White House sources expressed similar sentiments, with one saying Tillerson's "rage" toward Haley had drawn the disapproval of even the president. Tillerson's team disputed those accounts. Steven Goldstein, the under secretary of state for public diplomacy, called Tillerson "a very caring, decent, principled person" and attributed unflattering accounts from White House sources to disgruntled rivals. "Whenever you have a foreign policy decision, there are always competing interests and sometimes people aren't happy with the decisions made," he said. "But what is said is the furthest from the truth."

Tillerson, for his part, said his focus lay elsewhere. "The only person that I have to worry about is the president of the United States," he told me. "As long as he is happy with what I'm doing and wants me to keep doing it, that's what I'm going to do." But there were also reports of acrimony between Tillerson and Trump. In October 2017, a number of publications gleefully reported that Tillerson had, in one meeting, even referred to the president as a "moron." Tillerson's Texas swagger, the source close to the White House said, irked Trump. "You just can't be an arrogant alpha male all the time with Trump. You have to do what Mattis does, which is '*Mr. President, you're the president, you're smarter than me, you won, your instincts are always right, but let me just give you the other view, sir.*' Then you have this guy coming in," the source said, referring to Tillerson, "going 'Well, I guess because I worked for so many years in the oil business, I have something to say. You don't know much about the region, so let me start with that.' I mean, honestly, condescending." Tillerson aides said their boss spent more time with the president than most cabinet members, and Tillerson insisted accounts of a rift were overstated. "The relationship that he and I have is not like a lot of secretaries of state had with the presidents they've served," he explained, "because we did not know each other at all. So some of the dynamic between he and I is just learning who each other is. We didn't know each other, and I'm a very different style of manager than he is, and sometimes those differences are evident to other people. It doesn't mean we don't work together, though." The president, it came to pass, had a different view.

When I mentioned the White House's role in rumors of his demise, Tillerson made no effort to feign surprise. "Mhm," he said, nodding. He'd been waiting for the question. "How do you deal with that?" I asked. "I ignore it," he said flatly. He arched an eyebrow. "When you say the White House, who are you talking about?" It was a rhetorical question. "I'm not asking you to reveal sources. You understand the question though. The White House is comprised of how many people?" Brian Hook, Tillerson's director of policy planning, chimed in that the answer was perhaps in the thousands. Tillerson waved him off. "But people that *matter*, people that might have an interest in whether I stay or leave, there's about one hundred and sixty of them . . ." Tillerson leaned in and, for a moment, I realized it must be unpleasant to be fired by him. "I'm not gonna reveal *my* sources, cause I know who it is. I *know* who it is. And they know I know."

According to three people who had heard Tillerson speak directly of the matter behind closed doors, this was a reference to Trump's son-in-law-turned-adviser Jared Kushner. Tillerson, according to those sources, was convinced that Kushner, collaborating with another senior White House official, had been working to engineer Haley into the secretary of state job, to clear his own ascent to secretary of state. After Tillerson's departure, sources close to him continued to maintain that Kushner had played an instrumental role in his demise. Tensions between the two men had been flaring regularly, often in the form of a public relations proxy war. When Tillerson prevailed in reinstating some of the humanitarian funds for the UN agency for Palestinian refugees that Haley had sought to withhold, press items discussing potential negative repercussions for Kushner's Middle East peace efforts began appearing. Tillerson aides accused Kushner of planting them. The source close to the White House said Kushner had attempted to work with Tillerson and met with resistance. "Here's what I saw: a president who surprised [Kushner] on the spot and said 'you're doing Mideast peace' after the campaign. A guy who tried to brief Rex every single week but could never even get a call back or a meeting. . . . And it wasn't just Jared. It was many people across the government, including fellow cabinet members, who complained." A Tillerson aide bristled at the characterization of Kushner as a polite recipient of unexpected mandates, saying Tillerson had been forced to "have a pointed conversation" with Kushner, reminding him who was secretary of state.

But, when I asked Tillerson whether he had been frustrated when core mandates typically led by the secretary of state were handed to Kushner, he was surprisingly passive. "Uh, no," he said. "It's not a point of frustration because I think, in most areas, there was clarity up front. It was pretty clear in the beginning the president wanted him to work on the Middle East peace process, and so we carved that out." Had he pushed back? I asked. "No," he said. "That's what the president wanted to do." Tillerson remained involved. Kushner would "come over" periodically to update him, "so at least we had full connectivity between that and all the other issues that we're managing with the same countries and same leaders. We would give them input and suggestions: 'probably want to think about this,' 'that's going to be a non-starter . . .'" Tillerson seemed passionate about fighting stories of his ouster. Surrendering Middle East peace, he greeted with a shrug. Hook, the director of policy planning, went a step further. "It's important for parties in the region to know our peace team has the full backing of the president. . . ." he said. "I know past administrations made different divisions of labor on Mideast peace, but ours is built around new approaches and much closer proximity to the president." Having the imprimatur of the president's son-in-law, he suggested, was a good thing.

But the messy division of labor between Tillerson and Kushner had real consequences for American policy. When Tillerson began to work as a mediator in a dispute that saw Saudi Arabia and a number of Gulf States cut off relations with Qatar, an important counterterrorism ally, Trump veered off course, issuing a vociferous, off-the-cuff takedown of Qatar. It was a 180-degree turn from the narrative Tillerson had been pushing on the Sunday shows just a day before. Kushner, according to White House sources, had sided with the Saudis based on his close relationship with Crown Prince Mohammed bin Salman, whom Kushner considered a promising reformer. Middle East policy had been given to both men, and it appeared that Kushner, with a background in real estate and being the president's son-in-law, was winning the tug-of-war.

Colin Powell recalled similar turf wars with then–vice president Dick Cheney, and not fondly. "I've been in similar situations, where I suddenly discovered we've created military commissions. Wait a minute—that's a legal matter and a legal matter the State Department has primacy on." Did he have advice, I asked, for Tillerson? "I can't tell. He may love it," Powell said with a shrug. "I can't tell that he objects." And then, with a wry smile: "Maybe if we had ambassadors there, they'd pick it up—that's what they do." Powell was poking at a broader consequence of the Trump administration's approach to State: a building increasingly unmanned and cut down to size.

In March 2018, Tillerson himself became the latest diplomat to receive a pink slip. "Mike Pompeo, Director of the CIA, will become our new Secretary of State," Trump tweeted. "He will do a fantastic job! Thank you to Rex Tillerson for his service!" As was increasingly the norm, the State Department was the last to learn. "The Secretary had every intention of staying ..." read a statement from Goldstein, Tillerson's spokesperson. "The Secretary did not speak to the President and is unaware of the reason."

Pompeo, a former Republican congressman from Kansas, had little by way of diplomatic experience, and was more of a hawk than Tillerson. He had backed Trump's saber-rattling calls to dismantle the Iran deal with his own, equally hardline statements and tweets. And he appeared to have internalized some of the lessons cited by White House officials about dealing with Trump's ego. The president, he had said during his tenure as CIA Director, "asks good, hard questions. Make[s] us go make sure we're doing our work in the right way." Trump, likewise, said he and Pompeo were "always on the same wavelength. The relationship has always been good and that is what I need as secretary of state."

In the weeks leading up to the firing, Tillerson had attempted to communicate more support for the institution he ran, praising the value of the foreign service. The guillotine finally descending suggested that message was unwelcome. American diplomacy would be downsized, and there would be less dissent as it happened. Pompeo would step into a State Department where that mission was already well underway.

23

THE MOSQUITO AND THE SWORD

TILLERSON HAD STUDIED engineering in college, a fact he mentioned with some frequency and which seemed to inform his hard-nosed approach to management. When I asked him what kind of a legacy he envisioned leaving behind as secretary of state, he spoke of institutional reform before policy. "I'm a very systems, process guy," he said. And so, in April 2017, he began with a comprehensive survey, retaining a private consulting firm, Insigniam, to diagnose the health of America's diplomatic organs.

Over the course of several months, at a cost just north of $1 million, consultants surveyed more than 35,000 Department of State and USAID employees. This was regarded first as a good idea, and then, upon the delivery of the survey, a frustrating one. "It just made people crazy," a Foreign Service officer in the Department's Bureau of International Narcotics and Law Enforcement Affairs (INL) remembered. "I had to walk away from my computer for an hour before I could look at those questions."

"What should the Department stop doing?" the survey asked bluntly. What was a diplomat's mission in six words (so the firm could make word clouds)? "It's preposterous . . . a copy and paste from what a corporation would use, and even then, at almost any corporation, this would not have been customized enough," the Foreign Service officer in INL told me. "What the hell?" the Operations officer agreed. "I have some words for your cloud, but they all have four letters." BuzzFeed declared the survey "straight out of *Office Space*," and promptly made it into a listicle.

But the results were revealing. Some of the officers' complaints were quotidian. "The technology is terrible," the survey concluded, noting that the DC-based Department used servers in Miami for some reason, and quoting a distraught employee's lament that "with some PCs, you have to turn them upside down or they will burn out." Rex Tillerson focused on these practicalities when I asked him about his objectives for reform. "We need to update and modernize ourselves," he said. "I'm sure we're using the same IT system that we were using when you were here." Like a diplomatic Marie Kondo, he wanted to remove "clutter in the way people have to work."

But the survey also reflected more existential concerns. "People do not speak optimistically about the future," the firm concluded. "The absence of a clear vision of the future allows room for speculation and rumor about what the future could bring, such as further USAID integration into [State] or the militarization of foreign policy." One officer interviewed pleaded: "I am concerned that the dramatic reduction in budget, paired with extended staffing gaps at the most senior level, will result in the loss of not only an exceptionally talented group of people from our ranks, but will hamper our impact to fulfill our mission for decades to come." Of the Trump administration and Rex Tillerson's team at State, the Insigniam report concluded, "[p]eople question if these two groups understand the role the Department of State plays in forwarding the interests of the United States in the world." Many "perceived [a] lack of support from the administration, from Congress, and from the new [State] leadership, and from the American people."

Rex Tillerson's quest to de-clutter, it came to pass, was not about to allay these fears.

THE ADMINISTRATION'S FIRST BUDGET floated to Congress proposed a 27 percent slash to the State Department's funding—roughly $10 billion of the Department's $52.78-billion budget. The White House wanted to eliminate all funding for the United States Institute of Peace and its mission to "guide peace talks and advise governments; train police and religious leaders; and support community groups opposing extremism." It would gut health programs on HIV, malaria, and polio, and halve the United States' contributions to United Nations peacekeeping missions. It hoped to shutter the State Department's Office of Global Criminal Justice, responsible for setting policy on war crimes. More radically, the administration sought to move the bureaus of refugee issues and consular affairs—responsible for the passport stamping and hostage extricating that are perhaps the Department's most recognizable core competency—out of State entirely and into the Department of Homeland Security. Even the State Department's mission statement was sized up for cuts. For the first time, an administration proposed removing "just" and "democratic" from the list of qualities the United States sought to encourage around the world.

Few thought that the programs targeted for cuts were without need for reform. But there was steadily gathering outrage at the broad and seemingly cavalier nature of the cutbacks. Opposition reached a head in early 2018, when USAID, which reports to the State Department, took the unprecedented step of announcing that it would not comply with Tillerson's efforts to reorganize his building and its own. "Per direction from the Front Office, we are suspending all USAID involvement . . ." an official said in an email to senior staff. "You should not work on any joint Redesign activities." This was mutiny.

That move had been preceded by months of bipartisan pushback against Tillerson's plans. In a deco, wood-paneled hearing room in the Dirksen Senate Office Building, Tillerson faced off against arched eyebrows and grandstanding from both sides of the aisle when he presented the administration's first proposed budget. "After about five minutes" of reviewing the proposal, Senator Bob Corker, the Republican chair, reportedly recalled, "I said, 'This is a total waste of time. I don't want to do this anymore.' And the reason it's a waste of time is, I think you know, the budget that's being presented is not going to be the budget we're going to deal with."

"We'll write our own budget, but I do think it has a chilling impact on State Department, with the career people trying to carry out their missions," added Ben Cardin, the ranking Democrat. "Seventy years ago this month one of your predecessors, George Marshall, delivered a speech that helped cement his reputation as a key architect of the post-War effort to build a liberal international order. He was 'present at the creation.' My concern today, quite frankly, is that your Administration will go down in the history books as being 'present at the destruction' of that order we have worked so hard to support—and that has so benefited our security and prosperity and ideals."

Dirksen was a 1950s addition to the Hill. Its hearing rooms were among the first built with television in mind, eschewing round tables for rostrums designed for spectators. C-SPAN cameras picked up Tillerson nodding almost imperceptibly, a frown flickering across his face. But he gamely defended the deep cuts to his own organization, through hours of drubbing. Over the following year, Congress essentially tried to throw money at the Department, which Tillerson declined. He refused to accept $80 million in congressional funding earmarked for State to counter Russian propaganda, to the bafflement of many officials. It was almost unheard of for a cabinet official to refuse money already appropriated for his or her agency, and it raised eyebrows after the intelligence and defense communities asserted that Russia had been

using propaganda to meddle in the presidential election. An aide said
Tillerson feared the funds might anger Russia. Tillerson's relations on
the Hill frayed. One prominent Republican senator called the White
House and threatened to subpoena Tillerson if he wasn't more cooperative, according to a source at the White House and another on the Hill.

Several former secretaries of state of both parties regarded with
astonishment Tillerson's pushback against funds for his Department.
"Senators who believed in the State Department wanted to restore
some of the money, or not agree to the cuts," Madeleine Albright
recalled. "Tillerson didn't want the money. For me, I've never heard
about anything like that."

When I pressed him on his defense of the budget, Tillerson
appeared conflicted. He admitted, for the first time, that he had pushed
back on the budget behind closed doors. "In fact, I had people around
here who said, 'You know, you need to leak your passback letter, you
need to leak your appeals letter.' And I said, 'No, that's not how I do
things.'" Tillerson said he'd looked at the numbers proposed by the
White House Office of Management and Budget (OMB) and assumed
he could count on "plus ten, plus twenty percent, because we figure
the congress is going to give us something there." No other living
secretary of state said they'd conducted budget advocacy this way, asking for less and leaving it to Congress to fight for their institution.
Tillerson conceded he may have simply lacked experience. "Having
been here one month, I didn't have a real basis to do much other than
work with OMB to understand what were their objectives. I'll be honest with you: I didn't get myself embroiled so much in the numbers
themselves as much as trying to understand, 'What are we trying to
achieve here?'" In the end, Trump would replace Tillerson with complaints about needing to be on the same "wavelength" as his secretary
of state anyway. Even the modest pushback behind closed doors had,
apparently, been too much.

Ironically, the greatest champions of State Department funding were sometimes on the military side: the generals, flush with cash in their own institution, seeking to spread the wealth. "If you don't fund the State Department fully, then I need to buy more ammunition ultimately," Trump's secretary of defense James Mattis told members of Congress in 2013, when he was CENTCOM commander. "I think it's a cost-benefit ratio. The more that we put into the State Department's diplomacy, hopefully, the less we have to put into a military budget." But by 2017, even he appeared to flip that logic while advocating for a new era of increased defense spending: "Our military must ensure that the president and our diplomats always negotiate from a position of strength." He had little to worry about. The same budget that eviscerated America's civilian foreign policy apparatus proposed a $52-billion hike in defense spending.

The Mahogany Row massacre had been nothing compared to the planned casualties of the budget offensive. More than 1,300 diplomats would get pink slips. New hiring was also frozen. Initially, it was announced that there would be no new classes of Foreign Service officers—the so-called "A 100" recruits who file off for training at a sort of Hogwarts for diplomats in the Virginia countryside before becoming full-fledged officers. Rangel and Pickering fellows, who are drawn from underrepresented communities and had already been promised spots in those classes, were suddenly left without a future. Outrage was so swift and decisive that some new recruits were reinstated. State also abruptly suspended its participation in the Presidential Management Fellows program, a prestigious apprenticeship long used to draw talent to the profession. The effect was tangible: the number of new recruits taking the Foreign Service entrance exam plummeted by 26 percent from the year before. It was the lowest level of interest in nearly a decade. Under the best of circumstances, the State Department faced intense competition from the private sector when it came to recruiting great minds. "Imagine today, when the handwriting is on the wall that Trump doesn't value the State

Department?" John Kerry said. "Imagine what that does to the best people?"

There seemed to be just as little interest in filling the core leadership roles that had been left intact. Hundreds of senior positions sat empty. The building was being run almost entirely by deputies elevated to "acting" assistant secretary status, many of whom had decades less experience than their unceremoniously removed predecessors. When I asked Tillerson whether the unfilled posts were a source of anxiety, he puffed his chest and smirked. "I don't *have anxiety*," he said. This particular matter was, however, "a point of concern . . . the posts have been open too long. It's not something I'm happy about."

Tillerson said he met with officials overseeing personnel every other week to address the problem. "They've not been easy," he said of conversations with the White House about filling the open jobs. "The process over there has not been the most efficient and they've changed personnel trying to improve it, I mean, many, many times . . . it was very slow, it was very cumbersome, it was frustrating at times because you couldn't get a sense of, 'What's the issue'? Someone seems to be kind of sitting in idle over there . . ." Tillerson sighed. "I would tell 'em, 'Just give me a no, at least with a no, I'll go get another name.'" He was reported to have exploded at White House personnel director Johnny DeStefano over meddling in his staffing decisions—including a rejection of his initial choice for deputy, Elliott Abrams, who was deemed too critical of Trump during the campaign. That role would sit empty for nearly five months. This was the problem across the Department. In one early conversation, a Tillerson aide gave me a specific reason he couldn't respond to detailed questions about the budget cuts: "We're just so thinly staffed, I don't have time to get into that."

EVEN THE STATE DEPARTMENT'S most ardent champions often agree that the bureaucracy is no model of efficiency. Richard Holbrooke, in his 1970s complaint in *Foreign Policy* magazine, "The Machine that Fails," decried the "sheer, unimaginable size" of the system and its stultifying procedures and protocols. James Baker, George H. W. Bush's secretary of state, took a similar view, complaining of "too many bureaucratic layers, which can lead sometimes to sclerotic decision-making."

Aides to Tillerson invoked a similar logic. The goal, one told me, was to strip back the roving envoys and pet projects and restore power to the regional bureaus.

"How do you restore power to the regional bureaus if there are no heads of regional bureaus in the building?" I asked, genuinely curious.

"I don't know what your experience with the Foreign Service is—"

"Mixed," I admitted.

"It's mixed. There are some bureaus where I can hand something to someone and I know with 100 percent confidence that I don't have to look again. There are some where I have to start at the one-yard line and march it ninety-nine yards."

Like any large organization, and especially government organizations with little relationship between merit and compensation, the Foreign Service had its clock punchers and sullen, bored lifers. But it also had plenty of wonderful, dedicated public servants: men and women well qualified to make more money elsewhere, sacrificing much to protect American lives. In the end, the doubts behind the aide's skepticism were self-fulfilling. American leadership no longer valued diplomats, which led to the kind of cuts that made diplomats less valuable. Rinse, repeat.

Several former secretaries of state agreed with the premise of expansive cuts, but virtually all, spanning generations, took issue with the extent and execution of the ones championed by Tillerson. The most supportive of significant downsizing, Baker, said that he believed in the urgency of restraining government spending in general and had "long believed that the State Department's budgets could benefit from a review. . . . Of course," he was quick to add, "I cannot respond to the scale of recent employee cutbacks at the State Department because I have not been briefed about them."

George P. Shultz, who served in Nixon's and Reagan's cabinets, said: "I think it's a drastic cut. There's no doubt that some things can be cut down like the special envoys. But fundamentally . . . you have to have regional bureaus, you have to have ambassadors, you have to have people who know the layout." Shultz and Tillerson had both spent years in the private sector, Shultz at Bechtel, the construction and civil engineering company. Transitioning from a large corporation to a government organization, he said, "You don't start out with the idea that you're going to cut everything before you even know what's going on." The fact that Tillerson had moved so swiftly toward downsizing was "astonishing. Whether he was told to do that by the president, that was part of a condition of taking the job, I don't know. On the other hand, if the president insists on something like that, I think it's unacceptable. You can turn a job down."

Condoleezza Rice, who once served as a budget officer at Stanford University, was a believer in efficiency. "I don't say 30 percent," she told me in that clipped cadence retaining just a trace of her Alabama roots. "But I can't say that there isn't some tightening up that could be done at State . . . Some of these auxiliary positions, things grow like Topsy and nobody ever prunes them." But, she said, other efforts to scale back under Tillerson, like dropping democracy from the United States' diplomatic mandate, "would be a spectacularly bad idea." And even she questioned the battery of unfilled positions across the Department: "I don't understand any reform that's not going to have an assistant secretary for Europe and Latin America and Asia."

Other former secretaries were more exercised about the state of the Department. "I believe it is incalculable damage that's been caused," Madeleine Albright said. "What became very evident to me the minute the budget was proposed was that it was in fact cutting not just fat, but into the system." Hillary Clinton described "getting rid of Arabic speakers, Korean speakers, Mandarin speakers, cutting back the number of young people who want to be Foreign Service officers who have language experience or are willing to take the two to three years necessary to master a difficult language" as "foolishness."

Colin Powell offered a similarly blunt assessment. The new administration was "ripping the guts out of the organization. Worse than that, they're not filling these positions they're planning to keep." The hiring freeze was especially stinging for a secretary who had invested so personally in the workforce. "Any organization that stops bringing in new blood is hurting itself in the present and in the future. It's a mistake. When you stop bringing people in or when you make it an undesirable place to be, then you are mortgaging your future." He grinned. Powell had kept some of his more incisive observations on background. This one, he said, "you can use."

"It's enormously costly," John Kerry told me of what was, in the eyes of many in the building, becoming a relentless pummeling of the Department and the profession. "Look, in a couple years, if we get a presidency of either party that values diplomacy, you can fix a budget, you can invest again in the State Department, but it takes years to undo what's happening because it takes years to build up expertise and capacity."

The effect on morale was immediate for those at a working level, watching their profession get dismantled as they tried to do their jobs. "It's undisciplined and not based on effectiveness," said Chris LaVine, the career official who had been working on Syria policy at State when news of the cuts hit. "It's the equivalent of taking a sword to a mosquito."

24

MELTDOWN

As Foggy Bottom emptied, America's diplomatic foot-hold in confrontations around the world began to slip. In July 2017, Rex Tillerson and President Trump sat at the White House, shouting at each other about Iran. The deal to contain that country's nuclear development, struck under Tillerson's predecessor, John Kerry, required the administration to certify Iranian compliance to Congress every ninety days. The two men were meeting ahead of the latest of these milestones. "Why should I certify?" Trump demanded again and again, according to a source familiar with the meeting. Two of Trump's hard-line advisers, Steve Bannon and Sebastian Gorka, backed him up, insisting the deal was hurting American national security interests.

Where Tillerson had been a seemingly enthusiastic enforcer of budget cuts, on several of these policy matters, he appeared to lay down in front of the bulldozer of the Trump administration. Tillerson's response to Trump's insistent questioning—that all evidence indicated that Iran had complied with and passed inspections by international investigators—agitated the president. By the end of the meeting, the source said, he was furious. A Tillerson spokesperson later claimed accounts of the showdown were exaggerated, and that the president was "appreciative" of the input. But even he conceded, choosing his words delicately, that "not everyone in the room agreed with what the secretary was saying." Public reports drawing on White House sources later gave the meeting a simpler description: a "meltdown." Trump told his White House advisers to come up with alternative rationales for killing the deal. If the State Department wouldn't give him what he wanted, he would simply work around it.

The Iran deal had vexed Trump since the campaign. On the trail, he had said that his "number one priority" was "to dismantle the disastrous deal with Iran." In one stump speech, he'd offered his own rendition of the multilateral negotiations process that led to the agreement: "Can you imagine?" he asked, head bobbing animatedly over a microphone, royal blue tie dangling, as ever, four inches longer than customary. He put a hand to his ear in a pantomime of a phone. "You call them: 'We hear you're making nukes.' 'OK, well let us check.' They call: 'No, we're not making nukes there, you dumb son of a bitch.'" Trump mouthed the last words under his breath, like a kid in the back of class. Mike Pompeo, Trump's appointee as CIA Director—and, later, as Tillerson's successor at State—tweeted shortly after his nomination for the former job: "I look forward to rolling back this disastrous deal with the world's largest state sponsor of terrorism." Trump himself had offered his share of Twitter condemnations. "Iran has been formally PUT ON NOTICE for firing a ballistic missile," he tweeted on one occasion. "Should have been thankful for the terrible deal the U.S. made with them!" And then: "Iran is playing with fire—they don't appreciate how 'kind' President Obama was to them. Not me!"

The Iranians argued that their ballistic missiles were for self-defense and unrelated to the nuclear deal. But Western powers were concerned about the country's expanding conventional arsenal—and nearer targets, like Israel, doubly so. Iran's human rights record was similarly unredeemed. At the time of Trump and Tillerson's showdown over certification in July 2017, at least three American citizens were being held by Iran on fabricated charges.

Still, Iran was complying with the letter of the deal. The group responsible for enforcing the agreement's rigorous inspections had, again and again, reported that the country was not cheating. Other than the United States, the many countries behind the deal were unanimous: there were no grounds for rolling it back. That went for even Trump's fellow hard-liners elected abroad. "The nuclear deal with Iran was controversial but it has neutralised the possibility of the Iranians acquiring nuclear weapons for more than a decade," UK prime minister Theresa May insisted, amid otherwise tough rhetoric.

Initially, Trump continued to certify that Iran was in compliance. But each time, the administration made it clearer that they were doing so unhappily. After the ballistic missile test, the administration imposed a round of new sanctions, prompting the Iranians to claim the United States, not they, had violated the terms of the deal. In September 2017, US ambassador to the United Nations Nikki Haley was dispatched to a conservative think tank, the American Enterprise Institute, to make the case for exiting the deal. A few weeks later, Trump was openly threatening to do so. "We are not going to stand what they are doing with our country," he said. "They've violated so many different elements, and they've also violated the spirit of that deal." Even Rex Tillerson was falling in line: "In our view," he said, parsing his words carefully, "Iran is clearly in default of these expectations."

OTHER DIPLOMATIC FEATS of the past received the same treatment. Trump pulled out of the Paris Agreement on climate change, making the United States only the third country to shun it after Syria and Nicaragua, both of which later changed course and joined.

"Whoever believes that the world's problems can be solved by isolationism and protectionism," Angela Merkel said of Trump's decision, "is making an enormous error." "It's just an incredible walking back of American leadership, and everywhere I go, I hear about it," John Kerry later told me. "Foreign ministers wonder whether the president ever bothered to read or understand the Paris Agreement that let us set our own commitments in the first place. Why we wanted to abandon our seat at the table—why a businessman would do that, especially— is beyond me. Other countries are leading instead and their industries will be advantaged, making incredible amounts of money doing it. It's self-defeating. China especially is reaping the benefits of us stepping back."

At the US embassy in Beijing, it fell to the second-in-command, career officer David H. Rank, to notify the Chinese of the United States' withdrawal from the Paris Agreement. He resigned instead, ending a twenty-seven-year career in the Foreign Service. His explanation, published in the *Washington Post*, was a lament for diplomacy in the modern age. "I worry about the frequently politically motivated portrayal of those who work for the American people as members of some mythical elite, separate and suspicious," he explained. "I worry about the denigration of expertise at a time when a complex world demands it more than ever." Finally, he wrote, "I worry at the erosion of the bipartisan consensus on the need for US leadership. . . . If that leadership does not come from us, it will come from elsewhere."

In front of a crowd of Cuban-Americans in Miami's Little Havana neighborhood, Trump announced another diplomatic reversal, "canceling the last administration's completely one-sided deal with Cuba." It was, in some ways, symbolic: the US embassy in Havana would remain open. But there were real rollbacks of progress, too. Americans traveling to Cuba once again faced tighter restrictions. They were banned from doing business with a new list of hotels and other enterprises deemed to be connected to the Cuban government. The move was intended to be tough on that government, but critics argued those hurt most would be small businesses like bed-and-breakfasts. As was typical of these rollbacks, the State Department was the last to learn. "Poor WHA," said one career official, referring to the Western Hemisphere bureau ostensibly in charge of Cuba policy. No permanent assistant secretary had been nominated to run that office. The acting assistant secretary "was not informed about the Cuba policy change until the day of." The new administration seemed intent on laying waste to the few diplomatic accomplishments its predecessors had left behind.

IN OTHER CASES, the Trump era squandered diplomatic leadership by dint of chaos and blunder. These moments were bigger than the secretary of state and the sidelining of his department. They were born of a unique moment in American politics and the unique character of a reckless president hooked on Twitter. But they threw into relief the importance of muscular diplomacy, and the perils of its absence.

Again and again the president's off-the-cuff remarks threatened delicate areas of foreign policy. "We have plenty of options for Venezuela, and by the way, I'm not going to rule out a military option," Trump said in 2017 as political turmoil roiled that country. He stood outdoors at his golf course in New Jersey, flanked by Tillerson (chewing his lip nervously) and Haley (attempting to break a world record for brow furrowing). Trump's remark sparked a diplomatic row, with Venezuela's defense minister calling it "an act of madness" and "supreme extremism" and the White House refusing a call from Venezuelan president Nicolás Maduro. This kind of hardball approach might well have found a place in aggressive diplomacy with Venezuela, but officials in the State Department's Latin America bureau said that they had little insight into or ability to temper the president as he hurtled toward a standoff.

A similar pattern played out in Trump's relationships with European allies. Tillerson was among a group of officials—including National Security Advisor H. R. McMaster and Secretary of Defense James Mattis—who worked overtime to ensure President Trump included a commitment to collective defense when addressing NATO leaders during his first trip to Europe. It was a pledge considered nonnegotiable by every president since Truman. After months of aides' careful planning to insert the concept into prepared remarks, Trump ad-libbed and omitted the line. It took weeks for him to rectify the error, a tense period in which career officials engaged in triage, struggling to soothe alarmed allies.

TRUMP SHOWED STILL LESS CAUTION after millions of people in northern Japan awoke to a beeping alert on their cell phones in late August 2017, telling them North Korea had launched missiles over their country. He issued an astonishing ultimatum: "North Korea best not make any more threats to the United States," he warned, once again from the golf course in New Jersey. "They will be met with fire, fury and frankly power the likes of which this world has never seen before." Presidential historians called it the most aggressive language from a commander-in-chief since Truman warned Japan of "a rain of ruin from the air, the like of which has never been seen on this earth," though no one could figure out if the parallel language was intentional. It was also exactly the kind of statement regional experts at the State Department, steeped in the sensitive trigger points of the complex relationship with North Korea, would have been well equipped to temper. But as far as anyone could tell, no expert of any kind had weighed in. "President Trump's comment was unplanned and spontaneous," said one senior official of the outburst. Pyongyang immediately threatened to retaliate by striking US territory in Guam. The president took to Twitter to double down. "Military solutions are now fully in place, locked and loaded, should North Korea act unwisely," he wrote. "Hopefully Kim Jong Un will find another path!"

A month later, Trump was at the green marble rostrum of the United Nations General Assembly for the first time as president, thundering at the North Korean regime and its despot, to whom he assigned a taunting schoolyard nickname: "Rocket Man." "No nation on Earth has an interest in seeing this band of criminals arm itself with nuclear weapons and missiles," Trump said, narrowing his eyes. In the audience, General John Kelly, the White House chief of staff, put a palm to his face and rubbed his temples, appearing to have an existential crisis. "The United States has great strength and patience," Trump went on. "But if it is forced to defend itself or its allies, we will have no choice but to totally destroy North Korea."

Kim Jong Un fired back, calling the speech "unprecedented rude nonsense" and warning: "I will surely and definitely tame the mentally deranged US dotard with fire." The word "dotard," suggesting age and senility, dated back to the fourteenth century. It quickly became a viral sensation. (The Korean version of the text used *neulg-dali-michigwang-i*: "old lunatic.") As the North Koreans continued their public offensive, Trump offered another Twitter rejoinder: "Just heard Foreign Minister of North Korea speak at UN. If he echoes thoughts of Little Rocket Man, they won't be around much longer!"

Rex Tillerson, striking a very different tone, announced that the administration was in direct contact with the North Korean regime. "We ask, 'Would you like to talk?'" he said. "We have lines of communication with Pyongyang." Tillerson insisted that he and the president were "completely aligned" on North Korea. "The President's policy on North Korea is a complete, verifiable, and irreversible denuclearization of the Korean peninsula. And the President wants to achieve that through diplomatic efforts," he told me. But that statement was hard to reconcile with the Tweet Trump sent shortly after Tillerson announced his diplomatic overtures to Pyongyang. "I told Rex Tiller-

son, our wonderful Secretary of State, that he is wasting his time trying to negotiate with Little Rocket Man," the President wrote. "Save
your energy Rex, we'll do what has to be done!"

The escalation of the North Korean standoff divided America's
allies. From Germany, a weary Chancellor Angela Merkel refused to
say whether her country would stand by the United States in a military
confrontation with North Korea, and called, again, for negotiations.
"I am against threats of this kind," she intoned solemnly after the UN
speech. "And speaking for myself and the government, I must say that
we consider any type of military solution absolutely inappropriate and
we are counting on diplomatic efforts. This must be vigorously imple-
mented. In my opinion, sanctions and enforcing these sanctions are the
right answer. But anything else with regard to North Korea I think is
wrong. And that is why we clearly disagree with the US president."

Japanese prime minister Shinzo Abe, rattled in the wake of missile
launches over his country, hewed closer to Trump, laying out a history
of diplomatic failures with North Korea. "Again and again, attempts
to resolve issues through dialogue have all come to naught," he said.
"In what hope of success are we now repeating the very same failure a
third time?"

BOTH WERE RIGHT. Diplomacy of one kind had failed in North
Korea. But diplomacy of a different kind was also, in the eyes of those
most intimately familiar with the decades of engagement Abe was
referring to, the only way out of the world's most dangerous standoff.

Both the Clinton and second Bush administrations had made
considerable diplomatic inroads with the Hermit Kingdom. In 1994,
the United States actually succeeded in brokering a denuclearization agreement in which Pyongyang agreed to freeze and dismantle
its entire program. North Korea cheated, purchasing equipment for
highly enriched uranium development. But some veterans of North

Korea diplomacy maintain that the United States sealed the doom of the agreement by failing to live up to its own commitments. Pledges to build light-water reactors and provide fuel to Pyongyang were both sabotaged amidst political fights between the Clinton administration and a Republican Congress. Bush sealed the demise of the agreement when he took office, walking away altogether. Over the course of his first term, the administration adopted a more bellicose stance, listing the North Korean regime as one it might have to use nuclear weapons against and returning to saber-rattling condemnations.

In George W. Bush's second term, however, Condoleezza Rice tried anew. She sent a career diplomat named Christopher Hill, who had been part of the negotiating team that brokered peace in the Balkans under Richard Holbrooke, to lead six-party talks on denuclearizing North Korea. "This administration has fought two wars," Rice told Hill wearily. "And now we are looking for a few diplomats." Hill and a team of tireless Foreign Service officers—including Yuri Kim, who, a decade later, became embroiled in Trump's Mahogany Row massacre—threw themselves into the challenge for years. They endured weeks away from their families, long hours on flight across the world, and twelve- to thirteen-hour negotiation marathons in Beijing. The North Koreans were among the thorniest opponents in the world. Even in the Balkans, there had been moments of personal ice-breaking—discussions of children and grandchildren, sports and hobbies. The North Koreans had a "robotlike" reputation, according to Hill. After years of tense late nights together, he felt he barely knew them.

Throughout the ups and downs, Hill tried to carry forward the lessons of diplomats past, including his boss in the Balkans. When the Chinese didn't show for a promised meeting and proceeding without them meant going rogue and defying his marching orders, his first thought was, "would Holbrooke have canceled the meeting?" and he persevered. Later, at a low point in the negotiations, Holbrooke himself showed up to rally Hill's team. They were a part of history, he told them, as he later told me in Afghanistan. They should enjoy the moment. "You may never have another like it."

It was through those years of high-wire diplomacy that Chris Hill found himself, in the fall of 2007, standing in a white gown and hood, surveying an aging plutonium plant about two hours north of Pyongyang. Sections of the facility's thick pipes were being sawed to pieces. American and international "disablers" were on hand to supervise. Seven months later, North Korea would blow up the plant's cooling tower. It was historic: the first time North Korea had deactivated a reactor since 2001.

In the end, it wasn't enough. Pyongyang submitted a visibly incomplete accounting of its nuclear activities, then grew cold at demands for more. But talks had left behind a considerable legacy to build upon. Rifts had been closed in a rocky relationship with South Korea. And cooperation had been established, to a degree once thought impossible, with China—the single most important player in any resolution of the North Korean crisis to this day.

And so it was a surprise, for many of the career diplomats involved, when the Obama administration repeated the same mistake the Bush administration made in its first term and walked away from those years of diplomatic inroads entirely. "Frankly, I think what really happened was the Obama administration looked at the heat everyone got for trying to do something with North Korea, whether it was the Clinton administration or the second Bush term," Hill reflected. "The Obama Administration just decided, 'We have other priorities and this thing will wither on the vine.' They never got serious." I asked Hillary Clinton whether she regretted that turn away from North Korea. "No, we—" she stammered, "Chris Hill was continuing his negotiations when we were there." When I told her Hill felt the effort was sidelined, she said, "I can't speak to that. I don't know that. I'm not going to agree or disagree with him." I'd never heard her sound so tired. "Maybe he didn't feel there was [support] from the White House or

Pentagon," she went on. "But we certainly tried to get things going at the State Department as best we could."

HILL, AND THE OTHER DIPLOMATS who presided over the effort, remain in agreement about one thing: diplomacy is still the only way forward. "If we get out of the North Korean situation, it's probably going to be because of diplomacy," Condoleezza Rice said. In Hill's view, that might not mean more talks with North Korea—at least not right away—but it had to mean intensive talks with China. "If you can't get serious about working directly with the North Koreans, which I totally understand," he pled as Donald Trump ramped up his rhetoric at the UN, "then at least get serious with China . . . that's where I think we need to have a lot more serious diplomacy—and by that I mean we can't just be sending them messages in the night via Twitter accounts, we need to really sit down and have a no-kidding discussion about our mutual interests." The Chinese agreed. By 2017 they were making public calls for six-party talks. It was a way to appear responsible without committing to the cutting of ties with North Korea it had long resisted—just the kind of stance on which a team of skilled American diplomats might move the needle.

Brian Hook, Rex Tillerson's policy planning director, said that behind closed doors, Tillerson had, "through sheer diplomatic persistence," pressed China into a tougher stance on North Korea. "It began when he sat down with Chinese officials during his visit to Beijing and said, 'You can do this the easy way or the hard way, but you guys have to play a much greater role in denuclearizing the Korean Peninsula,'" he told me.

Whether those efforts could have prevailed would remain a question mark: Trump forced Tillerson out before they could bear fruit. Instead, Trump astonished allies when, in a meeting with a South Korean delegation, he agreed on the spot to personally meet with

North Korean leader Kim Jong Un. This was announced, almost casually, by the South Koreans after the meeting. Rex Tillerson, who had just hours earlier said the United States was still "a long way from negotiations," told the press that the president hadn't spoken to him beforehand, surprising no one. But as far as anyone could tell, Trump hadn't told any other officials either.

White House and State Department personnel scrambled to adjust course. The agreement was a curveball. Some hoped it would thaw relations. But many in the foreign policy establishment feared the move, undertaken out of the blue and absent broader diplomatic context, would be taken by North Korea as recognition of its status as a nuclear power. And officials worried that Trump, mercurial to begin with, would have little by way of a diplomatic team behind him to guide the talks. It was hard to see the United States' capacity for diplomacy in the region as anything but downsized. At the State Department, the sizable North Korea unit led by Yuri Kim a decade earlier no longer existed. A year into Trump's tenure, there wasn't even a permanent assistant secretary for East Asia.

THE REST OF THE WORLD has not stood by as America relinquishes its leadership in diplomacy and development. The balance of global diplomatic power is shifting. During Tillerson's first trip to China as secretary of state, he and President Xi Jinping sat in matching taupe leather armchairs in front of a mural of Chinese pastoral beauty: cranes soaring over pristine valleys and forests. They wore matching red ties and dark jackets. And, in a move that left close followers of US-Chinese relations agape, they used matching language. President Xi urged the United States to "expand cooperative areas and achieve win-win results." Tillerson agreed: "The US side is ready to develop relations with China based on the principle of no conflict, no confrontation, mutual respect, and win-win cooperation."

A lay observer might have blinked and missed it, but Asia experts at the State Department and beyond saw something unusual immediately. Tillerson had all but copy-pasted earlier statements by Xi who, just a few months before, had expressed hope that President Trump would "uphold the principles of non-conflict, non-confrontation, mutual respect, and win-win cooperation." That was the most recent of many examples of Xi, and other communist officials, using that coded sequence of terms to describe a new balance of powers, with China as an equal to the United States, and the US deferring to Chinese prerogatives on contentious issues from Taiwan to territorial disputes in the South China Sea. State-run media instantly picked up on the dog whistle. "Tillerson has implicitly endorsed the new model of major power relations," crowed the communist-affiliated *Global Times*, saying Tillerson's language had given "US allies in the Asia Pacific region an impression that China and the US are equal . . . " as "Barack Obama refused to do."

Several officials at the State Department told me the Bureau of East Asian and Pacific Affairs, home to regional experts attuned to the significance of such language, had not been consulted on the statement. Instead, it had been drafted by the White House—according to several sources there, by the office of Jared Kushner. Brian Hook, Tillerson's director of policy planning, did not dispute this account of events, but said that an acting official from the Asia bureau was on the trip. Was the acting official involved in drafting the statements, I asked?

"I don't recall," Hook said. "You've been on these trips. You know. They're a blur."

"Did Tillerson intend to mirror their language?" I asked.

"He is not intending to mirror their language."

"But is he aware that's what he did?"

"He—he signs off on every statement he delivers. He believes in win-win. He believes that China and the US can work together." Later, Hook added that Tillerson "assigns different meanings than the Chinese do to stock formulations. For example, the secretary believes in win-win, but that doesn't mean two wins for China." Hook described Tillerson's approach to China as "results-based," with a willingness to "count[er] any Chinese actions that harm our interests." But in the eyes of some career diplomats, those goals were being undermined by the steadfast refusal to draw on expertise within the system. An official in the Asia bureau said watching that trip unfold, with no contact between Tillerson and the experts back home that would typically be consulted on such statements, was like being locked outside watching an enthusiastic dog tear up your upholstery.

As America's diplomats face budget cuts, China's coffers are more flush with each passing year. Beijing has poured money into development projects, including a $1.4-trillion slate of infrastructure initiatives around the world that would dwarf the Marshall Plan, adjusted for inflation. Its spending on foreign assistance is still a fraction of the United States', but the trend line is striking, with funding growing by an average of more than 20 percent annually since 2005. The rising superpower is making sure the world knows it. In one recent year, the US State Department spent $666 million on public diplomacy, aimed at winning hearts and minds abroad. While it's difficult to know exactly what China spends on equivalent programs, one analysis put the value of its "external propaganda" programs at about $10 billion a year.

In international organizations, Beijing looms large behind a retreating Washington, DC. As the US proposes cuts to its UN spending, China has become the second-largest funder of UN peacekeeping missions. It now has more peacekeepers in conflicts around the world than the four other permanent Security Council members combined. The move is pragmatic: Beijing gets more influence, and plum appointments in the United Nations' governing bodies.

Around the world, the same transformation is playing out. The caricature of China's foreign policy offered by Western powers— ruthless economic expansion, unmoored from either ethical compunction or willingness to engage diplomatically—was accurate for years. Now, in Afghanistan, China is exploring a mediating role in that country's complex relationship with neighboring Pakistan. In Sudan, China for decades maintained a policy of "non-interference," buying oil from the notorious National Islamic Front/National Congress Party in Khartoum as that regime massacred civilians in Darfur and South Sudan. Sudan's brutalized population pleaded in vain for China to use its unique leverage to demand peace. Now, China's Africa envoy shuttles around the region, offering to facilitate mediations and trying to craft a settlement to the violence that still engulfs South Sudan. Beijing called the hands-on approach a "new chapter" in its foreign policy.

The impact is starker in Asia. As the Trump administration abandoned the Trans-Pacific Partnership (TPP), a regional trade agreement that the Obama administration had led and nurtured since 2009, China swiftly stepped in with its own massive trade pact. And in countries around the region, the difference is being felt on the ground. The Trump administration proposed cutting assistance to Kazakhstan and Turkmenistan entirely. These were small programs, but they were the only visible manifestation of American influence in countries strategically located adjacent to both the war in Afghanistan and the United States' showdown with Russia. They're also home to brand new train lines delivered under China's sweeping "One Belt, One Road" initiative.

"It's a completely self-inflicted wound," John Kerry said of China's encroachment on the kind of diplomacy and development the United States once dominated. "It worries me a lot more than many of the other issues consuming the public debate most days . . . in terms of a big, powerful, ambitious country setting the agenda and executing on it—they're eating our lunch today, and this president has invited it because he thinks our retreat is some kind of accomplishment." China is no global hero. It would be an oversimplification to argue that these first forays into diplomatic leadership can fully counter the United States' deeply rooted legacy of engagement. And Beijing brings to the table a very different kind of leadership: still ruthless, still burdened by its refusal to confront its own human rights abuses. But the trajectory is meaningful. Already, for the child born in Kazakhstan today, one world power's leadership will be evident, and the other's will not. Already, from Sudan to Pakistan, I have spoken to young people who grew up with more visible and aggressively branded Chinese infrastructure. If China can mature as a diplomatic power as rapidly as it has as a force for economic development, America will have ceded one of the most important ways in which great powers shape the world.

EPILOGUE

THE TOOL OF FIRST RESORT

VIENNA, 2015

> There are two types of military dispute, the one settled by negotiation and the other by force. Since the first is characteristic of human beings and the second of beasts, we must have recourse to the second only if we cannot exploit the first.
>
> —CICERO, *ON DUTIES*

THE STEADY DISSOLUTION of the State Department under the Trump administration may appear to be a logical outcome of years of imbalanced foreign policy, but it is not an inevitable one. The trend of sidelined diplomats and ascendant soldiers and spies since September 11, 2001 has not been linear. Diplomats who served in the Bush administration point to the return of North Korea diplomacy through Christopher Hill's efforts, and initiatives like PEPFAR, the President's Emergency Plan for AIDS Relief, which channeled billions into lifesaving medical treatment in developing countries.

And, taken together, the Iran deal and the Paris Climate Accord represented a rearguard action for diplomacy. They were the more striking for the contrast they represented, after a first term of the Obama administration that was comparatively dismissive of diplomats and barren of large-scale diplomatic endeavor. Ben Rhodes, Obama's deputy national security advisor, attributed the late breakthroughs partly to the slow-burn nature of diplomacy and partly to course correction.

"The centerpieces of our second-term foreign policy were much more diplomatic in nature than in our first term, and you also had an effort to . . . " he paused, seeming to reflect on the failures of the Holbrooke era. "The kind of superstar-general dynamic, the Petraeus, McChrystal dynamic, was not present in the second term. Not that generals weren't stars, it's just that they weren't these giant public figures who sucked up oxygen in certain parts of the world. I think there was a slow, admittedly, but steady reprioritization of diplomacy."

The results were controversial: proof points of diplomacy's power for some, and of its folly for others. But, even as Trump withdrew the United States from Paris and as fierce debate over the Iran deal and its virtues and vices continued, it could not be denied that these were serious foreign policy initiatives, born of hard-fought, old-school diplomacy. Little surprise that the most controversial of those initiatives, the Iran deal, would begin and end with shouting.

It was night when one of those rounds of shouting began, echoing off gilt- and white-paneled walls, and rococo chairs, and an ornate marble fireplace with a mantle held up by cherubs. Half of the shouts were from Iran's foreign minister, backtracking on how many years his country would assent to constraints on its nuclear program. Half were from the American secretaries of state and energy, telling the Iranians to, in not so many words, go to hell. "I've *had it* with this," John Kerry was shouting. "You cannot do what you're threatening to do." If Iran wanted to renegotiate basic terms, the United States was more than happy to walk away.

It was July 2015, and Iranian, American, British, French, Chinese, Russian, German, and European Union negotiators had converged on Vienna for a final, tortured stretch of diplomacy. The hyperluxe Palais Coburg, where Johann Strauss had once conducted in the glittering ballroom and where the Saxe-Coburg-Gotha dynasty had schemed and inbred and reclined in scented baths until its last princess expired in the 1990s, was selected as the venue for the talks, partly because its thirty-four rooms allowed for few guests to overhear conversations like this. Still, those who could afford to stay at the Palais Coburg—spies and diplomats, bankers and barons—had keen ears. And by then, six hundred reporters had descended on hushed Vienna for just such gossip.

The Americans, in the next dining room over, were nervous. "Kerry kind of lost it, lost his temper," Jon Finer—Kerry's chief of staff and, later, the director of policy planning at State—remembered. "A lot of us were gathering in the dining area, outside where this meeting was, and people were able to hear the shouts coming through the walls." Kerry's longtime body man, Jason Meininger, finally opened the doors and interrupted. He delicately informed the Americans and the Iranians that random guests were hearing the intimate details of the most sensitive diplomacy in the world. There turned out to be some truth to this. Over breakfast the next morning, Germany's foreign minister—and later president—Frank-Walter Steinmeier drily congratulated Kerry for what he assumed were productive talks, seeing as the whole hotel heard them.

Ultimately, the most powerful diplomats in the world would spend eighteen days trapped in splendor. Night after night, negotiations stretched into the small hours of the morning. The red-eyed US team went through ten pounds of strawberry-flavored Twizzlers, twenty pounds of string cheese, thirty pounds of mixed nuts and dried fruit, and hundreds of Rice Krispies Treats and espresso pods.

THE NIGHT AFTER the shouting match, the showdown had a reprise in a larger meeting of the ministers of the "P5+1"—the permanent members of the UN Security Council plus Germany. As Iranian foreign minister Javad Zarif tried to insist on a more lenient time frame, the EU's Federica Mogherini said she'd sooner go home than consider it. "Never threaten an Iranian!" Zarif bellowed. "Or a Russian," added Russian foreign minister Sergei Lavrov slyly, cutting the tension. But, in fact, Russia had fallen in line with the Americans and Europeans. Again and again, Lavrov helped the US break logjams—a remarkable fact as the Ukraine crisis worsened and US-Russian relations went into a deep freeze. It was one of the many unusual characteristics of an unusual diplomatic effort: a unified front. Even China signed up to play an important role helping to modify one of Iran's reactors.

The process was also an anachronistic showcase of diplomatic grit. For Bill Burns, it was the last mission of a decades-long career in the Foreign Service that had taken him from ambassadorships in Russia and Jordan to, at the time of the Iran negotiations, the second-in-command job at the State Department. Burns was what you'd picture when you envision a career diplomat. He was lanky, with a salt-and-pepper moustache and a creaky, soft voice that seemed impossibly patient and even-tempered. He was, a *Washington Post* headline declared upon his retirement, a "diplomat's diplomat." When John Kerry told me about the challenges of encouraging young diplomats, he referred to the importance of "finding the next generation of talented foreign service, the next Bill Burns so to speak."

Burns was a living testament to the irreplaceable role Foreign Service officers could still play. He had been involved in American diplomacy with Iran dating back thirty years, to when he joined the National Security Council staff at the White House immediately after the Iran-Contra affair. "As a relatively young diplomat," he said, "the perils of Iran diplomacy were driven home to me because of how badly that all ended." But Iran had a gravitational pull for him. Years later, he had run the Middle East bureau in Colin Powell's State Department and grown distressed at the shrinking space for diplomacy and the growing emphasis on policy made out of the Pentagon. "I saw first-hand the inversion of diplomacy and the use of force that was so characteristic of the run up to the Iraq War," he continued. That inversion, he felt, was one reason why earlier opportunities to approach Iran, when its nuclear program was still in its infancy, were shunned. It wasn't until the very last year of the Bush administration, when Burns was serving as the under secretary for political affairs under Condoleezza Rice, that the administration began to warm to the idea of a diplomatic approach. It was that summer that Burns sat, for the first time, directly opposite the Iranians, in a meeting of world powers in Geneva. "That really opened up a new phase in a sense," Burns reflected. "Which, you know, Obama drove through much more ambitiously."

In the summer of 2009, the United States discovered a secret uranium enrichment facility, not far from the holy city of Qom, and responded with a wave of new sanctions squeezing every aspect of Iran's economy. This entailed careful diplomacy. State Department and Treasury officials appealed to country after country to cut ties, creating a unified front of economic warfare. The impact was devastating: "Their oil exports dropped by 50 percent," Burns recalled. "The value of their currency dropped by 50 percent."

That pressure set the stage for talks. In March 2013, at a military officers' beach house in Oman—which had demonstrated its pull with Tehran by brokering the release of several imprisoned American hikers—Burns and four colleagues held their first secret talks with the Iranians. Over the course of three days, he and the head of the Iranian delegation walked the grounds and spent long hours in a light-filled conference room with a wide view of the Arabian Sea. "I think we left with the sense that there might be an opening here," Burns said. The Iranians were still on a tight leash from Tehran. But they were working-level *diplomats,* not the national security hard-liners who had shown up for international talks before. That distinction would be important on both sides.

Talks gathered steam when Iran surprised the world by electing as president Hassan Rouhani, a perceived moderate who ran on a platform of thawing the freeze on Iran's economy. He installed Javad Zarif, a Western-educated *Charlie Rose* regular, as foreign minister. Over the following year, Burns would lead nine or ten secret negotiations in capitals around the world. In one case, "we did a patch of negotiations in Muscat, then flew to Beijing, then flew back to Oman then back to Beijing," remembered Jon Finer, who was present for many of the later talks. As the months dragged on, the negotiators began to develop a personal rapport. When one of the American diplomats, Wendy Sherman, and her counterpart, Majid Takht-Ravanchi, both became grandparents in the fall of 2013, they shared pictures. Kerry and Zarif held such long meetings that *New York* magazine later Photoshopped a cloud of hearts between the two men and place them atop a listicle entitled "The Most Romantic Moments of the Iran-Deal Negotiations." By the end of 2013, an interim agreement had been signed. In April 2015, that progressed to a framework agreement. And over the following three months, the fight to translate the commitments developed over the previous years into a final deal played out in Vienna.

AS THE SECRET TALKS advanced, some aspects of the American position softened. "Obama made a very critical policy decision . . . which was the US might consider a very, very limited enrichment program if Iran agreed to very strict monitoring and verification," recalled Sherman. Iran having a nuclear program would happen with or without our blessings, the thinking went. The sanctions, Sherman, Burns, and the rest of the Americans became convinced, could only slow that down. Negotiations offered the only hope of ensuring oversight of Iran's activities. The concession of allowing a civil nuclear program— a source of rebuke from opponents of the deal to this day—was an inflection point, one of the most significant factors in making the cascade of agreements that followed possible.

Sherman compared the deal to a Rubik's Cube, with each twist messing up another facet of the negotiations. (Later, a Department of Energy official gave Rubik's Cubes to forty of the American negotiators, including Finer and Sherman, as a gag gift, the word "gag" loosely applied.) The talks literally broke several members of the team. Wendy Sherman broke her nose slamming into a door while rushing to brief Kerry on a secure line, and ruptured her pinky finger tumbling down a staircase en route to one of the team's many Senate briefings defending the negotiations against political attacks. She put her finger on ice and carried on with the briefing anyway. ("I was quite focused, it was a really good briefing," she said. After answering the last question, she burst into tears.) In one heated negotiation in Geneva in 2015, John Kerry slammed his hand on the table so hard a pen went flying and hit one of the Iranian negotiators. Still rattled the day after, he'd gone for a bike ride in the French Alps to clear his head, which is a thing you do if you're John Kerry and you're too far from the coast to windsurf. Distracted by a passing motorcycle, he slammed into a barrier and went flying, shattering his femur.

From Muscat to New York and Geneva to Vienna, they persevered, and entreated allies to do the same. In July 2015—after one last push that stretched until 3 a.m.—the ministers lined up at the United Nations in Vienna, looking tired in front of a row of their countries' flags as flashbulbs went off. Together, they announced a deal that would constrain Iran's nuclear ambitions for at least a decade. The rogue nation that had flouted sustained diplomacy with the outside world for more than thirty years had consented to rigorous, intrusive checks and verifications.

John Kerry took the opportunity to defend the deal against what he knew would be years of outrage, from those who opposed the very idea of talks, and those who would argue that the United States got snookered. "I will just share with you, very personally, years ago when I left college, I went to war," he told the assembled press, referring to his time in Vietnam. "And I learned in war the price that is paid when diplomacy fails. And I made a decision that if I ever was lucky enough to be in a position to make a difference, I would try to do so." His voice, hoarse and weary, cracked with emotion. "I know that war is the failure of diplomacy and the failure of leaders to make alternative decisions."

THE DEAL WAS A LIGHTNING ROD for criticism. Getting to the finish line required what some considered to be unacceptable compromises. Back in 2009 Obama had ordered the CIA and the State Department to stand down from supporting anti-government protesters in Iran's Green Revolution, fearing regime change would explode the secret diplomatic entrees. Some critics argued that the Obama administration's obsessive pursuit of the deal had also contributed to its inaction in Syria, after Iran threatened to pull out of talks if the United States interfered with the Tehran-allied Syrian regime. And the deal itself—affording Iran the right to a low level of nuclear enrichment insufficient for weapons production, and featuring some restraints that would expire after a decade—was no clean victory.

Others argued it was a deal with the devil. From stoning rape victims, to imprisoning journalists, including Americans, Iran was hardly a reformed actor. When the Trump administration set about lobbying against the deal—and failed to gain traction on claims that Iran had cheated—many of its arguments were instead premised on this. US Ambassador to the United Nations Nicki Haley talked at length about Iran's history, since 1979, as a rogue nation and sponsor of terrorism, urging the world to view Iran as a "jigsaw puzzle," incorporating more pieces than the nuclear issue.

The deal's negotiators were the first to admit its imperfections. But this was, they argued, what a diplomatic victory looked like. The deal was narrowly focused on the singular, pressing challenge of

Iran's nuclear ambitions. Nowhere did it seek to address the country's human rights record, or its support for anti-US elements in Syria, or its nonnuclear weapons tests. It was hard to envision, the deal's proponents said, how taking nuclear talks off the table would do anything but diminish the United States' ability to address any of those other issues. "We recognized that there were a lot of other elements of Iranian behavior that would threaten our interests and the interests of our friends," Bill Burns told me. "But being able to resolve the nuclear issue without a shot being fired, in a way that serves our interests, is a pretty significant step."

There were also few alternatives. Without the agreement, Kerry argued, "You were going to have near-term military action, period. Breakout time was down to a couple months. So, either on our watch or early in [Trump's] presidency, without [the deal] you were going to have a confrontation." The Obama administration had reviewed the military options and they looked bleak. They could temporarily debilitate specific sites, but there was no way to keep the Iranians from rebuilding. "You were going to be in the situation of doing it once, then making diplomacy totally impossible because once you've bombed them," Finer recalled of the administration's view of tactical options. "They're pretty unlikely to sit at the table and negotiate with you, they're going to try to race to a bomb covertly, away from monitoring. And then you're going to be in a position where you have to find it and bomb it again, maybe in two years down the road and so you're in perpetuity in this cycle."

"There is this notion out there that there is a better deal or a perfect deal to be had and life's not like that," Burns added. "You can make an argument that, had we seriously engaged with the Iranians a decade earlier, when they were spinning sixty-four centrifuges and a very primitive effort of an enrichment program, maybe we could have produced sharper limits on their nuclear program. The reality was, at the beginning of 2013, when we began the secret talks in earnest, they were spinning almost nineteen thousand centrifuges. . . . And there was no way in which you could bomb or wish that away. The challenge in diplomacy was always going to produce something short of a perfect solution." This was how complex negotiated settlements looked: twenty years earlier, the agreement Richard Holbrooke brokered in Dayton had compromised deeply, too, attaching rights of political representation to ethnic groups, and creating a bloated, unwieldy government in an effort to satisfy everyone.

Several of the diplomats behind the Iran deal, including Sherman and Finer, banded together to take the fight to Congress and the media. They argued that withdrawal would diminish the United States' influence, and that China and Russia would seize on the opportunity to drive a wedge between the US and its European allies, which were significantly invested in the deal. Most of all, the diplomats feared how the destruction of the world's most significant nonproliferation deal with a hostile state might echo across the world, in another great crisis. "If we ditch this deal," Finer said, "What are the North Koreans going to think? What incentive do the North Koreans have to even contemplate negotiating anything?"

FOR ALL ITS FLAWS, it was a deal, and one that offered lessons on the factors that can still converge to make diplomacy work in the present day. The Iran negotiators prevailed through their trials partly because the president offered full-bodied support, with little micromanagement. Before each round of negotiations, Obama ran through his "red lines" with Kerry and Sherman, then reminded them they were empowered to walk away if they saw fit. By the end of the yearslong journey to Vienna, dozens of State Department officials had been involved in the deal. I spoke to many of them: uniformly, they recalled feeling empowered by the White House, and how integral that was to their work.

If there was to be a road map for the future of American diplomacy, many career diplomats told me, it was this: embracing the compromise and imperfection of the deals, realizing that they could avert
war and save lives; investing in working-level diplomats and giving
them a long enough leash to do their jobs; and installing leadership
with a visionary belief in large-scale diplomatic initiatives like the ones
the Trump administration seemed bent on dismantling. Those proposals looked, in their way, not unlike the reforms that had reshaped State
in the years after World War II.

"On Iran, Cuba, and Paris—I think it's really, frankly, just three
policies where whichever administration came in after us was handed
a series of opportunities, big ones, and frankly had some diplomatic
openings that past secretaries would've loved to have teed up to
explore," John Kerry said. The worst-case scenario of the Iran deal,
he continued to believe as the Trump administration began its pushback, was that Iran would resist compliance, isolating the Iranians,
not the Americans. The consequences of the United States unilaterally imploding the deal were, he argued, far worse. "Trump's done it
backwards, with bluster. He's isolated us. If the [deal] goes belly up, the
world will blame us not Iran. . . ." Kerry went for a jab: "If that's the
art of the deal, you can see why this guy filed for bankruptcy seven
times." It was a sound bite from another era, when you could shame
someone into seeing the error of their ways; when a crystal-clear case,
a sound argument, could make a difference. But, in American politics,
that time had passed.

Ultimately, more than eighty arms control specialists signed a letter defending the Iran deal as a "net plus for international nuclear nonproliferation efforts" and warning that "unilateral action by the United
States, especially on the basis of unsupported contentions of Iranian
cheating, would isolate the United States." But that message didn't
penetrate the Trump administration, which continued to publicly
excoriate Iran. The time of specialists playing a formative role in for-

eign policy, some career officials feared, may have passed too. Just days after assuming power, the new administration had, of course, fired its top in-house expert on nonproliferation.

So IT WAS THAT, on a cold Sunday in January 2017, Tom Countryman found himself clearing out his office at the State Department. It was the end of thirty-five years of service, but he was unsentimental. "There was so much to do," he said with a shrug. "I'm not sure I pondered it." On most Sundays, the Department was eerily empty. But on this one, Countryman wasn't alone. Under Secretary Patrick Kennedy, after forty-four years in the Foreign Service, was cleaning out his desk as well. The two graying diplomats took a break from their boxes of paperwork and family photos to reminisce. Kennedy had been in the thick of the Iraq War as chief of staff for the Coalition Provisional Authority. Countryman had been in Egypt as that country joined the Gulf War. It was an improbably quiet end to a pair of high-stakes careers: memories and empty desks, as the State Department stood still.

A few days had passed since Countryman was fired while on a mission in Jordan, and he had done his best to wrap up what he could. There hadn't been time to talk to most of his 260 employees in the Bureau of International Security and Nonproliferation. In any case, there was little to say that could provide clarity about what was to come.

The following Tuesday, he had one last chance to say goodbye. More than a hundred career officers crammed into a reception area on the first floor with a stained ceiling and industrial gray carpeting. The crowd clutched white Styrofoam cups as Countryman took to a podium. Since his firing less than a week before, Tom Countryman had become something of a minor celebrity, a symbol of an embattled profession. One colleague compared the end of his career to Obi-Wan Kenobi getting cut down by Darth Vader in *Star Wars,* which Countryman found touching. (Another, he added archly, compared it to the scene where Princess Leia strangles Jabba the Hutt. "And I found that confusing.")

He had spent days thinking through a message, a lesson, something of worth to leave behind. Countryman was not, he told the crowd of beleaguered diplomats, disgruntled. He was, in fact, "probably the most gruntled person in the room." He told them about a career that had given him a firsthand view of world and diplomatic history. He spoke of "ambassadors legendary" and of the bright young officers who, he was convinced, still rose from the ranks of the Foreign Service.

But he also sounded a warning. "A foreign policy without professionals is," he said, "by definition, an amateur foreign policy."

Stay, he urged the assembled officers—even as he acknowledged that theirs was a profession out of step with the times. "Our work is little understood by our fellow Americans, a fact that is sometimes exploited for political purpose." Only they, he said, could serve as a bulwark against an increasingly transactional and militarized approach to the world. "Our consular officers are the first of many lines of defense against those who would come to the US with evil purpose. We want the families of America's heroes—our servicemen—to know that their loved ones are not put into danger simply because of a failure to pursue nonmilitary solutions. . . . If our interaction with other countries is only a business transaction, rather than a partnership with allies and friends, we will lose that game too. China practically invented transactional diplomacy, and if we choose to play their game, Beijing will run the table."

These were the fears of the surviving diplomats who remembered a different time, when talking and listening counted for something, and the State Department was an indispensable instrument of American power. "We have unilaterally disarmed basically," Wendy Sherman reflected. "If you don't have diplomacy as a tool, you have unilaterally undermined your own power. Why would we do that?" She sighed. "Why we would take that away from ourselves is unfathomable to me and why we would become a military-first foreign policy is unfathomable to me."

"There's a real corrosion of the sense of American leadership in the world and the institutions that make that leadership real," added Bill Burns. "You end up creating a circumstance where you wake up fifteen years from now and say 'Where are all those Foreign Service officers who should be just short of the mark of becoming ambassadors?' and they're not going to be there." He remembered vividly the "inversion" of diplomacy and military might he had witnessed during the run-up to the war in Iraq. As he watched the precious few diplomatic accomplishments of the modern era fall like dominoes under the Trump administration, he couldn't help but see the parallel. "Diplomacy really ought to be the tool of first resort internationally. It can sometimes achieve things at far less cost, both financially and in terms of American lives, than the use of the military can," Burns remarked. Some of the tilt toward military policymaking would be hard to undo, he conceded—but, he was convinced, there was always a path back. He still believed in the quality of Americans drawn to serve in his unglamorous but necessary line of work.

I was reminded of something Richard Holbrooke had written, as the State Department weathered the brutal budget cuts of the Clinton era, in the introduction of *To End a War*, his grand history of Bosnia and, of course, himself. "Today, public service has lost much of the aura that it had when John F. Kennedy asked us what we could do for our country. To hear that phrase before it became a cliché was electrifying. . . . Public service can make a difference. If this book helps inspire a few young Americans to enter the government or other forms of public service, it will have achieved one of its goals." Holbrooke was an impossible blowhard but his belief in America—and its power to make peace, not just war—was achingly earnest. After he died, I remember sitting at my cubicle, under the gray lights of the State Department's first floor, staring at that passage, and thinking that, for all his faults, he had achieved that goal for the group of staffers he nurtured in Afghanistan. Years later, I pulled the volume off a shelf and opened it to the same dog-eared page, and realized that I had written in pencil along the margin: "miss you, Ambassador."

As long as people continued to believe in civilian public service, Burns felt, the institutions would survive. "The Foreign Service has often gotten the shit beaten out of it," he observed, sounding, for the first time, undiplomatic. It had always survived before. This time, he and virtually all of his peers agreed, it had to. "In a world where power is more diffuse . . . in which there's so much that's in flux, that actually makes diplomacy far more important and far more relevant than it ever was before, contrary to the fashionable notion that with information technology, 'who needs embassies?' "

Tom Countryman was among those out of fashion. After his speech, he packed his bags and took a vacation. So it was that I caught up with him, sucking down e-cigarettes and looking out at the wide blue Puget Sound from his brother's modest one-story house in Tacoma, Washington. Several months later, I asked Brian Hook, the first policy planning director at State during the Trump era, what he would identify as that administration's signature diplomatic mission. Hook thought for a moment, as if turning over the question for the first time. In later conversations, he mentioned a broader range of priorities, including confronting ISIL. But in that first exchange, he said, finally, "Nonproliferation around dangerous states like Iran and North Korea." At the time, there was no one in charge of those issues at the State Department. For the following year, the job Tom Countryman once held would sit empty, like so many others.

ACKNOWLEDGMENTS

I CONDUCTED OVER two hundred interviews for *War on Peace*. I owe much to the sources whose eyewitness accounts, documents, and insights run through every page. Some of your names I may never be able to make public. For every one of you who spoke, sometimes at personal or professional risk: thank you. To the career diplomats, especially—Tom Countryman, Erin Clancy, Robin Raphel, Anne Patterson, Bill Burns, Christopher Hill, Chris LaVine, and too many others to list here—I hope this book is a fitting examination of the work you do. I hope it is the same for Richard Holbrooke and his complicated and important legacy. Without him, this book wouldn't exist.

I am equally grateful to the secretaries of state who were gracious enough to go on the record: Henry Kissinger, George P. Shultz, James Baker, Madeleine Albright, Colin Powell, Condoleezza Rice, Hillary Clinton, John Kerry, and Rex Tillerson. They were generous with their time and their candor. The same thanks go to the other military and civilian leaders who spoke: David Petraeus, Michael Hayden, Leon

Panetta, John Allen, James Stavridis, William Caldwell, and many others.

Shana Mansbach, my indefatigable research assistant, was involved in hundreds of hours of interviews, proofing, and footnoting. She refused to drop the project, even when it ran longer than anticipated, and she had better damn things to do. She was preceded by the wonderful Arie Kuipers and Nathan Kohlenberg. All of us were given a safety net by Andy Young, my meticulous fact-checker, who made time to review manuscripts while being a full-time traveling companion to Lady Gaga, for some reason.

My agent, Lynn Nesbit, fought hard to keep *War on Peace* alive. She is the best ally a writer could have. She's represented fifty years of literary luminaries, she's the toughest negotiator I know, and she manages regular Kettlebell workouts. We should all be Lynn Nesbit.

I also owe thanks to the team at W. W. Norton, which published Dean Acheson's *Present at the Creation* in 1969, making this, in a sense, a very dark sequel. John Glusman was a patient and compassionate editor. Drake McFeely believed in the project when others were fickle and abandoned it and me. Many of their colleagues also worked hard: Louise Brockett, Rachel Salzman, Brendan Curry, Steven Pace, Meredith McGinnis, Steve Attardo, Julia Druskin, Nancy Palmquist, and Helen Thomaides among them. Books, like diplomacy, are an institution buffeted by changing times. Research-heavy ones take commitment from good and serious people like these.

Several foreign policy experts I respect, including Ian Bremmer, Richard Haass, and Samantha Vinograd, looked at manuscripts and gave notes they didn't have time to give. They informed these pages greatly. David Remnick, David Rohde, and my other editors at *The New Yorker* gave invaluable advice and politely tolerated the time I had to take off to finish the thing.

Lastly, nothing I do would be possible without my family and the friends I have left after this book made me unpleasant and unavailable for half a decade. My mother was there for every excited call accompanying a breakthrough, and every despairing one as things nearly fell apart. Jon Lovett, who usually charges for this sort of thing, gave countless notes. Jennifer Harris, I am sorry I missed your wedding to go interview a warlord. I really did rehearse that song.

NOTES

PROLOGUE: MAHOGANY ROW MASSACRE

ix *[A]ppoint an ambassador: The Laws of Manu.* Translated by George Bühler. Amazon Digital Services LLC, 2012, loc. 1818. Kindle.

x *"We'd build a moat if we could":* Conversation with a Foreign Service officer who requested anonymity due to the critique of embassy security implicit in the remark, 20 February 2012.

x *His trip that January:* Goldschmidt, Pierre. "A Realistic Approach Toward a Middle East Free of WMD." *Carnegie Endowment for International Peace*, 7 July 2016, carnegieendowment.org/2016/07/07/realistic-approach-toward-middle-east-free-of-wmd-pub-64039.

x *"a fairly quixotic quest":* Author interview with Thomas Countryman, 22 June 2017.

x *"It was an important meeting":* Author interview with Thomas Countryman, 22 June 2017.

xi *"I'm trying":* Author interview with Thomas Countryman, 22 June 2017.

xii *"one of those faceless bureaucrats":* "The Case of Thomas Countryman." *Seattle.Politics Google Group*, 26 February 2017, https://groups.google.com/forum/#!topic/seattle.politics/hVTxKDgCdbU.

xii *"King of the party":* "Former Assistant Secretary of State Rocks Bodacious Mullet on MSNBC." *Washington Free Beacon*, 1 February 2017, freebeacon.com/national-security/former-assistant-secretary-of-state-rocks-bodacious-mullet-on-msnbc/.

xii *"This is not happy news":* Author interview with Thomas Countryman, 22 June 2017.

xii   *"I didn't have any idea":* Author interview with Thomas Countryman, 22 June 2017.

xiii   *"What about the Rome meeting?":* Author interview with Thomas Countryman, 22 June 2017.

xiv   *"It's not fair":* Author interview with Thomas Countryman, 22 June 2017.

xiv   *"Nobody can do that better than me":* Gharib, Malaka. "From AIDS To Zika: Trump On Global Health And Humanitarian Aid." NPR, 9 November 2016, https://www.npr.org/sections/goatsandsoda/2016/11/09/501425084/from-aids-to-zika-trump-on-global-health-and-humanitarian-aid and Clarke, Hilary et al. "Alarm bells ring for charities as Trump pledges to slash foreign aid budget." CNN, 1 March 2017, www.cnn.com/2017/02/28/politics/trump-budget-foreign-aid/index.html.

xv   *"none of those things were true":* Author interview with Thomas Countryman, 22 June 2017.

xv   *"deep distrust for professional public servants:"* Author interview with Thomas Countryman, 22 June 2017.

xv   *"in the arms-control bureau":* Author interview with Thomas Countryman, 22 June 2017.

xv   *"dump everyone they could dump":* Author interview with Thomas Countryman, 22 June 2017.

xvi   *"To this day":* Author interview with Thomas Countryman, 22 June 2017.

xvi   *"That was just petty":* Author interview with Thomas Countryman, 22 June 2017.

xvii   *"Hold on the line":* Author interview with Thomas Countryman, 22 June 2017.

xvii   the Ferraris of State Department personnel: Author interview with Erin Clancy in Los Angeles, 1 June 2017.

xvii   *"have you heard this rumor?":* Author interview with Erin Clancy in Los Angeles, 1 June 2017.

xviii   *"We just found out":* Author interview with Erin Clancy in Los Angeles, 1 June 2017.

xviii   *"No reason":* Author interview with Erin Clancy in Los Angeles, 1 June 2017.

xviii   *"We're all being fired":* Author interview with Erin Clancy in Los Angeles, 1 June 2017.

xix   *"We are truly seen as outsiders":* Author interview with Erin Clancy in Los Angeles, 1 June 2017.

xx   *"I'm not familiar with that one":* Author interview with Rex Tillerson, 4 January 2018.

xxi   *"Unprecedented":* Gramer, Robbie, De Luce, Dan, and Lynch, Colum. "How the Trump Administration Broke the State Department." *Foreign Policy*, 31 July 2017, foreignpolicy.com/2017/07/31/how-the-trump-administration-broke-the-state-department; Chalfant, Morgan. "Trump's War on the State Department." *The Hill*, 14 July 2017, thehill.com/homenews/administration/341923-trumps-war-on-the-state-department and see, e.g., Dreyfuss, Bob. "How Rex Tillerson Turned the State Department into a Ghost Ship." *Rolling Stone*, 13 July 2017, www.rollingstone.com/politics/features/rex-tillerson-turned-the-state-department-into-a-ghost-ship-w492142.

xxi   *" 'diplomacy works best when it comes in a mailed fist' ":* Author interview with James Baker, 22 January 2018.

xxii   *the nosedive accelerated:* Konyndyk, Jeremy. "Clinton and Helms Nearly Ruined State. Tillerson Wants to Finish the Job." *Politico,* 4 May 2017, www .politico.com/magazine/story/2017/05/04/tillerson-trump-state-department-budget-cut-215101.

xxii   *Over the course of the 1990s:* "A Foreign Affairs Budget for the Future: Fixing the Crisis in Diplomatic Readiness." Stimson Center, October 2008, https:// www.stimson.org/sites/default/files/file-attachments/A_Foreign_Affairs_ Budget_for_the_Future_11_08pdf_1.pdf.

xxii   *Here's what happened:* "A Foreign Affairs Budget for the Future: Fixing the Crisis in Diplomatic Readiness." Stimson Center, October 2008, https:// www.stimson.org/sites/default/files/file-attachments/A_Foreign_Affairs_ Budget_for_the_Future_11_08pdf_1.pdf.

xxii   *fewer embassies and consulates:* Lippman, Thomas. "U.S. Diplomacy's Presence Shrinking." *Washington Post,* 3 June 1996, https://www.washingtonpost.com/ archive/politics/1996/06/03/us-diplomacys-presence-shrinking/4d1d817e-a748-457d-9b22-1971bb1cb934/?utm_term=.d3faf19815ad.

xxii   *jerry-rig a satellite dish:* Lippman, Thomas. "U.S. Diplomacy's Presence Shrinking." *Washington Post,* 3 June 1996, https://www.washingtonpost.com/archive/ politics/1996/06/03/us-diplomacys-presence-shrinking/4d1d817e-a748-457d-9b22-1971bb1cb934/?utm_term=.d3faf19815ad.

xxiii   *had been wiped out:* "The Last Time @StateDept Had a 27% Budget Cut, Congress Killed A.C.D.A. and U.S.I.A." *Diplopundit,* 31 March 2017, https://diplopundit .net/2017/03/31/the-last-time-statedept-had-a-27-budget-cut-congress-killed-acda-and-usia/.

xxiii   *"sake of the present":* Friedman, Thomas. "Foreign Affairs; the End of Something." *New York Times,* 26 July 1995, www.nytimes.com/1995/07/26/opinion/ foreign-affairs-the-end-of-something.html.

xxiii   *undertrained and under-resourced:* "A Foreign Affairs Budget for the Future: Fixing the Crisis in Diplomatic Readiness." Stimson Center, October 2008, https://www.stimson.org/sites/default/files/file-attachments/A_Foreign_ Affairs_Budget_for_the_Future_11_08pdf_1.pdf.

xxiii   *"like never before":* Author interview with Colin Powell in Washington, DC, 29 August 2017.

xxiii   *"Soft" categories:* For example, Economic Support Funds (ESF) tripled from $2.3 billion in Fiscal Year 2001 to $6.1 billion in FY 2017, with $3.7 billion of $3.8-billion increase coming from OCO. Similarly, OCO accounted for nearly all of the increase in International Disaster Assistance, which rose from $299 million to $2 billion. Same goes for the increase in Migration and Refugee Assistance budget ($698 million to $2.8 billion). At the same time, Inter-American Foundation, African Development Foundation, and other "soft" budget categories flatlined. "Congressional Budget Justification Department of State, Foreign Operations, and Related Programs: Fiscal Year 2017," United States State

Department and "Congressional Budget Justification, Foreign Operations, Fiscal Year 2002," United States State Department.

xxiv   *"ceded a lot of authority"*: Author interview with Madeleine Albright, 15 December 2017.

xxiv   *"The VP had very, very strong views"*: Author interview with Colin Powell in Washington, DC, 29 August 2017.

xxiv   *"The temptations of propinquity"*: Author interview with Henry Kissinger, 4 December 2017.

xxv   *"we didn't take over the country to run a country"*: Author interview with Colin Powell in Washington, DC, 29 August 2017.

xxv   *deadly insurgency:* Konyndyk, Jeremy. "Clinton and Helms Nearly Ruined State. Tillerson Wants to Finish the Job." *Politico*, 4 May 2017, www.politico.com/magazine/story/2017/05/04/tillerson-trump-state-department-budget-cut-215101.

xxv   *Taxpayer dollars:* Lake, Eli. "SIGIR Audit Finds Some U.S. CERP Funds Went to Insurgents in Iraq." *Daily Beast*, 29 April 2012, www.thedailybeast.com/sigir-audit-finds-some-us-cerp-funds-went-to-insurgents-in-iraq.

xxv   *The State Department's legal adviser:* Boumediene v. Bush, 553 US 723 (2008).

xxvi   *proved toxic:* Konyndyk, Jeremy. "Clinton and Helms Nearly Ruined State. Tillerson Wants to Finish the Job." *Politico*, 4 May 2017, www.politico.com/magazine/story/2017/05/04/tillerson-trump-state-department-budget-cut-215101.

xxvi   *"Events in Iraq":* "Text: Obama's Cairo Speech." *New York Times*, 4 June 2009, http://www.nytimes.com/2009/06/04/us/politics/04obama.text.html.

xxvi   *Lute as Jones's deputy:* "Donald Trump Would Have the Most Generals in the White House Since WWII." *ABC News*, 8 December 2016, http://abcnews.go.com/Politics/donald-trump-generals-white-house-world-war-ii/story?id=44063445.

xxvii   *Obama administration sold more arms than any other:* Weisgerber, Marcus. "Obama's Final Arms-Export Tally More than Doubles Bush's." *Defense One*, 8 November 2016, www.defenseone.com/business/2016/11/obamas-final-arms-export-tally-more-doubles-bushs/133014 and Farid, Farid. "Obama's Administration Sold More Weapons Than Any Other Since World War II." *Vice News*, 3 January 2017, https://motherboard.vice.com/en_us/article/qkjmvb/obamas-administration-sold-more-weapons-than-any-other-since-world-war-ii.

xxvii   *"more right than wrong":* Author interview with Hillary Clinton, 20 November 2017.

xxvii   *"pure mil-think":* "SUBJECT: AT THE CROSSROADS." Memo from Richard Holbrooke to Hillary Clinton, 10 September 2010. See detailed discussion infra.

xxvii   *"back-channel" communication:* DeYoung, Karen. "How the Obama White House Runs Foreign Policy." *Washington Post*, 4 August 2015, https://www.washingtonpost.com/world/national-security/how-the-obama-white-house-runs-foreign-policy/2015/08/04/2befb960-2fd7-11e5-8353-1215475949f4_story.html?utm_term=.ffae45cd1509 and DeYoung, Karen. "Obama's NSC Will Get New Power." *Washington Post*, 8 February 2009, www.washingtonpost.com/wp-dyn/content/article/2009/02/07/AR2009020702076.html.

xxviii *the* New York Times *offered:* Buckley, Cara. "A Monster of a Slip." *New York Times,* 16 March 2008, www.nytimes.com/2008/03/16/fashion/16samantha.html.

xxviii *"ivory-toned":* Roig-Franzia, Manuel. "Samantha Power: learning to play the diplomat's game." *Washington Post,* 4 April 2014, https://www.washingtonpost.com/lifestyle/magazine/samantha-power-learning-to-play-the-diplomats-game/2014/04/03/1ea34bae-99ac-11e3-b88d-f36c07223d88_story.html.

xxviii *"sky-blue backdrop":* Sullivan, Robert. "Samantha Power Takes on the Job of a Lifetime as Ambassador to the U.N." *Vogue,* 14 October 2013, www.vogue.com/article/samantha-power-americas-ambassador-to-the-un.

xxviii *"Enough With Samantha Power's Flowing Red Hair":* Carmon, Irin. "Enough With Samantha Power's Flowing Red Hair." *Jezebel,* 30 March 2011, www.jezebel.com/5787135/have-you-heard-about-samantha-powers-flowing-red-hair.

xxviii *"The bottleneck is too great":* Author interview with Samantha Power, 10 July 2017.

xxviii *exerted even tighter control over policy:* Author interview with anonymous senior official.

xxix *"That is ever the charge from the agencies":* Author interview with Susan Rice, 19 January 2018.

xxix *"learned helplessness":* Author interview with Susan Rice, 19 January 2018.

xxix *"felt that they couldn't move":* Author interview with Samantha Power, 10 July 2017.

xxx *"trying to kill it":* Author interview with Susan Rice, 19 January 2018.

xxx *working above their level of experience:* Davidson, Joe. "Gaps Persist in Midlevel Foreign Service Positions." *Washington Post,* 16 July 2012, https://www.washingtonpost.com/blogs/federal-eye/post/gaps-persist-in-midlevel-foreign-service-positions/2012/07/16/gJQAHEdwoW_blog.html?tid=a_inl&utm_term=.7eccb98aee1d.

xxx *a decline from even the 1990s:* "Five Year Workforce and Leadership Succession Plan FY2016 to FY2020." Department of State, Bureau of Human Resources, September 2016, https://www.state.gov/documents/organization/262725.pdf.

xxx *just a quarter did:* "American Diplomacy at Risk." American Academy of Diplomacy, reprinted by the Association for Diplomatic Studies and Training, April 2015, http://adst.org/american-diplomacy-at-risk.

xxx *"you have to conduct a global diplomacy":* Author interview with George P. Shultz, 19 January 2018.

xxx *"80 percent chance of a discussion":* Author interview with Henry Kissinger, 4 December 2017.

xxxi *"There isn't really time for the bureaucratic processes":* Author interview with Condoleezza Rice, 3 August 2017.

xxxi *"tilt more to the Pentagon":* Author interview with Condoleezza Rice, 3 August 2017.

xxxii *"new institutions have arisen":* Author interview with Henry Kissinger, 4 December 2017.

xxxii *"Diplomacy . . . is under the gun":* Author interview with Hillary Clinton, 20 November 2017.

PART I: THE LAST DIPLOMATS

1: AMERICAN MYTHS

4 **Pact of Paris:** "Diplomatic Gains in the Early 19th Century." State Department, Office of the Historian, https://history.state.gov/departmenthistory/short-history/conc1 and "A Return to Isolationism." State Department, Office of the Historian, https://history.state.gov/departmenthistory/short-history/return.

4 **"fear of cholera":** "A Foreign Policy of Inaction." State Department, Office of the Historian, https://history.state.gov/departmenthistory/short-history/inaction.

4 **tripled its workforce:** "Embarrassment Brings Change." State Department, Office of the Historian, https://history.state.gov/departmenthistory/short-history/embarrasment.

5 **that came to define the Cold War:** Rojansky, Matthew. "George Kennan is Still the Russia Expert America Needs." *Foreign Policy*, 22 December 2016, foreignpolicy.com/2016/12/22/why-george-kennan-is-still-americas-most-relevant-russia-expert-trump-putin-ussr/.

5 **"the supposed best and the brightest got plenty of our friends killed in Vietnam":** Author interview with John Kerry, 21 November 2017.

6 **"It's one great American myth":** Author interview with Henry Kissinger, 4 December 2017.

2: LADY TALIBAN

8 **even had an acronym:** "Pakistan: Extrajudicial Executions by Army in Swat." Human Rights Watch, 16 July 2011, https://www.hrw.org/news/2010/07/16/pakistan-extrajudicial-executions-army-swat.

9 **had bankrolled Pakistan:** "Factbox: U.S. has allocated $20 billion for Pakistan." Reuters, 21 April 2011, http://www.reuters.com/article/us-pakistan-usa-aid-factbox-idUSTRE73K7F420110421.

12 **sleepy lumber town:** Mathieu, Stephanie. "Home Grown: Native Travels Globe as Diplomat." *Daily News* (WA), 16 November 2007, http://tdn.com/business/local/home-grown-native-travels-globe-as-diplomat/article_c1384a98-0a14-51d0-9fde-5b03d87ab082.html.

13 **She prided herself on it:** Author interview with Robin Raphel, 30 June 2016.

13 **Raphel . . . started dating:** Griffin, Tom. "Rarified Air: UW Rhodes Scholars Since 1960." University of Washington, March 2004, https://www.washington.edu/alumni/columns/march04/rhodes04.html.

13 **politician named Bill Clinton:** Stanley, Alessandra. "Most Likely to Succeed." *New York Times*, 22 November 1992, http://www.nytimes.com/1992/11/22/magazine/most-likely-to-succeed.html?pagewanted=all.

13 **Clinton considered various strategies:** "The 1992 Campaign; A Letter by Clinton on His Draft Deferment: 'A War I Opposed and Despised.'" *New York Times*, 13 February 1992, http://www.nytimes.com/1992/02/13/us/1992-campaign-letter-clinton-his-draft-deferment-war-opposed-despised.html.

13 *"passionate about being dispassionate"*: Author interview with Robin Raphel, 30 June 2016.

3: DICK

15 *revolving door behind you:* Halberstam, David. *War in a Time of Peace: Bush, Clinton, and the Generals.* New York: Scribner, 2001, p. 186.

16 *"He's not entirely housebroken"*: Halberstam, David. *War in a Time of Peace: Bush, Clinton, and the Generals.* New York: Scribner, 2001, p. 17.

16 *"mountain climbing"*: Holbrooke, Richard. *To End a War.* New York: Random House, 2011, loc. 179. Kindle.

16 *visited Holbrooke's class:* Gordon, Meryl. "Ambassador A-List." *New York*, http://nymag.com/nymetro/news/people/features/1748/index3.html.

17 *"worst diplomatic fiasco"*: Chollet, Derek and Power, Samantha. *The Unquiet American: Richard Holbrooke in the World.* New York: PublicAffairs, 2012, p. 47. Kindle.

17 *muggy June night:* Chollet, Derek and Power, Samantha. *The Unquiet American: Richard Holbrooke in the World.* New York: PublicAffairs, 2012, p. 78. Kindle.

18 *"free soap"*: Unpublished memo, rpt. in Chollet, Derek and Power, Samantha. *The Unquiet American: Richard Holbrooke in the World.* New York: PublicAffairs, 2012, p. 86. Kindle.

18 *"time in the field"*: Halberstam, David. *War in a Time of Peace: Bush, Clinton, and the Generals.* New York: Scribner, 2001, p. 181.

18 *"Americans in such disarray"*: "Memorandum from Richard Holbrooke of the White House Staff to the President's Special Assistant (Komer)." Foreign Relations of the United States, 1964–1968. Volume IV, Vietnam, 1 December 1966, Document 321.

18 *"faultily conceived"*: Chollet, Derek and Power, Samantha. *The Unquiet American: Richard Holbrooke in the World.* New York: PublicAffairs, 2012, p. 90. Kindle.

19 *hustling for a spot:* Halberstam, David. *War in a Time of Peace: Bush, Clinton, and the Generals.* New York: Scribner, 2001, p. 188.

19 *"Holbrooke wants to always talk"*: Packer, George. "The Last Mission." *New Yorker*, 28 September 2009, http://www.newyorker.com/magazine/2009/09/28/the-last-mission.

19 *to scuttle the talks:* Farrell, John Aloysius. "Yes, Nixon Scuttled the Vietnam Peace Talks." *Politico Magazine*, 9 June 2014, http://www.politico.com/magazine/story/2014/06/yes-nixon-scuttled-the-vietnam-peace-talks-107623.

19 *the team wasted two months:* Holbrooke, Richard. *To End a War.* New York: Random House, 2011, loc. 3111. Kindle.

19 *"A negotiated end"*: Holbrooke, Richard. *To End a War.* New York: Random House, 2011, loc. 8208-8211, Kindle.

19 *"I was wondering how long"*: Clemons, Steve. "Afghanistan War: What Richard Holbrooke Really Thought." *Huffington Post*, 17 May 2011, https://www.huffingtonpost.com/steve-clemons/afghanistan-war-what-rich_b_862868.html.

20 *"That was the wrong question"*: Author interview with Henry Kissinger, 4 December 2017.

20 *"trying to apply in Vietnam"*: Holbrooke, Richard. "The American Experience in Southeast Asia, 1946–1975." Washington, DC, 29 September 2010, Keynote Address.

4: THE MANGO CASE

21 *danced and acted:* Leiby, Richard. "Who is Robin Raphel, the State Department Veteran Caught up in Pakistan Intrigue?" *Washington Post*, 16 December 2016, https://www.washingtonpost.com/lifestyle/style/who-is-robin-raphel-the-state-department-veteran-caught-up-in-pakistan-intrigue/2014/12/16/cfa4179e-8240-11e4-8882-03cf08410beb_story.html?utm_term=.c44eab67b086.

21 *"It was great"*: Author interview with Robin Raphel, 30 June 2016.

22 *"finger-wagging demanded"*: Author interview with Robin Raphel, 30 June 2016.

22 *"IF YOU DON'T READ BOOKS"*: Crile, George. *Charlie Wilson's War*. New York: Grove Press, 2007, loc. 352. Kindle.

23 *"This means more money"*: "December 26, 1979: Memo to President Carter Gives Pakistan Green Light to Pursue Nuclear Weapons Program." *History Commons*, 2007, www.historycommons.org/timeline.jsp?timeline=aq_khan_nuclear_network_tmln&aq_khan_nuclear_network_tmln_us_intelligence_on_pakistani_nukes=aq_khan_nuclear_network_tmln_soviet_afghan_war_connections.

23 *pursuing the atom bomb:* "Reflections on Soviet Intervention in Afghanistan," memorandum for the President from Zbigniew Brzezinski, December 26, 1979, rpt. by the Cold War International History Project.

23 *swelled from tens to hundreds of millions:* Coll, Steve. *Ghost Wars*. London: Penguin, 2004, p. 65. Kindle.

23 *"Take care of the Pakistanis"*: Coll, Steve. *Ghost Wars*. London: Penguin, 2004, pp. 55, 58. Kindle.

23 *"effectively dead"*: "Your Meeting with Pakistan President . . ." Memo from Shultz to Reagan, November 29, 1982, and "Visit of Zia-ul-Haq," from Shultz, also dated November 29, 1982, rpt. in the Cold War International History Project, Wilson Center.

23 *"we succeeded"*: Author interview with George P. Shultz, 19 January 2018.

24 *easy to overlook:* Coll, Steve. *Ghost Wars*. London: Penguin, 2004, p. 66. Kindle.

24 *Zia lied:* Coll, Steve. *Ghost Wars*. London: Penguin, 2004, p. 64. Kindle.

24 *"no question"*: Hersh, Seymour. "On the Nuclear Edge." *New Yorker*, 29 March 1993, http://www.newyorker.com/magazine/1993/03/29/on-the-nuclear-edge.

24 *"versus the long-term"*: Smith, Hedrick. "A Bomb Ticks in Pakistan." *New York Times Magazine*, 6 March 1988, http://www.nytimes.com/1988/03/06/magazine/a-bomb-ticks-in-pakistan.html?pagewanted=all.

24 *skinning captured soldiers:* Crile, George. *Charlie Wilson's War*. New York: Grove Press, 2007, loc. 379. Kindle.

25 *"I really should have shot him"*: Author interview with Milton Bearden, 28 April 2016.

25 *favored jihadis:* Coll, Steve. *Ghost Wars*. London: Penguin, 2004, pp. 86, 153. Kindle.

25 *declared the covert war cost-effective:* Coll, Steve. *Ghost Wars*. London: Penguin, 2004. p. 68. Kindle.

25 *the love of Robin Raphel's life:* Entous, Adam. "The Last Diplomat." *Wall Street Journal*, 2 December 2016, https://www.wsj.com/articles/the-last-diplomat-1480 695454.

25 *Hercules:* Robert MacFarlane. "The Late Dictator." *New York Times*, 15 June 2008, p. BR12.

25 *hand-selected:* Epstein, Edward Jay. "Who Killed Zia." *Vanity Fair*, September 1989.

26 *kept the CIA away:* Epstein, Edward Jay. "Who Killed Zia." *Vanity Fair*, September 1989.

26 *in a secret report:* Epstein, Edward Jay. "Who Killed Zia." *Vanity Fair*, September 1989.

26 *"But life goes on":* Author interview with Robin Raphel, 30 June 2016.

26 *"we won":* Crile, George. *Charlie Wilson's War*. New York: Grove Press, 2007, loc. 110. Kindle.

27 *"Speaking for Pakistan":* Fineman, Mark. "She Hails U.S. Support for Pakistani Democracy: Bhutto Wins Ovation in Congress." *Los Angeles Times*, 8 June 1989, http://articles.latimes.com/1989-06-08/news/mn-1927_1_bhutto-pakistani-democracy-pro-democracy.

27 *one person who was present that day:* Author interview with anonymous American lobbyist for Pakistan, 17 March 2017.

27 *irrefutable evidence:* Windrem, Robert. "Pakistan's Nuclear History Worries Insiders." *NBC News*, 6 November 2007, www.nbcnews.com/id/21660667/ns/nbc_nightly_news_with_brian_williams/t/pakistans-nuclear-history-worries-insiders/#.WPj5OfnyuUl.

27 *Pressler Amendment:* "U.S. Legislation on Pakistan (1990–2004)." PBS, 3 October 2006, http://www.pbs.org/wgbh/pages/frontline/taliban/pakistan/uspolicychart.html.

28 *"we screw 'em":* Author interview with Milton Bearden, 28 April 2016.

28 *install Hekmatyar:* Tomsen, Peter. *The Wars of Afghanistan: Messianic Terrorism, Tribal Conflicts, and the Failures of Great Powers*. New York: Public Affairs, 2001, pp. 405–408. Kindle.

28 *a bloody fight for Kabul:* Coll, Steve. *Ghost Wars*. London: Penguin, 2004. p. 263. Kindle.

28 *"students of Islam":* "U.S.-Pakistan Relations (1954–Present)." Council on Foreign Relations, 2017, http://www.cfr.org/interactives/CG_Pakistan/index.html#timeline.

28 *"I do not regret not dealing with the Taliban":* Author interview with Madeleine Albright, 13 December 2017.

28 *Pakistan, as the Taliban's benefactor:* Inderfurth, Karl. "Pushing for Peace in Afghanistan." US Department of State cable to the Secretary of State, 25 March 2009, http://nsarchive.gwu.edu/NSAEBB/NSAEBB227/33.pdf.

29 *legislation to ease restrictions on assistance:* Entous, Adam. "The Last Diplomat," *Wall Street Journal*, 2 December 2016, https://www.wsj.com/articles/the-last-diplomat-1480695454.

29 *assistance to the Taliban:* State Department cable, April 14, 1996, rpt. in Coll, Steve. *Ghost Wars*. London: Penguin, 2004, p. 298. Kindle.

29 *while lying about it to the Americans:* Coll, Steve. *Ghost Wars*. London: Penguin, 2004, p. 298. Kindle.

29 *"I didn't believe Bhutto"*: Author interview with Robin Raphel, 5 January, 2018.

29 *helped secure assistance for Pakistan:* Coll, Steve. *Ghost Wars*. London: Penguin, 2004, pp. 298–299. Kindle.

29 *"own limitations":* Declassified cable, "A/S Raphel Discusses Afghanistan," 22 April 1996, quoted in Coll, Steve. *Ghost Wars*. London: Penguin, 2004, p. 329. Kindle.

29 *"they have demonstrated staying power":* Transcript of remarks in closed-door session at UN, obtained by Rashid, Ahmed, rpt. in Rashid, Ahmed. *Taliban: Militant Islam, Oil and Fundamentalism in Central Asia*. Second Edition. New Haven, CT: Yale University Press, 2010, p. 178.

29 *"If Robin had lasted":* Author interview with Husain Haqqani, 28 May 2015.

30 *"emotionally driven":* Author interview with Robin Raphel, June 30, 2016.

30 *"I was ahead of my time!":* Author interview with Robin Raphel, June 30, 2016.

30 *Their investigation came up empty:* Entous, Adam. "The Last Diplomat," *Wall Street Journal*, 2 December 2016, https://www.wsj.com/articles/the-last-diplomat-1480695454.

30 *the firm had two Pakistani contracts:* "Exhibit A to Registration Statement Pursuant to the Foreign Agents Registration Act of 1938, as amended." United States Department of Justice. Cassidy & Associates, Embassy of the Islamic Republic of Pakistan, 2005, https://www.fara.gov/docs/5643-Exhibit-AB-20071004-4.pdf.

31 *"Brazenly pro-Pakistan":* Rajghattal, Chidanand. "Pakistan Lobbyist Robin Raphel Under Lens for Alleged Spying." *Times of India*, 7 November 2014, http://timesofindia.indiatimes.com/world/us/Pakistan-lobbyist-Robin-Raphel-under-lens-for-alleged-spying/articleshow/45073087.cms.

31 *"for three weeks":* Author interview with Robin Raphel, June 30, 2016.

31 *30 percent premium:* "Top Hardship Assignments in the Foreign Service." *Diplopundit*, 14 July 2009, https://diplopundit.net/2009/07/14/top-hardship-assignments-in-the-foreign-service.

31 *turn back to public service:* Leiby, Richard. "Who is Robin Raphel, the State Department veteran caught up in Pakistan intrigue?" *Washington Post*, 16 December 2014, https://www.washingtonpost.com/lifestyle/style/who-is-robin-raphel-the-state-department-veteran-caught-up-in-pakistan-intrigue/2014/12/16/cfa4179e-8240-11e4-8882-03cf08410beb_story.html?utm_term=.59cd5ed4b662.

5: THE OTHER HAQQANI NETWORK

32 *named Husain:* Public papers of William J Clinton, 5 May 1993, available at https://books.google.com/books?id=MSPhAwAAQBAJ&pg=PA1263&lpg=PA

1263&dq=Ranasinghe+Premadasa+funeral&source=bl&ots=WvCzewwlRN&s
ig=Sn2i7_SLyqKJSktRdC6qDIkCUeQ&hl=en&sa=X&ved=0ahUKEwi0kejcoI
rTAhXoiFQKHRMzAjQ4ChDoAQhJMAk#v=onepage&q=raphel&f=false.

33 *clawed his way up:* Author phone interview with Husain Haqqani, 29 March
2017.

33 *soaked in Western perspectives:* Haqqani, Husain. *Pakistan: Between Mosque and
Military.* Washington, DC: Carnegie Endowment for International Peace, 2005,
loc. 101. Kindle.

33 *citing the Quran:* Haqqani, Husain. "The Day I Broke With the Revolution."
Asian Wall Street Journal, 23 April 1998, p. 7. Haqqani, Husain. *Magnificent Delu-
sions: Pakistan, the United States, and an Epic History of Misunderstanding.* New York:
PublicAffairs, 2013, p. 3. Kindle.

33 **Far Eastern Economic Review:** Fineman, Mark. "Million Mourn at
Funeral for Pakistan's Zia." *Los Angeles Times,* 21 August 1988, articles.latimes.
com/1988-08-21/news/mn-1149_1_president-zia/2.

33 *"might be able to bring some balance":* Author interview with Husain Haqqani,
28 March 2015.

34 *"material support":* Haqqani, Husain. *Magnificent Delusions: Pakistan, the United
States, and an Epic History of Misunderstanding.* New York: PublicAffairs, 2013, p.
271. Kindle.

34 *pushed him into a waiting car:* Landler, Mark. "Adroit Envoy States Case for
Pakistan." *New York Times,* 8 May 2009, www.nytimes.com/2009/05/09/world/
asia/09envoy.html.

34 *He credits the call with saving his life:* "Pakistan: Country Reports on Human Rights
Practices." US Department of State. Bureau of Democracy, Human Rights and
Labor, 23 February 2000, https://www.state.gov/j/drl/rls/hrrpt/1999/441.htm.

35 *"I came to the US":* Author interview with Husain Haqqani, 29 March 2017.

35 *"rentier state":* Haqqani, Husain. *Magnificent Delusions: Pakistan, the United States,
and an Epic History of Misunderstanding.* New York: PublicAffairs, 2013, pp. 323–
324. Kindle.

35 *"new relationship":* Haqqani, Husain. *Magnificent Delusions: Pakistan, the United
States, and an Epic History of Misunderstanding.* New York: PublicAffairs, 2013, p.
324. Kindle.

35 *"I wld hold":* "Bhutto Said She'd Blame Musharraf if Killed." CNN, 28 December 2007, edition.cnn.com/2007/WORLD/asiapcf/12/27/bhutto.security.

36 *Supporters swarmed:* Farwell, James. *The Pakistan Cauldron: Conspiracy, Assassination & Instability.* Lincoln, NE: Potomac Books, 2011, p. 135.

36 *among bodies:* Rashid, Ahmed. *Descent into Chaos: The U.S. and the Disaster in Paki-
stan, Afghanistan, and Central Asia.* London: Penguin, 2009, loc. 7980; Schmidle,
Nicholas. *To Live or to Perish Forever: Two Tumultuous Years in Pakistan.* New York: St.
Martin's Griffin, 2010, p. 207; and Coleman, Isobel. *Paradise Beneath Her Feet: How
Women Are Transforming the Middle East.* New York: Random House, 2013, p. 127.

36 *corruption allegations:* Walsh, Declan. "Zardari Rejects Claim of al-Qaida
Link to Bhutto's Murder." *Guardian* (Manchester), 1 January 2008, https://
www.theguardian.com/world/2008/jan/01/pakistan.international1.

36 ***During Bhutto's exile:*** Haqqani, Husain. *Magnificent Delusions: Pakistan, the United States, and an Epic History of Misunderstanding.* New York: PublicAffairs, 2013, p. 323. Kindle.

36 ***he headed to Washington:*** "Haqqani Presents Credentials to Bush." *Dawn*, 7 June 2008, https://www.dawn.com/news/306395.

36 ***"extension of the United States":*** Rashid, Ahmed. *Descent into Chaos: The U.S. and the Disaster in Pakistan, Afghanistan, and Central Asia.* London: Penguin, 2009.

37 ***"loyal to the pigs":*** Khan, Asad Rahim. "The Magnificent Delusions of Husain Haqqani." *Express Tribune*, 28 September 2015, https://tribune.com.pk/story/963896/the-magnificent-delusions-of-husain-haqqani/.

6: DUPLICITY

39 ***at least 100,000 people:*** "Bosnia war dead figure announced." BBC. 21 June 2007, http://news.bbc.co.uk/2/hi/europe/6228152.stm and Tabeau, Ewa and Bijak, Jakub. "Casualties of the 1990s War in Bosnia-Herzegovina: A Critique of Previous Estimates and the Latest Results." Demographic Unit, Office of the Prosecutor, International Criminal Tribunal of the former Yugoslavia, 15 September 2003, http://archive.iussp.org/members/restricted/publications/Oslo03/5-con-tabeau03.pdf.

39 ***"Who else?":*** Chollet, Derek and Power, Samantha. *The Unquiet American: Richard Holbrooke in the World.* New York: PublicAffairs, 2012, pp. 203–204. Kindle.

40 ***agreement untenable:*** "Kosovo, Genocide and the Dayton Agreement." *Wall Street Journal.* 1 December 2005.

40 ***"Hasta la vista":*** Chollet, Derek and Power, Samantha. *The Unquiet American: Richard Holbrooke in the World.* New York: PublicAffairs, 2012, p. 164. Kindle.

40 ***strikes authorized:*** Chollet, Derek and Power, Samantha. *The Unquiet American: Richard Holbrooke in the World.* New York: PublicAffairs, 2012, p. 2. Kindle.

40 ***dangling on a wire:*** "Richard Holbrooke Image in TIME Magazine Calling Him Diplomatic Acrobat of the Week." *The History Project*, 1 January 1996, https://www.thehistoryproject.com/media/view/6236.

41 ***"I know he wanted to be Secretary of State":*** Author interview with Madeleine Albright, 15 December 2017.

41 ***Gore administration:*** Traub, James. "Holbrooke's Campaign." *New York Times Magazine*, 26 March 2000, www.nytimes.com/2000/03/26/magazine/holbrooke-s-campaign.html and *The Diplomat.* Dir. David Holbrooke. HBO Documentary Films, 2015, 1:04:48: "I will say most people were justified in believing he was first in line."

41 ***collaborated with Pakistan:*** Woodward, Bob and Ricks, Thomas. "CIA Trained Pakistanis to Nab Terrorist But Military Coup Put an End to 1999 Plot." *Washington Post*, 3 October 2001, www.washingtonpost.com/wp-dyn/content/article/2007/11/18/AR2007111800629.html.

41 ***lock down Pakistan's support:*** Rashid, Ahmed. *Descent into Chaos: The U.S. and the Disaster in Pakistan, Afghanistan, and Central Asia.* London: Penguin, 2009, pp. 25-30.

41 ***"And he reversed the direction":*** Iftikar, Ali. "Powell Defends U.S. support to Pakistan." *Nation*, 9 September 2004, ref. in Rashid, Ahmed. *Descent into Chaos: The U.S. and the Disaster in Pakistan, Afghanistan, and Central Asia.* London: Penguin, 2009.

42 ***"not necessarily agree with all the details":*** Rashid, Ahmed. *Descent into Chaos: The U.S. and the Disaster in Pakistan, Afghanistan, and Central Asia.* London: Penguin, 2009, p. 28, quoting Foreign Minister Abdul Sattar.

42 ***a break in the bombing:*** Filkins, Dexter and Gall, Carlotta. "Pakistanis Again Said to Evacuate Allies of Taliban." *New York Times*, 24 November 2001 and Hersh, Seymour. "The Getaway." *New Yorker*, 28 January 2002, http://www.newyorker.com/magazine/2002/01/28/the-getaway-2.

42 ***Rumsfeld insisted:*** Haider, Masood. "No Pakistani Jets Flew into Afghanistan Says U.S." *Dawn*, 2 December 2001 and Rashid, Ahmed. *Descent into Chaos: The U.S. and the Disaster in Pakistan, Afghanistan, and Central Asia.* London: Penguin, 2009, p. 91. Kindle.

42 ***"it was a mistake":*** Author interview with anonymous CIA source, 19 July 2016.

43 ***"is never 100 percent truth":*** Author interview with Husain Haqqani, 29 March 2017.

43 ***The United States had "not had a better partner":*** Warrick, Joby. "CIA Places Blame for Bhutto Assassination." *Washington Post*, 18 January 2008, www.washingtonpost.com/wp-dyn/content/article/2008/01/17/AR2008011703252.html and author interview with General Michael Hayden, in person at his offices in Washington, DC, 17 May 2017.

43 ***"deal with the devil":*** Author interview with General Michael Hayden, in person at his offices in Washington, DC, 17 May 2017.

44 ***"the whole truth!!":*** "Email from Gen. Pasha to Ronan Farrow." 22 September 2016.

44 ***"Look, I mean":*** Author interview with General Michael Hayden, in person at his offices in Washington, DC, 17 May 2017.

44 ***devastating attacks:*** Rashid, Ahmed. *Taliban: Militant Islam, Oil and Fundamentalism in Central Asia.* Second Edition. New Haven, CT: Yale University Press, 2010, p. 227.

45 ***America was losing:*** Rashid, Ahmed. *Taliban: Militant Islam, Oil and Fundamentalism in Central Asia.* Second Edition. New Haven, CT: Yale University Press, 2010, p. 234, and "Deadliest Month Yet for U.S. in Afghanistan." *CBS News*, 30 August 2011, www.cbsnews.com/news/deadliest-month-yet-for-us-in-afghanistan.

7: THE FRAT HOUSE

47 ***"documentation just isn't what it used to be":*** Holbrooke, Richard. "The American Experience in Southeast Asia, 1946–1975." Washington, DC, 29 September 2010, Keynote Address.

47 ***for bipartisan schmoozing:*** Roberts, Roxanne. "Don't Gloat, Don't Pout: The Golden Rule of Elite Washington Inaugural Parties." *Washington Post*, 17 January 2017, https://www.washingtonpost.com/lifestyle/style/dont-gloat-dont-pout-the-golden-rule-of-elite-washington-inaugural-parties/2017/01/17/f0c512da-d8f5-11e6-9a36-1d296534b31e_story.html?utm_term=.15242dfb588a.

48   ***"One could not be with him":*** Halberstam, David. *War in a Time of Peace: Bush, Clinton, and the Generals.* New York: Scribner, 2001, p. 181.

48   ***He worked the phones:*** Packer, George. "The Last Mission." *New Yorker*, 28 September 2009, http://www.newyorker.com/magazine/2009/09/28/the-last-mission.

49   ***"Why weren't you there?":*** "Richard Holbrooke." *Charlie Rose*, published 8 August 2008, ttps://charlierose.com/videos/11639.

49   ***"pipsqueak":*** Ioffe, Julia. "Susan Rice Isn't Going Quietly." *New Republic*, 20 December 2012, https://newrepublic.com/article/111353/susan-rice-isnt-going-quietly and Milibank, Dana. "Susan Rice's Tarnished Resume." *Washington Post*, 16 November 2012, https://www.washingtonpost.com/opinions/dana-milbank-susan-rices-tarnished-resume/2012/11/16/55ec3382-3012-11e2-a30e-5ca76eeec857_story.html?utm_term=.b42e179a05cc.

50   ***soon fall out of favor:*** Woodward, Bob. *Obama's Wars.* New York: Simon & Schuster, 2011, p. 377. Kindle.

50   ***Holbrooke State Department:*** Allen, Jonathan and Parnes, Amie. *HRC: State Secrets and the Rebirth of Hillary Clinton.* New York: Crown/Archetype, 2014, p. 73. Kindle.

50   ***"none of the baggage":*** Woodward, Bob. *Obama's Wars.* New York: Simon & Schuster, 2011, p. 377. Kindle.

50   ***"frat house":*** Mastromonaco, Alyssa. "To Bro or Not to Bro?" *Lenny Letter*, 22 March 2017, www.lennyletter.com/work/advice/a766/to-bro-or-not-to-bro/ and Leibovich, Mark. "Man's World at White House? No Harm, No Foul, Aides Say." *New York Times*, 24 October 2009, www.nytimes.com/2009/10/25/us/politics/25vibe.html.

51   ***"I think his whirlwind":*** Author interview with Hillary Clinton, 20 November 2017.

51   ***Two days after:*** Kurtz, Howard. "Media Notes: Making Nice." *Washington Post*, 18 November 2008, www.washingtonpost.com/wp-dyn/content/article/2008/11/18/AR2008111800923_2.html.

51   ***"That's a joke":*** *The Diplomat.* Dir. David Holbrooke. HBO Documentary Films, 2015, 1:05:44.

51   ***Obama was annoyed:*** Woodward, Bob. *Obama's Wars.* New York: Simon & Schuster, 2011, p. 211. Kindle. (Note: This anecdote has passed into legend. Woodward places it later, immediately before Holbrooke accepted his job in the administration. According to Gelb and others, it took place during that first meeting in Chicago.)

51   ***"with some condescension":*** Author interview with Henry Kissinger, 4 December 2017.

52   ***"by many metrics," the most difficult:*** *The Diplomat.* Dir. David Holbrooke. HBO Documentary Films, 2015, 1:07:27.

52   ***"test myself":*** Holbrooke, Richard. *To End a War.* New York: Random House, 2011, loc. 1101–1102. Kindle.

8: MISSION: IMPOSSIBLE

53 *"India, Pakistan and Afghanistan":* Kamen, Al. "Special Envoys Give Career Diplomats Special Heartburn." *Washington Post*, 15 December 2008, www.washingtonpost.com/wp-dyn/content/article/2008/12/14/AR2008121401898.html.

53 *"require regional agreements":* Holbrooke, Richard. "The Next President: Mastering a Daunting Agenda." *Foreign Affairs*, September/October 2008, https://www.foreignaffairs.com/articles/2008-09-01/next-president.

53 *In Bosnia:* Chollet, Derek and Power, Samantha. *The Unquiet American: Richard Holbrooke in the World.* New York: PublicAffairs, 2012, p. 204. Kindle.

54 *"infinitely complex":* "President Obama Delivers Remarks to State Department Employees." *Washington Post*, 22 January 2009, www.washingtonpost.com/wp-dyn/content/article/2009/01/22/AR2009012202550.html.

54 *"importance of diplomacy":* "President Obama Delivers Remarks to State Department Employees." *Washington Post*, 22 January 2009, www.washingtonpost.com/wp-dyn/content/article/2009/01/22/AR2009012202550.html.

54 *"my former roommate":* "State Department Personnel Announcement." rpt. in CSPAN, 22 January 2009, https://www.c-span.org/video/transcript/?id=981.

54 *sui generis title:* Packer, George. "The Last Mission." *New Yorker*, 28 September 2009, http://www.newyorker.com/magazine/2009/09/28/the-last-mission.

55 *an article in* **Foreign Policy***:* Holbrooke, Richard. "The Machine That Fails." *Foreign Policy*, 14 December 2010, foreignpolicy.com/2010/12/14/the-machine-that-fails/.

55 *"This is where you want to be":* Nasr, Vali. "The Inside Story of how the White House Diplomacy Let Diplomacy Fail in Afghanistan." *Foreign Policy*, 4 March 2013, http://foreignpolicy.com/2013/03/04/the-inside-story-of-how-the-white-house-let-diplomacy-fail-in-afghanistan.

55 *"I'm very efficient":* Packer, George. "The Last Mission." *New Yorker*, 28 September 2009, http://www.newyorker.com/magazine/2009/09/28/the-last-mission.

58 *"Fuck that":* Google Chat with a then-recent Yale Law School graduate who requested anonymity due to concerns about his political career.

58 *"the journey will be very painful":* "U.S. Diplomat Holbrooke Dies After Tearing Aorta." *NBC News*, 14 December 2010, www.nbcnews.com/id/40649624/ns/politics/t/us-diplomat-holbrooke-dies-after-tearing-aorta/#.WPoYJtLyvIV.

59 *a senior military leader told me:* Author interview with senior military official who requested anonymity due to the sensitivity of the statement.

59 *"absolutely brilliant":* Author interview with Hillary Clinton, 20 November 2017.

59 *"more airplanes than I have":* Packer, George. "The Last Mission," *New Yorker*, 28 September 2009, http://www.newyorker.com/magazine/2009/09/28/the-last-mission.

60 **They tried, and failed, to catch him:** "David Petraeus LITERALLY Runs Away From Bilderberg Questions." YouTube. WeAreChange, 11 June 2016, https://www.youtube.com/watch?v=a3x0mSdGY9I.

60 *M-16 shot to the chest:* "Lasting Ties Mark Gen. Petraeus' Career." NPR, 6 February 2007, www.npr.org/templates/story/story.php?storyId=7193883.

60 *one meal a day:* Ackerman, Spencer. "The Petraeus Workout." *American Prospect*, 4 September 2007, prospect.org/article/petraeus-workout and McDougall, Christopher. "The Petraeus Workout." *Daily Beast*, 25 June 2010, www .thedailybeast.com/articles/2010/06/25/general-petraeus-workout-routine .html.

61 *events outside his control:* Cambanis, Thanassis. "How We Fight: Fred Kaplan's 'Insurgents,' on David Petraeus." *New York Times*, 24 January 2013, www.nytimes .com/2013/01/27/books/review/fred-kaplans-insurgents-on-david-petraeus .html; Taqfeed, Mohammed. "Al-Sadr Extends Mehdi Army Cease-Fire." CNN, 22 February 2008, www.cnn.com/2008/WORLD/meast/02/22/iraq.main/index .html.

61 *COIN to the test:* Allen, Jonathan and Parnes, Amie. *HRC: State Secrets and the Rebirth of Hillary Clinton.* New York: Crown/Archetype, p. 72. Kindle.

61 *"aggressive counterinsurgency":* Author interview with Hillary Clinton, 20 November 2017.

62 *said he was more comfortable:* Landler, Mark. *Alter Egos: Hillary Clinton, Barack Obama, and the Twilight Struggle Over American Power.* New York: Random House, 2016, loc. 1680. Kindle.

62 *"His job should be":* Chandrasekaran, Rajiv. *Little America: The War Within the War for Afghanistan.* New York: Vintage, loc. 3620. Kindle.

62 *"'I am Barack Obama'":* Chandrasekaran, Rajiv. *Little America: The War Within the War for Afghanistan.* New York: Vintage, loc. 3620. Kindle.

63 *"General, I appreciate you're doing your job":* Woodward, Bob. *Obama's Wars.* New York: Simon & Schuster, 2011, p. 80. Kindle.

63 *"third co-chair":* Broadwell, Paula and Loeb, Vernon. *All In: The Education of General David Petraeus.* New York: Penguin, 2012.

63 *"ghosts":* Woodward, Bob. *Obama's Wars.* New York: Simon & Schuster, 2011, p. 97. Kindle.

64 *"really talk like that":* Landler, Mark. *Alter Egos: Hillary Clinton, Barack Obama, and the Twilight Struggle Over American Power.* New York: Random House, 2016, loc. 1488. Kindle.

64 *voice sounding tired:* The Diplomat. Dir. David Holbrooke. HBO Documentary Films, 2015, 1:31:25.

64 *"He was incredibly unhappy":* Author interview with Hillary Clinton, 20 November 2017.

64 *"military domination":* Rosenberg, Matthew. "Richard C. Holbrooke's Diary of Disagreement With Obama Administration." *New York Times*, 22 April 2015, https:// www.nytimes.com/2015/04/23/world/middleeast/richard-c-holbrookes-diary-of-disagreement-with-the-obama-administration.html.

64 *were going unread:* Nasr, Vali. "The Inside Story of how the White House Diplomacy Let Diplomacy Fail in Afghanistan." *Foreign Policy*, 4 March 2013, http:// foreignpolicy.com/2013/03/04/the-inside-story-of-how-the-white-house-let-diplomacy-fail-in-afghanistan.

65 *"I was convinced":* Author interview with Hillary Clinton, 20 November 2017.
66 *"My position":* The Diplomat. Dir. David Holbrooke. HBO Documentary Films, 2015, 1:14:00.
66 *"there will be a 'low-risk' option":* Nasr, Vali. "The Inside Story of how the White House Diplomacy Let Diplomacy Fail in Afghanistan." *Foreign Policy*, 4 March 2013, http://foreignpolicy.com/2013/03/04/the-inside-story-of-how-the-white-house-let-diplomacy-fail-in-afghanistan.
67 *with an expiration date:* Landler, Mark. "At U.S.-Afghan Meetings, Talk of Nuts and Bolts." *New York Times*, 13 May 2010, www.nytimes.com/2010/05/14/world/asia/14karzai.html.
67 *"no discussion at all of diplomacy":* Nasr, Vali. "The Inside Story of how the White House Diplomacy Let Diplomacy Fail in Afghanistan." *Foreign Policy*, 4 March 2013, http://foreignpolicy.com/2013/03/04/the-inside-story-of-how-the-white-house-let-diplomacy-fail-in-afghanistan.

9: WALKING ON GLASS

69 *"You're here because of the stories":* Author interview with Umar Cheema, via Skype to his home in Pakistan, 5 September 2016.
69 *"I thought of my son":* Author interview with Umar Cheema, via Skype to his home in Pakistan, 5 September 2016.
70 *The CIA later intercepted:* Mazzetti, Mark. *The Way of the Knife: The CIA, a Secret Army, and a War at the Ends of the Earth.* New York: Penguin, 2014, p. 292.
70 *67 percent of deaths:* "60 Journalists Killed in Pakistan Since 1992/Motive Confirmed." Committee to Protect Journalists, https://cpj.org/killed/asia/pakistan.
70 *Countless reporters:* Gall, Carlotta. *The Wrong Enemy: America in Afghanistan, 2001–2014.* Boston: Houghton Mifflin Harcourt, 2014, p. xx (prologue).
71 *"There was literally no word":* Author interview with Umar Cheema, via Skype to his home in Pakistan, 5 September 2016.
71 *"Can I count on your assistance":* Author interview with General Michael Hayden, in person at his offices in Washington, DC, 17 May 2017.
71 *"When we found out":* Author phone interview with Leon Panetta, 6 May 2016.
72 *"You were always walking":* Author phone interview with Leon Panetta, 6 May 2016.
73 *"It was so weird":* Author interview with Ambassador Anne Patterson, 12 May 2016.
73 *"Which is actually true":* Author interview with Ambassador Anne Patterson, 12 May 2016.
73 *"I come here, Mr. President":* Author interview with Ambassador Anne Patterson, 12 May 2016.
73 *"never have to acknowledge":* Author phone interview with Leon Panetta, 6 May 2016.
73 *"Let Leon have his say!!!!":* Text message sent from General Pasha to author.
74 *"had a US technical team":* Author interview with Pakistani General, at Pakistani embassy in Washington, DC, 6 January 2017.

75   *no strike came:* Author interview with Pakistani General, at Pakistani embassy in Washington, DC, 6 January 2017.

75   *"Nobody is asking":* Author interview with Pakistani general, January 2017.

76   *"a very transactional relationship":* Author interview with General David Petraeus, in person at his offices in New York City, 25 May 2016.

76   *hand over the flight data:* Haqqani, Husain. *Magnificent Delusions: Pakistan, the United States, and an Epic History of Misunderstanding.* New York: PublicAffairs, 2013, p. 342. Kindle.

77   *hundreds of applications:* Haqqani, Husain. *Magnificent Delusions: Pakistan, the United States, and an Epic History of Misunderstanding.* New York; PublicAffairs, 2013, p. 342. Kindle.

77   *"papering over a lot of problems":* Author interview with Husain Haqqani, in person, Hudson Institute office, Washington, DC, 6 January 2017.

10: FARMER HOLBROOKE

78   *$800 million more:* Chandrasekaran, Rajiv. *Little America: The War Within the War for Afghanistan.* New York: Vintage, 2013. Kindle.

79. *enhanced poppy cultivation:* Chandrasekaran, Rajiv. *Little America: The War Within the War for Afghanistan.* New York: Vintage, 2013, loc. 1525. Kindle.

79   *"soup-to-nuts agricultural support":* Chandrasekaran, Rajiv. *Little America: The War Within the War for Afghanistan.* New York: Vintage, 2013, loc. 1646. Kindle.

80   *Farmer Holbrooke:* Landler, Mark. "At U.S.-Afghan Meetings, Talk of Nuts and Bolts." *New York Times,* 13 May 2010, www.nytimes.com/2010/05/14/world/asia/14karzai.html.

80   *ten to one:* Tarnoff, Curt. "Afghanistan: U.S. Foreign Assistance." Congressional Research Service, 12 August 2010, https://fas.org/sgp/crs/row/R40699.pdf.

80   *From 2008:* Tarnoff, Curt. "Afghanistan: U.S. Foreign Assistance." Congressional Research Service, 12 August 2010, https://fas.org/sgp/crs/row/R40699.pdf.

80   *a sea of development projects:* "Recipient Profile: International Medical Corps." USAspending.gov, https://www.usaspending.gov/transparency/Pages/RecipientProfile.aspx?DUNSNumber=186375218&FiscalYear=2012.

80   *"enable COIN-focused, unstable communities":* Request for Application RFA 306-09-545, Community Based Stability Grants (CBSGs) Program, USAID, September 3, 2009, p. 4.

82   *They began lobbying:* Rozen, Laura. "Special Liaison: Holbrooke Appoints Mia Farrow's Son as NGO Liaison." *Politico,* 22 October 2009, www.politico.com/blogs/laurarozen/1009/Special_liaison_Holbrooke_appoints_Mia_Farrows_son_as_liaison_to_NGOs.html.

11: A LITTLE LESS CONVERSATION

85   *"Remember one thing":* Author interview with Husain Haqqani, 29 March 2017.

85 *"all three sides were willing to let their people die":* Holbrooke, Richard. *To End a War.* New York: Random House, 2011, loc. 2930–2931. Kindle.

85 *"In the subcontinent":* Author interview with Husain Haqqani, 29 March 2017.

86 *Holbrooke's desired region-wide role:* Kessler, Glen. "Mitchell and Holbrooke to be Named Envoys." *Washington Post,* January 2009, www.voices.washingtonpost .com/44/2009/01/mitchell-and-holbrooke-to-be-n.html.

86 *nix any India envoy:* Rozen, Laura. "India's Stealth Lobbying Against Holbrooke's Brief." *Foreign Policy,* 24 January 2009, foreignpolicy.com/2009/01/24/ indias-stealth-lobbying-against-holbrookes-brief.

87 *"What will satisfy":* Author interview with Husain Haqqani, 29 March 2017.

88 *"That is a respectable IPO":* Nasr, Vali. "The Inside Story of how the White House Diplomacy Let Diplomacy Fail in Afghanistan." *Foreign Policy,* 04 March 2013, http://foreignpolicy.com/2013/03/04/the-inside-story-of-how-the-white-house-let-diplomacy-fail-in-afghanistan.

88 *"worked that very hard on the Hill":* Author interview with General David Petraeus, in person at his offices in New York City, 25 May 2016.

88 *"didn't care about democracy":* Author interview with Alan Kronstadt, 18 August 2016.

89 *"An affront":* "Pakistan Media Reaction: Kerry-Lugar Bill, Terrorism, India-American-Pakistan October 20, 2009." Cable released by Wikileaks, 09ISLAM-ABAD2543, 1 October 2009, www.scoop.co.nz/stories/WL0910/S02256/ cablegate-pakistan-media-reaction-kerry-lugar-bill-terrorism.htm/.

89 *expressed outrage:* Perlez, Jane and Khan, Ismail. "Aid Package from U.S. Jolts Army in Pakistan." *New York Times,* 7 October 2009, www.nytimes .com/2009/10/08/world/asia/08pstan.html.

89 *"Haqqani did something very stupid":* Author phone interview with Mohsin Kamal, 14 November 2016.

89 *"the c word":* Holbrooke, Richard. "Special Briefing on Secretary Clinton's Recent Trip to Afghanistan and Pakistan." US Department of State, 23 November 2009, https://2009-2017.state.gov/p/sca/rls/rmks/2009/132307.htm.

90 *refurbished Toyota:* Entous, Adam. "The Last Diplomat." *Wall Street Journal,* 2 December 2016, https://www.wsj.com/articles/the-last-diplomat-1480695454.

91 *never became a reality:* Author interview with Robin Raphel, 30 June 2016.

91 *"The fact is":* Author interview with Robin Raphel, 30 June 2016.

92 *"I didn't realize":* Author interview with Robin Raphel, 30 June 2016.

92 *"better branded than us":* Sullivan, Jake. "Baseball Cap." Email to Hillary Clinton, 15 September 2010, released by WikiLeaks, https://wikileaks.org/ clinton-emails/emailid/1751.

93 *"US Government's label":* Salmon, Felix. "U.S.A.I.D.'S PR Problem." Reuters, 13 October 2010, blogs.reuters.com/felix-salmon/2010/10/13/usaids-pr-problem/ and Crilly, Rob. "Pakistan Aid Workers in Row with U.S. Over Stars and Stripes 'Logo.'" *Telegraph* (UK), 11 October 2010, www.telegraph.co.uk/news/ worldnews/asia/pakistan/8056123/Pakistan-aid-workers-in-row-with-US-over-Stars-and-Stripes-logo.html.

93 ***"Don't put a target on our backs":*** Worthington, Samuel. "We're Aiding Pakistan. Don't Put a Target on our Backs." *Washington Post*, 10 October 2010, http://www.washingtonpost.com/wp-dyn/content/article/2010/10/08/AR2010 100802665.html.

93 ***make the case:*** Subject: INTERACTION OP-ED ON BRANDING IN PAKISTAN, Email exchange between Judith McHale and Hillary Clinton, 10 October 2010, obtained via WikiLeaks, https://wikileaks.org/clinton-emails/emailid/1476.

95 ***op-ed from Rajiv:*** Shah, Rajiv. "From the American People." *Huffington Post*, www.huffingtonpost.com/dr-rajiv-shah/from-the-american-people_1_b_772736 .html.

95 ***"Humanitarian aid siphoned":*** Author interview with Alan Kronstadt, 18 August 2016.

96 ***gushed to reporters:*** "U.S., Pakistan Seek to Build Trust With Talks." NPR, 25 March 2010, www.npr.org/templates/story/story.php?storyId=125153658.

96 ***had been stalled:*** Landler, Mark. "Afghanistan and Pakistan Sign a Trade Deal, Representing a Thaw in Relations." *New York Times*, 18 July 2010, www.nytimes.com/2010/07/19/world/asia/19diplo.html.

96 ***India began to signal its willingness:*** Raman, Sunil. "Why India Wants to Enter Af-Pak Trade and Transit Agreement." *Swarajya*, 7 January 2016, https:// swarajyamag.com/world/why-india-wants-to-enter-af-pak-trade-and-transit-agreement.

96 ***water policy:*** "Agriculture Secretary Vilsack Announces U.S. Members of Three Working Groups Under the U.S.-Afghanistan-Pakistan Trilateral." USDA, No. 0529.09, 26 October 2009, webcache.googleusercontent. com/search?q=cache:zX-i8OahGE8J:www.usda.gov/wps/portal/usda/ usdamobile%3Fcontentid%3D2009/10/0529.xml+&cd=1&hl=en&ct =clnk&gl=us.

97 ***Drought could trigger:*** Qiu, Jane. "Stressed Indus River Threatens Pakistan's Water Supplies." *Nature*, 29 June 2016, www.nature.com/news/stressed-in dus-river-threatens-pakistan-s-water-supplies-1.20180.

97 ***shrinking glaciers:*** Mandhana, Niharika. "Water Wars: Why India and Pakistan are Squaring Off Over Their Rivers." *Time*, 16 April 2012, content.time.com/ time/world/article/0,8599,2111601,00.html.

97 ***whether he was kidding:*** Woodward, Bob. *Obama's Wars*. Kindle Ed., Simon & Schuster, 2011, p. 210.

97 ***Indus Waters Treaty:*** Kugelman, Michael. "Why the India-Pakistan War Over Water Is So Dangerous." *Foreign Policy*, 30 September 2016, http://foreign policy.com/2016/09/30/why-the-india-pakistan-war-over-water-is-so-dangerous-indus-waters-treaty.

98 ***" 'This thing is really working' ":*** Author interview with General David Petraeus, in person at his offices in New York City, 25 May 2016.

12: A-ROD

99 *choosing his words carefully:* Ahmed, Rashid. *Pakistan on the Brink*. New York: Penguin, 2013. p. 114.

100 *Steiner lip-syncing:* "Steiner Stirbt den Bollywood-Tod." *Spiegel TV,* 25 April 2015, www.spiegel.de/video/indien-botschafter-michael-steiner-bollywood-video-video-1572700.html.

100 *Taliban websites:* Reuter, Christopher, Schmitz, Gregor Peter, and Stark, Holger. "How German Diplomats Opened Channel to Taliban." *Spiegel,* 10 January 2012, www.spiegel.de/international/world/talking-to-the-enemy-how-german-diplomats-opened-channel-to-taliban-a-808068-2.html.

100 *triple agent:* "How a Triple Agent Duped the CIA." *Daily Beast,* 20 June 2011, http://www.thedailybeast.com/articles/2011/06/20/cia-base-attack-in-afghanistan-how-a-triple-agent-duped.

100 *traditional German castles:* Ahmed, Rashid. *Pakistan on the Brink*. New York: Penguin, 2013, p. 114.

101 *Harry's Tap Room:* Clinton, Hillary. *Hard Choices*. New York: Simon & Schuster, 2014, loc 2747. Kindle.

101 *"Remember this moment":* Clinton, Hillary. *Hard Choices*. New York: Simon & Schuster, 2014, loc.2729. Kindle.

102 *love of the Yankees:* Gordon, Meryl. "Ambassador A-List." *New York,* http://nymag.com/nymetro/news/people/features/1748/index3.html.

102 *"If this thing works":* Nasr, Vali. "The Inside Story of how the White House Diplomacy Let Diplomacy Fail in Afghanistan." *Foreign Policy,* 4 March 2013, http://foreignpolicy.com/2013/03/04/the-inside-story-of-how-the-white-house-let-diplomacy-fail-in-afghanistan.

103 *"are not reconcilable":* "White Paper of the Interagency Policy Group's Report on U.S. Policy toward Afghanistan and Pakistan." United States Government, Office of the White House, 2009, edocs.nps.edu/govpubs/wh/2009/Afghanistan_Pakistan_White_Paper.pdf.

103 *"taboo word":* *The Diplomat*. Dir. David Holbrooke. HBO Documentary Films, 2015, 1:19:40.

104 *"on board":* Chandrasekaran, Rajiv. *Little America: The War Within the War for Afghanistan*. New York: Vintage, loc. 3599. Kindle.

104 *a violent reminder:* Marquez, Miguel. "Holbrooke Gets Very Close Look at Afghan War." *ABC News,* 21 June 2010, http://abcnews.go.com/WN/Afghanistan/ambassador-holbrookes-plane-attacked-marja-afghanistan/story?id=10973713.

105 *"not another email":* Hastings, Michael. "The Runaway General." *Rolling Stone,* 22 June 2010, http://www.rollingstone.com/politics/news/the-runaway-general-20100622.

105 *"if we just tried a little harder":* Author interview with General David Petraeus, in person at his offices in New York City, 25 May 2016.

106 *"Not now":* Chandrasekaran, Rajiv. *Little America: The War Within the War for Afghanistan*. New York: Vintage, loc. 3610. Kindle.

106 **dead-ended:** Chandrasekaran, Rajiv. *Little America: The War Within the War for Afghanistan.* Kindle Ed., New York: Vintage, loc. 3554. Kindle.

107 **"We don't outsource our foreign policy":** Chandrasekaran, Rajiv. *Little America: The War Within the War for Afghanistan.* New York: Vintage, loc. 3569. Kindle.

107 **"constant uphill struggle":** The Diplomat. Dir. David Holbrooke. HBO Documentary Films, 2015, 1:20:00.

108 **had the president's trust:** Chandrasekaran, Rajiv. *Little America: The War Within the War for Afghanistan.* New York: Vintage, loc. 3515. Kindle.

108 **plan his exit strategy:** Chandrasekaran, Rajiv. *Little America: The War Within the War for Afghanistan.* New York: Vintage, loc. 3515. Kindle.

108 **"White House aides told me":** Author interview with Hillary Clinton, 20 November 2017.

109 **"confident edging on arrogance":** The Diplomat. Dir. David Holbrooke. HBO Documentary Films, 2015, 1:29:00.

109 **A frequent fixture:** Schulman, Daniel. "State Department Launches Afghanistan Leak Probe." *Mother Jones,* 27 January 2010, http://www.motherjones.com/politics/2010/01/state-department-launches-afghan-leak-probe.

109 **not a leaker:** Landler, Mark. *Alter Egos: Hillary Clinton, Barack Obama, and the Twilight Struggle Over American Power.* New York: Random House, 2016, loc. 1746. Kindle.

109 **he did like talking to reporters:** "State Department Launches Afghan Leak Probe." *Mother Jones,* January 2010, www.motherjones.com/politics/2010/01/state-department-launches-afghan-leak-probe.

110 **replete with pictures:** Packer, George. "The Last Mission." *New Yorker,* 28 September 2009, http://www.newyorker.com/magazine/2009/09/28/the-last-mission.

110 **"you shouldn't be making":** Conversation with Kati Marton, 13 April 2017.

110 **"Obviously Richard strayed":** Clinton, Hillary. "PACKER ARTICLE." Message to Cheryl Mills. 16 September 2009. Email released by WikiLeaks, https://wikileaks.org/clinton-emails/emailid/15835.

110 **"You don't understand":** Hirsch, Michael. "Richard Holbrooke's Decline and Fall, as Told in Clinton Emails." *Politico,* 1 July 2015, www.politico.com/story/2015/07/richard-holbrookes-hillary-clinton-emails-119649.

13: PROMISE ME YOU'LL END THE WAR

112 **"I think I've got it":** Hirsch, Michael. "Richard Holbrooke's Decline and Fall, as Told in Clinton Emails." *Politico,* 1 July 2015, www.politico.com/story/2015/07/richard-holbrookes-hillary-clinton-emails-119649.

113 **"I still believe":** "SUBJECT: AT THE CROSSROADS." Memo from Richard Holbrooke to Hillary Clinton, 10 September 2010.

114 **only India:** Wright, Tom. "No Pakistan on President Obama's India Trip." *Wall Street Journal,* 21 October 2010, https://blogs.wsj.com/indiarealtime/2010/10/21/no-pakistan-on-president-obama%E2%80%99s-india-trip.

117 *"The best we can achieve":* "SUBJECT: AT THE CROSSROADS." Memo from Richard Holbrooke to Hillary Clinton, 10 September 2010.

118 *"always hoping": The Diplomat.* Dir. David Holbrooke. HBO Documentary Films, 2015, 1:33:00.

120 *"Finally the president": The Diplomat.* Dir. David Holbrooke. HBO Documentary Films, 2015, 1:34:00.

120 *looked flushed:* Landler, Mark. *Alter Egos: Hillary Clinton, Barack Obama, and the Twilight Struggle Over American Power.* New York: Random House, 2016, loc. 1768. Kindle.

120 *her own internist: The Diplomat.* Dir. David Holbrooke. HBO Documentary Films, 2015, 1:35:00; Clinton, Hillary. *Hard Choices.* New York: Simon and Schuster, 2014, loc. 2779; Alter, Jonathan. "Richard Holbrooke's Lonely Mission." *Newsweek,* 16 January 2011, www.newsweek.com/richard-holbrookes-lonely-mission-67057; and Roig-Franzia, Manuel. "Searching for Richard Holbrooke." *Washington Post,* 20 October 2015, https://www.washingtonpost.com/lifestyle/style/searching-for-richard-holbrooke/2015/10/20/84d62ee4-7747-11e5-b9c1-f03c48c96ac2_story.html?utm_term=.da8936547d62.

121 *"You have to promise":* Landler, Mark. *Alter Egos: Hillary Clinton, Barack Obama, and the Twilight Struggle Over American Power.* New York: Random House, 2016, loc. 1781. Kindle.

121 *Holbrooke was joking:* Chandrasekaran, Rajiv and DeYoung, Karen. "Holbrooke's War Remark Called Banter, Not Entreaty." *Washington Post,* 15 December 2010, www.washingtonpost.com/wp-dyn/content/article/2010/12/14/AR2010121407701.html.

122 *merge it with a Holbrooke tribute event:* "Holiday Reception." US Department of State, 13 December 2010, https://video.state.gov/detail/videos/category/video/709543962001/?autoStart=true.

124 *when she got the call:* Mills, Cheryl. "FW: Harper's Bazaar: 'Hillary Clinton: Myth and Reality." Message to Hillary Clinton. 17 February 2017. Email released by WikiLeaks, No. C05777693, 7 January 2016, https://wikileaks.org/clinton-emails/Clinton_Email_January_7_Release/C05777693.pdf.

125 *"that December":* Author interview with Hillary Clinton, 20 November 2017.

14: THE WHEELS COME OFF THE BUS

127 *"he wouldn't stand out":* McKelvey, Tara. "The CIA's Last-Minute Osama bin Laden Drama." *Daily Beast,* 9 May 2011, www.thedailybeast.com/articles/2011/05/10/raymond-davis-the-cias-last-minute-osama-bin-laden-drama.html.

127 *casualty of an American dream:* Conrad, Jim. "The Walls Come Down at Powell Valley High." WCYB, 21 May 2014, www.wcyb.com/news/virginia/the-walls-come-down-at-powell-valley-high_20160524074842261/14089434.

127 *"peaceful and confident":* Walsh, Declan. "A C.I.A. Spy, a Hail of Bullets, Three Killed, and a U.S.-Pakistan Diplomatic Row." *Guardian* (Manchester), 20 February 2011, https://www.theguardian.com/world/2011/feb/20/cia-agent-lahore-

civilian-deaths and Mazzetti, Mark. *The Way of the Knife: The CIA, a Secret Army, and a War at the Ends of the Earth*. New York: Penguin, 2014, p. 2.

127   *Minutes later:* Yasif, Rana. "Raymond Davis Case: The Forgotten Victim." *Express Tribune*, 18 March 2011, https://tribune.com.pk/story/134313/the-forgotten-victim.

128   *"not subject":* Tapper, Jake and Ferran, Lee. "President Barack Obama: Pakistan Should Honor Immunity for 'Our Diplomat.'" *ABC News*, 15 February 2011, abc news.go.com/Blotter/raymond-davis-case-president-barack-obama-urges-pakistan/story?id=12922282.

128   *"he's not one of ours":* Mazzetti, Mark. *The Way of the Knife: The CIA, a Secret Army, and a War at the Ends of the Earth*. New York: Penguin, 2014, p. 264.

128   *"If we have to play":* Author phone interview with Leon Panetta, 6 May 2016.

129   *"Hey, where are you":* Author phone interview with Mohsin Kamal, 14 November 2016.

129   *"a most unpredictable man":* Author phone interview with Mohsin Kamal, 14 November 2016.

130   *No American:* Author phone interview with Mohsin Kamal, 14 November 2016.

130   *pulling dozens of its undercover operatives out:* Mazzetti, Mark. *The Way of the Knife: The CIA, a Secret Army, and a War at the Ends of the Earth*. New York: Penguin, 2014, p. 276.

130   *"The wheels just came off":* Author interview with General David Petraeus, in person at his offices in New York City, 25 May 2016.

130   *Clinton canceled:* DeYoung, Karen and Brulliard, Karin. "U.S.-Pakistan Relations Strained Further With Case of Jailed Diplomat." *Washington Post*, 8 February 2011, www.washingtonpost.com/wp-dyn/content/article/2011/02/07/AR2011020705790.html.

131   *leaving behind:* Schmidle, Nicholas. "Getting Bin Laden." *New Yorker*, 8 August 2011, www.newyorker.com/magazine/2011/08/08/getting-bin-laden and Meyers, Steven Lee and Bumiller, Elisabeth. "Obama Calls World 'Safer' After Pakistan Raid." *New York Times*, 2 May 2011, http://www.nytimes.com/2011/05/03/world/asia/osama-bin-laden-dead.html.

131   *the Pakistanis were incompetent:* "U.S.-Pakistani Relations After the bin Laden Raid." Stratfor, 2 May 2011, https://www.stratfor.com/analysis/us-pakistani-relations-after-bin-laden-raid.

131   *"We are still talking":* Brulliard, Karin and DeYoung, Karen. "Pakistani Military, Government Warn U.S. Against Future Raids." *Washington Post*, 6 May 2011, https://www.washingtonpost.com/world/pakistan-questions-legality-of-us-operation-that-killed-bin-laden/2011/05/05/AFM2l0wF_story.html?tid=a_inl&utm_term=.9dce5bb83301.

131   *not accepted:* Brulliard, Karin and Hussain, Shaiq. "Pakistani Spy Chief Offers to Resign." *Washington Post*, 13 May 2011, https://www.washingtonpost.com/world/2011/05/12/AFdoRh1G_story.html?utm_term=.e556f2485d1a.

131   *"People just don't understand":* Author interview with General David Petraeus, in person at his offices in New York City, 25 May 2016.

132 *"politics took over"*: Author phone interview with Leon Panetta, 06 May 2016.

132 *how to get tougher:* Brulliard, Karin and DeYoung, Karen. "Pakistani Military, Government Warn U.S. Against Future Raids." *Washington Post*, 6 May 2011, https://www.washingtonpost.com/world/pakistan-questions-legality-of-us-operation-that-killed-bin-laden/2011/05/05/AFM2l0wF_story.html?tid=a_inl&utm_term=.9dce5bb83301.

132 *"pulled the veil back":* Author interview with General Michael Hayden, in person at his offices in Washington, DC, 17 May 2017.

132 *tipping off al-Qaeda fighters:* Crilly, Rob. "Pakistan Accused of Tipping Off al-Qaeda Fighters Ahead of Raids." *Telegraph* (UK), 12 June 2011, www.telegraph.co.uk/news/worldnews/al-qaeda/8571134/Pakistan-accused-of-tipping-off-al-Qaeda-fighters-ahead-of-raids.html.

133 *"he was **pissed**":* Author phone interview with Leon Panetta, 6 May 2016.

133 *"as a veritable arm":* Barnes, Julian, Rosenberg, Matthew, and Entous, Adam. "U.S. Accuses Pakistan of Militant Ties." *Wall Street Journal*, 23 September 2011, https://www.wsj.com/articles/SB10001424053111904563904576586760263338104.

133 *recriminations:* DeYoung, Karin and Partlow, Joshua. "Afghans Saw Commando Unit Was Attacked Before Airstrike Was Called on Pakistan." *Washington Post*, 28 November 2011, https://www.washingtonpost.com/world/afghans-say-unit-was-attacked-before-airstrike/2011/11/28/gIQAX6ZY5N_story.html?hpid=z1&utm_term=.f70a1c3d2b3a.

133 *GLOCs:* Coleman, Jasmine. "Pakistan Halts NATO Supplies After Attack Leaves Soldiers Dead." *Guardian* (Manchester), 26 November 2011, https://www.theguardian.com/world/2011/nov/26/pakistan-halts-nato-supplies-attack.

134 *sixty days of supplies:* Phone interview with General John Allen, 2 September 2016.

134 *it worked:* Martinez, Luis. "Afghanistan War: Closed Pakistan Routes Costing U.S. $100 Million a Month." *ABC News*, 13 June 2012, abcnews.go.com/blogs/politics/2012/06/afghanistan-war-closed-pakistan-routes-costing-u-s-100-million-a-month.

134 *"spell 'relief'":* Sherman, Wendy. "THANK YOU." Email to Hillary Clinton, 2 July 2012, released by WikiLeaks, https://wikileaks.org/clinton-emails/emailid/20254 and Clinton, Hillary. "Re; Thanks." Email to Bill Burns, 3 July 2012, released by WikiLeaks, https://wikileaks.org/clinton-emails/emailid/7553.

134 *"sad state":* Author phone interview with General John Allen, 2 September 2016.

134 *biggest dent:* Author interview with Alan Kronstadt, 18 August 2016.

135 *"work together":* Clinton, Hillary. *Hard Choices*. New York: Simon & Schuster, 2014, loc. 3457-3458. Kindle.

135 *Afghans in the lead:* Yusufzai, Mushtaq, Williams, Abigail, Burton, Brinley. "Taliban Begins Secret Peace Talks With U.S., Afghan Officials: Sources." *NBC News*, 18 October 2016, www.nbcnews.com/news/world/taliban-begins-secret-peace-talks-u-s-afghan-officials-sources-n668131.

15: THE MEMO

137 *"would go bad":* Author interview with Husain Haqqani, Hudson Institute Office, Washington, DC, 6 January 2017.

138 *"eliminate hardline elements":* Ijaz, Mansoor. "Time to Take on Pakistan's Jihadi Spies." *Financial Times*, 10 October 2011, https://www.ft.com/content/5ea9b804-f351-11e0-b11b-00144feab49a and "Confidential Memorandum: Briefing for Adm. Mike Mullen, Chairman, Joint Chiefs of Staff." 9 May 2011, *Washington Post*, www.washingtonpost.com/wp-srv/world/documents/secret-pakistan-memo-to-adm-mike-mullen.html.

138 *to issue visas:* "Gilani Granted Controversial Visa-Issuing Powers to Haqqani, Letter Reveals." *GeoTV News*, 24 March 2017, https://www.geo.tv/latest/135334-Gilani-granted-controversial-visa-issuing-powers-to-Haqqani-letter-reveals.

138 *not to approve visas:* "Hussain Haqqani Renewed Visas to 36 C.I.A. Agents in Pakistan Despite Foreign Office Warning." *Times* (Islamabad), 25 March 2017, https://timesofislamabad.com/hussain-haqqani-renewed-visas-to-36-cia-agents-in-pakistan-despite-foreign-office-warning/2017/03/25.

138 *a turncoat:* Author interview with Husain Haqqani, Hudson Institute Office, Washington, DC, 6 January 2017.

139 *"completely out of his depth":* Author interview with Husain Haqqani, Hudson Institute Office, Washington, DC, 6 January 2017.

139 *"God gave you":* Ignatius, David. "Mansoor Ijaz, Instigator Behind Pakistan's 'Memogate.'" *Washington Post*, 22 January 2012, https://www.washingtonpost.com/blogs/post-partisan/post/mansoor-ijaz-instigator-behind-pakistans-memogate/2012/01/22/gIQAcRdjJQ_blog.html?utm_term=.a2243babdf37.

140 *similarly colorful:* Ignatius, David. "Mansoor Ijaz, Instigator Behind Pakistan's 'Memogate.'" *Washington Post*, 22 January 2012, https://www.washingtonpost.com/blogs/post-partisan/post/mansoor-ijaz-instigator-behind-pakistans-memogate/2012/01/22/gIQAcRdjJQ_blog.html?utm_term=.a2243babdf37 and Bergen, Peter. "What's Behind the Furor in Pakistan?" CNN, 25 November 2011, www.cnn.com/2011/11/24/opinion/bergen-memogate-pakistan.

140 *named him as the culprit:* Nelson, Dean. "Imran Khan Blame by Pakistan U.S. Envoy for Links to Army Plot." *Telegraph* (UK), 21 November 2011, www.telegraph.co.uk/news/worldnews/asia/pakistan/8904605/Imran-Khan-blamed-by-Pakistan-US-envoy-for-links-to-army-plot.html.

140 *downloading evidence:* Kiessling, Hein. *Faith, Unity, Discipline: The Inter-Service-Intelligence (ISI) of Pakistan.* London: Hurst, 2016, loc. 4277. Kindle.

140 *victim of his own politeness:* Author interview with Husain Haqqani, Hudson Institute Office, Washington, DC, 6 January 2017.

141 *"I'll be Houdini":* Author interview with Husain Haqqani, Hudson Institute Office, Washington, DC, 6 January 2017.

141 *changing of the guard:* Author interview with Husain Haqqani, Hudson Institute Office, Washington, DC, 6 January 2017.

142 *"material inaccuracies":* "Email from Mansoor Ijaz to Ronan Farrow." 11 March 2018.

143 *stage the bin Laden raid:* Haqqani, Husain. "Yes, the Russian ambassador met Trump's team. So? That's what we diplomats do." *Washington Post*, 10 March 2017, https://www.washingtonpost.com/posteverything/wp/2017/03/10/yes-the-russian-ambassador-met-trumps-team-so-thats-what-we-diplomats-do/.

143 *long-awaited confirmation:* "Pakistan Army Reacts to Hussain Haqqani's Article." *The News* (Pakistan), 29 March 2017, https://www.thenews.com.pk/latest/195267-Pakistan-Army-reacts-to-Hussain-Haqqanis-article.

143 *"The veracity":* Iqbal, Anwar. "Haqqani Claims His 'Connections' Led U.S. to Kill Osama." *Dawn*, 13 March 2017, https://www.dawn.com/news/1320175.

143 *A year after:* Author interview with Husain Haqqani, Hudson Institute Office, Washington, DC, 6 January 2017.

16: THE REAL THING

144 *"just a case":* Author interview with Robin Raphel, 6 January 2017, Garden Cafe in Washington, DC.

145 *Cassidy & Associates:* Author interview with Robin Raphel, 6 January 2017, Garden Cafe in Washington, DC.

145 *"In medical terms":* Author interview with Robin Raphel, 6 January 2017, Garden Cafe in Washington, DC.

145 *"no longer a Department employee":* Mazzetti, Mark and Apuzzo, Matt. "F.B.I. Is Investigating Retired U.S. Diplomat, a Pakistan Expert, Officials Say." *New York Times*, 7 November 2014, https://www.nytimes.com/2014/11/08/us/robin-raphel-fbi-state-department-search.html?_r=0.

146 *"was diplomacy":* Author interview with Ambassador Richard Olson, 28 September 2017.

147 *After a few months:* Entous, Adam. "The Last Diplomat." *Wall Street Journal*, 2 December 2016, https://www.wsj.com/articles/the-last-diplomat-1480695454.

147 *"Everybody hated Pakistan":* Author interview with Robin Raphel, 6 January 2017, Garden Cafe in Washington, DC.

147 *criminal charge:* Entous, Adam. "The Last Diplomat." *Wall Street Journal*, 2 December 2016, https://www.wsj.com/articles/the-last-diplomat-1480695454.

148 *"scope of work":* Author interview with Robin Raphel, 16 May 2016, at US Institutes of Peace.

149 *"Nobody is going to hire you":* Author phone interview with Robin Raphel, 30 June 2016.

149 *"I'm a working woman":* Author interview with Robin Raphel, 6 January 2017, Garden Cafe in Washington, DC.

150 *"I'm not a spy":* Author interview with Robin Raphel, 6 January 2017, Garden Cafe in Washington, DC.

150 *"they're clueless":* Author interview with Robin Raphel, 6 January 2017, Garden Cafe in Washington, DC.

151 *"criminalizing diplomacy":* Author interview with anonymous senior US official, 28 September 2016.

PART II: SHOOT FIRST, ASK QUESTIONS NEVER

153 *Corinthians:* The Holy Bible, English Standard Version.

17: GENERAL RULE

155 *"Whether we need an SRAP or not":* Author interview with Rex Tillerson, 4 January 2018.

156 *authority to launch raids:* Diamond, Jeremy. "How Trump is Empowering the Military—and Raising Some Eyebrows." *CNN Politics*, 26 June 2017, www.cnn.com/2017/06/24/politics/trump-pentagon-shift-war-power-military/index.html.

156 *rolling out a new surge:* Jaffe, Greg and Ryan, Missy. "Up to 1,000 more U.S. troops could be headed to Afghanistan this spring." Washington Post, 21 January 2018, https://www.washingtonpost.com/world/national-security/up-to-1000-more-us-troops-could-be-headed-to-afghanistan-this-spring/2018/01/21/153930b6-fd1b-11e7-a46b-a3614530bd87_story.html.

156 *ten of twenty-five:* Ryan, Missy and Jaffe, Greg. "Military's Clout at White House Could Shift U.S. Foreign Policy." *Washington Post*, 28 May 2017, https://www.washingtonpost.com/world/national-security/military-officers-seed-the-ranks-across-trumps-national-security-council/2017/05/28/5f10c8ca-421d-11e7-8c25-44d09ff5a4a8_story.html?utm_term=.e50c3e38d779.

156 *White House ended the practice of "detailing":* Wadhams, Nick. "Tillerson Tightens Limits on Filling State Department Jobs." *Bloomberg Politics*, 28 June 2017, https://www.bloomberg.com/news/articles/2017-06-28/tillerson-puts-tighter-limits-on-filling-state-department-jobs; author interviews with Foreign Service officers, 1 June 2017 and 30 July 2017.

157 *American arms sales:* Mehta, Aaron. "U.S. on Track for Record Foreign Weapon Sales." *Defense News*, 26 December 2016, www.defensenews.com/pentagon/2016/12/26/us-on-track-for-record-foreign-weapon-sales/.

157 *according to several Pentagon staffers:* Browne, Ryan. "Amid Diplomatic Crisis Pentagon Agrees $12 Billion Jet Deal with Qatar." *CNN Politics*, 14 June 2017, www.cnn.com/2017/06/14/politics/qatar-f35-trump-pentagon/index.html.

157 *resume the sale of F-16 fighter jets:* Morello, Carol. "State Department Drops Human Rights as Condition for Fighter Jet Sale to Bahrain." *Washington Post*, 27 March 2017, https://www.washingtonpost.com/world/national-security/state-department-drops-human-rights-as-condition-for-fighter-jet-sale-to-bahrain/2017/03/29/6762d422-1abf-406e-aaff-fbc5a6a2e0ac_story.html?utm_term=.ba9bb8036665.

157 *naked in a dream:* Lusher, Adam. "Senior U.S. Official Reduced to Very Awkward Silence When Asked About Saudi Arabia's Attitude to Democracy." *Independent* (UK), 31 May 2017, www.independent.co.uk/news/world/americas/us-politics/stuart-jones-state-department-saudi-arabia-democracy-iran-awkward-embarrassing-agonising-pause-most-a7764961.html.

158 *"fantastic":* Conway, Madeline. "Trump: 'We Are Very Much Behind' Egypt's

el-Sisi." *Politico*, 04 April 2017, https://www.politico.com/story/2017/04/ trump-praises-egypt-abdel-fattah-el-sisi-236829.

158 *"unbelievable":* Carter, Brandon. "Trump Praised Philippines' Duterte for 'Unbelievable Job' on Drugs: Reports." *The Hill*, 23 May 2017, thehill.com/policy/international/334858-trump-praised-philippines-duterte-for-unbelievable-job-on-drugs-report.

158 *"it is important that we deal with those leaders":* Author interview with James Baker, 22 January 2018.

158 *"what this president":* Author interview with John Kerry, 21 November 2017.

158 *they weren't informed:* Scahill, Jeremy, Emmons, Alex and Grim, Ryan. "Trump Called Rodrigo Duterte to Congratulate Him on His Murderous Drug War: 'You Are Doing An Amazing Job.'" *Intercept*, 23 May 2017, https://theintercept.com/2017/05/23/trump-called-rodrigo-duterte-to-congratulate-him-on-his-murderous-drug-war-you-are-doing-an-amazing-job/.

158 *"it's definitely me":* Author interview with Chris LaVine, 25 June 2017.

159 *"Hard underlying parts of the diplomacy":* Author interview with Chris LaVine, 25 June 2017.

159 *FSA arms:* "U.S.-Trained Syrian Rebels Gave Equipment to Nusra: U.S. Military." Reuters, 26 September 2015, www.reuters.com/article/us-mideast-crisis-usa-equipment-idUSKCN0RP2HO20150926.

159 *a terrorist organization:* Author interview with anonymous career officer, 25 June 2017.

159 *"They play shell games":* Author interview with Chris LaVine, 25 June 2017.

159 *"a very big mistake":* Author interview with Abdullah Al-Mousa, 12 September 2016.

159 *"Kurds, Turks, and Syrian rebels were all locked in battle":* Gilbert, Benjamin. "Three U.S. Allies Are Now Fighting Each Other in Northern Syria." *Vice News*, 29 August 2016, https://news.vice.com/article/three-us-allies-are-now-fighting-each-other-in-northern-syria and Bulos, Nabih, Hennigan, W. J. and Bennett, Brian. "In Syria, Militias Armed by the Pentagon Fight Those Armed by the CIA." *Los Angeles Times*, 27 March 2016, www.latimes.com/world/middleeast/la-fg-cia-pentagon-isis-20160327-story.html.

160 *"it's really a very big mistake":* Author interview with Abdullah Al-Mousa, 12 September 2016.

160 *"the Pentagon program is false":* Author interview with Osama Abu Zaid, 12 September 2016.

161 *covert support for rebel elements:* "Trump to Send Arms to Kurdish YPG in Syria." Al Jazeera, 10 May 2017, www.aljazeera.com/news/2017/05/trump-send-arms-kurdish-ypg-syria-170509190404689.html and Jaffe, Greg and Entous, Adam. "Trump Ends Covert C.I.A. Program to Arm Anti-Assad Rebels in Syria, A Move Sought By Moscow." *Washington Post*, 19 July 2017, https://www.washingtonpost.com/world/national-security/trump-ends-covert-cia-program-to-arm-anti-assad-rebels-in-syria-a-move-sought-by-moscow/2017/07/19/b6821a62-6beb-11e7-96ab-5f38140b38cc_story.html?utm_term=.ade66898dd5e.

161 *"completely corrosive"*: Author interview with Chris LaVine, 25 June 2017.

161 *"support the legitimate opposition"*: Author interview with Hillary Clinton, 20 November 2017.

161 *"on board with that"*: Author interview with Chris LaVine, 25 June 2017.

162 *"it's become impossible to have an honest policy disagreement"*: Author interview with Chris LaVine, 25 June 2017.

162 *the word "partner"*: ["]Full Transcript of President Obama's Commencement Address at West Point." *Washington Post*, 28 May 2014, https://www.washington post.com/politics/full-text-of-president-obamas-commencement-address-at -west-point/2014/05/28/cfbcdcaa-e670-11e3-afc6-a1dd9407abcf_story.html.

18: DOSTUM: HE IS TELLING THE TRUTH AND DISCOURAGING ALL LIES

165 *"fragments of skull"*: Author interview with Jennifer Leaning, 6 September 2016.

165 *Physicians for Human Rights:* Author interview with John Heffernan, 25 May 2015.

168 *"bulging biceps"*: Rashid, Ahmed. *Taliban: Militant Islam, Oil and Fundamentalism in Central Asia*, Second Edition. New Haven, CT: Yale University Press, 2010, p. 56. Kindle.

168 *meat slurry:* Rashid, Ahmed. *Taliban: Militant Islam, Oil and Fundamentalism in Central Asia*, Second Edition. New Haven, CT: Yale University Press, 2010, p. 56. Kindle.

168 *"You're a good fellow"*: Author interview with General Dostum, in person at the Vice Presidential Palace in Kabul, Afghanistan, 29–30 August 2016.

169 *"my friend"*: Williams, Brian Glyn. *The Last Warlord: The Life and Legend of Dostum, the Afghan Warrior Who Led U.S. Special Forces to Topple the Taliban Regime*. Chicago: Chicago Review Press, 2013, p. 80.

169 *"some baby!"*: Author interview with General Dostum, in person at the Vice Presidential Palace in Kabul, Afghanistan, 29–30 August 2016.

170 *to carry rifles:* Filkins, Dexter. "Taking a Break from War With a Game Anything but Gentle." *New York Times*, 2 January 2009, www.nytimes.com/2009/01/03/world/asia/03afghan.html.

170 *was unbeatable:* Author interview with General Dostum, in person at the Vice Presidential Palace in Kabul, Afghanistan, 29–30 August 2016.

170 *all fake lashes:* Crile, George. *Charlie Wilson's War*. New York: Grove Press, 2007, loc. 1288-1289. Kindle.

170 *Congress was allocating more money to the fighters:* Coll, Steve. *Ghost Wars*. London: Penguin, 2004, p. 101. Kindle.

171 *"they weren't suicides"*: Author interview with Milton Bearden, 28 April 2016.

171 *have had her lawyer saber rattle:* "Socialite Joanne Herring wins 'War.'" *New York Daily News*, 11 December 2007, http://www.nydailynews.com/entertainment/gossip/socialite-joanne-herring-wins-war-article-1.276411.

172 *mused openly about defecting:* Williams, Brian Glyn. *The Last Warlord: The Life*

and *Legend of Dostum, the Afghan Warrior Who Led U.S. Special Forces to Topple the Taliban Regime.* Chicago: Chicago Review Press, 2013, p. 80.

172 **balance of power:** Williams, Brian Glyn. *The Last Warlord: The Life and Legend of Dostum, the Afghan Warrior Who Led U.S. Special Forces to Topple the Taliban Regime.* Chicago: Chicago Review Press, 2013, p. 146.

172 **campaign of rapes:** Coll, Steve. *Ghost Wars.* London: Penguin, 2004, p. 262. Kindle.

173 **meetings with the Taliban:** Rubin, Michael. "Taking Tea with the Taliban." *Commentary*, 1 February 2010, https://www.commentarymagazine.com/articles/taking-tea-with-the-taliban.

173 **a freeze of Taliban assets:** Rashid, Ahmed. *Taliban: Militant Islam, Oil and Fundamentalism in Central Asia.* Second Edition. New Haven, CT: Yale University Press, 2010, p. 217.

173 **deepening bond with Osama bin Laden:** Rashid, Ahmed. *Descent into Chaos: The U.S. and the Disaster in Pakistan, Afghanistan, and Central Asia.* London: Penguin, 2009, p. 73.

173 **peaceful resolution:** "The Situation in Afghanistan and its Implications for International Peace and Security." United Nations General Assembly Security Council, 21 September 1999, https://unama.unmissions.org/sites/default/files/21%20September%201999.pdf.

174 **Pakistan worked with the Taliban:** Rashid, Ahmed. *Descent into Chaos: The U.S. and the Disaster in Pakistan, Afghanistan, and Central Asia.* London: Penguin, 2009, p. 53.

174 **"Short question":** Author interview with General Dostum, in person at the Vice Presidential Palace in Kabul, Afghanistan, 29–30 August 2016.

175 **"whatever you want":** Author interview with General Dostum, in person at the Vice Presidential Palace in Kabul, Afghanistan, 29–30 August 2016.

175 **warlords and brigands:** Mazzetti, Mark. *The Way of the Knife: The CIA, a Secret Army, and a War at the Ends of the Earth.* New York: Penguin, p. 32. Kindle.

176 **"it was such nonsense":** Author interview with Robin Raphel at US Institutes of Peace, 16 May 2016.

176 **"our biggest mistake":** Author interview with Robin Raphel at US Institutes of Peace, 16 May 2016.

176 **"The Bonn Agreement":** Rubin, Barnett. "What I Saw in Afghanistan." *New Yorker*, 1 July 2015, https://www.newyorker.com/news/news-desk/what-have-we-been-doing-in-afghanistan.

177 **slaughtering the elderly, children:** Coll, Steve. *Ghost Wars.* London: Penguin, 2004, p. 263. Kindle.

177 **forcing them into marriage:** "RIC Query—Afghanistan." United States Citizenship and Immigration Services, BCIS Resource Information Center, 27 May 2003, https://www.uscis.gov/tools/asylum-resources/ric-query-afghanistan-27-may-2003; "UN Opposes Afghanistan Bill Giving Immunity to War Criminals." Revolutionary Association of the Women of Afghanistan, 2 February 2007, http://www.rawa.org/temp/runews/2007/02/02/un-opposes-afghanistan-bill-giving-immunity-to-war-criminals.html.

177   *Noor's militias:* Raghavan, Sudarsan. "Afghanistan's Defining Fight: Technocrats vs. Strongmen." *Washington Post,* 12 April 2015, https://www.washingtonpost .com/world/asia_pacific/former-warlords-test-the-rise-of-a-new-afghanistan/ 2015/04/12/73e052ae-b091-11e4-bf39-5560f3918d4b_story.html?tid=a_ inl&utm_term=.6d12c65413a4.

177   *the agency had been developing its relationship:* Author interview with Hank Crumpton, 19 July 2016.

177   *" 'Hey, how ya doing' ":* *Legion of Brothers,* dir. Greg Barker, CNN films 2017, 9:30.

177   *" 'the horse was still moving' ":* *Legion of Brothers,* dir. Greg Barker, CNN films 2017, 9:30.

178   *"now we've gone back in time":* Author interview with Bart, 5 September 2016.

178   *"laying in a ditch":* *Legion of Brothers,* dir. Greg Barker, CNN films 2017, 9:30.

178   *"such a great country":* Author interview with General Dostum, in person at the Vice Presidential Palace in Kabul, Afghanistan, 29–30 August 2016.

179   *"accomplished on the battlefield":* Author interview with Hank Crumpton, by phone, 19 July 2016.

179   *Kunduz:* Anderson, Jon Lee. "The Surrender," *New Yorker,* 10 December 2001, http://www.newyorker.com/magazine/2001/12/10/the-surrender.

179   *surrendered peacefully:* Stewart, Richard W. "The United States Army in Afghan- istan, October 2001–March 2002: Operation Enduring Freedom," United States Army, http://www.history.army.mil/html/books/070/70-83/cmhPub_ 70-83.pdf.

179   *twice that:* Contemporaneous claims from US forces, Northern Alliance leaders, and independent journalists all vary significantly. See, e.g.: "Thousands of Taliban Fight- ers Surrender in Kunduz," *Haaretz,* 24 November 2001, http://www.haaretz.com/ news/thousands-of-taliban-fighters-surrender-in-kunduz-1.75571.

180   *"location which I can't talk about":* Author interview with Bart, 5 September 2016.

180   *killing one CIA agent:* Sennott, Charles M. "The First Battle of the 21st Century: Returning to the Site of America's Earliest Casualty in Afghanistan." *Atlantic,* 5 May 2015.

180   *"The bodies":* Author interview with General Dostum, in person at the Vice Presidential Palace in Kabul, Afghanistan, 29–30 August 2016.

180   *"the price we paid for going very fast":* Author interview with Hank Crumpton, 19 July 2016.

181   *"You mean the prisoners":* Author interview with Jennifer Leaning, 22 May 2015.

181   *Red Cross was barred:* James Risen of the *New York Times* also reported that US military officials blocked initial Red Cross inquiries: http://www.nytimes .com/2009/07/11/world/asia/11afghan.html.

181   *able to build rapport:* Author interview with Jennifer Leaning, 6 September 2016.

181   *" 'Where are the rest?' ":* Author interview with John Heffernan, 25 May 2015.

182   *sundry thuggery:* Raghavan, Sudarsan. "Afghanistan's Defining Fight: Technocrats vs. Strongmen." *Washington Post,* 12 April 2015, https://www.washingtonpost.com/

world/asia_pacific/former-warlords-test-the-rise-of-a-new-afghanistan/2015/04/12/73e052ae-b091-11e4-bf39-5560f3918d4b_story.html?tid=a_inl&utm_term=.fe112937980d.

182 *accused of harassing:* Center for American Progress. "Profiles of Afghan Power Brokers." 26 October 2009, https://www.americanprogress.org/issues/security/news/2009/10/26/6734/profiles-of-afghan-power-brokers/.

182 *spectacular corruption:* Human Rights Watch. *"Today We Shall All Die": Afghanistan's Strongmen and the Legacy of Impunity.* 2015, https://www.hrw.org/sites/default/files/report_pdf/afghanistan0315_4up.pdf.

182 *"broad range of criminal activity":* "Cable: 06KABUL2962_a," released by WikiLeaks, https://wikileaks.org/plusd/cables/06KABUL2862_a.html.

182 *similar havoc:* Peceny, Mark and Bosin, Yury. "Winning with Warlords in Afghanistan." *Small Wars & Insurgencies,* 22:4, 603–618, www.unm.edu/~ybosin/documents/winning_with_warlords_2011.pdf.

183 *"rather kill each other over cows":* Partlow, Joshua. "Dostum, a Former Warlord Who Was Once America's Man in Afghanistan, May Be Back." *Washington Post,* 23 April 2014, https://www.washingtonpost.com/world/dostum-a-former-warlord-who-was-once-americas-man-in-afghanistan-may-be-back/2014/04/23/9d1a7670-c63d-11e3-8b9a-8e0977a24aeb_story.html?utm_term=.61ff3c408558.

183 *"difficult to get rid of":* Author interview with Robert Finn, 2 June 2016.

184 *"how to use the Americans":* Author interview with Robert Finn, 2 June 2016.

184 *"little appetite":* Risen, James. "U.S. Inaction Seen After Taliban P.O.W.'s Died." *New York Times,* 10 July 2009, www.nytimes.com/2009/07/11/world/asia/11afghan.html.

184 *"Where do you start":* Risen, James. "U.S. Inaction Seen After Taliban P.O.W.'s Died." *New York Times,* 10 July 2009, www.nytimes.com/2009/07/11/world/asia/11afghan.html.

185 *"there are responsibilities":* CNN interview broadcast 12 July 2009. Transcript available via *Daily Kos* at https://www.dailykos.com/stories/2009/7/13/753057/-.

186 *sentenced to thirty months in prison:* "Ex-CIA officer Kiriakou 'made peace' with leak decision." *BBC News,* 28 February 2013, http://www.bbc.com/news/world-us-canada-21610806.

186 *" 'You kill it' ":* Author interview with John Kiriakou, 3 June 2016.

186 *"I was very disappointed":* Author interview with John Kiriakou, 3 June 2016.

187 *"never pulled punches":* Author interview with John Kerry, 21 November 2017.

187 *"might have interpreted":* Author interview with Frank Lowenstein, 5 August 2016. Lowenstein also questions Kiriakou's credibility, referencing criminal charges later brought against him for leaking classified information, and suggesting that "he's [Kiriakou's] not—let me figure out the most polite way to say this—not the world's most reliable guy."

187 *new inquiry:* Currier, Cora. "White House Closes Inquiry Into Afghan Massacre—and Will Release No Details," *ProPublica,* 31 July 2013, https://www.propublica.org/article/white-house-closes-inquiry-into-afghan-massacre-and-will-release-no-details.

187 *series of large holes:* Lasseter, Tom. "As Possible Afghan War-Crimes Evidence

Removed, U.S. Silent," McClatchy, 11 December 2008, www.mcclatchydc.com/news/nation-world/world/article24514951.html.

187 *"literal obstruction":* Author phone interview with Susannah Sirkin, 22 May 2015.

188 *"the rights of women":* Author interview with General Dostum, in person at the Vice Presidential Palace in Kabul, Afghanistan, 29–30 August 2016.

189 *"he is nonfunctional":* Author interview with former United States ambassador, who spoke on condition of anonymity due to the sensitivity of the remarks, 31 August 2016.

190 *"a different person":* Author interview with General Dostum, in person at the Vice Presidential Palace in Kabul, Afghanistan, 29–30 August 2016.

190 *charges of mass atrocities:* Nordland, Rod. "Top Afghans Tied to '90s Carnage, Researchers Say." *New York Times*, 22 July 2012, www.nytimes.com/2012/07/23/world/asia/key-afghans-tied-to-mass-killings-in-90s-civil-war.html.

190 *violent reprisals:* Wafe, Abdul Waheed. "Former Warlord in Standoff With Police at Kabul Home." *New York Times*, 4 February 2008, www.nytimes.com/2008/02/04/world/asia/04afghan.html; Gall, Carlotta. "Ethnic Uzbek Legislator Beaten, Afghans Confirm." *New York Times*, 30 June 2006, www.nytimes.com/2006/06/30/world/asia/30afghan.html.

190 *Junbish militias:* "Afghanistan: Forces Linked to Vice President Terrorize Villagers." Human Rights Watch, 31 July 2016, https://www.hrw.org/news/2016/07/31/afghanistan-forces-linked-vice-president-terrorize-villagers.

190 *"known killer":* Partlow, Joshua. "Dostum, a Former Warlord Who Was Once America's Man in Afghanistan, May Be Back." *Washington Post*, 23 April 2014, https://www.washingtonpost.com/world/dostum-a-former-warlord-who-was-once-americas-man-in-afghanistan-may-be-back/2014/04/23/9d1a7670-c63d-11e3-8b9a-8e0977a24aeb_story.html?utm_term=.353f99b7d698.

190 *denied him a visa:* Vasilogambros, Matt. "Afghanistan's Barred Vice President." *Atlantic*, 25 April 2016, http://www.theatlantic.com/international/archive/2016/04/afghanistan-dostum-barred/479922/.

191 *"they fabricate what they want":* Author interview with General Dostum, in person at the Vice Presidential Palace in Kabul, Afghanistan, 29–30 August 2016.

191 *had swooped in:* Nissenbaum, Dion. "When Hillary (Almost) Met the Warlord." McClatchy, 22 November 2009, blogs.mcclatchydc.com/jerusalem/2009/11/when-hillary-almost-met-the-warlord.html.

192 *"I have the key":* Author interview with General Dostum, in person at the Vice Presidential Palace in Kabul, Afghanistan, 29–30 August 2016.

192 *"We're partners":* Author interview with General Dostum, in person at the Vice Presidential Palace in Kabul, Afghanistan, 29–30 August 2016.

192 *did jumping jacks:* Rahim, Fazul, "Afghanistan's Warlord-Turned-VP Abdul Rashid Dostum Fights for Fitness." *NBC News*, http://www.nbcnews.com/news/world/afghanistans-warlord-turned-vp-abdul-rashid-dostum-fights-fitness-n265451.

193 *"peacelord":* Author interview with General Dostum, in person at the Vice Presidential Palace in Kabul, Afghanistan, 29–30 August 2016.

193 *"the prisoners":* Author interview with General Dostum, in person at the Vice Presidential Palace in Kabul, Afghanistan, 29–30 August 2016.

193 *"stacked like cordwood":* Risen, James. "U.S. Inaction Seen After Taliban P.O.W.'s Died." *New York Times*, 10 July 2009, http://www.nytimes.com/2009/07/11/world/asia/11afghan.html/.

194 *continued for days:* Barry, John. "The Death Convoy of Afghanistan." *Newsweek*, 25 August 2002, www.newsweek.com/death-convoy-afghanistan-144273 and Risen, James. "U.S. Inaction Seen After Taliban P.O.W.'s Died." *New York Times*, 10 July 2009, www.nytimes.com/2009/07/11/world/asia/11afghan.html.

194 *A top secret cable:* US diplomatic cable, from Department of State Bureau of Intelligence and Research to White House, OP 260221Z, 2008, accessed via FOIA request from Rubenstein, Leonard, Physicians for Human Rights, Case No. 200802926, 4 August 2008.

194 *"number of Taliban deaths":* Dasht-i-Leili FOIA'd State and DOD cables, p. 19 in State Dept pagination, p. 32 in PDF.

194 *"the actual number may approach 2,000":* Dasht-i-Leili FOIA'd State and DOD cables, p. 19 in State Dept pagination, p. 32 in PDF.

194 *"one container":* Author interview with General Dostum, in person at the Vice Presidential Palace in Kabul, Afghanistan, 29–30 August 2016.

195 *"his name was Hazarat Chunta":* Author interview with General Dostum, in person at the Vice Presidential Palace in Kabul, Afghanistan, 29–30 August 2016.

196 *He shrugged:* Author interview with General Dostum, in person at the Vice Presidential Palace in Kabul, Afghanistan, 29–30 August 2016.

196 *Raymond said:* "A Mass Grave In Afghanistan Raises Questions." NPR, 22 July 2009.

196 *"we worked very closely with [Dostum]":* Author interview with Mark Nutsch, 7 February 2018.

197 *"We did not witness":* Author interview with Mark Nutsch, 7 February 2018.

198 *"I'm over time!":* Author interview with General Dostum, in person at the Vice Presidential Palace in Kabul, Afghanistan, 29–30 August 2016.

199 *Taliban had ambushed:* "Afghan Vice-President Dostum Injured in Taliban Ambush." *Hindustan Times*, 17 October 2016, www.hindustantimes.com/world-news/taliban-militants-ambush-afghanistan-vice-president-s-convoy/story-UQdKiuhxtFoddiT6NUpwiK.html.

199 *Dostum can be seen:* Facebook video posted by Esmat Salehoghly Azimy, ATV footage, uploaded 25 November 2016, https://www.facebook.com/esmat.azimy/videos/vb.100002358908259/1170150113073608/?type=2&theater.

199 *Forensic evidence:* Rasmussen, Sune Engel. "Vice-President Leaves Afghanistan Amid Torture and Rape Claims." *Guardian* (Manchester), 19 May 2017, https://www.theguardian.com/world/2017/may/19/vice-president-leaves-afghanistan-amid-torture-and-claims; Masha, Mujiib and Abed, Fahim. "Afghan Vice President Seen Abducting Rival." *New York Times*, 27 November 2016, https://www.nytimes.com/2016/11/27/world/asia/afghan-vice-president-is-accused-of-assaulting-rival-and-taking-him-hostage.html?_r=0; Masha, Mujib and Abed,

Fahim. "Afghanistan Vice President Accused of Torturing Political Rival." *New York Times*, 13 December 2016, https://www.nytimes.com/2016/12/13/world/asia/political-rival-accuses-afghanistan-vice-president-of-torturing-him.html?rref=collection%2Ftimestopic%2FDostum%2C%20Abdul%20Rashid&action=click&contentCollection=timestopics&region=stream&module=stream_unit&version=latest&contentPlacement=8&pgtype=collection.

200 *charge of physical abuse:* Wafa, Abdul Waheed. "Former Warlord in Standoff with Police at Kabul Home." *New York Times*, 4 February 2008, www.nytimes.com/2008/02/04/world/asia/04afghan.html.

200 *"No one returns":* Ahmed, Azam. "Afghan First Vice President, an Ex-Warlord, Fumes on the Sidelines." *New York Times*, 18 March 2015, https://www.nytimes.com/2015/03/19/world/asia/afghan-first-vice-president-an-ex-warlord-fumes-on-the-sidelines.html.

200 *criminal investigation:* "Afghan Vice-President Dostum Accused of Sex Assault." BBC, 13 December 2016, www.bbc.com/news/world-asia-38311174.

200 *Ghani returned:* Nordland, Rod and Sukhanyar, Jawad. "Afghanistan Police Surround Vice President's House." *New York Times*, 21 February 2017, https://www.nytimes.com/2017/02/21/world/asia/abdul-rashid-dostum-afghanistan.html.

201 *smaller than al-Qaeda:* Bearak, Max. "Behind the Front Lines in the Fight to 'Annihilate' ISIS in Afghanistan." *Washington Post*, 23 July 2017, https://www.washingtonpost.com/world/asia_pacific/behind-the-front-lines-in-the-fight-to-annihilate-isis-in-afghanistan/2017/07/23/0e1f88d2-6bb4-11e7-abbc-a53480672286_story.html?utm_term=.391eec1930b5.

201 *"wasting our money":* Schwarz, Jon and Mackey, Robert. "All the Times Donald Trump Said the U.S. Should Get Out of Afghanistan." *Intercept*, 21 August 2017, https://theintercept.com/2017/08/21/donald-trump-afghanistan-us-get-out/.

201 *Mattis ordered:* "Full Transcript and Video: Trump's Speech on Afghanistan." *New York Times*, 21 August 2017, https://www.nytimes.com/2017/08/21/world/asia/trump-speech-afghanistan.html; and Gordon, Michael. "Mattis Orders First Group of Reinforcements to Afghanistan." *New York Times*, 31 August 2017, https://www.nytimes.com/2017/08/31/us/politics/trump-mattis-troops-afghanistan.html?rref=collection%2Ftimestopic%2FAfghanistan.

201 *America's troop commitments:* Rucker, Philip and Costa, Robert. "'It's a Hard Problem': Inside Trump's Decision to Send More Troops to Afghanistan." *Washington Post*, 21 August 2017, https://www.washingtonpost.com/politics/its-a-hard-problem-inside-trumps-decision-to-send-more-troops-to-afghanistan/2017/08/21/14dcb126-868b-11e7-a94f-3139abce39f5_story.html?utm_term=.3255b6d552c7.

201 *"We are with you":* Nordland, Rod. "The Empire Stopper." *New York Times*, 29 August 2017, https://www.nytimes.com/2017/08/29/world/asia/afghanistan-graveyard-empires-historical-pictures.html?rref=collection%2Ftimestopic%2FAfghanistan.

202 *"nobody knows":* Landay, Jonathan. "Despite Expected U.S. Troop Hike, No End in Sight to Afghan War." Reuters, 22 August 2017, https://www.reuters.com/

article/us-usa-trump-afghanistan-diplomacy/despite-expected-u-s-troop-hike-no-end-in-sight-to-afghan-war-idUSKCN1B2009.

202 *no permanent assistant secretary:* Toosi, Nahal. "State's Afghanistan-Pakistan Envoy Leaves, Spurring Confusion about U.S. Diplomacy in Region." *Politico*, 23 June 2017, www.politico.com/story/2017/06/23/trump-administration-dissolves-afghanistan-pakistan-unit-239901.

202 *"Childhood is childhood":* Author interview with General Dostum, in person at the Vice Presidential Palace in Kabul, Afghanistan, 29–30 August 2016.

19: WHITE BEAST

205 *"We're just ordinary people":* Author interview with Sally and Micheal Evans, 6 October 2016, in person at their home in Wooburn Green, England.

205 *to study Arabic:* "Sally Evans Slams UK Anti-Terror 'Failure.'" BBC. 4 February 2015, www.bbc.com/news/uk-england-beds-bucks-herts-31126913.

206 *"No god would guide you to this":* Author interview with Sally and Micheal Evans, 6 October 2016, in person at their home in Wooburn Green, England.

206 *"Thomas rang":* Author interview with Sally and Micheal Evans, 6 October 2016, in person at their home in Wooburn Green, England.

207 *and screams:* Author interview with Preeyam K. Sehmi, at the Westgate Mall, Nairobi, 13 December 2013.

207 *grisly torture:* Strauss, Gary. "Inside Kenya Shopping Mall, a House of Horrors." *USA Today*, 27 September 2013, http://www.usatoday.com/story/news/2013/09/27/mall-victims-tortured-maimed-in-al-shabab-attacks/2882299/.

207 *seventy-two people:* Soi, Nicholas and Dixon, Robyn. "Kenya says Nairobi mall siege is over, with 72 dead." *Los Angeles Times*, 24 September 2013, http://www.latimes.com/world/la-fg-kenya-mall-20130925,0,3451298.story#ixzz2pz9qg1hN.

207 *foreign meddling in Somalia:* Fieldstadt, Elisha. "Somali Terror Group al-Shabab Claims Responsibility for Kenya Mall Attack." *NBC News*. 21 September 2013, https://www.nbcnews.com/news/other/somali-terror-group-al-shabab-claims-responsibility-kenya-mall-attack-f4B11223876.

207 *seventy-six dead:* "Hunt for Terrorists Shifts to 'Dangerous' North Africa, Panetta Says." *NBC News*, 12 December 2011, https://archive.li/WOplo.

207 *"direct threat":* Kulish, Nicholas and Gettleman, Jeffrey. "U.S. Sees Direct Threat in Attack at Kenya Mall." *New York Times*, 25 September 2013, http://www.nytimes.com/2013/09/26/world/africa/us-sees-direct-threat-in-attack-at-kenya-mall.html?_r=0&pagewanted=all.

207 *"Selfishly":* *My Son the Jihadi*, Channel 4 documentary.

209 *"didn't lend itself":* Author interview with Princeton Lyman, 27 February 2017.

209 *"no need":* Vick, Karl. "Al Qaeda Ally in Somalia is in Tatters." *Washington Post*, 24 February 2002, https://www.washingtonpost.com/archive/politics/2002/02/24/al-qaeda-ally-in-somalia-is-in-tatters/4a0dd409-2bbf-4e76-8131-0a5c9e78e86a/?utm_term=.e6e20c5fc959.

209 *The courts could be brutally conservative:* Okeowo, Alexis. "The Fight Over Women's Basketball in Somalia." *New Yorker*, 11 September 2017.

209 *ninety-seven courts:* Hansen, Stig Jarle. *Al Shabaab in Somalia: The History and Ideology of a Militant Islamist Group, 2005–2012.* Oxford: Oxford University Press, 2013, p. 36. Kindle.

209 *ports and airports:* "Mogadishu's Port Reopened," AlJazeera.com, 23 August 2006.

209 *humanitarian access:* US diplomatic cable 06NAIROBI3441, from Economic Counselor John F. Hoover, US Embassy Nairobi, "Horn of Africa, State-U.S.A.I.D. Humanitarian Cable Update Number 8," 8 August 2006, released by WikiLeaks, http://wikileaks.org/cable/2006/08/06NAIROBI3441.html.

209 *warlords perceived to be secular:* Somali warlord Yusuf Mohammed Siad "told me he was first approached by the C.I.A. in Dubai in 2004." Scahill, Jeremy. *Dirty Wars: The World Is a Battlefield.* New York: Nation Books, 2013, p. 191. Kindle.

210 *flow of arms:* Author interview with Matthew Bryden, conducted by phone from Somaliland, 11 January 2014.

210 *many of them had fought:* "We fought some of these warlords in 1993 and now we are dealing with some of them again." Ted Dagne, the leading Africa analyst for the Congressional Research Service, as quoted by Wax and DeYoung, *Washington Post*, Id. at 47.

210 *"offered me money":* Scahill, Jeremy. "Blowback in Somalia." *Nation*, 7 September 2011, https://www.thenation.com/article/blowback-somalia.

211 *supposed Islamic terrorists:* Scahill, Jeremy. "Blowback in Somalia." *Nation*, 7 September 2011, https://www.thenation.com/article/blowback-somalia.

211 *capture-and-kill:* Wax, Emily and DeYoung, Karen. "U.S. Secretly Backing Warlords in Somalia." *Washington Post*, 17 May 2016, www.washingtonpost.com/wp-dyn/content/article/2006/05/16/AR2006051601625.html.

211 *"They are waiting":* Scahill, Jeremy. "Blowback in Somalia." *Nation*, 7 September 2011, https://www.thenation.com/article/blowback-somalia.

211 *"wondered aloud":* US diplomatic cable 06NAIROBI1484, from Ambassador William M. Bellamy, US Embassy Nairobi, "Ambassador to Yusuf: Alliance Against Terror Not Directed at TFG," 4 April 2006, released by WikiLeaks, http://wikileaks.org/cable/2006/04/06NAIROBI1484.html.

211 *"Just to be blunt":* Author interview with Jendayi Frazer, 12 January 2014.

212 *"high value targets":* US diplomatic cable 06NAIROBI2425 from Ambassador William Bellamy, US Embassy Nairobi, "Somalia: A Strategy for Engagement," June 2, 2006, released by WikiLeaks, http://wikileaks.org/ cable/ 2006/ 06/ 06NAIROBI2425. html.

212 *reassigned to Chad:* Graham, Bradley and DeYoung, Karen. "Official Critical of Somalia Policy is Transferred." *Washington Post*, 31 May 2006, www.washingtonpost.com/wp-dyn/content/article/2006/05/30/AR2006053001203.html.

213 *"no problem":* Author interview with Tekeda Alemu, 10 March 2017.

214 *was dispatched:* Oloya, Opiyo. *Black Hawks Rising: The Story of AMISOM's Successful War against Somali Insurgents, 2007–2014.* London: Helion, 2016, loc. 1175. Kindle.

214 *"IGAD deployment":* Oloya, Opiyo. *Black Hawks Rising: The Story of AMISOM's Successful War against Somali Insurgents, 2007–2014.* London: Helion, 2016, loc. 1175. Kindle.

214 *"tertiary sideshow":* Author interview with Colonel Richard Orth, 2 March 2017.

214 *"the agency was running":* Author interview with Colonel Richard Orth, 2 March 2017.

215 *"how superpowers behave":* Author interview with Tekeda Alemu, 10 March 2017.

215 *as a power grab:* Panapress. "U.S. Opposes Somalia Troops Deployment, Threatens Veto." *Panapress,* 17 March 2005, http://www.panapress.com/.

215 *brutal fighting:* Mazzetti, Mark. "U.S. Signals Backing for Ethiopian Incursion Into Somalia." *New York Times.* 27 December 2006.

216 *"totally uncontrollable":* Author interview with Tekeda Alemu, 10 March 2017.

216 *largest donor:* Staats, Sarah Jane. "What Next for U.S. Aid in Ethiopia." Center for Global Development, 27 August 2012, http://www.cgdev.org/blog/what-next-us-aid-ethiopia.

216 *most powerful in the region:* "Ethiopia has the most powerful military in the region, trained by American advisors and funded by American aid." Jeffrey Gettleman, "Ethiopian Warplanes Attack Somalia." *New York Times,* 25 December 2006, www.nytimes.com/2006/12/24/world/africa/24cnd-somalia.html.

216 *"Given the chaos":* Author interview with General Michael Hayden, in person at his offices in Washington, DC, 17 May 2017.

216 *"dismantling of the Islamic Union":* Author interview with Simiyu Werunga, conducted in Nairobi, 14 December 2013.

216 *in secret Ethiopian prisons:* Mitchell, Anthony. "U.S. Agents Visit Ethiopian Secret Jails." *Washington Post,* 3 April 2007, www.washingtonpost.com/wp-dyn/content/article/2007/04/03/AR2007040301042_pf.html.

217 *human rights abuses:* Gettleman, Jeffrey. "Ethiopian Warplanes Attack Somalia." *New York Times,* 25 December 2006, www.nytimes.com/2006/12/24/world/africa/24cnd-somalia.html.

217 *"Any Ethiopian action":* Memorandum from Azouz Ennifar, Deputy Special Representative for mission in Ethiopia and Eritrea, "Meeting with U.S. Assistant Secretary of State for African Affairs," 26 June 2006, released by WikiLeaks, http://wikileaks.org/wiki/US_encouraged_Ethiopian_invasion_of_Somalia:_UN_meeting_memo_with_Jenday_Frazer,_Secretary_of_State_for_African_Affairs,_2006.

217 *advisers and trainers:* Jelinek, Pauline. "U.S. Special Forces in Somalia." Associated Press, 10 January 2007, http://www.washingtonpost.com/wp-dyn/content/article/2007/01/10/AR2007011000438.html.

217 *own aircraft:* Vries, Lloyd. "U.S. Strikes in Somalia Reportedly Kill 31." CBS/AP, 8 January 2007, http://www.cbsnews.com/news/us-strikes-in-somalia-reportedly-kill-31/.

217 *"and we'll provide":* Author interview with senior defense official, 2 March 2017.

217 *"The Somalia job was fantastic":* Classified memorandum, January 7, 2007, released by WikiLeaks, http://wikileaks.org/cable/2007/01/07ABUDHABI145.html.

217 **Protests against the newly installed Ethiopian forces:** Scahill, Jeremy. *Dirty Wars: The World Is a Battlefield.* New York: Nation Books, 2013, p. 208. Kindle.

218 **"a legitimate jihad":** Author interview with Matthew Bryden, 11 January 2014.

218 **"invasion was quite helpful":** Author interview with Jendayi Frazer, 12 January 2014.

218 **tended to be hard-liners:** Author interview with Matthew Bryden, 11 January 2014.

218 **"defile" Somalia:** Remarks by Ahmed Iman Ali, available at http://www.metacafe.com/watch/7950113/al_kataib_media_lecture_by_ahmad_iman_ali_h.

218 **fortified its support:** "Al Qaeda saw Somalia as an ideal front line for jihad and began increasing its support for al Shabaab." Scahill, Jeremy. *Dirty Wars: The World Is a Battlefield.* New York: Nation Books, 2013, p. 223. Kindle.

218 **Recruitment rates:** "Ironically, the rise of Al-Shabaab was aided by the policy mistakes of the international community. Perhaps the best known factor was the Ethiopian occupation, which created a fertile environment for recruitment." Hansen, Stig Jarle. *Al Shabaab in Somalia: The History and Ideology of a Militant Islamist Group, 2005–2012.* Oxford: Oxford University Press, 2013, p. 49. Kindle.

218 **"period of greatest growth":** Author interview with Matthew Bryden, 11 January 2014.

218 **terrorist organization:** Office of the Coordinator for Counterterrorism, Designation of al-Shabaab as a Foreign Terrorist Organization, 26 February 2008, http://www.state.gov/j/ct/rls/other/des/102446.htm.

218 **global jihad:** "Al Qaeda's Morale Boost As It Formally Joins With Somalia's Al Shabaab," *Telegraph* (UK), 10 February 2012, http://www.telegraph.co.uk/news/worldnews/al-qaeda/9074047/Al-Qaedas-morale-boost-as-it-formally-joins-with-Somalias-al-Shabaab.html.

219 **"created the space":** Author interview with Jendayi Frazer, 12 January 2014.

219 **recalled Frazer:** Third parties have also reported that Ethiopia's presence in AMISOM was excluded "in the hope of preventing anti-Ethiopian nationalistic recruitment to Al-Shabaab." Hansen, Stig Jarle. *Al Shabaab in Somalia: The History and Ideology of a Militant Islamist Group, 2005–2012.* Oxford: Oxford University Press, 2013, p. 117. Kindle.

219 **dispatched Marines:** Edwards, Jocelyn. "U.S. Steps Up Training for African Force in Somalia." *Chicago Tribune,* 1 May 2012, http://articles.chicagotribune.com/2012-05-01/news/sns-rt-us-somalia-uganda-usabre84011e-20120501_1_shabaab-somalia-siad-barre.

219 **private contractors:** "Several private military corporations, most notably Bancroft, were involved in the build up and had advisers in the front line." Hansen, Stig Jarle. *Al Shabaab in Somalia: The History and Ideology of a Militant Islamist Group, 2005–2012.* Oxford: Oxford University Press, 2013, p. 118. Kindle.

219 **number of children:** Nichols, Michelle. "Somalia Cases of Killing, Maiming, Abuse of Children Halved: UN," Reuters, 3 June 2013, http://www.reuters.com/article/2013/06/03/us-somalia-un-idUSBRE95216420130603.

219   *al-Shabaab's hands:* Axe, David. "U.S. Weapons Now in Somali Terrorists' Hands." *Wired*, 2 August 2011, https://www.wired.com/2011/08/u-s-weapons-now-in-somali-terrorists-hands.

219   *"Its capabilities and tactics have become more sophisticated":* Author interview with Matthew Bryden, conducted by phone from Somaliland, 11 January 2014.

220   *more than twenty:* Roggio, Bill and Weiss, Caleb. "Al-Shabaab Releases Video Showing Deadly Raid on Somali Military Base." *Business Insider*, 13 November 2017, www.businessinsider.com/al-shabaab-attack-somali-military-base-video-2017-11?IR=T.

220   *fresh spate of air strikes:* "U.S. Mounts Air Strike Against al Shabaab Militants in Somalia." Reuters, 15 November 2017, https://www.reuters.com/article/us-usa-somalia/u-s-mounts-air-strike-against-al-shabaab-militants-in-somalia-idUSKBN1DF1ZK.

220   *"Do they have the aspiration":* Author interview with Anders Folk, 25 November 2013.

221   *"looked so skinny":* Author interview with Sally and Micheal Evans, 6 October 2016, in person at their home in Wooburn Green, England.

221   *" 'I love you, Mom' ":* Author interview with Sally and Micheal Evans, 6 October 2016, in person at their home in Wooburn Green, England.

221   *"It never goes away":* Author interview with Sally and Micheal Evans, 6 October 2016, in person at their home in Wooburn Green, England.

20: THE SHORTEST SPRING

223   *been warned:* "Egypt Police to Break up Sit-in Protests within 24 Hours." Associated Press, 11 August 2013, http://www.cbc.ca/news/world/egypt-police-to-break-up-sit-in-protests-within-24-hours-1.1372985.

223   *"tried to scream":* Interview with Teo Butturini, 17 January 2014.

223   *stashed in a boot:* Author interview with Teo Butturini, 18 January 2015.

223   *taking surviving protesters into custody:* Interview with Teo Butturini, 17 January 2014.

223   *Egypt's "Tiananmen Square":* The comparison has been employed by several commentators, including Amy Austin Holmes, assistant professor of sociology at the American University in Cairo who specializes in military and social mobilization issues in Egypt. See Holmes, "Why Egypt's Military Orchestrated A Massacre." *Washington Post*, 22 August 2014, http://www.washingtonpost.com/blogs/monkey-cage/wp/2014/08/22/why-egypts-military-orchestrated-a-massacre/.

223   *"excessive lethal force":* "All According to Plan: The Rab'a Massacre and Mass Killings of Protesters in Egypt." Human Rights Watch, August 2014, http://www.hrw.org/sites/default/files/reports/egypt0814web.pdf.

224   *to block exits:* "The Weeks of Killing, State Violence, Communal Fighting, and Sectarian Attacks in the Summer of 2013." Egyptian Initiative for Personal Rights, June 2014, eipr.org/sites/default/files/reports/pdf/weeks_of_killing_en.pdf.

224   *"had been our concern":* Author interview with Ambassador Anne Patterson, 12 May 2016.

224   *"intoxicated by power"*: Khalifa, Sherif. *Egypt's Lost Spring: Causes and Consequences.* Santa Barbara, CA: Praeger, 2015.

224   *"We talked"*: Author interview with Ambassador Anne Patterson, 12 May 2016.

225   *"made a difference"*: Author interview with John Kerry, 21 November 2017.

225   *"we'd said everything"*: Author interview with Ambassador Anne Patterson, 12 May 2016.

225   *"any pressure"*: Author interview with Hazem Beblawi, IMF offices, Washington, DC, 30 June 2017.

226   *"I have no regrets"*: Author interview with Hazem Beblawi, IMF offices, Washington, DC, 30 June 2017.

226   *"a cabinet decision"*: Author interview with Nabil Fahmy in New York City, 7 April 2017.

227   *"Transitions can be derailed"*: "In Tunisia, Clinton Cites Promise of Arab Spring." *CBS News,* 24 September 2012, https://www.cbsnews.com/news/in-tunisia-clinton-cites-promise-of-arab-spring/.

228   **Soviet sponsorship:** Williams, Carol. "Amid U.S.-Egypt Chill, el-Sisi Seeks Military Assistance from Russia." *Los Angeles Times,* 13 February 2014, http://articles.latimes.com/2014/feb/13/world/la-fg-wn-russia-egypt-sisi-putin-20140213.

228   **constant conflict:** Moaz, Zeev. *Defending the Holy Land: A Critical Analysis of Israel's Security & Foreign Policy.* Ann Arbor: University of Michigan Press, 2009.

228   **with Israel:** Aloni, Shlomo. *Arab-Israeli Air Wars 1947–1982.* Oxford: Osprey, 2001.

228   **over land:** Oren, Michael. Speech to the Washington Institute, 2 July 2002, http://www.washingtoninstitute.org/policy-analysis/view/the-six-day-war-and-its-enduring-legacy.

228   **reclaim the Sinai:** Pace, Eric. "Anwar el-Sadat, the Daring Arab Pioneer of Peace with Israel." *New York Times,* 7 October 1981, http://www.nytimes.com/learning/general/onthisday/bday/1225.html.

228   **continued into the 1970s:** Mørk, Hulda Kjeang. "The Jarring Mission" (master's thesis, University of Oslo), http://www.duo.uio.no/publ/IAKH/2007/58588/HuldaxMxrkxxMasteropgavexixhistorie.pdf.

228   **peace was the way:** Pace, Eric. "Anwar el-Sadat, the Daring Arab Pioneer of Peace with Israel. *New York Times,* 7 October 1981, http://www.nytimes.com/learning/general/onthisday/bday/1225.html.

228   **president Jimmy Carter:** "Walter Mondale, his Vice President, was surprised by the fact that on Carter's first day in office he announced that peace in the Middle East was a top priority. That seemed wildly naïve. . . . Carter's closest advisors told him that he should wait until his second term to risk any of his fragile political capital." Wright, Lawrence. *Thirteen Days in September: Carter, Begin, and Sadat at Camp David.* New York: Knopf, 2004, p. 6.

228   **Egypt and Israel at Camp David:** President Carter Speech on 25th Anniversary of Accords. Washington, DC, 16 September, 2003, https://www.cartercenter.org/news/documents/doc1482.html.

229   **would commit to:** Interview with Laurence Wright. "'13 Days In September' Examines 1978 Camp David Accords." NPR, 16 September 2014, https://

www.npr.org/2014/09/16/348903279/-13-days-in-september-examines-1978-camp-david-conference.

229 **bankrolling Egypt:** Sharp, Jeremy M. "Egypt: Background and U.S. Relations." Congressional Research Service, 5 June 2014, www.fas.org/sgp/crs/mideast/RL33003.pdf.

229 **at $1.3 billion:** Sharp, Jeremy M. "Egypt: Background and U.S. Relations." Congressional Research Service, 5 June 2014, www.fas.org/sgp/crs/mideast/RL33003.pdf.

229 **military aid:** Sharp, Jeremy M. "Egypt: Background and U.S. Relations." Congressional Research Service, 5 June 2014, www.fas.org/sgp/crs/mideast/RL33003.pdf.

229 **80 percent of Egypt's weapons:** Plumer, Brad. "The U.S. Gives Egypt $1.5 Billion a Year in Aid. Here's What it Does." *Washington Post*, 9 July 2013, http://www.washingtonpost.com/blogs/wonkblog/wp/2013/07/09/the-u-s-gives-egypt-1-5-billion-a-year-in-aid-heres-what-it-does/.

229 **13,500 times:** Thompson, Mark. "U.S. Military Aid to Egypt: An IV Drip, With Side-Effects." *Time*, 19 August 2016, www.swampland.time.com/2013/08/19/u-s-military-aid-to-egypt-an-iv-drip-with-side-effects/.

229 **Revolution was spreading:** "The January 25 Revolution." In *Arab Spring: A Research and Study Guide*, Cornell University Library, 2010, guides.library.cornell.edu/c.php?g=31688&p=200748%20%20Id.

229 **from mass unemployment:** "The January 25 Revolution." In *Arab Spring: A Research and Study Guide*, Cornell University Library, 2010, guides.library.cornell.edu/c.php?g=31688&p=200748%20%20Id.

230 **proclaimed the regime "stable":** "Our assessment is that the Egyptian government is stable and is looking for ways to respond to the legitimate needs and interests of the Egyptian people." The following day she encouraged "all parties to exercise restraint and refrain from violence"; "Clinton Calls for Calm, Restraint in Egypt." *CBS News*, 26 January 2011, https://www.cbsnews.com/news/clinton-calls-for-calm-restraint-in-egypt/.

230 **"must stay in office":** Fahim, Kareem, Landler, Mark and Shadid, Anthony. "West Backs Gradual Egyptian Transition." *New York Times*, 5 February 2011, www.nytimes.com/2011/02/06/world/middleeast/06egypt.html?pagewanted=all&_r=0.

230 **to step down:** Fahim, Kareem, Landler, Mark and Shadid, Anthony. "West Backs Gradual Egyptian Transition." *New York Times*, 5 February 2011, www.nytimes.com/2011/02/06/world/middleeast/06egypt.html?pagewanted=all&_r=0.

230 **little effect:** "The January 25 Revolution." In *Arab Spring: A Research and Study Guide*, Cornell University Library, 2010, guides.library.cornell.edu/c.php?g=31688&p=200748%20%20Id.

230 **first free elections:** Childress, Sarah. "The Deep State: How Egypt's Shadow State Won Out." *Frontline*, 17 September 2013, http://www.pbs.org/wgbh/pages/frontline/foreign-affairs-defense/egypt-in-crisis/the-deep-state-how-egypts-shadow-state-won-out/.

230 **Sam LaHood:** Monteforte, Filippo. "Egypt Cracks Down on NGOs." *Newsweek*, 6 February 2012, www.newsweek.com/egypt-cracks-down-ngos-65823.

230 **"really, really disruptive":** Interview with Ambassador Anne Patterson, 12 May 2016.

230 **securing the presidency:** Carlstom. Greg. "Meet the Candidates: Morsi vs Shafiq." Al-Jazeera, 24 June 2012, www.aljazeera.com/indepth/spotlight/egypt/2012/06 /201261482158653237.html.

231 **"bloodsuckers":** "Morsi Called Israelis 'Descendants of Apes and Pigs.'" *Haaretz*, 4 January 2013, https://www.haaretz.com/israel-news/morsi-called-israelis-descend ants-of-apes-and-pigs-in-2010-video-1.491979.

231 **harsh social policies:** Black, Ian. "Egypt's Muslim Brotherhood Poised to Prosper in Post-Mubarak New Era." *Guardian* (Manchester), https://www.theguardian.com/ world/2011/may/19/muslim-brotherhood-poised-prosper-egypt.

231 **faced street protests:** Black, Ian. "Egypt's Muslim Brotherhood Poised to Prosper in Post-Mubarak New Era." *Guardian* (Manchester), https://www.theguardian.com/ world/2011/may/19/muslim-brotherhood-poised-prosper-egypt.

231 **"a lot more brutal":** Interview with Ambassador Anne Patterson, 12 May 2016.

231 **at least 2,500 civilians:** Hamid, Shadi. "Rethinking the U.S.-Egypt Relationship: How Repression is Undermining Egyptian Stability and What the United States Can Do." Brookings, 3 November 2015, https://www.brookings.edu/testimonies/ rethinking-the-u-s-egypt-relationship-how-repression-is-undermining-egyptian-stability-and-what-the-united-states-can-do/.

231 **Egyptians were "disappeared":** Hamid, Shadi. "Rethinking the U.S.-Egypt Relation-ship: How Repression is Undermining Egyptian Stability and What the United States Can Do." Brookings, 3 November 2015, https://www.brookings.edu/testimonies/ rethinking-the-u-s-egypt-relationship-how-repression-is-undermining-egyptian-stability-and-what-the-united-states-can-do/.

231 **"scale unprecedented":** Hamid, Shadi. "Rethinking the U.S.-Egypt Relationship: How Repression is Undermining Egyptian Stability and What the United States Can Do." Brookings, 3 November 2015, https://www.brookings.edu/testimonies/ rethinking-the-u-s-egypt-relationship-how-repression-is-undermining-egyptian-stability-and-what-the-united-states-can-do/.

232 **were threatened:** Hamid, Shadi. "Rethinking the U.S.-Egypt Relationship: How Repression is Undermining Egyptian Stability and What the United States Can Do." Brookings, 3 November 2015, https://www.brookings.edu/testimonies/ rethinking-the-u-s-egypt-relationship-how-repression-is-undermining-egyptian-stability-and-what-the-united-states-can-do/.

232 **already died:** Hamid, Shadi. "Rethinking the U.S.-Egypt Relationship: How Repression is Undermining Egyptian Stability and What the United States Can Do." Brookings, 3 November 2015, https://www.brookings.edu/testimonies/ rethinking-the-u-s-egypt-relationship-how-repression-is-undermining-egyptian-stability-and-what-the-united-states-can-do/.

232 **"outside of a war zone":** Author interview with Frank Lowenstein, 5 August 2016.

232   *"recipe for radicalizing":* Author phone interview with Tony Blinken, 12 May 2016.

232   *"coup clause":* Office of Senator Patrick Leahy, Provisions Relevant to the Situation in Egypt in the FY12 State Department and Foreign Operations Appropriations Law, 3 July 2013, http://www.leahy.senate.gov/press/provisions-relevant-to-the-situation-in-egypt-in-the-fy12-state-department-and-foreign-operations-appropriations-law_.

232   *"duly elected":* Hughes, Dana and Hunter, Molly. "President Morsi Ousted: First Democratically Elected Leader Under House Arrest." *ABC News*, 3 July 2013, http://abcnews.go.com/International/president-morsi-ousted-democratically-elected-leader-house-arrest/story?id=19568447.

233   *"difficult contortions":* Hudson, John. "Obama Administration Won't Call Egypt's Coup a Coup." *Foreign Policy*, 8 July 2013, foreignpolicy.com/2013/07/08/obama-administration-wont-call-egypts-coup-a-coup.

233   *not be called a coup:* Ackerman, Spencer and Black, Ian. "U.S. Trims Aid to Egypt as Part of Diplomatic 'Recalibration.'" *Guardian* (Manchester), 9 October 2013, http://www.theguardian.com/world/2013/oct/09/obama-cuts-military-aid-egypt.

233   *resumed deliveries:* Broder, Jonathan. "The Winter of Egypt's Dissent." *Newsweek*, 6 January 2015, http://www.newsweek.com/2015/01/16/winter-egypts-dissent-296918.html.

233   *escalating crackdowns:* After what were widely reported to be sham trials, they were sentenced to seven years in prison each. One, an Egyptian-Canadian reporter named Mohammed Fahmy, was sentenced to an additional three years for picking up a spent bullet casing after a protest.

233   *temporarily froze:* Gordon, Michel R, and Landler, Mark. "In Crackdown Response, U.S. Temporarily Freezes Some Military Aid to Egypt." *New York Times*, 9 October 2013, available at: http://www.nytimes.com/2013/10/10/world/middleeast/obama-military-aid-to-egypt.html?pagewanted=all&_r=0.

233   *"Sinai stuff":* Interview with Ambassador Anne Patterson, 12 May 2016.

233   *"already committed":* Author interview with Sarah Leah Whitson, 17 March 2017.

234   *"cash flow financing":* Interview with Ambassador Anne Patterson, 12 May 2016.

234   *2016 audit:* Asher-Schapiro, Avi. "The U.S. Isn't Making Sure Its Military Aid to Egypt Stays Out of the Wrong Hands." *Vice News*, 17 May 2016, https://news.vice.com/article/the-us-isnt-making-sure-its-military-aid-to-egypt-stays-out-of-the-wrong-hands.

234   *billions of dollars:* Author interview with Congressman Adam Schiff, 20 January 2015.

234   *Saudi Arabia:* "Egypt Signs $350 mln in Oil, Power Financing Deals with Saudi." Reuters, 1 November 2014, https://www.reuters.com/article/idUSL5N0SR0H520141101.

234   *growing assistance packages:* "Russia, Egypt Seal Preliminary Arms Deal Worth $3.5 Billion: Agency." Reuters, 17 September 2014, http://www.reuters.com/article/2014/09/17/us-russia-egypt-arms-idUSKBN0HC19T20140917.

234   *"We certainly have influence":* Author interview with John Kerry, 21 November 2017.

235   *"the ultimate leverage":* Author interview with Frank Lowenstein, 5 August 2016.

235   *"'ruthless' is a good word":* Author interview with General Michael Hayden, in person at his offices in Washington, DC, 17 May 2017.

235   *"looked largely the same":* Author interview with Samantha Power, 10 July 2017.

236   *"money to Tunisia":* Author interview with Samantha Power, 10 July 2017.

236   *"two presidents talking":* Author interview with Nabil Fahmy in New York City, 7 April 2017.

236   *"they're shooting at us":* Author interview with Teo Butturini, 17 January 2014.

21: MIDNIGHT AT THE RANCH

240   *"They don't help anyone":* Author interview with Freddy Torres, 4 November 2016.

240   *Eventually, his suspicions bore out:* "IIR: Cashiered Colonel Talks Freely About the Army He Left Behind (Laser Strike)." Information Report, 178798311. Department of Defense to Director of Intelligence, Washington, DC, nsarchive2. gwu.edu//NSAEBB/NSAEBB266/19971224.pdf.

241   *more than 3,000:* "On Their Watch: Evidence of Senior Army Officers' Responsibility for False Positive Killings in Colombia." Human Rights Watch, 24 June 2015, https://www.hrw.org/report/2015/06/24/their-watch/evidence-senior-army-officers-responsibility-false-positive-killings.

241   *Directive #29:* "False Positives." *Colombia Reports*, 14 March 2017, https://colombiareports.com/false-positives/.

241   *"no evidence to suggest":* Statement by Professor Philip Alston, UN Special Rapporteur on Extrajudicial Executions Mission to Colombia 8-18 June 2009." United Nations Office of the High Commissioner on Human Rights, 18 June 2009, http://newsarchive.ohchr.org/EN/NewsEvents/Pages/DisplayNews.aspx?NewsID=9219&LangID=E.

241   *Researchers found:* "False Positives." *Colombia Reports*, 14 March 2017, https://colombiareports.com/false-positives/.

242   *Western Hemisphere Institute for Security Cooperation:* "The Rise and Fall of 'False Positive' Killings in Colombia: The Role of U.S. Military Assistance, 2000–2010." Fellowship of Reconciliation and Colombia-Europe-US Human Rights Observatory, May 2014, http://archives.forusa.org/sites/default/files/uploads/false-positives-2014-colombia-report.pdf.

242   *Jaime Lasprilla:* "The Rise and Fall of 'False Positive' Killings in Colombia: The Role of U.S. Military Assistance, 2000–2010." Fellowship of Reconciliation and Colombia-Europe-US Human Rights Observatory, May 2014, http://archives.forusa.org/sites/default/files/uploads/false-positives-2014-colombia-report.pdf.

242   *"aggressive anti-guerrilla activity":* "Unclassified Cable 200202961," from

American Embassy Bogota to Secretary of State, Washington, DC, http://nsarchive2.gwu.edu//NSAEBB/NSAEBB266/19941021.pdf.

242 *"history of assassinating":* "Colombian Counterinsurgency: Steps in the Right Direction." Central Intelligence Agency. Directorate of Intelligence Memorandum, Office of African and Latin American Analysis, 26 January 1994, nsarchive2.gwu.edu//NSAEBB/NSAEBB266/19940126.pdf.

242 *"the guerrilla body count":* "IIR: Cashiered Colonel Talks Freely About the Army He Left Behind (Laser Strike)." Information Report, 178798311. Department of Defense to Director of Intelligence, Washington, DC, nsarchive2.gwu.edu//NSAEBB/NSAEBB266/19971224.pdf.

243 *"the first stage of Plan Colombia":* Author interview with Andres Pastrana, 29 September 2016.

244 *"great deal" of concern:* "In U.S., 65% Say Drug Problem 'Extremely' or 'Very Serious,'" Gallup Polls, 28 October 2016, news.gallup.com/poll/196826/say-drug-problem-extremely-serious.aspx?g_source=position1&g_medium=related&g_campaign=tiles.

244 *"directly threaten":* Clinton, Bill. "Remarks at the Council of the Americas 30th Washington Conference." 2 May 2000, www.presidency.ucsb.edu/ws/?pid=58427.

244 *"two struggles that have become one":* Author interview with Ambassador Anne Patterson, 23 June 2016.

244 *human rights provisions:* "Clinton Waives Rights Standards." *CBS News*, 22 August 2000, https://www.cbsnews.com/news/clinton-waives-rights-standards/.

244 *set aside $1.3 billion:* Shifter, Michael. "Plan Colombia: A Retrospective." *Americas Quarterly*, Summer 2012, www.americasquarterly.org/node/3787.

245 *"you give them stones":* Dan Gardner, "Losing the Drug War," *Ottawa Citizen*,6 September, cited in Villar, Olivier and Cottel, Drew. *Cocaine, Death Squads,and the War on Terror: U.S. Imperialism and Class Struggle in Colombia*. New York:Monthly Review Press, 2011.

245 *"counter-propaganda functions":* US Army Special Warfare School, "Subject: Visit to Colombia, February 26, 1962." Declassified Documents Reference Series (Arlington, VA: Carrollton Press, 1976), cited in Villar, Olivier and Cottel, Drew. *Cocaine, Death Squads, and the War on Terror: U.S. Imperialism and Class Struggle in Colombia*. New York: Monthly Review Press, 2011.

245 *"hearts and mind" strategy:* "The History of the Military-Paramilitary Partnership." Human Rights Watch, 1996, https://www.hrw.org/reports/1996/killer2.htm.

246 *organize ordinary citizens:* Dyer, Chelsey. "50 Years of U.S. Intervention in Colombia." *Colombia Reports*, 4 October 2013, https://colombiareports.com/50-years-us-intervention-colombia/.

246 *"self-defense units":* 1963 Field Manual on US Army Counterinsurgency Forces (FM 31-22), 82-84, cited in Villar, Olivier and Cottel, Drew. *Cocaine, Death Squads, and the War on Terror: U.S. Imperialism and Class Struggle in Colombia*. New York: Monthly Review Press, 2011.

246 *courses like:* Michael McClintock, "Instruments of Statecraft: U.S. Guerrilla Warfare, Counterinsurgency, and Counterterrorism," 1992, cited in Villar, Oliv-

ier and Cottel, Drew. *Cocaine, Death Squads, and the War on Terror: U.S. Imperialism and Class Struggle in Colombia.* New York: Monthly Review Press, 2011.

246 **admitted to the moral contradiction:** Villar, Olivier and Cottel, Drew. *Cocaine, Death Squads, and the War on Terror: U.S. Imperialism and Class Struggle in Colombia.* New York: Monthly Review Press, 2011.

247 **"blood and capital accumulation":** Villar, Olivier and Cottel, Drew. *Cocaine, Death Squads, and the War on Terror: U.S. Imperialism and Class Struggle in Colombia.* New York: Monthly Review Press, 2011.

247 **Reagan's first term:** Villar, Olivier and Cottel, Drew. *Cocaine, Death Squads, and the War on Terror: U.S. Imperialism and Class Struggle in Colombia.* New York: Monthly Review Press, 2011.

248 **FARC's numbers:** Molano, Alfredo. "The Evolution of the FARC: A Guerrilla Group's Long History." NACLA, https://nacla.org/article/evolution-farc-guerrilla-groups-long-history.

248 **paramilitaries were everywhere:** "United Self-Defense Forces of Colombia." Stanford University, 28 August 2015, web.stanford.edu/group/mappingmilitants/cgi-bin/groups/view/85.

248 **they were brutal:** "United Self-Defense Forces of Colombia." Stanford University, 28 August 2015, web.stanford.edu/group/mappingmilitants/cgi-bin/groups/view/85.

248 **"narco-guerrillas":** Villar, Olivier and Cottel, Drew. *Cocaine, Death Squads, and the War on Terror: U.S. Imperialism and Class Struggle in Colombia.* New York: Monthly Review Press, 2011.

248 **as informants:** Smyth, Frank. "Still Seeing Red: The C.I.A. Fosters Death Squads in Colombia." *Progressive,* 3 June 1998, www.franksmyth.com/the-progressive/still-seeing-red-the-cia-fosters-death-squads-in-colombia/.

249 **The homicide rate:** Shifter, Michael. "Plan Colombia: A Retrospective." *Americas Quarterly,* Summer 2012, www.americasquarterly.org/node/3787.

249 **netting millions:** Marcella, Gabriel et al. "Plan Colombia: Some Differing Perspectives." June 2001, www.dtic.mil/dtic/tr/fulltext/u2/a392198.pdf.

249 **did not dare enter:** Shifter, Michael. "Plan Colombia: A Retrospective." *Americas Quarterly,* Summer 2012, www.americasquarterly.org/node/3787.

249 **More than 700,000 Colombians:** Shifter, Michael. "Plan Colombia: A Retrospective." *Americas Quarterly,* Summer 2012, www.americasquarterly.org/node/3787.

249 **cutting their victims apart:** Wilkinson, Daniel. "Death and Drugs in Colombia." Human Rights Watch, 2 June 2011, published in *New York Review of Books,* https://www.hrw.org/news/2011/06/02/death-and-drugs-colombia.

249 **"vile situation":** Author interview with General Barry McCaffrey, 22 June 2016.

249 **nationwide protest:** "Revolutionary Armed Forces of Colombia—People's Army." Stanford University, 15 August 2015, web.stanford.edu/group/mappingmilitants/cgi-bin/groups/view/89.

250 **"try and achieve peace":** Author interview with President Andres Pastrana and Chief of Staff Jaime Ruiz, 29 September 2016.

250 **political assassinations targeting leftists:** Villar, Olivier and Cottel, Drew. *Cocaine,*

Death Squads, and the War on Terror: U.S. Imperialism and Class Struggle in Colombia. New York: Monthly Review Press, 2011.

250 **US-made smart bombs:** Priest, Dana, "Covert Action in Colombia." *Washington Post,* 21 December 2013, www.washingtonpost.com/sf/investigative/2013/12/21/covert-action-in-colombia/?utm_term=.3c65ec066eb6.

250 **"secret state terror":** "Colombia: San Vicente del Caguan After the Breakdown of the Peace Talks" and Villar, Olivier and Cottel, Drew. *Cocaine, Death Squads, and the War on Terror: U.S. Imperialism and Class Struggle in Colombia.* New York: Monthly Review Press, 2011.

251 **"incarcerated" on farms:** Wilkinson, Daniel. "Death and Drugs in Colombia." Human Rights Watch, 2 June 2011, published in *New York Review of Books,* https://www.hrw.org/news/2011/06/02/death-and-drugs-colombia.

252 **"such poppycock":** Author interview with General Barry McCaffrey, 22 June 2016.

252 **Killings were cut nearly in half:** Shifter, Michael. "Plan Colombia: A Retrospective." *Americas Quarterly,* Summer 2012, www.americasquarterly.org/node/3787.

252 **launched peace talks:** "Colombia." Freedom House, 2007, https://freedomhouse.org/report/freedom-world/2007/colombia.

252 **"We tried to get Congress to do a Free Trade Agreement with Colombia":** Author interview with Condoleezza Rice, 3 August 2017.

253 **"the most successful policy intervention":** Author interview with General Barry McCaffrey, 22 June 2016.

PART III: PRESENT AT THE DESTRUCTION

22: THE STATE OF THE SECRETARY

258 **scenes of the American West:** Sanger, David, Harris, Gardiner, Landler, Mark. "Where Trump Zigs, Tillerson Zags, Putting Him at Odds with White House." *New York Times,* 25 June 2017, https://www.nytimes.com/2017/06/25/world/americas/rex-tillerson-american-diplomacy.html?_r=1.

259 **Rex Allen and John Wayne:** Filkins, Dexter. "Rex Tillerson at the Breaking Point." *New Yorker,* 16 October 2017, https://www.newyorker.com/magazine/2017/10/16/rex-tillerson-at-the-breaking-point.

259 **"drove a truck selling bread":** Filkins, Dexter. "Rex Tillerson at the Breaking Point." *New Yorker,* 16 October 2017, https://www.newyorker.com/magazine/2017/10/16/rex-tillerson-at-the-breaking-point.

259 **met through the Boy Scouts:** Osborne, James. "Exxon Mobil CEO Rex Tillerson Is an Eagle Scout to the Core." *Dallas Morning News,* 6 September 2014.

259 **a personal fortune:** Filkins, Dexter. "Rex Tillerson at the Breaking Point." *New Yorker,* 16 October 2017, https://www.newyorker.com/magazine/2017/10/16/rex-tillerson-at-the-breaking-point.

259 **"I didn't want this job":** McPike, Erin. "Trump's Diplomat." *Independent Journal Review,* 21 March 2017, https://ijr.com/2017/03/814687-trumps-diplomat/.

259 **"interesting":** Author interview with Rex Tillerson, 4 January 2018.

260 **"I'm the new guy":** "Welcome Remarks to Employees." Secretary of State Rex Tillerson, Washington, DC, 2 February 2017, https://www.state.gov/secretary/remarks/2017/02/267401.htm.

260 **"The buzz was okay":** Author interview with Erin Clancy in Los Angeles, 1 June 2017.

260 **"What a different choice":** Author interview with source close to the White House, 23 January 2018.

260 **"You have to take the press on the plane":** Author interview with associate of Condoleezza Rice, 23 January 2018. See also Stelter, Brian. "Journalists outraged by Tillerson's plan to travel without press." *CNN*, 10 March 2017, http://money.cnn.com/2017/03/10/media/rex-tillerson-state-department-no-press/index.html.

260 **"I can't assess what's going on inside":** Author interview with Condoleezza Rice, 3 August 2017.

260 **"I don't play the game outside the house":** Author interview with Rex Tillerson, 4 January 2018.

261 **"the Washington Post's claim":** Gearan, Anne, and Morello, Carol. "Secretary of State Rex Tillerson spends his first weeks isolated from an anxious bureaucracy." *Washington Post*, 30 March 2017, https://www.washingtonpost.com/world/national-security/secretary-of-state-rex-tillerson-spends-his-first-weeks-isolated-from-an-anxious-bureaucracy/2017/03/30/bdf8ec86-155f-11e7-ada0-1489b735b3a3_story.html?utm_term=.0ea61ef83e7d.

261 **enforced such a rule:** Author interview with member of Secretary Tillerson's security detail, 20 July 2017.

261 **"bottleneck":** Johnson, Eliana and Crowley, Michael. "The Bottleneck in Rex Tillerson's State Department." *Politico*, 4 June 2017, www.politico.com/story/2017/06/04/rex-tillerson-state-department-bottleneck-239107.

261 **" 'I can read a map' ":** Author interview with anonymous Foreign Service officer, 25 June 2017.

261 **three rows of the auditorium:** "Welcome Remarks to Employees." Secretary of State Rex Tillerson, Washington, DC, 2 February 2017, https://www.state.gov/secretary/remarks/2017/02/267401.htm; "Remarks to U.S. Department of State Employees." Secretary of State Rex Tillerson, Dean Acheson Auditorium, Washington, DC, 3 May 2017, https://www.state.gov/secretary/remarks/2017/05/270620.htm; anecdote about audience reaction from author interview with Foreign Service officer, 26 June 2017.

261 **"The fact is that Mr. Tillerson is not witting":** Author interview with Colin Powell in Washington, DC, 29 June 2017.

262 **"a lot of internal navel-gazing":** Author interview with anonymous Foreign Service officer, 28 July 2017.

262 **declined to take more than three a day:** Author interview with anonymous Foreign Service officer, 28 July 2017.

262 **"We just bombed Syria":** Author interview with anonymous Foreign Service officer, 28 July 2017.

263   *"two-page limit":* Author interview with anonymous career Foreign Service officer, 25 June 2017.

263   *"Forty years at Exxon, in the God Pod":* Author interview with source close to the White House, 23 January 2018.

263   *rumors of his demise were relentless:* Parker, Ashley et al., "White House readies plan to replace Tillerson with Pompeo at State, install Cotton at CIA." *Washington Post*, 30 November 2017, https://www.washingtonpost.com/news/post-politics/wp/2017/11/30/white-house-readies-plan-to-replace-tillerson-with-pompeo-install-cotton-at-cia/?utm_term=.5f455d49d416.

264   *virtually the same time:* Schwirtz, Michael. "US Accuses Syria of New Chemical Weapons Use." *New York Times*, 23 January 2018, https://www.nytimes.com/2018/01/23/world/middleeast/syria-chemical-weapons-ghouta.html.

264   *publicly undermining them:* Author interview with Tillerson aide, 24 January 2017.

264   *"I've never seen anything like the way he's treated her":* Author interview with source close to the White House, 23 January 2018.

264   *"a very caring, decent, principled person":* Author interview with Steven Goldstein, 24 January 2018.

264   *"The only person that I have to worry about":* Author interview with Rex Tillerson, 4 January 2018.

265   *"You just can't be an arrogant alpha male":* Author interview with source close to the White House, 23 January 2018.

265   *"we did not know each other at all":* Author interview with Rex Tillerson, 4 January 2018.

266   *reinstating some of the humanitarian funds:* Rogin, Josh. "Tillerson prevails over Haley on Palestinian funding." *Post and Courier*, 16 January 2018, https://www.postandcourier.com/opinion/commentary/tillerson-prevails-over-haley-on-palestinian-funding/article_2b1b2972-fafd-11e7-81e6-7f2974b7274f.html.

266   *"it wasn't just Jared":* Author interview with source close to the White House, 23 January 2018.

266   *"have a pointed conversation":* Author interview with Tillerson aide, 22 December 2017.

266   *"It's not a point of frustration":* Author interview with Rex Tillerson, 4 January 2018.

267   *"ours is built around new approaches":* Author interview with Brian Hook, 13 December 2017.

267   *Kushner, according to White House sources:* Labott, Elise and Borger, Gloria. "Kushner's foreign policy gamble fuels Tillerson feud." CNN, 4 December 2017, http://www.cnn.com/2017/12/04/politics/jared-kushner-rex-tillerson-middle-east/index.html.

267   *Powell recalled similar turf wars:* Author interview with Colin Powell in Washington, DC, 29 June 2017.

268   *"He may love it":* Author interview with Colin Powell in Washington, DC, 29 August 2017.

268   *"our new Secretary of State":* Tweet by Donald J. Trump, 13 March 2018, 5:44AM.

268   ***"did not speak to the president":*** Parker, Ashley, Rucker, Philip, et al., "Trump ousts Tillerson, will replace him as secretary of state with CIA chief Pompeo." *Washington Post*, 13 March 2018, https://www.washingtonpost.com/politics/trump-ousts-tillerson-will-replace-him-as-secretary-of-state-with-cia-chief-pompeo/2018/03/13/30f34eea-26ba-11e8-b79d-f3d931db7f68_story.html?utm_term=.04ffab6fcaab.

268   ***"asks good, hard questions":*** Erickson, Amanda. "The one interview that explains Mike Pompeo's foreign policy approach." *Washington Post*, 13 March 2018, https://www.washingtonpost.com/news/worldviews/wp/2018/03/13/the-one-interview-that-explains-mike-pompeos-foreign-policy-approach/?utm_term=.07fe3e4ee7a4.

268   ***"always on the same wavelength":*** Cohen, Zachary and Merica, Dan. "Unlike Tillerson, Trump says Pompeo 'always on same wavelength'." CNN, 13 March 2018, https://www.cnn.com/2018/03/13/politics/mike-pompeo-secretary-of-state-trump/index.html.

23: THE MOSQUITO AND THE SWORD

269   ***"I'm a very systems, process guy":*** Author interview with Rex Tillerson, 4 January 2018.

269   ***"I had to walk away":*** Author interview with anonymous Foreign Service officer, 25 June 2017.

270   ***"It's preposterous":*** Author interview with anonymous Foreign Service officer, 25 June 2017.

270   ***"I have some words for your cloud":*** Author interview with anonymous Foreign Service officer, 28 June 2017.

270   ***"straight out of Office Space":*** Hudson, John. "This State Department Employee Survey is Straight Out of 'Office Space.'" *BuzzFeed News*, 4 May 2017, https://www.buzzfeed.com/johnhudson/leaked-state-department-survey-suggests-diplomacy-work-is-a?utm_term=.wfJm3MEPYL#.gfYwg1GevR.

270   ***"they will burn out":*** Schwartz, Felicia. "State Department Workers Vent Grievances Over Trump, Tillerson, Cite Longer-Term Issues." *Wall Street Journal*, 4 July 2017, https://www.wsj.com/articles/state-department-workers-vent-grievances-over-trump-tillerson-cite-longer-term-issues-1499194852.

270   ***"People do not speak optimistically":*** Insigniam survey, 2017, p. 43, leaked by an anonymous Foreign Service source.

270   ***"and from the American people":*** Insigniam survey, 2017, p. 43, leaked by an anonymous Foreign Service source.

271   **The administration's first budget:** "America First: A Budget Blueprint to Make America Great Again." White House Office of Management and Budget. 16 March 2017, https://www.whitehouse.gov/sites/whitehouse.gov/files/omb/budget/fy2018/2018_blueprint.pdf.

271   **The White House wanted to eliminate all funding:** "What We Do." United States Institute of Peace, https://www.usip.org/.

271 ***It would gut health programs:*** Konyndyk, Jeremy. "Trump's aid budget is breath-takingly cruel—cuts like these will kill people." *Guardian* (Manchester), 31 May 2017, https://www.theguardian.com/global-development-professionals-network/2017/may/31/trumps-aid-budget-is-breathtakingly-cruel-cuts-like-these-will-kill-people.

271 ***passport stamping and hostage extricating:*** Van Schaack, Beth. "Why is Tillerson Shuttering the State Dept.'s Global Justice Bureau?" *Newsweek*, 18 July 2017, www.newsweek.com/why-tillerson-shuttering-state-depts-global-justice-bureau-638246 and Tapper, Jake. "White House Memo Suggests Moving Refugee Bureau from State Department to DHS." *CNN Politics*, 30 June 2017, www.cnn.com/2017/06/28/politics/refugee-bureau-state-department-dhs/index.html.

271 ***For the first time:*** Rogin, Josh. "State Department Considers Scrubbing Democracy Promotion from its Mission." *Washington Post*, 1 August 2017, https://www.washingtonpost.com/news/josh-rogin/wp/2017/08/01/state-department-considers-scrubbing-democracy-promotion-from-its-mission/?utm_term=.28ffdcf307e7.

271 ***"we are suspending all USAID involvement":*** Wadhams, Nick. "Tillerson's State Overhaul Faces Mutiny as USAID Weighs Its Role." *Bloomberg*, 24 January 2017, https://www.bloomberg.com/news/articles/2018-01-24/tillerson-s-overhaul-at-state-in-doubt-as-usaid-suspends-role.

272 ***"'This is a total waste of time'":*** Harris, Gardiner. "Will Cuts Hurt Diplomacy? Tillerson Tries to Ease Senate's Worries." *New York Times*, 13 June 2017, https://www.nytimes.com/2017/06/13/world/rex-tillerson-senate-state-department.html.

272 ***"'present at the destruction'":*** "Cardin Challenges Tillerson on Administration's State Dept., Foreign Assistance Budget Request." Senate Foreign Relations Committee, 13 June 2017, https://www.foreign.senate.gov/press/ranking/release/cardin-challenges-tillerson-on-administrations-state-dept-foreign-assistance-budget-request.

272 ***He refused to accept $80 million:*** Toosi, Nahal. "Tillerson spurns $80 million to counter ISIS, Russian propaganda." *Politico*, 2 August 2017, www.politico.com/story/2017/08/02/tillerson-isis-russia-propaganda-241218.

273 ***Tillerson's relations on the Hill frayed:*** Rubin, Jennifer. "Tillerson unites D's and R's—they all ridicule his testimony." *Washington Post*, 15 June 2017, https://www.washingtonpost.com/blogs/right-turn/wp/2017/06/15/tillerson-unites-ds-and-rs-they-all-ridicule-his-testimony/.

273 ***"Tillerson didn't want the money":*** Author interview with Madeleine Albright, 15 December 2017.

273 ***"'that's not how I do things'":*** Author interview with Rex Tillerson, 4 January 2018.

274 ***"cost-benefit ratio":*** Lockie, Alex. "Mattis Once Said if State Department Funding Gets Cut 'Then I Need to Buy More Ammunition.'" *Business Insider*, 27 February 2017, http://www.businessinsider.com/mattis-state-department-funding-need-to-buy-more-ammunition-2017-2.

274   ***"position of strength":*** Read, Russ. "Mattis: A Strong Military is Crucial to Effective Diplomacy." *Daily Caller,* 22 March 2017, http://dailycaller.com/2017/03/22/mattis-a-strong-military-is-crucial-to-effective-diplomacy.

274   *eviscerated America's civilian foreign policy:* "America First: A Budget Blueprint to Make America Great Again." White House Office of Management and Budget. 16 March 2017, https://www.whitehouse.gov/sites/whitehouse.gov/files/omb/budget/fy2018/2018_blueprint.pdf.

274   ***More than 1,300 diplomats would get pink slips:*** Harris, Gardiner. "State Department to Offer Buyouts in Effort to Cut Staff." *New York Times,* 10 November 2017, https://www.nytimes.com/2017/11/10/us/politics/state-department-buyouts.html.

274   ***Outrage was so swift:*** Harris, Gardiner. "State Dept. Restores Job Offers to Students After Diplomat Outcry." *New York Times,* 30 June 2017, https://www.nytimes.com/2017/06/30/us/politics/state-department-students-foreign-service.html.

274   ***abruptly suspended its participation:*** Hellman, Joel. "SFS Voices Concern for Suspension of Current Pickering, Rangel Fellows." Georgetown University, 21 June 2017, https://sfs.georgetown.edu/sfs-voices-concern-suspension-current-pickering-rangel-fellows/ and "State Department Withdraws from Top Recruitment Program, Sowing Confusion." *Foreign Policy,* 28 July 2017, http://foreignpolicy.com/2017/07/28/state-department-withdraws-from-top-recruitment-program-sowing-confusion/.

274   ***lowest level of interest in the profession:*** Lippman, Daniel and Toosi, Nahal. "Interest in U.S. diplomatic corps tumbles in early months of Trump." *Politico,* 12 August 2017, http://www.politico.com/story/2017/08/12/trump-state-department-foreign-service-interest-plummets-241551.

274   ***"when the handwriting is on the wall":*** Author interview with John Kerry, 21 November 2017.

275   ***"They've not been easy":*** Author interview with Rex Tillerson, 4 January 2018.

275   ***That role would sit empty:*** Dawsey, Josh, Eliana Johnson, and Alex Isenstadt. "Tillerson Blows Up at Top White House Aide." *Politico,* 28 June 2017, www.politico.com/story/2017/06/28/tillerson-blows-up-at-white-house-aide-240075.

275   ***"We're just so thinly staffed":*** Author interview with anonymous State Department aide, 5 July 2017.

276   ***"sheer, unimaginable size":*** Holbrooke, Richard. "The Machine That Fails." *Foreign Policy,* 14 December 2010, foreignpolicy.com/2010/12/14/the-machine-that-fails/.

276   ***"too many bureaucratic layers":*** Author interview with James Baker, 22 January 2018.

276   ***"march it ninety-nine yards":*** Author interview with anonymous State Department aide, 5 July 2017.

277   ***"I think it's a drastic cut":*** Author interview with George P. Shultz, 19 January 2018.

277   ***"a spectacularly bad idea":*** Author interview with Condoleezza Rice, 3 August 2017.

278   *"incalculable damage":* Author interview with Madeleine Albright, 15 December 2017.

278   *"foolishness":* Author interview with Hillary Clinton, 20 November 2017.

278   *This one, he said, "you can use":* Author interview with Colin Powell in Washington, DC, 29 June 2017.

278   *"It's enormously costly":* Author interview with John Kerry, 21 November 2017.

278   *"a sword to a mosquito":* Author interview with Chris LaVine, 25 June 2017.

24: MELTDOWN

279   *"Why should I certify?":* Gearan, Anne. " 'He threw a fit': Trump's anger over Iran deal forced aides to scramble for a compromise." *Washington Post*, 11 October 2017, https://www.washingtonpost.com/politics/he-threw-a-fit-trumps-anger-over-iran-deal-forced-aides-to-scramble-for-a-compromise/2017/10/11/6218174c-ae94-11e7-9e58-e6288544af98_story.html?utm_term=.0c4e86e19d9b.

280   *simply work around it:* Winter, Jana, Gramer, Robbie and de Luce, Dan. "Trump Assigns White House Team to Target Iran Nuclear Deal, Sidelining State Department." *Foreign Policy*, 21 Jul 2017, foreignpolicy.com/2017/07/21/trump-assigns-white-house-team-to-target-iran-nuclear-deal-sidelining-state-department/.

280   *"dismantle the disastrous deal":* "Full Speech of Donald Trump's Speech to AIPAC." *Times of Israel*, 22 March 2016, www.timesofisrael.com/donald-trumps-full-speech-to-aipac/.

280   *" 'you dumb son of a bitch' ":* Diamond, Jeremy. "Trump Suggests U.S. 'Dumb Son of a Bitch' on Iran Deal." *CNN Politics*, 17 December 2015, www.cnn.com/2015/12/16/politics/donald-trump-iran-deal-rally-arizona/index.html.

280   *"rolling back this disastrous deal":* Nakamura, David and Viebeck, Elise. "Trump chooses Sen. Jeff Sessions for attorney general, Rep. Mike Pompeo for C.I.A. director." *Washington Post*, 18 November 2016, https://www.washingtonpost.com/politics/trump-chooses-sen-jeff-sessions-for-attorney-general-rep-mike-pompeo-for-cia-director-transition-sources-say/2016/11/18/a0c170ae-ad8e-11e6-a31b-4b6397e625d0_story.html?utm_term=.828961f2e7c8.

280   *"Iran has been formally PUT ON NOTICE":* Parker, Ashley. "Trump to Iran: Be Thankful for 'Terrible' Nuclear Deal." *Washington Post*, 2 February 2017, https://www.washingtonpost.com/news/post-politics/wp/2017/02/02/trump-to-iran-be-thankful-for-terrible-nuclear-deal/?utm_term=.8c68545f04cc.

280   *"Iran is playing with fire":* Tweet from Donald J. Trump, 3 February 2017, 3:28 AM.

280   *Western powers were concerned:* Parker, Ashley. "Trump to Iran: Be Thankful for 'Terrible' Nuclear Deal." *Washington Post*, 2 February 2017, https://www.washingtonpost.com/news/post-politics/wp/2017/02/02/trump-to-iran-be-thankful-for-terrible-nuclear-deal/?utm_term=.8c68545f04cc.

281   *at least three American citizens were being held:* Rogin, Josh. "The U.N. General Assembly Gives Trump a Chance to Confront Iran on American Hostages." *Washington Post*, 18 September 2017, https://www.washingtonpost.com/opinions/global-opinions/the-un-general-assembly-gives-trump-a-chance-to-

confront-iran-on-american-hostages/2017/09/17/571e5884-9a52-11e7-82e4-
f1076f6d6152_story.html?utm_term=.2a1ca4033041.

281   *"The nuclear deal with Iran was controversial":* Pasha-Robinson, Lucy. "Theresa May Warns Donald Trump About 'Iran's Malign Influence' During
Speech to Republicans in Philadelphia," *Independent* (UK), 26 January 2017,
www.independent.co.uk/news/theresa-may-donald-trump-iran-malign-
influence-philadelphia-republican-speech-a7548491.html.

281   *After the ballistic missile test:* Morello, Carol and Gearan, Anne. "Trump Administration Sanctions Iran Over Missile Test." *Washington Post*, 3 February 2017, https://
www.washingtonpost.com/world/national-security/trump-administration-
sanctions-iran-on-missile-test/2017/02/03/dfb101ce-4107-409e-ab45-
f49449e92c1f_story.html?utm_term=.dc32d5c48c32 and Cunningham, Eric.
"Iran Calls New U.S. Sanctions a Violation of Nuclear Deal." *Washington Post*,
3 August 2017, https://www.washingtonpost.com/world/middle_east/iran-calls-
new-us-sanctions-a-violation-of-nuclear-deal/2017/08/03/f22d9464-7218-11e7-
8c17-533c52b2f014_story.html?utm_term=.234b3e17e8d3.

281   *"violated the spirit of that deal":* Morello, Carol. "U.S. Extends Waivers on
Iran Sanctions but Warns It's an Interim Move." *Washington Post*, 14 September
2017,   https://www.washingtonpost.com/world/national-security/us-extends-
sanctions-against-iran-but-warns-its-an-interim-move/2017/09/14/1d4ba5ee-
9953-11e7-b569-3360011663b4_story.html?utm_term=.50c1d20aaa10.

281   *"Iran is clearly in default":* Wadhams, Nick. "Tillerson Says Iran 'Clearly
in Default' of Nuclear Deal's Terms." Bloomberg, 14 September 2017,
https://www.bloomberg.com/news/articles/2017-09-14/tillerson-says-iran-
clearly-in-default-of-iran-deal-s-terms.

282   *"making an enormous error":* Stanley-Becker, Isaac and Kirchner, Stephanie.
"Angela Merkel Predicts Showdown with U.S. over Climate at G-20." *Washington Post*, 29 June 2017, https://www.washingtonpost.com/world/angela-merkel-
predicts-showdown-over-climate-at-g-20/2017/06/29/76bf6678-5a84-11e7-
aa69-3964a7d55207_story.html?utm_term=.fbe49000547c.

282   *"Other countries are leading instead":* Author interview with John Kerry, 21
November 2017.

282   *He resigned instead:* Morello, Carol. "Senior Diplomat in Beijing Resigns
over Trump's Climate Change Decision." *Washington Post*, 5 June 2017, https://
www.washingtonpost.com/world/national-security/senior-diplomat-in-beijing-
embassy-resigns-over-trumps-climate-change-decision/2017/06/05/3537ff8c-
4a2e-11e7-a186-60c031eab644_story.html?utm_term=.c89251a58514.

282   *"it will come from elsewhere":* Rank, David. "Why I Resigned From the Foreign Service after 27 Years." *Washington Post*, 23 June 2017, https://www
.washingtonpost.com/opinions/why-i-resigned-from-the-foreign-service-after-
27-years/2017/06/23/6abee224-55ff-11e7-ba90-f5875b7d1876_story.html?utm_
term=.b78438fb1b53.

283   *intended to be tough:* Kunovic, Martina. "Five Things You Need to Know
About Trump's Cuba Policy—And Who It Will Hurt." *Washington Post*, 22 June
2017,   https://www.washingtonpost.com/news/monkey-cage/wp/2017/06/22/

five-things-you-need-to-know-about-trumps-cuba-policy-and-who-it-will-hurt/?utm_term=.af14570d57d0.

283 *"not informed about the Cuba policy change":* Author interview with State Department official, 1 June 2017.

283 *"I'm not going to rule out a military option":* Fabian, Jordan and Greenwood, Max. "Trump Does Not Rule Out Military Action in Venezuela. *The Hill*, 11 August 2017, thehill.com/homenews/administration/346265-trump-does-not-rule-out-military-action-in-venezuela.

284 *Trump ad-libbed:* Glasser, Susan. "Trump National Security Team Blindsided by NATO Speech." *Politico*, 5 June 2017, www.politico.com/magazine/story/2017/06/05/trump-nato-speech-national-security-team-215227.

284 *"fire, fury and frankly power":* Vitali, Ali. "Trump Vows North Korea Threat Will Be Met With 'Fire and Fury'. *NBC News*. 9 August 2017, "http://www.nbcnews.com/politics/white-house/trump-vows-north-korea-could-be-met-fire-fury-n790896.

284 *"a rain of ruin":* Davos, Julie Hirschfeld. "Trump's Harsh Language on North Korea Has Little Precedent, Experts Say." *New York Times*, 8 August 2017, https://www.nytimes.com/2017/08/08/us/politics/trumps-harsh-language-on-north-korea-has-little-precedent-experts-say.html.

284 *"unplanned and spontaneous":* Walcott, Josh. "Trump's 'fire and fury' North Korea remark surprised aides: officials." *Reuters*, 9 August 2017, https://www.reuters.com/article/us-northkorea-missiles-usa-idUSKBN1AP26D.

284 *"fully in place, locked and loaded":* Berlinger, Joshua, et al. "Tillerson dials back rhetoric after Trump's North Korea 'fire and fury' threats." *CNN*, 9 August 2017, 7www.cnn.com/2017/08/09/politics/north-korea-donald-trump/index.html.

285 *put a palm to his face:* Selk, Avi. "John Kelly's Facepalm at Trump's U.N. Speech: Exasperation, Exhaustion or No Big Deal." *Washington Post*, 20 September 2017, https://www.washingtonpost.com/news/the-fix/wp/2017/09/20/john-kellys-facepalm-at-trumps-u-n-speech-exasperation-exhaustion-or-no-big-deal/?utm_term=.c596752186c4.

285 *"no choice but to totally destroy North Korea":* Trump, Donald. "Remarks by President Trump to the 72nd Session of the United Nations General Assembly." United Nations, New York, 19 September 2017.

285 *"old lunatic":* Griffiths, James. "What is a 'Dotard'?" CNN, 22 September 2017, www.cnn.com/2017/09/22/asia/north-korea-dotard/index.html and "Full Text of Kim Jong-un's Response to President Trump." *New York Times*, 22 September 2017, https://www.nytimes.com/2017/09/22/world/asia/kim-jong-un-trump.html?_r=0.

285 *"Little Rocket Man":* Tweet by Donald J. Trump, 23 September 2017, 8:08PM.

285 *"completely aligned":* Author interview with Rex Tillerson, 4 January 2018.

286 *"wonderful Secretary of State":* Tweet by Donald J. Trump, 01 October 2017, 7:30AM.

286 *Chancellor Angela Merkel:* Brechenmacher, Victor. "Merkel takes swipe at Trump's fiery North Korea comments." *Politico*, 8 August 2017, www.politico.eu/article/merkel-takes-swipe-at-trumps-fiery-north-korea-comments/.

286   ***"I am against threats of this kind":*** Thurau, Jens. "Chancellor Angela Merkel: 'There is a Clear Disagreement with Trump on North Korea." DW, 20 September 2017, www.dw.com/en/chancellor-angela-merkel-there-is-a-clear-disagree ment-with-trump-on-north-korea/a-40608769.

286   ***"repeating the very same failure":*** "Full Text of Abe's Address at U.N. General Assembly." *Japan Times*, 21 September 2017, https://www.japantimes.co.jp/news/2017/09/21/national/politics-diplomacy/full-text-abes-address-u-n-general-assembly/#.Wchp18iGPIU.

286   ***North Korea cheated:*** Hill, Christopher R. *Outpost: A Diplomat at Work.* New York: Simon & Schuster, 2015. Kindle.

287   ***walking away altogether:*** Lippman, Thomas. "N. Korea-U.S. Nuclear Pact Threatened." Washington Post, 6 July 1998, www.washingtonpost.com/wp-srv/inatl/longterm/korea/stories/nuke070698.htm and Ryan, Maria. "Why the US' 1994 Deal with North Korea Failed—and What Trump Can Learn From It." *The Conversation*, 19 July 2017, theconversation.com/why-the-uss-1994-deal-with-north-korea-failed-and-what-trump-can-learn-from-it-80578.

287   ***use nuclear weapons against:*** "Nuclear Posture Review." 8 January 2002, web. stanford.edu/class/polisci211z/2.6/NPR2001leaked.pdf.

287   ***saber-rattling condemnations:*** Ryan, Maria. "Why the US' 1994 Deal with North Korea Failed—and What Trump Can Learn From It." *The Conversation*, 19 July 2017, theconversation.com/why-the-uss-1994-deal-with-north-korea-failed-and-what-trump-can-learn-from-it-80578.

287   ***"we are looking for a few diplomats":*** Hill, Christopher R. *Outpost: A Diplomat at Work.* New York: Simon & Schuster, 2015, p. 195. Kindle.

287   ***"robotlike":*** Hill, Christopher R. *Outpost: A Diplomat at Work.* New York: Simon & Schuster, 2015, p. 229. Kindle.

287   ***"would Holbrooke have canceled":*** Author phone interview with Christopher Hill, 12 September 2017.

287   ***Holbrooke himself showed up:*** Hill, Christopher R. *Outpost: A Diplomat at Work.* New York: Simon & Schuster, 2015, pp. 215, 237, 253. Kindle.

288   ***"You may never have another like it":*** Hill, Christopher R. *Outpost: A Diplomat at Work.* New York: Simon & Schuster, 2015, p. 225. Kindle.

288   ***pipes were being sawed:*** Hill, Christopher R. *Outpost: A Diplomat at Work.* New York: Simon & Schuster, 2015, p. 229. Kindle.

288   ***"They never got serious":*** Author phone interview with Christopher Hill, 12 September 2017.

288   ***"I can't speak to that":*** Author interview with Hillary Clinton, 20 November 2017.

289   ***"If we get out":*** Author interview with Condoleezza Rice, 3 August 2017.

289   ***appear responsible without committing:*** "China Says Six-Party Talks Resumption Not Easy, But in the Right Direction." Reuters, 6 August 2017, https://www.reuters.com/article/us-asean-philippines-china-northkorea-mi/china-says-six-party-talks-resumption-not-easy-but-in-the-right-direction-id USKBN1AM089.

289   ***meet with North Korean leader Kim Jong Un:*** Gaouette, Nicole et al. "US starts to prep for North Korea summit even as Pyongyang remains silent." CNN, 13

March 2018, https://www.cnn.com/2018/03/13/politics/trump-korea-summit-early-prep/index.html.

290 *"a long way from negotiations":* Lauter, David. "Trump's risky, but bold approach to North Korea." *Los Angeles Times,* 9 March 2018, http://www.latimes.com/politics/la-pol-essential-politics-20180309-story.html.

290 *"many in the foreign policy establishment feared":* Lewis, Jeffrey. "Trump is walking into Kim Jong Un's Trap." *Washington Post,* 13 March 2018, https://www.washingtonpost.com/news/theworldpost/wp/2018/03/13/trump-north-korea/?utm_term=.4167c5ee8b24.

290 *President Xi urged the United States:* "President Xi meets U.S. Secretary of State." *Xinhua,* 19 March 2017, news.xinhuanet.com/english/2017-03/19/c_136140432.htm.

290 *"win-win cooperation":* Brunnstrom, David. "Tillerson Affirms Importance of Constructive U.S.-China Ties." Reuters, 22 February 2017, https://www.reuters.com/article/us-usa-china-tillerson/tillerson-affirms-importance-of-constructive-u-s-china-ties-idUSKBN1602TL?il=0.

291 *"Barack Obama refused to do":* Beech, Hannah. "Rex Tillerson's Deferential Visit to China." *New Yorker,* 21 March 2017, www.newyorker.com/news/news-desk/rex-tillersons-deferential-visit-to-china; "Did America's Top Diplomat Inadvertently Offer China a New Great Power Relationship?" *Japan Times,* 21 March 2017, http://www.japantimes.co.jp/news/2017/03/21/asia-pacific/politics-diplomacy-asia-pacific/americas-top-diplomat-inadvertently-offer-china-new-great-power-relationship/.

291 *"He believes in win-win":* Author interview with Brian Hook, 13 December 2017.

292 *watching an enthusiastic dog tear up your upholstery:* Author interview with anonymous State Department official, 1 June 2017.

292 *The trend line is striking:* Zhang, Junyi. "Order from Chaos: Chinese Foreign Assistance, Explained." *Order from Chaos* (Brookings blog), 19 July 2016, https://www.brookings.edu/blog/order-from-chaos/2016/07/19/chinese-foreign-assistance-explained/.

292 *$10 billion a year:* Shambaugh, David. "China's Soft-Power Push." *Foreign Affairs,* July/August 2015, https://www.foreignaffairs.com/articles/china/2015-06-16/china-s-soft-power-push.

292 *Beijing gets more influence:* Lynch, Colum. "China Eyes Ending Western Grip on Top U.N. Jobs With Greater Control Over Blue Helmets." *Foreign Policy,* 2 October 2016, http://foreignpolicy.com/2016/10/02/china-eyes-ending-western-grip-on-top-u-n-jobs-with-greater-control-over-blue-helmets/.

293 *China is exploring a mediating role:* Putz, Catherine. "Can China Help Mediate Between Afghanistan and Pakistan?" *Diplomat,* 13 June 2017, thediplomat.com/2017/06/can-china-help-mediate-between-afghanistan-and-pakistan/.

293 *Sudan's brutalized population:* Johnson, Keith. "China's African Adventure." *Foreign Policy,* 24 April 2014, foreignpolicy.com/2014/04/24/chinas-african-adventure/.

293 *unique leverage to press for peace:* Farrow, Ronan. "China's Crude Conscience." *Wall Street Journal,* 10 August 2016, https://www.wsj.com/articles/SB115515906133031402.

293 ***China swiftly stepped in:*** Morimoto, Andy. "Should America Fear China's Alternative to the TP?" *Diplomat*, 17 March 2016, thediplomat.com/2016/03/should-america-fear-chinas-alternative-to-the-tp/.

293 ***"One Belt, One Road" initiative:*** Ayres, Alyssa. "Trump To Cut Foreign Aid Budgets, Opening South and Central Asia's Door to Chinese Influence." *Forbes*, 4 May 2017, https://www.forbes.com/sites/alyssaayres/2017/05/04/trump-to-cut-foreign-aid-budgets-opening-south-and-central-asias-door-to-chinese-influence/#77e273a75f50.

293 ***"It's a completely self-inflicted wound":*** Author interview with John Kerry, 21 November 2017.

EPILOGUE: THE TOOL OF FIRST RESORT

295 ***two types of military dispute:*** Cicero. *De Officiis.* Translated by P. G. Walsh. Oxford: Oxford University Press, 2000, loc. 1014. Kindle.

296 ***"reprioritization of diplomacy":*** Author phone interview with Ben Rhodes, 18 August 2017.

297 ***"shouts coming through the walls":*** Author phone interview with Jon Finer, 11 September 2017.

297 ***the whole hotel heard them:*** Lakshmana, Indira A. R., "If You Can't Do This Deal . . . Go Back to Tehran." *Politico Magazine*, 25 September 2015, www.politico.com/magazine/story/2015/09/iran-deal-inside-story-213187?paginate=false.

297 ***Rice Krispies Treats:*** Viser, Matt. "Twizzlers, String Cheese, and Mixed Nuts (in Larger Quantities) Fuel Iran Nuclear Negotiations." *Boston Globe*, 7 July 2015, https://www.bostonglobe.com/news/world/2015/07/07/twizzlers-string-cheese-and-mixed-nuts-large-quantities-fuel-iran-nuclear-negotiators/zun8dliHFISaCV8yzrTVNO/story.html.

298 ***Zarif bellowed:*** Gay, John Allen. "Why is Iran's Foreign Minister So Angry?" *National Interest*, 9 July 2015, nationalinterest.org/blog/the-buzz/why-irans-foreign-minister-so-angry-13303.

298 ***a "diplomat's diplomat":*** Itkowitz, Colby. "Bill Burns, a 'Diplomat's Diplomat' Retires." *Washington Post*, 11 April 2014, https://www.washingtonpost.com/blogs/in-the-loop/wp/2014/04/11/bill-burns-a-diplomats-diplomat-retires/?utm_term=.4e10e71e949a.

298 ***"the next Bill Burns":*** Author interview with John Kerry, 21 November 2017.

299 ***"opened up a new phase":*** Author phone interview with William Burns, 14 September 2017.

299 ***squeezing every aspect of Iran's economy:*** Solomon, Jay. *The Iran Wars: Spy Games, Bank Battles, and the Secret Deals That Reshaped the Middle East.* New York: Random House, 2016, loc. 2385-2386. Kindle.

299 ***Oman:*** Author phone interview with William Burns, 14 September 2017.

299 ***"there might be an opening":*** Author phone interview with William Burns, 14 September 2017.

300 *"a patch of negotiations in Muscat":* Author phone interview with Jon Finer, 11 September 2017.

300 *"The Most Romantic Moments of the Iran–Deal Negotiations":* Fuller, Jaime. "The Most Romantic Moments of the Iran-Deal Negotiations." *New York*, 16 July 2015, nymag.com/daily/intelligencer/2015/07/most-romantic-moments-of-the-iran-deal.html.

300 *"very limited enrichment program":* Author interview with Wendy Sherman, 13 September 2017.

301 *a Rubik's Cube:* Author interview with Wendy Sherman, 13 September 2017.

301 *gag gift:* Lakshmana, Indira A. R., "If You Can't Do This Deal . . . Go Back to Tehran." *Politico Magazine*, 25 September 2015, www.politico.com/magazine/story/2015/09/iran-deal-inside-story-213187?paginate=false.

301 *"I was quite focused":* Author interview with Wendy Sherman, 13 September 2017.

302 *"war is the failure of diplomacy":* Kerry, John. "Iran Accord Address and Presser." Austria Center, Vienna, Austria, 14 July 2015, www.americanrhetoric.com/speeches/johnkerryiranaccord.htm.

302 *explode the secret diplomatic entrees:* Lake, Eli. "Why Obama Let Iran's Green Revolution Fail." *Bloomberg View*, 25 August 2016, https://www.bloombergquint.com/opinion/2016/08/24/why-obama-let-iran-s-green-revolution-fail.

302 *Iran threatened to pull out:* Solomon, Jay. *The Iran Wars: Spy Games, Bank Battles, and the Secret Deals That Reshaped the Middle East.* New York: Random House, 2016, loc. 219-225. Kindle.

302 *claims that Iran had cheated:* Gladstone, Rick. "Arms Control Experts Urge Trump to Honor Iran Nuclear Deal." *New York Times*, 13 September 2017, https://www.nytimes.com/2017/09/13/world/middleeast/iran-nuclear-deal-trump.html.

302 *view Iran as a "jigsaw puzzle":* Haley, Nikki. "Nikki Haley Address on Iran and the JCPOA." American Enterprise Institute, 5 September 2017.

303 *"without a shot being fired":* Author phone interview with William Burns, 14 September 2017.

303 *"you were going to have a confrontation":* Author interview with John Kerry, 21 November 2017.

303 *"race to a bomb covertly":* Author phone interview with Jon Finer, 11 September 2017.

304 *"something short of a perfect solution:"* Author phone interview with William Burns, 14 September 2017.

304 *how complex negotiated settlements looked:* Hronesvoa, Jessie. "A Flawed Recipe for How to End a War and Build a State: 20 Years Since the Dayton Agreement." *London School of Economics and Political Science Blog*, 14 December 2015, blogs.lse.ac.uk/europblog/2015/12/14/a-flawed-recipe-for-how-to-end-a-war-and-build-a-state-20-years-since-the-dayton-agreement/.

304 *"If we ditch this deal":* Author phone interview with Jon Finer, 11 September 2017.

305 *"Trump's done it backwards, with bluster":* Author interview with John Kerry, 21 November 2017.

305 ***more than eighty arms control specialists:*** Gladstone, Rick. "Arms Control Experts Urge Trump to Honor Iran Nuclear Deal." *New York Times*, 13 September 2017, https://www.nytimes.com/2017/09/13/world/middleeast/iran-nuclear-deal-trump.html.

306 ***"There was so much to do":*** Author interview with Thomas Countryman, 22 June 2017.

307 ***"I found that confusing":*** "Tom Countryman's Farewell: A Diplomat's Love Letter to America." *Diplopundit*, 2 February 2017, https://diplopundit.net/2017/02/02/tom-countrymans-farewell-a-diplomats-love-letter-to-america.

307 ***"ambassadors legendary":*** "Tom Countryman's Farewell: A Diplomat's Love Letter to America." *Diplopundit*, 2 February 2017, https://diplopundit.net/2017/02/02/tom-countrymans-farewell-a-diplomats-love-letter-to-america.

307 ***"foreign policy without professionals":*** "Tom Countryman's Farewell: A Diplomat's Love Letter to America." *Diplopundit*, 2 February 2017, https://diplopundit.net/2017/02/02/tom-countrymans-farewell-a-diplomats-love-letter-to-america.

307 ***"Beijing will run the table":*** "Tom Countryman's Farewell: A Diplomat's Love Letter to America." *Diplopundit*, 2 February 2017, https://diplopundit.net/2017/02/02/tom-countrymans-farewell-a-diplomats-love-letter-to-america.

307 ***"Why would we do that?":*** Author interview with Wendy Sherman, 13 September 2017.

308 ***"ought to be the tool of first resort":*** Author phone interview with William Burns, 14 September 2017.

308 ***"Public service can make a difference":*** Holbrooke, Richard. *To End a War*. New York: Random House, 2011, loc. 2930-2931. Kindle.

309 ***" 'who needs embassies?' ":*** Author phone interview with William Burns, 14 September 2017.

309 ***"nonproliferation around dangerous states":*** Author interviews with Brian Hook, 5 July 2017 and 13 December 2017.

INDEX